1006687659

Interconnecting Smart Objects with IP

Interconnecting Smart Objects with IP
The Next Internet

Jean-Philippe Vasseur

Adam Dunkels

ELSEVIER

AMSTERDAM • BOSTON • HEIDELBERG • LONDON
NEW YORK • OXFORD • PARIS • SAN DIEGO
SAN FRANCISCO • SINGAPORE • SYDNEY • TOKYO

Morgan Kaufmann Publishers is an Imprint of Elsevier

MORGAN KAUFMANN PUBLISHERS

Acquiring Editor: Rick Adams
Development Editor: David Bevans
Project Manager: Andre Cuello
Designer: Eric DeCicco

Morgan Kaufmann is an imprint of Elsevier
30 Corporate Drive, Suite 400, Burlington, MA 01803, USA

Library of Congress Cataloging-in-Publication Data
Application submitted

British Library Cataloguing-in-Publication Data
A catalogue record for this book is available from the British Library.

ISBN: 978-0-12-375165-2

Printed in the United States of America
10 11 12 13 14   10 9 8 7 6 5 4 3 2 1

Working together to grow
libraries in developing countries

www.elsevier.com | www.bookaid.org | www.sabre.org

ELSEVIER   BOOK AID
            International   Sabre Foundation

For information on all MK publications visit our website at www.mkp.com

Dedication

To the best gift life offered me : my wife Brigitte,
who gave me three exceptional children: Manon, Eleonore
and Louis who I love so much. I would also like to
dedicate this book to my wonderful parents.

JP Vasseur

Dedicated to my wonderful wife Maria and
our three fantastic sons Morgan, Castor,
and Olof — you bring so much love
into my life!

ADAM

About the Authors

JP Vasseur is a Cisco Distinguished Engineer where he works on IP/MPLS architecture specifications, focusing on IP, Traffic Engineering, network recovery and Sensor networks. Before joining Cisco, he worked for several Service Providers in large multi-protocol environments. He is an active member of the IETF (co-author of more than 30 IETF RFCs/Drafts), co-chair of the IETF PCE (Path Computation Element) and the ROLL (Routing Over Low power and Lossy networks (ROLL) Working Groups. JP is also the chair of the Technology Advisory Board of the IPSO (IP for Smart Object Alliance). JP is a regular speaker at various international conferences, he is involved in various research projects in the area of IP/Sensor Networks and the member of a number of Technical Program Committees. He has filed a number of patents in the area of IP/MPLS and Sensor Networks. He is the coauthor of "Network Recovery" (Morgan Kaufmann, July 2004) and "Definitive MPLS Network Designs" (Cisco Press, March 2005).

Adam Dunkels, PhD, is a senior scientist at the Swedish Institute of Computer Science where he has worked with IP networking for embedded and low-power wireless systems for eight years. He is the author of the open source Contiki operating system for networked embedded devices and the open source uIP and lwIP embedded TCP/IP stacks that are currently used in thousands of embedded systems in space, on earth, and on the seven seas. He has authored over 40 papers on embedded IP, wireless sensor networks and embedded programming, and has received prestigious awards for his work. Adam has also developed the Operating System for Smart object that become a de-facto standard.

Contents

Foreword

Vinton G. Cerf

The Internet has been around in concept since 1973 and in operation since 1983. Its usage exploded when the World Wide Web application became broadly available with the arrival of the commercial Netscape Navigator browser and server applications around 1994. Since that time, an avalanche of content and new applications have poured into the Internet, which has grown to include nearly 2 billion people and possibly that many servers, laptops, desktops, and mobile units. But the system is about to experience yet another explosive period of growth as smart devices become a part of the Internet environment. The trend has already become visible as sensor networks connect to the Internet along with some fraction of the 4 billion mobiles thought to be in use around the world. To these devices appliances of all kinds (home, office, portable, fixed and mobile sensors, etc.) will be added.

What will this "Internet of Things" be like? For one thing, many of these "Internet-enabled" devices will be using the relatively new IPv6 protocol for access. IPv6 was standardized by the Internet Engineering Task Force around 1996, but implementation has been sparse. It is expected to accelerate, partly to accommodate the huge number of potential devices that will be connected to the Internet and also to cope with the anticipated exhaustion of the original IPv4 address space. The latter provided for approximately 4.3 billion unique terminations. A combination of relatively sparse assignment practices and reuse of "private address space" through Network Address Translation (NAT) boxes has allowed operation of the limited IPv4 address space through the present, but it is expected that the last of the IPv4 addresses will be allocated by the Internet Corporation for Assigned Names and Numbers by mid-2011, and the Regional Internet Registries that assign address space to Internet Service Providers will exhaust their supplies not long thereafter. There are 340 trillion trillion trillion IPv6 addresses, and it is hoped that this will suffice for the foreseeable future.

Many of the "things" on the Internet will be appliances that can accept control inputs remotely or can report status information remotely. Sensor systems are good examples. I have a monitoring system in my home that tracks temperature, humidity, and light levels in every room in the house every 5 minutes. This information is captured and stored in a local database at home but is accessible remotely from anywhere on the Internet. One can easily envision security systems and a wide range of appliances that might be able to report their status and accept control information. The Smart Grid project in the United States is prototypical of the ideas behind the Internet of Things. For example, devices can not only report their energy usage but also be provided by users, or others on their behalf, with profiles to moderate energy usage during times of peak loads in exchange for reduced charges.

How often have you gone off on a trip, only to wonder whether a particular appliance was on or off, a light switch was set on or off, or some other home or office device was properly configured for your absence? The Smart Grid may provide a means to answer such questions remotely and securely and even allow remote interaction.

Standards to permit the interoperation of smart, Internet-enabled devices will also be essential. Such standards will also promote competitive provision of devices and services associated with them. Such potentially large-scale systems will make demands on designers to cope with billions of devices interacting in various subsets with each other. Emergent properties may well appear unexpectedly. Security and strong authentication of identity and authority will play key roles in making such systems safe to use.

Our ability to model, understand, and successfully operate such large-scale infrastructure will be challenged, and within that challenge there may dwell many Ph.D. dissertations as well as new and unexpected businesses. The law and policy will not escape the impact of this gigantic network with its billions of components. The potential for mischief, interference, and even significant infrastructure failures (deliberate or accidental) will be made even more complex by the global scope of the Internet and its connections. New frameworks for dealing with liability, risk, vulnerability, and criminal activity will be needed along with multilateral agreements to secure the benefits and protect users from harm.

The authors of this book offer a rich and thoughtful exploration of this new Internet canvas on which the twenty-first century will unfold. Predictions will be hard; we are all just going to have to live through it to find out what happens!

Vinton G. Cerf
Woodhurst
January 2010

Preface

The digital revolution of the 21st century will be much, much larger than previous digital revolutions. During the 20th century, the world underwent two major digital revolutions: computers were developed and found their way into offices and homes, and the Internet interconnected the computers and fundamentally changed the way we interact with the digital world.

We now stand before the digital revolution of the 21st century: smart objects – the Internet of Things – that interconnect the digital world with the physical world. Industry predicts the number of smart objects to be counted in billions within the next ten years. Over the course of the forthcoming decade, we will see this fundamentally change the way we interact with both the digital and the physical world.

A smart object is a small micro-electronic device that consists of a communication device, typically a low-power radio, a small microprocessor, and a sensor or actuator. The sensors give the smart objects the ability to sense the physical world, for example by measuring its temperature. Actuators make it possible for the smart objects to change the physical world, for example by controlling an engine.

We already see a number of emerging applications of smart objects. The power grid is about to be equipped with sophisticated smart objects networks to help better manage the grid, handle renewable sources of energy, and recharge electric cars. Office buildings can become more energy-efficient with temperature sensors that monitor the actual temperature in the building so that controllable radiators and air conditioners can better control the temperature. Cities will support intelligent transport systems, environmental monitoring, energy management, and even social networking using smart objects. Freighter containers can measure the climate inside the containers to make sure that foodstuffs are kept in a good environment.

But we are only beginning to scratch the surface of what smart objects can do; the emerging applications we see today are just the start. The true innovative power of smart objects comes from their interconnection. When innovators can begin to easily and rapidly build applications and systems that connect the physical and the digital world, a new level of serendipity begins.

The network architecture for the smart objects must be extremely open to future innovation. We cannot possibly know what the future holds for smart objects, as the field is still in its infancy. Innovation must be allowed to occur both in how we use smart objects and in the way the smart object technology itself is designed. The overall architecture is the fundament and must be extremely flexible to support new applications in the future, just like the Internet did over that past three decades.

So far, however, smart objects have largely been isolated islands whose interconnection has been made difficult because of a number of proprietary solutions, usually optimized for one specific application, that have not been possible to integrate.

OBJECTIVES

In this book, we explain why the Internet Protocol, IP, is the protocol of choice for smart object networks, providing an open and standard based technology for the endless number of applications to come. IP has already successfully showed that it can interconnect billions of digital systems on the global Internet and in private IP networks. Once smart objects can be easily interconnected, a whole new class of smart object systems can begin to evolve. Developers can build systems that integrate information physical-world phenomena with digital information from on-line sources. Businesses can make use of physical information both to make their own business more efficient but also to explore completely new business opportunities.

The interconnection of smart objects is not without significant technical challenges. First, the sheer number of potential devices that can be connected provides challenges for communication mechanisms, routing protocols, and communication architecture. Deployments of hundreds or thousands of smart objects are not uncommon. Second, the requirement for low-power operation affects every layer of the system, from hardware through software and to the data management architectures. To meet lifetime requirements, smart objects must be able to operate with power consumptions of less than one milliwatt. Third, the requirements for a small physical size, low power consumption, and low cost mean that each device must make very efficient use of their limited resources. Smart objects may have only a few kilobytes of memory. Still, IP-based smart object networks are being designed and deployed. This book tells you how this is achieved. But this is just the beginning of an exciting journey: the future of interconnected smart objects has just begun.

STRUCTURE OF THE BOOK

We spent a good amount of time thinking of the most appropriate structure for this book, in order to make it a reference for engineers and researchers but also provide materials valuable for non-expert in the field. We decided to organize the book around three main parts: the book starts with one part devoted to discussing the architectural foundation of the IP smart object networks, before the second part takes a deep dive into protocols and algorithms, and the third part concludes the book with a detailed review of seven important use cases and applications for IP-based smart objects.

Part I demonstrates why the IP architecture is well suited to smart object networks by contrast with non-IP based sensor network or other proprietary systems interconnect to IP networks (e.g. the public Internet of private IP networks) by means of hard to manage and expensive multi-protocol translation gateways that scale poorly. We start Part I with a description of smart objects. After a review of the architectural principles of IP, we explain why IP and in particular IPv6, that uses the same architecture as IPv4, is particularly well suited for smart objet networks. Several key networking features are reviewed from an architectural angle such as routing, transport, service discovery, security, and web services. Part I concludes with a discussion on potential connectivity models of IP smart objects to (private and public) IP networks.

The second part is a deep technology dive into the technologies. Part II starts with a detailed discussion on smart objects (hardware architecture, lightweight operating systems) and several of the low power link layers technologies used in these networks. Then follows a chapter devoted to standardization, a must for any technology to be widely adopted: this chapter discusses in details the standardization process of the standardization body in charge of IP protocols: the IETF (Internet Engineering Task Force). Then follows two chapters explaining in details two key areas of IP smart object networks: the 6LoWPAN adaptation layer specified to carry IPv6 packet over the IEEE 802.15.4 link layer and the newly defined routing protocol (called RPL) used in IP smart object network. This second part concludes with an overview of the IPSO (IP for Smart Object alliance) followed by a discussion on two non-IP technologies.

IP smart object networks will unavoidably change and improve our day to day quality of life, in a number of ways: these networks will radically increase the efficiency of power grids allowing for new sources of energy generation and energy savings, they will help better manage buildings and homes, make our cities smarter and these are only a few examples. Thus, instead of providing a few examples here and there, we decided to devote en entire part of this book to the applications of IP smart object networks: *"What will IP smart object network be used for?"* in a very near future. Each chapter in Part III of the book describes the use of smart object networks as opposed to the technology itself and follows a similar structure: for each use case, we start with a detailed description of the various applications (for example, how to enable new services in a smart city such urban environmental monitoring, social networking and intelligent transport systems) followed by a discussion on the technical challenges. Part III discusses in details seven major applications: smart grid, industrial automation, smart cities and urban networks, home automation, building automation, structural health monitoring, and container tracking.

Acknowledgements

There are number of persons to acknowledge in this section for their tremendous help in writing this book.

Our warm thank to Vinton Cerf, Internet Pioneer, for having accepted to write the foreword of this book.

We are extremely grateful to our reviewers, Paul Bertrand (Founder and Vice-President of Watteco) and Mijeom Kim (Senior Research Engineer, Korea Telecom) for their detailed review of the book.

Considering how broad the set of use cases for IP smart objects network is, we greatly benefited from the expertise of several world-wide experts in several of the uses cases discussed in Part III. The following people wrote the bulk of several of the chapters in Part III:

- Jonas Neander, Ewa Hansen, Tomas Lennvall, and Mikael Gidlund, (ABB AB, Corporate Research) – Chapter 21, Industrial Automation;
- Lin Zhang (Professor, Tsinghua University, China) – Chapter 22, Smart Cities and Urban networks;
- Bernd Grohmann (VP Marketing & Business Development, eQ-3 AG) – Chapter 23, Home Automation;
- Jerry Martocci (Lead staff engineer, Wireless communications, Johnson Controls) – Chapter 24, Building Automation;
- Jukka Manner (Professor, Aalto University School of Science and Technology) and Jaakko Hollmen (Chief Research Scientist, Aalto University School of Science and Technology) – Chapter 25, Structural Health Monitoring.

We are also extremely grateful to the number of people who reviewed chapters of the book: Danny Cohen, Julien Abeille, Jonathan Hui, Tim Winter, Pascal Thubert, Joakim Eriksson, Nicolas Tsiftes, Akiba, and Eric Sandberg.

Needless to say that this book would not have been possible without the tremendous support and professionalism of our editor Rick Adams, our development editor Heather Scherer and our project manager Andre Cuello.

SPECIAL ACKNOWLEDGMENTS

I would like to thank my company, Cisco Systems, for years of exiting work and opportunities and I would address very special thanks to several individuals: my former managers, Joel Bion and Bruce Davie for their support when I first started to work on IP Smart Objects networks several years ago while this was still a concept, of course my manager Alain Fiocco for his constant support and inspiration in many areas, but also Dave Oran for our fruitful discussion over the past decade and finally close collaborators I have been closely working with over past few years: Navneet Agarwal, Amit Phadnis, Mathilde Durvy, Julien Abeille and Pascal Thubert. Special thank to Patrick Wetterwald with whom I spend long hours working on IP smart objects for the last few years.

I would like to warmly thank several Cisco executives who supported the work other the years: Marthin De Beer, Laura Ipsen, Ben Fathi, Win Elfrink and Guido Jouret.

A particular thank to Jaudelice De Oliveira (Professor at Drexel University) for years of friendship and fruitful collaboration, and to Joydeep Tripathi for the collaboration to write a sensor network simulator that we used to provide several simulation results provided in the Chapter 17 of this book.

JP Vasseur

First and foremost, I would like to thank the large number of people who have contributed to the success of the Contiki operating system and of the uIP and lwIP TCP/IP stacks. In particular, I would like to thank the members of the Contiki core team, who have all put in a tremendous effort to make Contiki what it is today: Oliver Schmidt, Niclas Finne, Joakim Eriksson, Fredrik Österlind, Nicolas Tsiftes, Mathilde Durvy, and Julien Abeillé. I would also like to thank all members of my research group at the Swedish Institute of Computer Science: Joakim Eriksson, Niclas Finne, Zhitao He, Marcus Lundén, Luca Mottola, Shahid Raza, Nicolas Tsiftes, Thiemo Voigt, Dogan Yazar, and Fredrik Österlind, for conducting top-quality research, and for being such inspiring people to work with. Likewise, I am also in debt to all collaborators in the numerous research projects I am involved in and have been involved in over the years. Being surrounded by so many great people is a tremendous gift.

I would like to thank my current and former lab managers, Sverker Janson and Bengt Ahlgren, SICS CEO Staffan Truvé, and SICS business manager Janusz Launberg, for their support and their confidence in my work with IP-based smart objects over the past ten years.

Finally, I would like to thank my wife Maria for her great support and patience with me during the writing of this book.

Adam Dunkels

The Architecture

What Are Smart Objects?

1

This book is about smart objects, networks of smart objects, and how these networks can be interconnected using the Internet Protocol (IP). In this chapter, we define smart objects, give an overview of the history of smart object technology, and discuss the present challenges.

Smart object technology has many names. In this book, we use the term smart objects, but the technology and its applications have names such as the Internet of Things, the web of objects, the web of things, and cooperating objects. Even though there are slight differences in the connotations and definitions of those names, they represent the same fundamental type of technology.

One definition of smart objects is a purely technical definition — a smart object is an item equipped with a form of sensor or actuator, a tiny microprocessor, a communication device, and a power source. The sensor or actuator gives the smart object the ability to interact with the physical world. The microprocessor enables the smart object to transform the data captured from the sensors, albeit at a limited speed and at limited complexity. The communication device enables the smart object to communicate its sensor readings to the outside world and receive input from other smart objects. The power source provides the electrical energy for the smart object to do its work.

For smart objects, size matters. They are significantly smaller than both laptops and cell phones. For smart objects to be embedded in everyday objects, their physical size cannot exceed a few cubic centimeters.

Although this technical definition of a smart object is important — we review it at length in Part II — it does not help us understand the behavior, interaction, and other implications of smart objects. Thus we must define smart objects based on their behavior.

We already know that smart objects are able to interact with the physical world by performing limited forms of computation as well as communicate with the outside world and with other smart objects. But what do smart objects, given their technical abilities, actually do?

The answer to this question is not as easy as it seems. First, the behavior of a smart object depends heavily on where and how it is used. A smart object deployed in a freighter container to monitor its temperature behaves differently than a smart object that monitors parking spaces. Second, and more important, we cannot know at this point how future smart objects will be used. Even though we can accurately predict future smart object uses based on how smart objects are used today, we cannot know exactly what the future usage patterns will be. This is an important point, because it tells designers of smart object systems that they must future-proof their systems, protocols, and architectures.

Despite not knowing the exact behavior of a smart object, there are two behavioral properties common to any smart object: interaction with the physical world and communication.

Interconnecting Smart Objects with IP. DOI: 10.1016/B978-0-12-375165-2.00001-6

Smart objects interact with the physical world by obtaining information from the physical world with their sensors and by affecting the physical world with their actuators. Smart objects use their sensors to sense physical properties ranging from simple and easy-to-measure properties such as light, temperature, and air humidity, to more complex properties such as air pollution, the presence of a car, or when an industrial machine is about to break down. Smart objects affect the physical world using different forms of actuators. This may be as simple as switching on a small LED or as complex as switching on the heat in a particular part of a building.

Smart objects communicate. Even though a single smart object can be very useful, by turning on the light in a doorway when the door opens, for example, the real power of smart objects comes from their ability to communicate. The smart object that would previously switch on the door light is now able to communicate that the door was opened to every other nearby smart object. These smart objects may turn on other lights in the house, turn up the heat, and so forth. Likewise, smart objects in an industrial plant that sense the vibration of machinery may communicate their vibration reading both to each other and to the plant's operator. Communication is essential to the behavior of smart objects, thus we frequently use the term *smart object networks* throughout this book.

In Part III of this book, we further explore the question of how smart objects behave through detailed case studies of deployed smart object networks. These case studies provide important insights into how smart objects are used now and how they are intended to be used in the near future to support the myriad of applications impacting our day-to-day lives, but they do not allow us to look into the future. We have to use the available tools — knowledge of history, understanding and experience, and sound engineering practices — to build this technology for the future.

1.1 WHERE DO SMART OBJECTS COME FROM?

Smart objects come from a number of different technology areas and scientific disciplines with each area making its own imprint on the technology.

To understand the origins of smart objects, we must look at the conceptual developments as well as the technological progress that makes smart objects possible. The concepts and the technology have coexisted for a long time and the developments in their respective areas are intertwined, but they have largely progressed and matured independently of each other.

Computing and telephony are two disparate strands of development that have led to the development of smart objects. Both computing and telephony play a large part in the formulation of smart objects, but the two technologies have different cultural and technical histories.

The roots of computing can be traced back to the academic environments that spun out of the aftermath of World War II. Computer scientists such as John von Neumann, who were employed by the US military during WW II, continued their work in the US academic system, often funded by the US military. It was this environment that developed the first computers, the first operating systems, and subsequently the Internet. This culture was often characterized by witty engineering, the development of evolvable systems, and the desire to make the most out of available tools. Frequently, the systems developed in this environment were never intended to have a world-wide distribution, but because they were built to evolve and built on solid engineering principles, they often succeeded in reaching monumental importance. Examples of this include the UNIX family of operating systems whose heirs support most of the Internet today, and indeed, the global Internet itself.

The roots of telephony are older than those of computing, and have taken a slightly different path. The first patent on telephony was filed by Alexander Graham Bell in 1876 (even though others had built telephones prior to Bell). In its humble beginnings, telephony was available only to a lucky few. Installation of a telephone in one's house required a significant investment in infrastructure. Not only were wires needed within the house, but they also had to be drawn all the way from a central switchboard to the house. Furthermore, to connect these wires together across larger distances, the switchboards had to be connected using wires drawn across long distances and each switchboard could even be operated by a different company. All in all, large investments were needed up front, before the system would be able to work, and once the system was installed, it was of utmost importance that it worked. This led to a culture where systems were rigorously specified before they were ever implemented. Without rigorous specification, it would be extremely difficult, if not impossible, to connect disparate operators and their various equipment. To make things even more difficult, the telephony companies have always been monitored by legislators and governments, requiring even more rigorous attention to detail.

Smart objects represent the middle ground between computing and telephony, borrowing from both. From its computing heritage, smart objects have assumed the culture of engineering evolvable systems. This is important because at this point, it is impossible to fully specify the expected behavior of future smart object systems, even if we have a good idea of where smart objects are heading today. From its telephony heritage, smart objects have applied the principles from connecting disparate systems that may be managed by different companies and organizations. Smart objects are not manufactured by a single organization, but by multitudes of different people and parties. Smart object technology must be both evolvable and standardized.

In the remainder of this chapter, we discuss areas leading up to today's smart objects as shown in Figure 1.1: embedded systems, ubiquitous and pervasive computing, mobile telephony, telemetry, wireless sensor networks, mobile computing, and computer networking. Some of these areas come from the computing heritage and some from the telephony heritage. Some have sprung out of academic research communities, some from an industrial background. What they have in common,

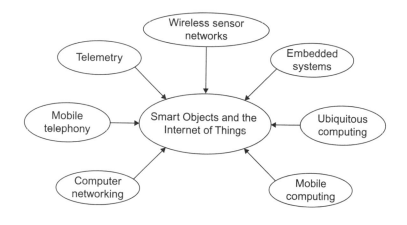

FIGURE 1.1

Smart objects are the intersection of embedded systems, ubiquitous computing, mobile telephony, telemetry, wireless sensor networks, mobile computing, and computer networking.

however, is that they either deal with computationally assisted connectivity among physical items, wireless communication, or with interaction between the virtual and the physical world.

1.1.1 Embedded Systems

An embedded system is a computer embedded in something other than a computer. Under this definition, any system that has a microprocessor is an embedded system with the exception of PCs, laptops, and other equipment readily identified as a computer. Thus this definition of an embedded system would include smart objects. Figure 1.2 illustrates different types of embedded systems.

Traditionally, at least until the late 1990s, embedded systems were thought to be synonymous with real-time control systems. Real-time control systems are computer-based systems used to control physical processes such as the pressure of a nozzle, the rudder of a ship, or the temperature of a radiator. In these control systems, an embedded computer typically is used to control the signals to an actuator that controls the phenomenon to be controlled. For a control system to work, it is imperative that the embedded computer produces signals to control the actuator with precise timing. Precise timing is required because the controller interacts with the physical world. A ship's rudder without precise timing would not be able to reliably steer a ship. This type of precise timing requirement is embodied in the concept of *real-time*. A real-time system is a system that always responds to external input, or a timer, in a pre-specified amount of time. The software for these devices needs to be strict

FIGURE 1.2

Embedded systems are microprocessor-equipped systems and devices that interact with the physical world. Examples include traffic lights, a ship's rudder controllers, and washing machine controllers.

about its timing, and operating systems that provide this strict timing are called Real-Time Operating Systems (RTOS).

Although the traditional definition of an embedded system focuses on its real-time aspects, not all embedded systems have real-time requirements. With the widespread adoption of microcontrollers in everyday items such as TV remote controls, wireless car keys, and toys, a new class of embedded systems has emerged. These systems do not have the same strict real-time requirements as the traditional embedded control systems, but are built using the same type of hardware. Many of these systems use RTOS similar to the real-time systems because this is the kind of software technology widely available for the class of hardware used.

Embedded and real-time systems share many properties with smart objects. The hardware used in embedded systems is typically similar to or the same as that used for smart objects. Embedded systems typically have similar constraints in terms of computational power and memory. Often the same types of microcontrollers used in embedded systems are used in smart objects. Thus much of the software used for embedded systems can be used for smart objects and vice versa.

The primary difference between a traditional embedded system and a smart object is that communication is typically not considered a central function for embedded systems, whereas communication is a defining characteristic for smart objects. Although there are many examples of communicating embedded systems, such as car engines with embedded microprocessors that can communicate their status information to a computer connected to the engine at service time, these systems are not defined by their ability to communicate. A car engine that cannot communicate can still operate as a car engine. In contrast, a smart object such as a wireless temperature sensor deprived of its communication abilities would no longer be able to fulfill its purpose.

1.1.2 Ubiquitous and Pervasive Computing

Ubiquitous computing, also called pervasive computing, is a field of study based on the concept of what happens when computers move away from the desktop and become immersed in the surrounding environment as illustrated in Figure 1.3. Ubiquitous computing, as a research discipline, originated in the mid-1980s. The term was coined by Mark Weiser, a professor at MIT, in 1988. Weiser published two short notes titled "Ubiquitous computing #1" and "Ubiquitous computing #2." In these texts, he laid out a future where computing, as we know it, was no longer done by desktop computers. Instead, he believed computing would move into our daily environment, living in "the woodwork of everywhere" as exemplified in Figure 1.3.

Mark Weiser criticized the trend of making computers exciting objects in their own right. He took a different perspective: instead of making computers the central object, they would become invisible. Weiser further argued that as technology became successful, it became invisible.

One example of how successful technology becomes invisible is the motor. At the start of the twentieth century, the US-based Sears mail-order catalog sold a "home motor." The home motor, which was fairly substantial, was designed to be placed at a central location in people's homes. The purpose of the home motor was to run various types of external equipment. Together with the motor, customers could purchase connectors that would let the motor run sewing machines, meat grinders, and hair dryers.

Today, motors have become the type of successful technology that has become invisible. Motors are found in various types of equipment and machines such as toothbrushes, hair dryers, car windows,

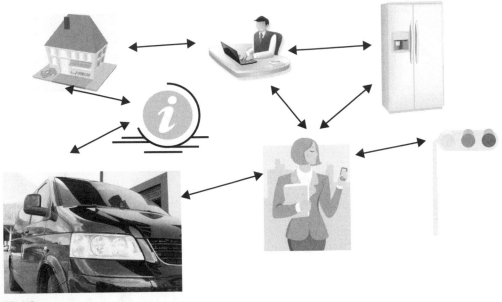

FIGURE 1.3

Ubiquitous computing is a vision for the future of computers where computing moves into everyday objects.

and automatic locks. Yet very few of us ever consider that a motor drives these everyday items. Of course, if we stop and think about it, we can imagine that there are small motors inside these systems, but we never see the motor as a defining feature. Motors have become invisible.

Ubiquitous computing has become an established academic research field with several major annual conferences and a number of scientific journals. Hundreds of doctoral theses have been written about this topic over the last two decades.

As an academic discipline, ubiquitous computing places a strong focus on building real systems that embody its ideas. There is a long string of important prototype systems that come from the ubiquitous computing community. These prototypes have been instrumental in pursuing the field of ubiquitous computing as well as demonstrating the feasibility of an ever-connected world.

One early example of a ubiquitous prototype system is the Active Badges system developed at the AT&T laboratory in Cambridge, UK, in the late 1980s and early 1990s [253]. The Active Badges system was composed of badges worn by people in an office and a set of readers dispersed throughout the office environment. The badges uniquely identified each wearer and the readers enabled the system to keep track of the location of all badge wearers. This location would be recorded and displayed on an application running on the participant's desktop PC. With the system each participant knew where everyone was and where to contact them.

The ubiquitous community has moved toward interacting with ubiquitous systems immersed in an ambient environment. In 1996 the ambientROOM project at MIT was developed [133] as an example of enriching an environment with ubiquitous computing. The ambientROOM was fully equipped with interaction devices. The walls were used to display an abstract pattern of light that changed based on outside input. Ambient sound was played that indicated activity on the local network.

Wearable computing is a field that has grown out of the ubiquitous computing community. With wearable computing, the computing infrastructure moves onto the body of its users [165] or into their clothing [89]. Wearable computers make ubiquitous computing truly person-centric.

Smart objects owe much of their history to ubiquitous computing. Many of the early developments and vision in ubiquitous computing directly apply to smart objects. Whereas ubiquitous computing is interested in the interaction between ubiquitous computing systems and humans, the area of smart objects takes a more technical approach. Much of the technology developed for smart objects has a direct applicability to ubiquitous computing. Similarly, much of the designs that have been developed within the ubiquitous computing community can be applied to smart objects as well.

1.1.3 Mobile Telephony

Mobile telephony grew out of the telephony industry with the promise of ubiquitous access to telephony. Today, mobile telephony not only provides telephony everywhere, but also Internet access. Even though the first steps toward mobile telephony were taken in the mid-twentieth century, it was not until the 1980s that the first commercial mobile telephony operators started gaining momentum. In the late 1990s, nearly 20% of the population in the developed world had a mobile telephone. In 2008, there were more than 4 billion mobile telephony subscribers.

Mobile telephony is often called cellular telephony, and mobile phones are called cell phones, because of the structure of the wireless networks in which mobile phones operate. The network is divided into cells where each phone is connected to exactly one cell at any given time. A cell covers a physical area whose size is determined by the network operator. Since each cell typically handles a limited number of simultaneous phone calls, network operators plan their networks so that cells are smaller and more numerous in areas where operators expect more people to make phone calls. Each cell is operated by a cell tower on which a wireless transceiver base station is mounted. The base station maintains a wireless connection to all active phones in its cell. When the user and the phone move to another cell, the base stations perform an exchange called a handover.

Mobile telephony has given rise to long-range wireless networking technology such as Global System for Mobile communications (GSM), General Packet Radio Service (GPRS), Enhanced Data Rates for GSM Evolution (EDGE), and Universal Mobile Telecommunications System (UMTS) as well as short-range wireless communication technology such as Bluetooth (IEEE 802.15.1). Long-range communication is used to transmit voice and Internet data from the mobile phone to the nearest base station. Short-range wireless communication is used for communication between the phone and wireless accessories such as wireless headsets.

Mobile telephony has revolutionized the way we think of personal connectivity. Telephony used to be restricted to a few physical locations: we had a phone at the desk in our office and a few phones at strategic locations in our homes, such as the kitchen or next to the TV. As telephony became mobile, we stopped thinking about telephony as location-bound, but as a ubiquitous always-on service, available everywhere.

Mobile telephony not only revolutionized person-to-person access, but changed the way we view network access. In the late 1990s, the Internet was confined to PCs. Establishing an Internet connection required an expressed action: switch on the modem, open the modem dialing program on the PC, and click the "Connect" button. After half a minute of noise from the modem, the Internet connection was established. The interaction was anything but seamless.

With modern smartphones, Internet access is no longer confined to PCs; it is truly ubiquitous. With a few quick button presses, e-mail, instant messaging, and the World Wide Web are immediately available. Instant Internet access is equally available in foreign countries, even if it sometimes costs a small fortune.

The way mobile telephony changed the general view on connectivity is an important factor for the continued development of smart objects. As we are now accustomed to think of connectivity as ubiquitous, we are equally accustomed to think of access to smart objects as ubiquitous. This view was not as widespread in the early 2000s.

1.1.4 Telemetry and Machine-to-machine Communication

The word telemetry is a portmanteau of the Greek words *tele* (remote) and *metron* (to measure). Telemetry is, as the name implies, about performing remote measurements. Machine-to-machine communication is a generalization of telemetry that implies autonomic communication between non-human operated machines and is central to the concept of telemetry. Telemetry is used to transmit information about current temperature, humidity, and wind from distant weather stations (Figure 1.4). Telemetry is used to transmit fuel consumption data from trucks so that the owner can optimize the truck's routes to save on fuel costs, and as a consequence reduce pollution.

The concept of machine-to-machine communication and telemetry is also used in shorter distances. Today's pacemakers (devices that are implanted in the hearts of people who have had a heart attack) frequently include a device called a "telemetry coil." This allows a doctor to monitor the pacemaker's activity without surgery. Instead, the doctor uses a device that creates a low-power electromagnetic field near the patient. The telemetry coil reacts to the electrical field by modulating it creating a low-power communication mechanism with which information can be transferred from the patient's heart to the doctor.

FIGURE 1.4

Telemetry allows reading measurements from remote systems such as weather stations. Data are typically transported using mobile telephony systems.

Telemetry and machine-to-machine communication are similar to smart objects because they are both used to perform large-scale measurements. With telemetry, these measurements can be performed from a remote site without direct physical access. Remote access using telemetry is most often performed with existing mobile telephony networks such as GSM or 3G (UMTS), or via dedicated networks such as the Inmarsat satellite network. Smart objects are not only used for measurements and sensing, but also affect their environment by using actuators. Nevertheless, much of the remote access technology developed for telemetry systems can be used with and applied to smart object systems.

1.1.5 Wireless Sensor and Ubiquitous Sensor Networks

Wireless sensor networks have evolved from the idea that small wireless sensors can be used to collect information from the physical environment in a large number of situations ranging from wild fire tracking and animal observation to agriculture management and industrial monitoring. Each sensor wirelessly transmits information toward a base station. Sensors help each other to relay the information to the base station, as illustrated in Figure 1.5. The research field of wireless sensor networks has been very active since the early 2000s with several annual conferences, many journals, and a large number of annual workshops. Wireless sensor networks are sometimes called ubiquitous sensor networks to highlight the ubiquity of the sensors.

Early work in wireless sensor networks envisioned sensor networks to be composed of so-called smart dust [142]. Smart dust would be composed of large numbers of tiny electronic systems with

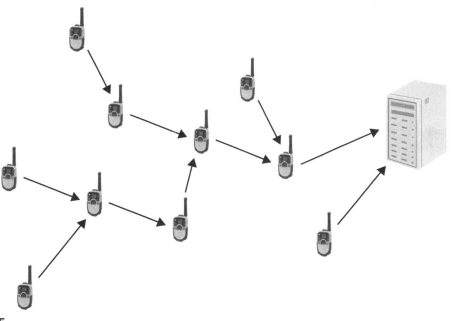

FIGURE 1.5

Wireless sensor networks provide large-scale measurements of physical properties using large amounts of sensors that transport their data wirelessly to a base station.

sensing, computation, and communication abilities. It would be spread over an area where a phenomenon, such as humidity or temperature, was to be measured. Because the dust specks would be so small, they could be dispersed using mechanisms such as air flow. The applications of smart dust would initially be used by the military to track the location of enemies, to signal an alarm when intruders were found, or to detect the presence of a vehicle.

The concept of smart dust was, however, too restrictive for most uses. The limited physical size of the dust specks severely limited possible communication mechanisms and the computational capability of the nodes. Instead, many research groups started building hardware prototypes with a larger physical size that were easier to use for experimentation [200].

The research community around wireless sensor networks has developed many important mechanisms, algorithms, and abstractions. Wireless sensor networks are intended to have a long lifetime. Since wireless sensors typically use batteries, having a long lifetime translates into reducing the power consumption of the individual nodes. Thus, several power-saving mechanisms have been designed, deployed, studied, and evaluated both in simulators and in actual deployments. Many of these have a direct applicability to smart objects.

Wireless sensor networks have further spurred work in standardization for industrial automation and monitoring. Many of the recent standards in wireless industrial networking, such as WirelessHART and ISA100a, have their roots in the wireless sensor networking community.

The concept of wireless sensor networks is similar to that of smart objects, and much of the development in smart objects has occurred in the community around wireless sensor networks. Wireless sensor networks are composed of small nodes, equipped with a wireless communication device, that autonomously configure themselves into networks through which sensor readings can be transported. Smart object networks are less focused on pure data gathering, but are intended for a large number of other tasks including actuation and control. Furthermore, wireless sensor networks are primarily intended to be operated over a wireless radio communications device. In contrast, the concept of smart objects is not tied to any particular communication mechanism, but can run over wired as well as wireless networks.

1.1.6 Mobile Computing

Mobile computing is the field of wireless communication and carry-around computers, such as laptop computers. In some ways the mobile computing field spun out of work initialized within the ubiquitous computing area. Likewise, the early focus on wireless networking led to wireless communication mechanism research. Work on these mechanisms began in the mid-1980s and led up to the standards around wireless local area networks (WiFi) that started forming in the late 1990s.

The field of mobile computing has benefited greatly from the technical advances in computing technology such as low-power PC processors, small-size digital memory technology, and inexpensive display systems. The combination of those technologies has created the field of laptop computing, which has led to the creation of the new class of inexpensive laptops called netbooks. Netbooks are designed with wireless communication in mind.

Mobile computing has further permeated wireless network access. Today, so-called WiFi hot spots at public places such as coffee houses, libraries, and airports are common. Users may connect to the Internet through this wireless network either gratis or for a fee.

In academia, the field of mobile computing also carried over into the research field of Mobile Ad hoc NETworks (MANETs). MANET research focuses on networking mechanisms for wireless computers where no network infrastructure exists. In such situations, routing protocols and other network mechanisms must quickly establish an ad hoc network. The network formation is made in a distributed manner where each node that participates in the network must take part in the network's mechanisms such as routing and access control. The MANET community has developed several important routing protocols for these networks such as the standardized AODV and DSR protocols.

Just as with mobile telephony, the use of mobile computing has permeated the understanding that network access is ubiquitous. As WiFi access has become widespread, we now take connectivity for granted anywhere, instantly.

1.1.7 Computer Networking

Computer networking is about connecting computers to allow them to communicate with each other. Computers are connected using networks as shown in Figure 1.6. These networks were initially wired, but with the advent of mobile computing, wireless networks are available.

The field of computer networking is significantly older than that of mobile computing. Computer networking began in the early 1960s when the breakthrough concepts of packet-switched networking were first described by Leonard Kleinrock at UCLA [151]. Earlier telephony networks were circuit-switched, and each connection (phone call) created a circuit through the network where all data were transported. With packet-switched networking, no circuits were constructed through the network. Instead, each message was transported as a packet through the network where each node would switch the packet depending on its destination address.

After Kleinrock's breakthrough, ARPANET was created as the first large-scale computer network built on the concepts of a packet-switched network. During the late 1970s and early 1980s,

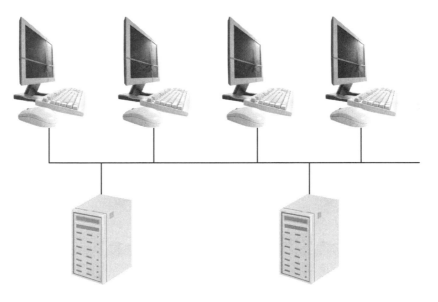

FIGURE 1.6

Computer networking allows computers and systems to communicate with each other. It forms the basis of today's Internet.

ARPANET was gradually replaced with the early versions of the Internet. ARPANET started to use the IP protocol suite in 1983 before becoming the Internet.

The ARPANET and the Internet were built on a powerful concept called the end-to-end principle of system design, named by an influential paper by Jerome H. Saltzer, David P. Reed, and David D. Clark [218]. The end-to-end principle states that functionality in a system should be placed as long as possible toward the end points. For the Internet, this meant that the end systems, the computers that connected to the Internet, should perform most of the work in the communication over the network with the network acting relatively dumb. Thus the network would only provide a mechanism for sending packets to and from the end points. This principle has arguably been one of the most important aspects of the design of the Internet system, because it allowed the system to gracefully support an ever-growing flora of applications from simple e-mail and file transport of the 1980s through the Web revolution of the 1990s transmission to high-speed, real-time video, and audio transmissions of the 2000s. The end-to-end principle allowed the network to evolve separately from these applications, thus making it possible to support an ever-growing number of users and uses, without requiring complex re-engineering of the entire network and its protocols.

The connection between computer networking and smart objects is evident: communication is one of the defining characteristics of smart objects. In this book, we argue that many of the concepts, protocols, and mechanisms that have been developed in the computer networking community are suitable for smart object networks.

1.2 CHALLENGES FOR SMART OBJECTS

As with any novel technology, there are technical and non-technical challenges in the development of smart objects. Some of these challenges are novel to the area of smart objects, but many are shared with existing systems and other developments, such as those outlined in the previous section.

The technical challenges for smart objects include the node-level internals of each smart object, such as power consumption and physical size, as well as the network-level mechanisms and structures formed by the smart objects. To make matters more complex, the two aspects often affect each other. For example, the power consumption of a smart object is affected by the communication patterns of the network in which the smart object participates. Likewise, the design of the network protocols for smart objects must take power consumption into account, when, for example, deciding when and where to send data.

There are also a number of non-technical challenges that need to be tackled before the widespread adoption of smart objects occurs. These non-technical challenges may even prove to be more challenging than the technical ones. Whereas the technical challenges revolve around how to design protocols and mechanisms for smart objects, the non-technical challenges are about spreading both the technology and the awareness the technology. Without general awareness of the technology, even the most beautifully engineered and technically perfect solutions will fail to achieve any large-scale impact.

The Internet Protocol for Smart Objects (IPSO) Alliance was set up for the purpose of spreading the awareness of the technology around smart objects. It was founded around the idea that smart objects need evolvable technology and that the technology around the IP, as well as the mechanisms and culture in which the technology is developed, would provide just that technology. We return to the IPSO Alliance in Chapter 18.

1.2.1 **Node-level Challenges**

The node-level challenges of smart objects primarily have to do with power consumption, physical size, and cost. Power consumption is a critical factor with smart objects because they are often either battery-powered or use an external low-power energy source such as physical vibrations or low-power electromagnetic fields. Physical size is important because the size and form factor determines the potential applications for a given smart object system — smart objects must be small. Cost is important with smart objects because of large-scale deployments. With deployments of many thousands of smart objects, cost savings of a few dollars quickly add up to significant amounts of money.

The severe power consumption constraints have design implications for the hardware, software, the network protocols, and even the network architecture. For the hardware designer, it is imperative to choose low-power hardware components and arrange them to minimize current leakage and to provide a power-efficient sleep mode. The software designer must be able to use the hardware to make the most out of the limited resources. The software must switch off unused components and put the hardware into sleep mode as often as possible. To aid the software developer, smart objects run operating systems that provide mechanisms for low-power operation.

Power efficiency significantly affects network architectures and protocol designs as well. Because communication consumes power, it is important to steer the communication patterns so they efficiently use available resources. To help the network protocols to do this, the hardware and software keep track of the spent energy and provide this information to the network layer. Additionally, to save power, the system designer must put the device into sleep mode as much as possible. Sleep modes affect the communication latency of the system, often in ways that are difficult to predict beforehand.

Physical size and cost have profound implications for both the hardware and software designer. For the hardware designer, the implications are that the hardware must be small, the number of components must be low, and each component must be small and inexpensive. The implications for the software designer are less obvious but equally profound. With low cost, low physical size, and low power consumption, the microprocessors on which the software runs become smaller as their computational speed and memory size are reduced.

The software designer for a smart object system often has only a few thousand bytes of memory to work with compared to the millions or billions of bytes of memory that software designers for general purpose computing systems have at their disposal. Thus the software for smart objects must not only be power-efficient but must be able to run within a severely resource-scarce environment.

The resource constraints that so deeply affect the node level also have implications at the network level. With the limitations on the amount of memory in each smart object, the network protocols must be designed so they limit the amount of information each node keeps about the network and about other nodes in the network. Like the power constraints, the memory constraints have a two-way effect: the network architecture is affected by the node-level effects and the network-level effects affect the node level.

We return to the node-level challenges of smart objects in detail in Part II.

1.2.2 **Network-level Challenges**

The node-level challenges of smart objects deal with the *small* scale of available resources, whereas the network-level challenges deal with the *large* scale of the smart object networks. As we see in Part III of this book, even if there are numerous examples of small-scale smart object networks, many networks can potentially be very large—on the order of thousands of nodes.

Smart object networks are potentially very large scale both in terms of the number of nodes involved in a system and in the number of data items generated by each node. As we see in the case studies in Part III, many of the situations in which smart objects are used call for a large set of individual data collection points. Individual networks consisting of thousands of nodes are common.

In each of these smart object networks, each node will generate several millions of data items over its lifetime. Consider a smart object network that samples the temperature inside a building. Temperature is generally a slow-moving phenomenon, so the nodes do not need to sample very often. Still, people in the building may forget to close a window or leave the outer door halfway open, and the system should be prepared to detect this within a reasonable time frame. Considering these requirements, the building manager instructs the system to sample the temperature twice every minute. With a sampling rate of two readings per minute, 2880 readings are taken each day, or 737,280 readings per year. Because the system is designed to work for ten years, there will be over seven million readings, from each node, during the lifetime of the system. This example is taken from a situation with a relatively slow sampling rate, but it makes it clear that smart object networks work at large scales in terms of both network and data size.

The challenges of network and data size are in some ways disparate but in other ways entwined.

The network size impacts the protocol design used for message routing in smart object networks. Routing is the process by which the network determines what paths messages should take through the network. Routing can be made either centrally, where a central server computes a route map for the entire network, or distributed, where each node makes individual decisions on where to send each message.

The design of the routing protocols is important because it affects both network performance in terms of the amount of data the network can sustain, the speed of which these data can be successfully transported through the network, and, in most cases, the achievable lifetime of the network as a whole. For most smart object systems, the act of communication requires energy, and nodes that communicate often drain their energy faster than those that are silent. Thus the routing protocol must make well-informed choices when planning how messages are transported through the network.

For a node to make a well-informed routing choice, it typically requires information about both the network as a whole and about the node's nearest neighbors. This information requires memory, but as we have already discussed, each node has a limited amount of memory. So the routing protocol must carefully choose what information to keep about the network and the neighbors and what information to disregard.

To make matters worse, smart object networks often run over unreliable communication media. Such communication media include low-power wireless communication standards as well as Powerline communication, where the communication takes place over the electrical grid. In these communication media, it is uncertain if a message sent by one node is received by the node for which it was intended. The message may be disrupted or may be entirely blocked on its way, perhaps because a large body of metal just happened to be placed between the wireless sender and the wireless receiver. Even if the message was not entirely blocked, its bits may have been altered in transit so that the receiver cannot make any sense of it.

The unreliable nature of smart object networks is often referred to as being "lossy." Lossyness is best thought of as an inherent property of smart object networks. Even if smart objects use communication technologies that are less lossy than others, by preparing for the worst a system can be created that is stable both for lossy and non-lossy networks.

The lossy nature of smart object networks is an additional challenge for routing protocols. Protocols must take the lossyness into account when deciding where to route messages and if messages should be re-sent. Messages should be routed so that the risk of them getting lost is lessened. But if a message has been routed over a path that happens to become lossy, the message may need to be re-sent a few times, in case it did not make it through on the first try.

Lossyness is an illusive property, particularly in wireless networks. Lossyness is affected by environmental factors such as temperature and humidity of the air as well as the physical surroundings of the smart object networks. For example, if a microwave oven is switched on, the electromagnetic field it creates can interfere with wireless transmissions on the 2.4 GHz band. Likewise, a WiFi computer network may interfere with a smart object network so that the smart object network sees more lossy behavior at daytime, when people are using the WiFi network, than during nighttime. Routing protocols for smart object networks must be prepared for this illusiveness.

The large-scale nature of smart object networks complicates addressing the nodes. In a large-scale network, each individual node must be addressable so that messages can be sent to it. The address must be long enough for each node to have an individual address, even in a large network. And even if the network is small, it may interact with external smart object networks. In this case, the addresses of the nodes in the two networks must be unique. As the number of smart object networks that potentially can interact with each other grows, we must be prepared for the scale to grow exponentially. Thus the addressing scheme chosen for smart object networks must uniquely identify several millions or even billions of individual nodes.

Given the large scale of smart object networks, network management becomes a daunting challenge. With smart object networks comprised of potentially thousands of nodes, traditional network management practices are not immediately applicable. Traditional management requires manual fine-tuning of the network infrastructure by a systems administrator. With smart objects forming ad hoc, the network must be prepared to manage itself, without any human network operator in the loop. Furthermore, in traditional computer-based networks, each computer connected to the network requires manual or semi-manual configuration. The person at the computer may need to, for example, enter a password to access the network. For smart object networks, it is not feasible for a person to manually enter a password into each smart object every time it needs to access its network.

The scale of the smart object networks not only pertains to the number of devices and the amount of data, but also to the amount of different environments and types of systems in which smart objects are used. For smart objects, no single communication technology suffices for all potential needs. For example, a smart object network operating in a highly controlled industrial environment has different requirements and cost structures than a smart object network operating in an office or home environment. Thus smart object networks must be prepared to run over a set of different underlying communication technologies, both wireless and wired.

Finally, a smart object network must provide mechanisms for external access to itself. There are situations where a smart object network is useful in isolation, but more often data produced by the smart object network need to be extracted so they can be processed or stored elsewhere. Also, the smart object network may need to be reconfigured or altered during operation. In either case, the smart object network must be able to be accessed externally.

As with the node-level challenges, we return to the network-level challenges later in this book, both in this part and, in more detail, in Part II.

1.2.3 **Standardization**

Standardization is a critical success factor for smart objects. Smart object systems are characterized not only by large numbers of devices and applications, but by a significant amount of different parties, manufacturers, and companies interested in contributing to the technology. Different technology manufacturers have different specializations. An equipment manufacturer that specializes in high-precision humidity sensors may not be interested in IT systems. Yet, these two must work together in a building automation system where the humidity sensors produce valuable input to the control of the environment in the building. The environment control system is controlled by an advanced IT system that receives its input from the humidity sensors.

Without standardization, equipment manufacturers and system integrators would need to build new systems from the ground up on every installed system. Alternatively, manufacturers and integrators would use a proprietary technology from a single vendor. Such proprietary technology might provide benefits in the short term, but it effectively creates vendor lock-in where both manufacturers and integrators have difficulties evolving their systems beyond the proprietary technology provided by the vendor. Furthermore, since the technology is proprietary, the vendor controls the future of the technology and manufacturers and integrators cannot control where their systems are going.

With standardized technology, the technology is independent of its vendors, producers, and users. Any vendor may choose to provide systems based on the technology, and equipment manufacturers and system integrators may choose to base their systems on technology from any vendor.

Standardized technology has a major advantage in terms of acceptance. When the technology is standardized, vendors, manufacturers, and system integrators can easily adopt the technology without risks of vendor lock-in. This level of acceptance is critical to the success of smart objects as a technology because of the large number of different devices, the large number of applications, and the multitude of existing and potential vendors.

Before continuing we must note that when we discuss standards, we are explicitly referring to the open standards produced through established practices of international standardization organizations. Even though it is possible to define a specification that has properties similar to a standard, such specifications typically have not been thoroughly vetted. Open standards reviewed by established organizations are also assessed in terms of intellectual property claims. Existing standardization organizations have policies stating that any intellectual property claims, such as patents, for technology that is standardized through them have to be openly published and sometimes freely licensed to anyone who wishes to adopt the standard. This is intended to provide a form of protection against so-called submarine patents, where a patent holder keeps a patent a secret, only to later come forth, as the technology has been widely adopted, to lay claim to the technology.

Standardization of smart object technology is a challenge not only in terms of technology but also in terms of organizations. Smart objects comprise many different levels of technology from low-power communication technologies, through networking and routing, and to application-level access and IT system integration. Each of these levels has their own technical challenges, but more important, standardization in each level is managed by different bodies.

For smart objects, as with any emerging technology, several standards and non-standard specifications have been produced. These range from specific specifications for particular low-power radio protocols to full protocol families. Although these specifications provide a technically viable solution to specific applications, their status as non-standard or proprietary is problematic for many vendors and manufacturers.

1.2.4 **Interoperability**

Interoperability is the ability of equipment and systems from different vendors to operate together. Interoperability is a must as smart objects emerge as a large-scale technology. Interoperability is essential both between smart objects from different manufacturers and between smart objects and existing infrastructures.

For smart objects, interoperability is as multifaceted as standardization. Smart objects must interoperate from the physical layer up to the application or integration layer. Physical layer interoperability occurs when equipment from different vendors physically communicates with each other. At the physical level, smart objects must agree on matters such as the physical frequencies at which communication takes place, what type of modulation the physical signals should carry, and the rate at which information is transferred. At the network level, nodes must agree on the format of the information that is sent and received over the physical channel and how nodes are addressed, as well as how messages should be transported through a network of smart objects. At the application or integration level, smart objects must share a common view on how data should be entered or extracted from a smart object network, as well as how the smart objects should be reached from outside systems.

The challenges of interoperability are in the technical definition of smart objects as well as the standardization and implementation and testing processes. To achieve interoperability, it is imperative that the technical architecture of smart objects is defined to ease interoperability. If the architecture either disallows interoperability or makes interoperability cumbersome, it is very difficult to achieve interoperability later. Likewise, the standardization process must make interoperability a primary concern. To do this, smart object standards cannot be tied to any particular hardware or communication technology. After standardization is complete, a testing or certification procedure helps to achieve and ensure interoperability between different devices and vendors.

As with standardization, interoperability poses several challenges for smart objects. First, the technical architecture for smart objects is still an open issue. In this book, we choose one such architecture for smart objects: the IP architecture. Second, although some of the standards for smart objects are still under development, those standards that already exist can be reused. We return to this ongoing standardization process in Part II. Third, interoperability test suites and conformance tests are still an open issue. Ideally, such interoperability test suites should test many levels of interoperability such as physical, networking, and application levels. There is an ongoing effort to develop such test suites for smart objects by the IPSO Alliance. The IPSO Alliance is further discussed in Chapter 18.

1.3 **CONCLUSIONS**

Smart objects can be defined in several dimensions: through the technology on which each smart object is based, on their operation, or though their intended use. Each smart object consists of a microprocessor, a communication device, a sensor or actuator, and a power source. The microprocessor provides the smart object with the necessary computational power to make it smart. The communication device allows the smart object to communicate with other smart objects as well as other systems. The sensors or actuators connect the smart object with the physical world, allowing it to measure or affect the physical phenomena. A power source is needed to run the electronics in the smart object. These include batteries or renewable energy such as solar cells or piezoelectric devices that produce energy from vibrations or movement. In either case, the power source is severely limited in terms of the amount of energy it can produce.

Smart objects are defined by their communication, their interaction with the physical world, their relatively small physical size, and their low cost. They communicate with other smart object as well as the surrounding systems through their communication device. Interaction with the physical world, such as sensing or actuation, is made through the sensors or actuators built into the smart objects. Physical size is important because smart objects are typically integrated in other items or deployed in places where a large physical size would be obtrusive. Low cost is important because smart objects are manufactured and deployed in large numbers. A cost reduction of a few dollars translates into a large saving of the system as a whole.

Smart objects have emerged from many different directions, yet they have roots both in the computing and telecommunications industries. The history of smart objects can be traced to ubiquitous and pervasive computing, mobile telephony and telemetry, mobile computing and computer networking, and embedded systems and wireless sensor networks.

Although smart objects, as a technology, are quickly emerging, it is not without challenges. These challenges are at both the node and the network levels. At the node level, the restrictions in terms of physical size, cost, and power consumption are challenges that have to be considered when understanding and designing smart object systems. At the network level, the scale of nodes in smart object networks and the power consumption and memory constraints of the nodes must be examined.

The challenges in the base smart object technology are reflected in the challenges of standardization and interoperability. Standardization is essential to the success of future smart object systems, as the technology will be produced by many different parties. Likewise, interoperability is essential between smart object devices and between smart objects and the surrounding IT ecosystem.

It is important that mechanisms and standards for smart objects evolve, as we have only seen a few glimpses of what this technology is able to do.

We believe the future for smart objects in terms of technology, standardization, and interoperability is the Internet Protocol, IP. When we first introduced the idea of using IP for smart objects several years ago [64,67], we were met by a healthy skepticism. Today, after a significant amount of work by many different groups of people [1,66,68,73,125,161,176,180,207,221,257,260], these ideas have become widespread in the industry as well as in the research community. The aim of this book is to present the architecture, the technology, and the applications of IP for smart objects.

In Chapters 2 and 3, we present arguments for why IP is the right choice for smart objects, followed by a discussion of the details of the protocols in the IP protocol suite, and how they map onto smart objects. In Part II, we review in detail both the smart object technology and how IP runs on top of this technology, showing the benefits of the IP architecture for smart objects. In Part III, we discuss case studies that show how IP has successfully been used in smart objects in the past and how IP is being used in the smart object systems of the future.

IP Protocol Architecture

2.1 INTRODUCTION

If there was an award for technical design excellence, it should certainly be given to Vint Cerf and Robert Kahn, the original designers of TCP/IP. The TCP/IP architecture, designed about 30 years ago, is now used on billions of devices around the world ranging from portable devices and laptop to super computers. The IP protocol suite has been enhanced to support multicast, Quality of Service (QoS), traffic engineering, and real-time services with the architecture fully preserved. This chapter discusses the original design goals and why this architecture must be preserved.

2.2 FROM NCP TO TCP/IP

Who has not heard of the ARPANET that gave birth to the Internet Protocol? ARPANET was a project funded by the Advanced Research Project Agency (ARPA). One of the first protocols developed was the 1822 protocol, which was quickly replaced by the Network Control Protocol (NCP). This protocol was developed in 1970 with the objective of interconnecting computers with Interface Message Processor (IMP) between various sites over a backbone network provided by BBN. During this time IMPs were interconnecting leased lines of a few K/bits per second (Kbps). Today, these IMPs are routers called smart objects and are deployed using a variety of link types on a much larger scale.

By the end of 1971, 15 sites were interconnected using the NCP protocol, forming the first nucleus of the Internet. Robert Kahn and Vint Cerf later designed TCP to replace NCP (at that time TCP/IP was called TCP since both protocols were not yet decoupled). ARPANET was the first operational network using the concept of packet switching, which was at that time a revolutionary approach for inter-host communication.

The next generation of protocol, IPv4 (Version 4 of TCP), was designed in 1981 and the Internet migrated to it. That protocol was only running on a few systems at that time. It is now running on hundreds of millions of hosts. This is the result of technical excellence.

The National Science Foundation (NSF) played a major role in the development of the Internet and the National Science Foundation Network (NSFNET), which was operational in 1986 using the TCP/IP protocol suite compatible with the ARPANET protocol. NSFNET started with the interconnection of regional and academic networks, the starting point of today's worldwide Internet. Note that major protocols such as BGP [212] were designed during that period. The development of the Internet research was transferred in the late 1980s from DARPA to NSFNET. The NSFNET network was then

Interconnecting Smart Objects with IP. DOI: 10.1016/B978-0-12-375165-2.00002-8

expanded to interconnect all of the regional academic networks in the United States. It is only during the mid-1990s that the NSFNET regional networks further extended to commercial networks, which have driven the exponential growth of the Internet until now.

Then followed the emergence of the new revision of IP (IPv6). IPv6 has not changed the TCP/IP architecture originally specified for IPv4, it is just a revision of IP that brings a series of new features and enhancements in addition to a significantly larger address space.

2.3 FUNDAMENTAL TCP/IP ARCHITECTURAL DESIGN PRINCIPLES

These were the original TCP/IP goals:

- Internet communication must continue despite loss of networks or gateways ("in presence of link or node failures" in today's terms).
- The Internet must support multiple types of communication services.
- Internet architecture must:
  - Accommodate a variety of networks ("networks" means link and physical layers)
  - Permit distributed management of its resources
  - Be cost-effective
  - Permit host attachment with little effort
- Resources used in the Internet architecture must be accountable.

The original objective of the TCP/IP protocol was to design a *single* protocol, but it quickly became evident that such an objective was unrealistic. Indeed, the second goal of the Internet architecture was to support a variety of services, characterized by different requirements such as delay, bandwidth, and jitter, just to name a few. Some services such as file transfers were very tolerant of delays but required high bandwidth in contrast to packetized voice traffic requiring short delays and jitter but low bandwidth.

It was evident very early that TCP could not easily accommodate such a wide scope of requirements. In particular, real-time applications such as digitized voice would typically not require high reliability but would be very intolerant of network delays and jitter. The most predominant component of network jitter was the set of mechanisms used to provide high reliability due to the retransmission of lost packets. It is preferable to drop a packet than to use a reliable transport protocol that would increase reliability using retransmission of lost packets.

This gave birth to the fundamental concept of "layering." The IP layer provides a best-effort service on top of which the transport layer would be chosen according to the applications requirements. So it was decided to decouple IP and TCP and design a new transport protocol (UDP) with IP supporting both UDP and TCP. It was not easy to support this architecture independently due to the nature of the media used. For example, by running UDP/IP over X25, service would still be reliable (thus potentially involving network delays due to retransmission because X25 was not designed to support a variety of services). This observation is still valid for existing link layer protocols, and is even more problematic when redundant services are offered at multiple layers (see multilayer routing architecture discussed in Chapter 5).

Another important goal was the ability to operate over a wide variety of links and physical layers (ARPANET, X25, satellite links, packet radio networks, serial links, etc.). This was achieved by making a *very minimal assumption* about lower layers and the function they provide.

Here is a very interesting note from Dave Clark in 1988:

Since Internet does not insist that lost packets be recovered at the network level, it may be necessary to retransmit a lost packet from one end of the Internet to the other. This means that the retransmitted packet may cross several intervening nets a second time, whereas recovery at the network level would not generate this repeat traffic. This is an example of the trade-off resulting from the decision, discussed above, of providing services from the end-points. The network interface code is much simpler, but the overall efficiency is potentially less.

For further discussion see [39].

Thus the objectives of the Internet were to build a highly flexible, reliable network capable of supporting a variety of services while using a variety of links and physical layers.

Such flexibility was provided by the adoption of a layered architecture. The TCP/IP architecture exceeded these expectations: the current Internet and private IP networks use a plethora of physical and link layers (e.g., SONET/SDH, Optical, ATM, Ethernet, Wireless links such as IEEE 802.11, Powerline communication, Frame Relay, etc.). The number of applications requiring a wide set of services using either TCP or UDP is quite impressive including e-mail or file transfers to real-time applications such as voice, video, and other industrial time-critical applications.

The reliability of IP networks has reached an extremely impressive level due to a number of protection/restoration techniques such as IP Fast Reroute, MPLS Traffic Engineering Fast Reroute, Fast Convergence of BGP, In-service software upgrade, and so on. Today's IP networks provide a level of reliability equivalent to highly redundant networks such as SONET/SDH with restoration times in the order of a few dozen milliseconds and no packet loss in various failure cases.

Furthermore, the range of supported devices supporting the TCP/IP protocol suite is also extremely impressive from an 8-bit microcontroller to powerful servers hosted in data centers.

Last but not least, TCP/IP has proven to be extremely scalable. The growth of the Internet regarding traffic and number of interconnected devices has been remarkably growing from 9 computers in the original ARPANET in 1970 (note that the ARPANET migrated to TCP/IP in 1983) to several billion computers today (see Figure 2.1).

Note that some of the lower ranked objectives were harder to reach. For example, resource management and accounting were initially difficult goals due to one of the most brilliant inventions — the store-and-forward paradigm (in contrast to telephone circuit switching). But new mechanisms such as Simple Network Management Protocol (SNMP; [107]) and Netflow [38] dramatically help accounting. Network resources management was handled by the IP-based signaling mechanism supporting call admission control (CAC) using RSVP [21] for IP and RSVP-TE [14]. RSVP was mostly deployed at the edge of the network for CAC due to the limited scalability of the protocol considering the millions of flows handled by core routers in the Internet. RSVP was also widely used to signal MPLS Traffic Engineering Label Switch Paths (TE LSPs) carrying large chunks of traffic between pairs of routers.

One of the drawbacks of such a flexible architecture is that it requires network engineering to understand the set of supported services since an IP network can be deployed in many ways with different sets of services; a variety of protocols may be used at different layers. Thus the network design requires a good understanding of each layer's respective capabilities to make the appropriate protocol choice.

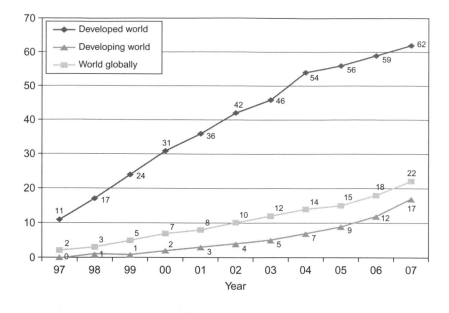

FIGURE 2.1

Level of penetration of the Internet regarding user number.

As previously discussed, the concept of layers is one of the core design foundations that leads to an extremely flexible architecture. The concept of layering was then extended to the current four layers of the TCP/IP protocol and the seven-layer OSI ([OSI]) model as shown in Figure 2.2.

[19] is one of the Internet Engineering Task Force (IETF) specifications that introduced the notion of layers in TCP/IP protocol architecture based on a four-layer model:

- Link layer: Usually refers to the physical and data link layers (the use of the PHY/MAC acronym is fairly common). At a high level the link layer is responsible for forwarding the IP packet on a link between two devices. This involves several functions such as media access control (MAC), error detection and (sometimes) retransmission, and flow control. Link layer protocol information is added in the form of a frame that carries the IP packet. Some links provide a very limited set of functions whereas others implement fairly sophisticated services that often include a link layer "routing" function (see Chapter 5 for more details). Note that the link layer may offer point-to-point or point-to-multipoint service.
- Internet layer (IP): Responsible for providing an unreliable service for sending a packet between a source and a destination across the network, where host and routers are uniquely identified by their IP (IPv4 or IPv6) address, using a hierarchical addressing scheme. The IPv6 addressing architecture is discussed in detail in Chapter 15. Routing is one of the main tasks accomplished by the IP layers and is extensively discussed in Chapter 5 and in Chapter 17 in the context of smart object networks. Protocols such as ICMP, see [203] and [42]) and IGMP [29] for multicast traffic are both considered part of the IP layer.
- Transport layer: Responsible for end-to-end communication between two devices where states are maintained (as opposed to within the network). A transport protocol such as TCP (detailed in

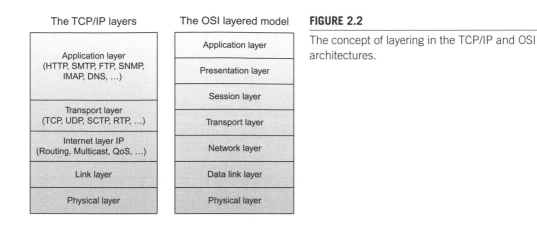

The TCP/IP layers

The OSI layered model

FIGURE 2.2

The concept of layering in the TCP/IP and OSI architectures.

Chapter 6) provides a reliable transport mechanism with error detection and retransmission, flow control using dynamic windowing techniques, security mechanisms, and so forth. In contrast the UDP [202] transport protocol is stateless and mostly used for application addressing and optional error detection (done by an optional checksum in IPv4; note that the UDP checksum is mandatory in IPv6). Other transport protocols have been developed such as the message stream transport protocol SCTP (Stream Control Transmission Protocol, see [229]) offering additional capabilities such as the bundling of multiple user messages in a single SCTP packet, the support of multi-homing, and so forth. Real-time Transport Protocol (RTP, see [220]) is another transport protocol designed for real-time applications such as streaming audio traffic and video.

- Application layer: Refers to higher level protocol(s) that supports the applications. The list of application layer protocols is fairly long, but few well known include File Transfer Protocol (FTP, see [205]), Trivial File Transfer Protocol (TFTP, see [224]), SNMP (see [108] to [206]), Hypertext Transport Protocol (HTTP, see [149]), and Telnet.

One of the key reasons for the impressive success of TCP/IP is its open, non-proprietary nature:

Dr. Cerf said part of the reason their protocols took hold quickly and widely was that he and Dr. Kahn made no intellectual property claims to their invention. They made no money from it, though it did help their careers. "It was an open standard that we would allow anyone to have access to without any constraints," he said.

Dr. Cerf said he was "pretty amazed" by what the Internet had become. He was quick to add, "I suppose anyone who worked on the railroad, or power generation and distribution, would have similar feelings about how amazing it is after you create infrastructure."

Dr. Cerf is also quite realistic about the recognition his contribution deserves. Creating a tool is one thing, he said, but credit for what people do with it is something no inventor can claim.

2.4 THE DELICATE SUBJECT OF CROSS-LAYER OPTIMIZATION

As discussed in previous sections, strict layer isolation brings a myriad of advantages such as flexibility because of the lack of interdependency between layers.

On the other hand, functions performed at a lower layer may be ignored by a higher layer and vice versa, thus leading to potential redundancy (error recovery or congestion management are typical examples). Cross-layering (also called horizontal separation) may be more cost-effective and reliable [28], a risky proposition when considering the trade-off between optimization and lack of flexibility. Indeed, it is fairly well known that a lack of flexibility usually leads to frequent network protocol architecture redesign, which is a very costly operation.

Increased layering may lead to costly operation where each layer performs duplicate functions (network recovery, QoS, routing, etc.). A good example is the IP over ATM over SONET/SH architecture. Such a network design was extremely inefficient and quickly replaced by "IP over glass" (IP over optical link), but this was a network design choice, not a purposely designed protocol architecture. These technologies were designed in parallel, and the objective was not to specify a link layer for IP networks. The same reasoning applies to SONET/SDH. When it clearly appeared that these technologies would not replace TCP/IP, network architects looked at how they could be used in conjunction with each other, which led to costly, inefficient network architecture.

It is sometimes mentioned that the "everything over IP" (EOIP) model is not the most OPEX and CAPEX efficient [28]:

> An example of where EOIP would not be the most OPEX and CAPEX efficient transport would be in those cases where a service or protocol needed SONET — like restoration times (e.g., 50 ms). It is not hard to imagine that it would cost more to build and operate an IP network with this kind of restoration and convergence property (if that were even possible) than it would to build the SONET network in the first place.

This was proven to be an incorrect statement. IP networks do provide SONET/SDH restoration time for a very reasonable cost with OPEX and CAPEX (please refer to [246] for a reference on this subject matter).

Still, it might be tempting to introduce some form of cross-layer optimizations. A notorious example of cross-layer optimization in smart object networks is known as "content routing." This consists of routing the traffic in the network according to the content of the packet at an application layer as opposed to using the IP destination. For some traffic it might be interesting to direct the traffic to its destination, not according to the shortest (constrained) path calculated by the routing protocol but, for example, to a traffic aggregator performing data aggregation and/or data fusion. In this case the objective is to limit the amount of traffic in the network, which is always desirable in constrained networks. This is a typical example where similar results can be achieved while using a layered architecture. IP packets could be marked by the upper layer to reflect the nature of their content and the routing protocol can be designed to route packets to their destinations along a path traversing traffic aggregators: this is precisely what the routing protocol for smart object networks (Chapter 16) does.

There are other circumstances where complete separation between layers is not always achievable. One example is security requiring deep packet inspection techniques: upon receiving a packet, routers/firewalls in the network inspect the packet to detect various attacks.

Cross-layer optimization always looked like an appealing approach to smart object network *designers* considering the high-constrained nature of these networks. A famous example of its appeal is the attempt to mingle the network and the link layer. Several attempts were made to add functionalities to the link layer beyond medium access control, error recovery, and so forth by adding routing functionality. The argument was that maintaining two layers was too costly for constrained networks and a more optimal approach would be to "collapse these layers." A second argument was to consider the specifics of the link layer when computing the routes, which would allow routing at the link layer. Such a strong inter-layer dependency led to the inevitable — a rigid architecture with no flexibility. As new link layers emerged, there was a critical need for a "convergence" layer (IP).

The solution? First, the a priori assumption that a layered protocol architecture such as TCP/IP would be too heavy for such constrained devices was proven wrong. As discussed in great detail in Chapter 12, the current lightweight IPv6 stacks only require a few kilobytes of RAM and few dozen kilobytes of Flash with limited processing power and can run on low-end, 8-bit microcontrollers. Don't forget that IPv4 was first developed on computers (called IMP in the ARPANET) with similar processing power and memory interconnected by low speed links. Second, the solution for routing while considering the characteristics of link layers simply consists of specifying new metrics reflecting these characteristics at a higher layer. Such metrics are discussed in Chapter 16.

Other attempts at cross-layer optimizations were made where upper layers would use addresses used by lower layers thus introducing another type of inter-layer dependency. Once again, designers had to step away from this approach because the emergence of new applications and lower layers forced them to redesign other layers.

So in conclusion, there is a trade-off. Layering provides a remarkable level of flexibility but requires a better knowledge of the set of features supported by various layers during the network design phase. Cross-layer optimization may, in some cases, lead to more optimal networking stacks. What we learned from the past is that technologies always evolve faster than we think, requiring a high level of flexibility. This is even more true for smart objects networks. Cross-layer optimization is achievable without violating the principles of layering due to a level of layer abstraction. For example, link layer properties may be reflected at the network layer because of routing metrics (Chapter 16).

2.5 WHY IS IP LAYERING ALSO IMPORTANT FOR SMART OBJECT NETWORKS?

Discussing the reasons that led to the current TCP/IP architecture shows why TCP/IP has been so successful.

It also demonstrates why TCP/IP is well suited for smart object networks. The question Why IP for Smart Objects? is addressed in Chapter 3, but it is worth spending more time on the adequacy of the TCP/IP protocol suite for smart object networks from an architectural standpoint.

As previously discussed, a plethora of proprietary or semi-closed protocol stacks have been designed over the past decade that advocated for a different model consisting of collapsing layers with no clear demarcation between the various functions handled by the network protocols. The main motivation for such an approach was to try to improve the efficiency of the networks, considering the high degree of constraints placed on smart object networks regarding the devices as well as the links interconnecting these devices.

By collapsing the layers, these architectures proved to be extremely rigid in the following ways:

• Link layer dependency: In most cases, architectures were tied to a specific link layer. Although there were a very limited number of low-power link layers designed for smart object networks a few years ago (e.g., IEEE 802.15.4), the emergence of a number of new low-power link layers could be easily predicted. As discussed in Chapter 12, several low-power link layers are now used in smart object networks, both wired and wireless. These include link layers such as low-power WiFi or Powerline communication. These architectures could not support the new links without performing protocol translation, which is a very costly and inefficient approach.

- Dependency between the various networking functions of the networking stack: This was also a major showstopper for innovation. In contrast to the layered TCP/IP architecture, the addition of new functionalities had consequences for a number of networking functions. With TCP/IP new applications are developed on a daily basis without having to change the transport or IP layers. If functions are collapsed into a single core component, this creates a dependency that dramatically slows down the support of additional functionalities.

2.6 CONCLUSIONS

The design of the TCP/IP architecture was a model of technical excellence with a degree of flexibility that allowed the Internet to grow from a few hosts to more than a billion hosts, supporting a myriad of services over a variety of media.

Looking back, the initial goals of TCP/IP include:

- Internet communication must continue despite loss of networks or gateways ("in the presence of link or node failures," to use nowadays terms).
- The Internet must support multiple types of communication services.
- Internet architecture must:
  - Accommodate a variety of networks ("networks" means link and physical layers)
  - Permit distributed management of its resources
  - Be cost-effective
  - Permit host attachment with a little effort
- Resources used in the Internet architecture must be accountable.

The main goals for smart object networks are the same list as outlined above. The additional requirement is the support of large-scale networks made of billions of unattended and constrained devices for which new IP technologies (detailed in Part II) have been developed.

The fundamental architectural principles of TCP/IP further illustrate why the TCP/IP protocol architecture is extremely well suited for smart object networks. Whereas semi-closed or proprietary protocols that try to collapse layers unavoidably lead to non-viable and non-scalable approaches (leading to local optimum), TCP/IP seeks a global optimum and provides the required foundations for smart object networks.

Why IP for Smart Objects?

In this chapter we argue that IP is the future for smart object networks. There is already a significant momentum for IP-based smart objects as demonstrated by the growing amount of products and systems built upon the principles laid out in this book. In this chapter, we review the challenges inherent to smart object networks, as presented in Chapter 1, and review them in light of the IP architecture discussed in Chapter 2.

Although we advocate the use of the IP architecture and protocols for smart objects, we do not advocate that all smart object networks should be connected to the public Internet. There are some smart objects connected to the Internet, for example, to send data to a central database, but this is an exception, not the norm.

First, a brief recap of the challenges of smart object networks:

- Evolvability: Although we have an idea of where the application space of smart objects is heading, we cannot know what direction it will take in the future. Therefore, smart object technology must inherently support the notion of evolvability. The mechanisms developed for smart objects should not be constrained by today's ideas, but must allow for the next generation of applications to take full advantage of the technology in pursuing its own application goals.
- Scale: Smart object networks have a large number of nodes per system. Existing smart object systems have thousands of nodes, and they are likely to develop into systems composed of hundreds of thousands or even millions of nodes. Thus, smart object architecture must support an increasing number of nodes through its addressing, routing, and management mechanisms.
- Diversity of applications: The number of applications for smart objects is large, and so is the number of differences in each application (as seen in Part III). A home automation application does not share all of the properties of an industrial automation application. Smart object technology tailored to one specific application therefore may not work for other applications.
- Diversity of communication technologies: Depending on the application and the environment in which the system is deployed, smart objects can use a wide range of communication technologies. Wireless communication is appropriate in many situations because of its deployment convenience, whereas wired communication is more suitable in other places. Many smart object systems use combinations of disparate technologies in the same deployment.
- Interoperability: Smart object networks need interoperability between the smart object devices and between the smart objects and existing network infrastructures. With the large base of existing systems that smart objects enhance, a smart object architecture that makes interoperability and interconnection difficult or cumbersome will not prevail.

Interconnecting Smart Objects with IP. DOI: 10.1016/B978-0-12-375165-2.00003-X

- Standardization: Mechanisms and protocols that define the operation of smart objects must be standardized using open standards through well-established standardization practices. Any patents covering the standardized technology must be disclosed and made available to be used by third parties. Open standards make the entry barrier low for manufacturers, and allow them to freely choose between different vendors. As seen in Chapter 2, open standards was a key to the success of IP.
- Potentially lossy communication technology: Many of the communication technologies used for smart objects are inherently lossy (data sent are not guaranteed to reach their destinations). Smart object protocols and mechanisms need to take this into account when determining where and how to send data as well as determining when and how often.
- Lifetime: Because of the large-scale installations and demanding applications for smart objects, smart object networks are meant to remain functional for many years. This lifetime has implications both for the performance requirements of smart object mechanisms, which must be power-efficient, and for the mechanisms as such, which must remain operational over the lifetime of the system.
- Low-power consumption: Smart objects have severe power constraints. Many smart objects are powered by batteries that cannot easily be replaced or recharged. Other smart objects draw their energy from their surroundings, such as vibration or electromagnetic energy. In either case, power consumption must be low for the system to achieve its optimal lifetime. The power requirement affects both the network protocols and the construction of nodes. The memory size and computational complexity of the nodes are limited by the power consumption constraints.
- Low cost: Smart objects are deployed in large numbers; therefore a small reduction in per-device costs quickly translates into large savings in the cost of the entire system. Just as the power consumption constraints affect the memory size and computational complexity of the nodes, so do cost constraints. Because of constrained resources such as memory, power, and computation, any smart object architecture must be lightweight.

Given these challenges, we now investigate the IP architecture to find out how well it meets them and their implications.

3.1 INTEROPERABILITY

Interoperability is a predominant characteristic of the IP architecture. It is interoperable because it runs over link layers with very different characteristics, providing interoperability among them (Figure 3.1), and because IP provides interoperability with existing networks, applications, and protocols. We examine these two aspects beginning with how IP provides interoperability between different link layers.

IP was originally designed to provide interoperability at the network layer because it works on top of different types of link layers. A single IP network operates across a variety of underlying media such as Ethernet or WiFi. Within the IP architecture, an IP network operates across both wired and wireless link layers without requiring any external mechanisms or add-ons. Operating over a variety of media has always been the prime objective of the IP architecture.

Interoperability within and across different link layers is very important for smart objects. Smart object networks are composed of a wide variety of link layers and transmission mechanisms. Smart object networks extend from low-power wireless nodes to high-power data coordination

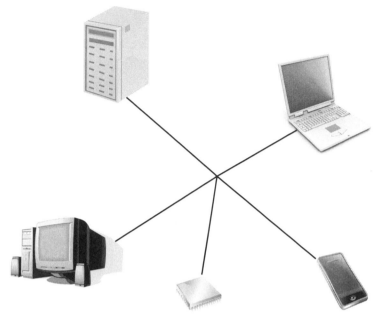

FIGURE 3.1

IP is interoperable across different platforms, devices, and underlying communication mechanisms.

servers. Because of the fundamentally different properties of these devices, it is unlikely they will share a single link layer. A low-power wireless node typically runs a low-power, low-data-rate radio link layer, whereas the high-power data coordination server runs over a wired, high-speed Ethernet network. Still, these systems need to communicate with each other. Because of its layered architecture, IP provides interoperability between these devices without any special servers, gateways, or custom software that connects the systems. IP naturally connects these two. The interoperability of IP is not just an artifact of IP protocols, but occurs because of the architectural choices that support the IP architecture.

The second characteristic of interoperability within the IP architecture is the widespread adoption of IP in today's networked ecosystem. Consequently, an IP-enabled device can interoperate with a large number of devices, computers, and servers. IP is not only the standard protocol that defines the Internet, it is also the de facto standard protocol used for networking computers outside the Internet. IP-based smart objects are able to communicate with any given device without any additional hardware or software.

IP is available in most, if not all, operating systems for general purpose computers and servers, and there is an ever-growing body of software available for IP networking for the type of microcontrollers used in smart objects. Both commercially licensed and open source implementations are generally available: general purpose operating systems such as Microsoft Windows and Linux or microcontroller operating systems such as Contiki, TinyOS, and FreeRTOS. Most software packages also provide the necessary device drivers for the underlying communication hardware.

The ubiquity of IP is also evident in the ever-growing number of communication technologies, or link layers in IP terminology, that support IP. IP runs not only high-speed, high-throughput communication technology such as the optical links that provide swift communication between servers in data centers, but also low-power, low-data-rate links such as those used for smart objects. This is important for smart object systems designers. With IP, any communication technology the designer chooses will interoperate with other parts of the network infrastructure.

IP-enabled smart objects interoperate with other systems and devices that run IP, but the IP architecture contains other protocols as well. The IP suite contains a set of protocols running on top of IP that include the transport protocols UDP and TCP; application layer protocols such as the Hypertext Transfer Protocol (HTTP), for web-style interaction and web service infrastructure; and the Simple Network Management Protocol (SNMP) for network configuration. Thus a smart object that runs IP is able to interoperate with a large number of external systems.

Interoperability at the application layer is as important for system builders as it is for system integrators. For the system builder, the ability to interoperate with existing application protocols not only makes the act of building the system easier, as existing applications can be used when developing the system, but also when deploying the system. When existing applications are able to interact without any additional mechanisms or heavily tailored software, deployment time is significantly reduced. For the system integrator, system integration becomes much easier when the different parts of the system immediately interoperate with each other.

Standardization plays a large part in the success of IP's interoperability. IP is standardized by an established standardization organization that provides mechanisms through which new standards are reviewed and vetted. This process puts a large amount of effort into ensuring that the mechanisms and protocols proposed as standards can be efficiently implemented. In Part II of this book we describe this process in detail. Furthermore, the standardization body has policies and practices that deal with how patents are to be handled.

3.2 AN EVOLVING AND VERSATILE ARCHITECTURE

The IP architecture has proven to be evolvable due to the way applications, protocols, and mechanisms running on top of the architecture have evolved, and the way that protocols within the architecture have evolved. The ability to evolve and the versatility in applications are due to the end-to-end principle that provides the foundation of the IP architecture.

From the outset the IP architecture was designed to allow application layer protocols and mechanisms to evolve independently of the underlying network protocols and mechanisms. The end-to-end principle states that application layer functionality should be held in the end points of the network (computers, or hosts, connected at the fringes of the network). The network does not contain any application-level intelligence. This is maintained solely by the network end points. The network only transports data between the end points (Figure 3.2).

The network does not know if it is transporting a temperature reading from a temperature sensor, a piece of sound from a voice conversation, a control command, or a piece of a larger file. It only knows that it has been given a string of bits to transport from one end of the network to another. It is up to the applications running at the end points to make sense of the bits.

The end-to-end principle is the primary reason today's IP networks work with a diverse number of applications. If we take the public Internet as an example and look at its history, it shows that the applications running on top of the Internet have evolved since the inception of the Internet in the early

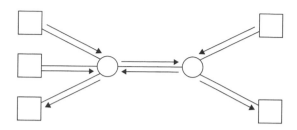

FIGURE 3.2

Versatility is seen when the applications run on the end points and the network only transports data between them, which allows the system to evolve.

1980s. In the 1980s, the Internet was mostly used for transporting text and files; the main applications were e-mail and file transfer between universities. In the 1990s, the World Wide Web was deployed, and by the late 1990s data traffic caused by the Web dominated the traffic on the Internet. In the early 2000s, peer-to-peer file sharing and Internet video transport emerged as new applications, and in 2010 these applications constitute the bulk of Internet traffic.

Without the end-to-end principle, designers might have been impelled to push application functionality into the fabric of the network. For example, the World Wide Web could have been encoded in the routers that make up the interconnected network of the Internet. Placing application functionality within the network may have yielded a slightly higher performance, because data may have needed to travel slightly shorter distances, but evolving the network to support new applications would have been extremely difficult. Inserting a new application into the network would have needed technical cooperation between a large number of parties, and globally agreeing what applications should be supported by the network would have been close to impossible.

In addition to promoting evolvable applications, the end-to-end principle and the resulting architecture embodied in IP have had a profound impact on the interoperability of existing IP networks. If application functionality had been placed deeply in the network fabric, network operators would have needed to negotiate complex deals on how to connect the applications. And once these negotiated deals were in place, adding new applications or evolving new ones would have been difficult.

Thus far we have discussed how the technical architecture that supports IP enables applications running on top of IP to evolve. But there are other elements in the mix that allow the system as a whole to evolve.

We have already touched upon the standards process of IP as an important factor in its interoperability, but the standardization process has implications for the evolution of the architecture too. The well-defined standardization process for IP provides mechanisms through which new features can be introduced to the architecture. The most common example of this is when a new link layer technology is introduced. The standardization process provides a way for vendors to agree on how to use the new link layer to transport IP packets within the IP architecture.

3.3 STABILITY AND UNIVERSALITY OF THE ARCHITECTURE

We have been discussing how the application layer protocols and the underlying link layer mechanisms have allowed IP architecture to evolve. Although evolvability is important, because it shows that the protocols are not tied to one particular application use that may change in the future, stability of the foundations of the architecture is also important. For smart objects, such stability is very important because individual smart object systems are designed to have a long lifetime, often up to ten years.

Such investments require the base technology to be stable enough to remain available toward the end of the system life cycle.

The IP architecture has existed for nearly 30 years. Although there is room in the IP architecture for evolving protocols both at the application layer and at the link layer, throughout the years the architecture as a whole has remained exceptionally stable. Standards have been updated several times over the 30 years, but its foundation as a packet-based communication technology has remained firm. The network layer, the core of the IP architecture, exists in two versions — version four (IPv4) and version six (IPv6). The major difference between the two is that IPv6 provides more addresses. There are, however, no major architectural differences between the two versions.

Because IP forms the basis of the public Internet, the IP architecture and its surrounding standards will continue to exist well into the future. The prevalence of the Internet not only implies that IP has a large installed user base regarding hardware and software that supports it, but there is also a large installed network infrastructure. IP networking equipment and IP network access are both readily available and will continue to be so as long as the Internet exists.

The stability and prevalence of the IP architecture also have implications on the knowledge and education of users and network administrators. IP architecture and its protocols are part of the core curriculum in courses and training material at all levels of the educational system ranging from day-long network training courses to multiyear university programs. Ever year, thousands of new engineers graduate with knowledge of IP protocols and the architecture.

The number of books and training material on IP architecture and its protocols is immense, continues to increase, and is available in many different languages. There is a vast amount of material freely available online both as text, recorded seminars, and animated videos. Again, material is available in many different languages and for different audiences.

3.4 SCALABILITY

The IP architecture has been thoroughly field-proven regarding scalability through the use of IP over the public Internet. Few communication architectures have ever seen such a large-scale deployment. Through the global deployment of the Internet, IP has both shown that it can be deployed over a large number of systems and that it can run across a vast variety of different implementations of its protocols.

But we need not go as far as to the public Internet to witness the scalability of IP. Most larger companies run internal networks to support the activities within the company. These networks are often not connected to the public Internet, yet they can span many thousands of individual computers or servers.

3.5 CONFIGURATION AND MANAGEMENT

Through its wide adoption and large-scale deployment, IP has evolved numerous mechanisms and protocols for network configuration and management. These mechanisms are a necessity when networks grow to thousands of hosts. Network management tools allow for a single person to manage large networks, without manual configuration of each host.

The IP architecture provides advanced configuration and management mechanisms as well as automatic configuration mechanisms. Configuration mechanisms are provided at many layers of the system: from the network layer, where managed and automatic mechanisms for assigning network addresses are widely used, to the routing protocols, where routing mechanisms are both self-healing and automatically configurable.

IP provides management mechanisms at all layers. Address assignment mechanisms such as the Dynamic Host Configuration Protocol (DHCP) allow network administrators to assign addresses both individually to singular nodes and in bulk to others. Routing protocols allow management of both network configuration and engineering.

Protocols such as the widely used SNMP provide means by which a network administrator can inspect the network, its configuration, and its performance. A plethora of tools for interacting with SNMP-enabled networks, and visualizing their performance, exist. The widespread adoption of SNMP also means there is a large body of knowledge and people experienced with these tools. Additional tools such as Cisco Netflow provide large amounts of data about the network health and traffic statistics.

For smart object networks, configuration, management, installation, and commissioning are clearly an issue. Even though traditional management mechanisms cannot be directly applied to smart object networks, due to their large scale and number of nodes, the ability to leverage existing mechanisms and tools is important. It provides not only technical advantages, but also non-technical advantages such as the availability of skilled people.

3.6 SMALL FOOTPRINT

Low energy consumption, small physical size, and low cost are three of the node-level challenges of smart objects. Taken together, these challenges translate into severe memory constraints and software complexity on the nodes. A network architecture for smart objects must be able to run within these tight bounds, and yet perform its task.

The IP architecture was long thought to be a heavyweight due to its perceived need for processing power and memory. The protocols were seen as too large to fit into the constrained environment of typical smart object systems. A typical smart object has only a few tens of kilobytes of memory, whereas existing implementations of the IP protocol family for general purpose computers would need hundreds of kilobytes. For this reason, several non-IP stacks were developed [120,222].

In the early 2000s, however, this view was challenged by lightweight implementations of the IP protocol family for smart objects such as the uIP stack [64]. uIP showed that the IP architecture would fit nicely into the typical constraints of smart objects, without removing any of the essential mechanisms from IP. Note that these resources, which we consider constrained today, are fairly close to the resources of general purpose computers that were available when IP was designed. Since its initial release, the uIP stack has become widely used in networked embedded and smart object systems.

In addition to uIP, there are many small IP stacks available, both as open source and closed source. Many of the early embedded IP stacks were adaptations of the IP stack from the open source BSD UNIX operating system [172].

Recently, a number of implementations of IPv6 for memory-constrained systems have appeared. uIP has been extended to support the IPv6 protocol, which is the first IPv6 stack for smart objects to

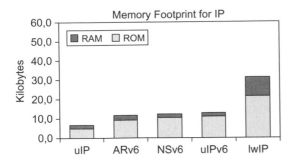

FIGURE 3.3

The memory footprint of uIP, lwIP, and two commercially available IPv6 stacks: the Arch Rock stack (ARv6), and the Sensinode NanoStack (NSv6). The footprint includes transport layer protocols UDP and TCP for uIP and lwIP.

be certified under the IPv6 Ready program [73]. Other independent implementations of the IPv6 stack have also appeared [1,125]. The footprints of the stacks are shown in Figure 3.3. The graph shows the memory requirements of the uIP and uIPv6 stacks [64,73], the stack by Hui and Culler [125], and the lwIP stack [64]. Figure 3.3 shows that there are many options for IP software that fit into the resource constraints in smart object nodes.

In Chapter 13 we take a detailed look at the uIP stack to see how it implements the IP architecture in a way that fits with the smart object resource challenges.

3.7 WHAT ARE THE ALTERNATIVES?

We have now seen that the IP architecture is interoperable across devices and communication technologies, evolving and versatile while still stable, scalable, and manageable, and simple enough that a resource-constrained smart object can easily run it. We have painted a very bright picture of the IP architecture, but is it really as good as we say? What are the alternatives?

The IP architecture was arguably not designed for smart objects. It was designed in the 1970s for connecting general purpose computers using wired networking technologies such as Ethernet. Could we do it better if we made a clean-slate redesign that specifically targets the challenges that smart object networks pose? To help answer our question, we turn to those who did this.

The challenges of low-power operation and the large scale of smart object networks have spurred several years of research in the wireless sensor networks research community. Although wireless sensor networks are a subset of smart object networks, they share many of the properties such as the low-power operation, the large scale of the networks, and the resource constraints.

At the outset, the wireless sensor network community rejected the IP architecture based on the assumption that it would not meet the challenges of wireless sensor network systems [110]. For an emerging research field, this clearly was the right choice. Consequently, many novel network architectures have been investigated, where the layers in the networking stack have been turned upside down [111], where the layers have been intermingled [168], and where the network itself processes the data produced by the end points [162]. After several years, however, the community started to lean toward layered network architectures, because of the benefits of modularity and separation of concerns [35,46,71,93]. In fact, many have moved to IP because of the interoperability with existing systems and the well-engineered architecture based on the end-to-end architecture [67,73,125,207].

The industry around low-power wireless communication has made a similar transition. In the late 1990s, there was a strong movement toward defining a new network architecture for the networking system under the brand name ZigBee. ZigBee was designed to perform control applications, such as controlling lights and appliances in homes, over a low-power wireless communication medium. ZigBee initially defined a networking stack that would work well over low-power wireless links, but that was incompatible with existing network standards such as IP. In 2009, however, ZigBee announced that they were moving toward adopting IP as its communication mechanism. In Part II of this book, we return to ZigBee to discuss the choices made in the original ZigBee architecture.

Even if we were designing our own network architecture for smart objects, at some point they would need to communicate with someone outside the network. Our electrical meter would need to report its data to a collection server. Our industrial vibration sensor would need to send its latest sensor reading to a database. Our radiator controller would need to be given instructions on how much to turn up the heat in its room. To reach the smart objects, we need to insert a translation point between our smart object network and the outside network. This translation point is called a gateway, and it introduces a number of problems.

3.8 WHY ARE GATEWAYS BAD?

At a first sight, gateways offer an alternative to adopting the IP end-to-end principle, which allowed for interconnecting non-IP-based smart object networks to an IP network.

Such gateways were designed and deployed in a number of networks about a decade ago, when IP was not yet the networking protocol of choice. At that time, several legacy networking protocols such as IBM's Systems Network Architecture (SNA), and Novell's Internetwork Packet Exchange protocol (IPX), and many other ones were deployed mostly in private networks. As IP networks were deployed, network administrators required gateways to interconnect these networks by means of multiprotocol translation gateways supporting these protocols, which led to several deployments models. Some protocols were tunneled over IP (encapsulated in IP packet to transport non-IP traffic over an IP network), while others were translated.

Although such gateways were deployed, most networks very quickly migrated to IP. But why? There are two main reasons for the move away from gateways: the inherent complexity of gateways and the lack of flexibility and scalability.

3.8.1 Inherent Complexity

The mode of operation of a multiprotocol translation gateway is a complex language translation mechanism with subtle nuances in semantics in addition to the actual translation. Network protocol translation is more complex than just a packet format conversion. Networking protocols use different mechanisms and logic for routing, Quality of Service (QoS), error recovery, transport, management, troubleshooting, and security models. Trying to translate the semantics of QoS between two networking protocols, for example, is not limited to the setting of a new field value in a packet and may sometimes not even be possible. Routing is similarly affected: when two routing domains are using different routing architectures, routing metrics, and paradigms the introduction of protocol translation gateways introduces several limitations. This is true for a number of network aspects where such gateways break the networking models on both sides.

Furthermore, with gateways, management and troubleshooting become cumbersome. Imagine traffic flows between three smart objects implementing different networking protocols. This requires as many as six protocol translations. Such a system is extremely difficult to manage and troubleshoot, especially when the gateway is not managed by a networking expert.

3.8.2 Lack of Flexibility and Scalability

The lack of flexibility and scalability is undoubtedly a real issue. As already pointed out, the evolvability and scalability essential to all networks are required for smart object networks because of the myriad of future innovative applications. Protocol translation gateways inherently do not scale and become networking bottlenecks. Each protocol enhancement implies changes in the gateways, which become the least common denominator factor of the architecture. Furthermore, such gateways introduce an undesirable state in the networks, which impacts not only the overall scalability but also the overall reliability with single points of failure.

The use of multiprotocol gateways helped integrate disparate networks in the late 1990s when network administrators had to deal with several legacy protocols and when networks were significantly smaller. Now that IP has become the networking protocol of choice, the use of multiprotocol translation gateways would ineluctably lead to the wrong architectural choice.

3.9 CONCLUSIONS

Smart object networks and their applications give rise to challenges both at the node and the network level. To meet these challenges we need a network architecture that is interoperable across a wide range of communication technologies, that evolves as the field of smart objects evolves, and is scalable enough to meet the challenges imposed by large-scale smart object networks while lightweight enough for the node-level resource constraints. We argue that the IP architecture meets these goals while providing unprecedented interoperability with existing networks, applications, and services.

IPv6 for Smart Object Networks and the Internet of Things

4

4.1 INTRODUCTION

IPv4 has been widely and very successfully deployed on hundreds of millions of hosts and routers in a number of private and public networks around the world. Considering that IPv4 was initially designed in 1982 [48], such a growth and adoption rate is remarkable. Very early on, considering the impressive growth of IP networks, the Internet Engineering Task Force (IETF) in charge of standardizing the IP protocol suite had identified the need to specify a new version of IP: several task force groups were formed and these initiatives led to the specification of IPv6 in 1998 [53].

IPv6 is an *evolution* of IPv4 and builds on IPv4 with no change in the fundamental and architectural principles of the IP protocol suite discussed in Chapter 2. Some protocols added to IPv4 to sort out specific issues have been natively embedded into IPv6, the header has been modified in particular to allow for a large address space. A few new features have been added but IPv6 fundamentally preserves the architectural principles of IP. This was imperative considering the power of the IP protocol suite architecture. Many of the existing protocols such as the transport protocols (UDP and TCP) have not been modified. Drastically simplifying layer 3 and the overall architecture as well as going back to the most fundamental architectural principle of IP were done in IPv6. More details on these aspects are discussed in Chapter 5 in the section Layer 2 versus Layer 3 Routing.

Why is IPv4 still so prevalent? The answer is somewhat fairly simple: cost and complexity of migration. With more than one billion devices using IPv4, the migration to a new version of the protocol is not entirely straightforward and usually requires a business driver. IPv6 undoubtedly enhances many of the IPv4 functionalities, offers a much larger address pool, and provides better support for security and mobility while preserving the fundamental protocol architecture of IPv4, but the "cost" of migration has slowed down the adoption rate of IPv6.

The question Why IPv6? is now obsolete, and the IP community fully agrees that IPv6 will replace IPv4 with a smooth transition (to that end a number of technologies and migration strategies have been designed by the IETF).

Over the past decade, several technologies have been developed to postpone the migration of IPv4 to IPv6 such as Network Address Translation (NAT), which has been used extensively (see Chapter 5 for more details). Multiprotocol Label Switching Virtual Private Network (MPLS VPN) also uses private addresses (non-routable over the global Internet) over a common (usually service provider) infrastructure. Basically, private networks are interconnected at the edge of the network and, upon receiving an IP packet using a private IP address, the router connected to this network pushes a (VPN)

First Three-Network Test of Internet

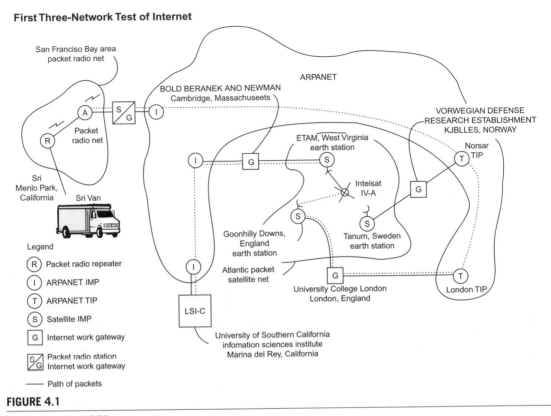

FIGURE 4.1

The Internet in 1972.

label that uniquely identifies the private address (using to a new address family called VPNv4). A second label is then added to forward the packet to the router connected to the destination private network where the VPN label is removed. See [217] for more details on MPLS VPN or [247] for more information on MPLS technology. Note that MPLS not only allows the interconnection of networks using private addressing over a common infrastructure but also enhances IP networks with sophisticated traffic engineering techniques.

But the situation is radically changing. First, the exhaustion rate of public IPv4 addresses is extremely concerning.

Figures 4.1 and 4.2 show the evolution of the Internet in the past 30 years from about a dozen devices to more than a billion. Imagine the number of devices (not yet) connected to both the public Internet and a myriad of IP private networks: this shows why IPv6 is the only viable option for smart object networks.

In many cases the use of NAT is not an option as detailed later in this chapter, in Section 4.3. Even in private networks composed of a large number of devices the use of IPv6 is the preferred option.

Smart Grid networks are good examples. Most of the devices connected to the grid will not be connected to the public Internet for security reasons. Still, these networks will likely contain hundreds

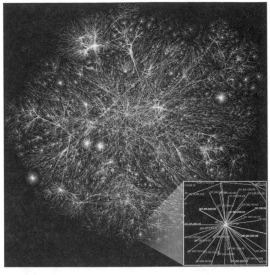

FIGURE 4.2

The same Internet in 2007.

(Source: Wikipedia.)

of millions of devices (please refer to Chapter 20 for more details). More than likely in less than 10 years such networks will connect millions of monitoring and control devices in the production and distribution part of the Smart Grid network. Smart meters will also be connected to the network, again with millions of devices. To support end-to-end applications such as demand-response, the Smart Grid will require communication with end devices in the home via a home energy controller. Simple math shows that the number of IP-enabled home devices running IP in the home area network (HAN) and smart objects in the grid networks including smart meters will quickly exceed billions of devices. The Smart Grid is only one example among many including Smart Cities, Industrial Automation, and so forth.

It is worth noting that the motivation for IPv6 in large-scale networks applies to both private IP networks and the public Internet.

Although the address space in undoubtedly one of the main motivations for using IPv6 (and the reason why a large proportion of this chapter is devoted to IPv4 address space exhaustion), it is not the only one. IPv6 provides a number of powerful features such as stateless autoconfiguration (discussed in detail in Chapter 15), which allows the network to support dynamic address assignment without requiring heavy state management in the network. This is only one of the value-added services provided by IPv6.

IPv6 is undoubtedly the only viable option for IP networks deployed today and in the future with many more IP devices connected to both private and public networks. This is why several IETF Working Groups in charge of standardizing IP protocols for smart objects decided to specify these new protocols for IPv6 only.

4.2 THE DEPLETION OF THE IPv4 ADDRESS SPACE

Who could have expected that the 32-bit address space of IPv4 would at some point be too restricted and 4,294,967,296 IPv4 would not be sufficient? First, the address space is not totally available and is fragmented: in reality, the number of available IPv4 addresses is far below the theoretical 4,294,967,296 number. The address space is divided into blocks of addresses that are partially used. Several indicators have been specified to evaluate the address space fragmentation ratio (see [72] and [126]). Such indicators were also used to determine the number of bits that would be required for IPv6 addresses.

As previously stated, considering the exponential growth of the Internet and the address allocation rate, the IETF demonstrated admirable foresight by starting several initiatives in the early 1990s to design the next version of IP, which led to the current IPv6 version.

Early predictions (made at the time IPv6 was in its early phase of design) were that IPv4 address depletion would take place as early as 2002. This triggered active work from the IETF community to find solutions to slow down the pace at which IP addresses were allocated while waiting for IPv6 (the ultimate solution to address exhaustion) to be widely adopted on the Internet.

Several mitigation strategies were developed:

- The first cure consisted of not allocating class B addresses to companies without a strong justification but allocate class C address blocks instead.
- Classless inter-domain routing (CIDR) is a variable length subnet mask technique that specifies a prefix length of arbitrary size. Furthermore address aggregation was used to reduce the routing table sizes (see also [88]).
- NAT was (and is still) a solution to temporary mitigate the issues of address exhaustion.

Although these mitigation strategies helped postpone IPv4 address depletion, the IPv4 address pool exhaustion is inexorable.

4.2.1 Current IPv4 Address Pool Exhaustion Rate

It is fairly difficult to predict exactly when IPv4 address exhaustion will occur, so we can only try to predict it based on statistical analysis according to the current IPv4 address allocation policy used by the Regional Internet Registries (RIR). Figures 4.3 to 4.7 are based on the IPv4 address report (http://www.potaroo.net/tools/ipv4/index.html) and provide a good indication of the IPv4 consumption rate and "prediction" of the IPv4 address depletion date. According to this model, which takes into account a number of positive factors such as the use of CIDR and reclaiming of addresses that have been allocated but are not advertised in the Internet, the date at which the unallocated address poll distribution occurs will be **March 2012**. But bear in mind that this date is an estimated prediction.

Let's take a closer look at a few interesting data points to understand the address allocation process.

First, it is worth reminding how IP addresses are being allocated. IANA, the Internet Assigned Numbers Authority (IANA; http://www.iana.org/) managed the allocation of the address pool. Then it was decided to decentralize the address space allocation to regional entities (RIR) and that Internet Service Providers (ISPs) would own the address and perform route aggregation in the core and limit the size of the routing tables. Examples of RIRs include AFRINIC (Africa), APNIC (Asia/Pacific), ARIN (North America), LACNIC (Latin America), and RIPE NCC (Europe). IANA allocates /8 address blocks to an RIR as soon as the RIR available space falls below the equivalent of a /9 address block or the equivalent of 9 months of allocation. An /8 address block corresponds to addresses where the first 8 bits are allocated (e.g., 15.X.X.X). The new /8 block allocation then provides enough addresses for the equivalent of 18 more months of allocation. Then the RIR allocates address blocks to the Local Internet Registries (LISPs) and ISPs. The RIRs have their own address allocation policy according to the regional policy forum in line with the RIR policy.

Not all of the 256 /8 address blocks are available to the public Internet. As noted in [128], a number of /8 address blocks have been reserved for special purposes such as loopback, "reserved for some unspecified future use," private addressing (e.g., 10.0.0.0), local identification (0.0.0.0), and "public data networks" along with other special uses (e.g., multicast). This is illustrated in Figure 4.3, where the allocated number pool is managed by the RIRs. IANA has a pool of unallocated addresses,

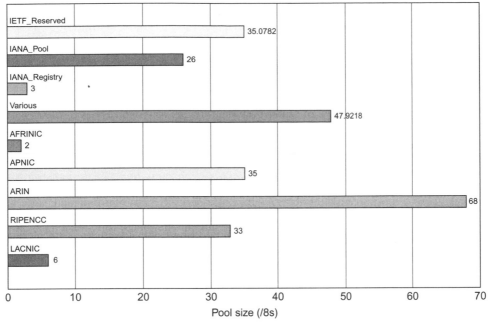

FIGURE 4.3

Address block allocation.

while the remainder have already been allocated by IANA for further downstream assignment by RIRs. The pool size labeled VARIOUS refers to the IANA IPv4 address registry where a number of blocks were assigned prior to the existence of RIRs (http://www.iana.org/assignments/ipv4-address-space/).

Figure 4.4 illustrates the allocation distribution of the 256 /8 block address as of May 2009.

It is interesting to note that any address can be in either of the following states:

- Reserved for special use (e.g., loopback address, private address, etc.)
- Available and not yet allocated by IANA (IANA_Pool_Pool)
- Part of the pool assigned to an RIR
- Assigned to an end user but not advertised in the Internet (thus it could be reclaimed at some point)
- Assigned to an end user and advertised in the Internet

What does the rate at which IPv4 address blocks are allocated mean?

As shown in Figure 4.5, with the exception of more recently allocated address space, about 90% of allocated address space is visible in the routing tables of the Internet.

Figure 4.6 illustrates a predictive model that shows when the address space will effectively be exhausted. It also shows the total amount of address space allocated by IANA to the various RIRs, the total amount of address space that has been allocated to end users by the RIRs, the total amount of address space effectively advertised in the Internet, the total amount of address space that has been allocated but not advertised in the Internet, and the total amount of address space still available in the RIR pool.

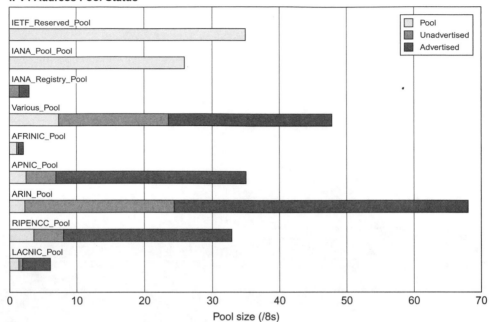

FIGURE 4.4

Pool size per RIRs.

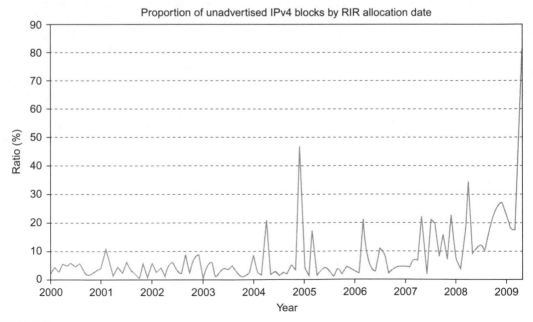

FIGURE 4.5

Proportion of addresses visible in the Internet routing table.

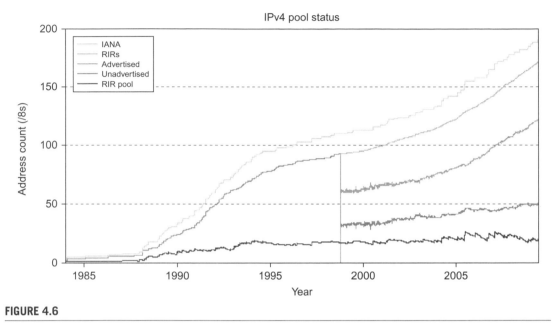

FIGURE 4.6

Overall status of the IPv4 address pool.

Figure 4.6 was used to construct a predictive model to extend the series and estimate the date at which IPv4 address space will be exhausted. A number of statistical models have been used to perform extrapolations: a linear best fit, exponential best fit, and a second order polynomial best fit (derived from the application of a linear best fit to the first order differential of the data).

The model that was selected to predict address poll exhaustion consisted of projecting the number of advertised addresses in the Internet forward (observing according to Figure 4.6 that an average of 95% of the allocated address were advertised). Detailed models have been derived for the RIR address allocation models. All of the studies managed to build an overall model of address consumption as shown in Figure 4.7.

In this model the point of exhaustion occurs when the RIR pools are exhausted but no address pool from IANA is available to replenish them. The best-fit predictive model suggests this may occur in March 2012.

A word of caution: this date is only "predictive." New allocation models could be put in place to reduce the allocation rate. On the other hand, some companies may request addresses at a higher rate than expected to get a public IPv4 address before they are exhausted.

4.3 NAT: A (TEMPORARY) SOLUTION TO IPv4 ADDRESS EXHAUSTION

NAT has been *the* solution to the IPv4 address space exhaustion, allowing the use of one public address to connect private IP networks [213]. In a nutshell, NAT enables millions of devices to hide behind one public address with less than 65,000 possible addresses since ports are coded over 16 bits.

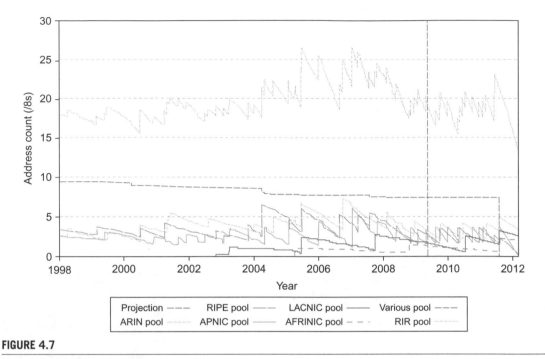

FIGURE 4.7

Model of address consumption.

NAT has been a useful technology and widely deployed over the Internet. It is worth understanding the issues outlined in this section, in light of the ongoing deployments of large-scale IP networks, to understand why NAT is not a long-term solution. This is specially true for smart object networks.

Most of these issues occur because NATs introduce states in the network between end points, since address conversion NATs also need to maintain various protocol states.

One of the key aspects of the end-to-end principle is that "state should be maintained only by end points, in such a way that the state can only be destroyed when the end point itself breaks." This leads to the notion of "fate-sharing" [32].

The introduction of NATs in the network breaks this model since NAT failures have a major impact on the communication between end devices without fast network recovery in the network. This is in contrast to router failures. Not only can paths be quickly recomputed around the failed router because of fast recovery techniques, but when the router recovers, flows can be routed again through the router. This is not the case with a NAT (because the address translation maps may have changed). The use of alternate NATs in which states would be replicated turns out to be fairly difficult.

Furthermore, beyond the issue of impacting the end-to-end reliability, the introduction of states in the network has an impact on the overall network scalability that always benefits from pushing states at the edge of the networks whenever possible.

NAT also has a strong impact on the security models and is problematic for several authentication techniques (e.g., for SNMPv3).

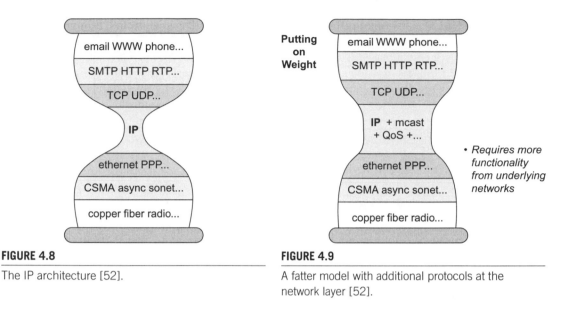

FIGURE 4.8

The IP architecture [52].

FIGURE 4.9

A fatter model with additional protocols at the network layer [52].

Some applications using IP addresses in their data stream may not work through NATs, thus requiring the deployment of an application layer gateway (ALG) coupled with NAT, which may be cumbersome to manage. By intervening along the forwarding path, ALGs combined with NATs require software updates as new applications are deployed on hosts. Workarounds have been found for some updates, but this shows how the introduction of NATs in the network impacts the development of new applications.

Without entering into detailed explanation, NATs introduce TCP state violations.

The objective of listing the drawbacks of NATs is to highlight that NATs are not a "free" solution. They were successfully used as a temporary solution until a massive deployment of IPv6 and are still useful.

4.4 ARCHITECTURAL DISCUSSION

The "hourglass" model proposed by Steve Deering in 2001 [52] illustrates the ability of IPv6 to move back to the initial IP protocol architectural principles that made IP successful.

The IP architecture started with a set of principles discussed in detail in Chapter 2 that are illustrated in Figure 4.8.

As new IP technologies such as multicast and Quality of Service (QoS) mechanisms were added to the IP layer, the model got fatter (Figure 4.9), but was still in line with the architecture principles of IP.

The next "step" was more problematic. As discussed previously, the introduction of NATs and ALGs in the network temporarily solved the IPv4 address exhaustion problem but also "broke" the architecture, as illustrated in Figure 4.10. The term "break" is probably a bit too strong and other technologies involving security mechanisms introduced by firewalls had similar effects. Still, the

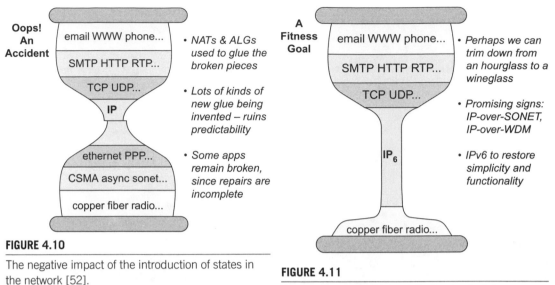

FIGURE 4.10

The negative impact of the introduction of states in the network [52].

FIGURE 4.11

Back to the original IP architectural principles.

introduction of states in the network had a negative effect on the architecture with a serious loss of network transparency.

IPv6 offers the possibility of returning to the root foundation of IP. This is done with a thin IP layer (see Figure 4.11) in charge of routing the traffic across the network with full support of IP multicast and QoS over a variety of link layers on top of which multiple transport protocols and applications can be used with total transparency, unique addresses, and application independence, which are required features for IP smart object networks.

IPv6 allows the return to main architectural principles of the IP architecture in line with the main goals of the Internet (as a reminder from Chapter 2):

- Internet communication must continue despite loss of networks or gateways ("in the presence of link or node failures").
- The Internet must support multiple types of communication services.
- Internet architecture must:
  - Accommodate a variety of networks ("networks" means link and physical layers)
  - Permit distributed management of its resources
  - Be cost-effective
  - Permit host attachment with a little effort
- Resources used in the Internet architecture must be accountable.

4.5 CONCLUSIONS

IPv4 has been deployed at a scale unimaginable by its original designers and is currently used by more than a billion devices. Early on, it was well understood that a new revision of IP would be needed because of the exponential growth of IP connected devices. Although the adoption of IPv6 has been delayed because of migration cost, the migration to IPv6 is inevitable and has already started. The most accurate models predict an exhaustion of the IPv4 address pool by March 2012.

The need to connect billions of IP smart objects makes IPv6 the IP protocol version of choice for smart object networks. From an architectural standpoint, IPv6 is built on the fundamental architectural principles of IP: it is not a new protocol but an evolution of IPv4 offering address space an order of magnitude larger than with IPv4 along with very useful features for smart object networks such as stateless configuration, which is explored in detail in Chapter 15.

Routing

5

5.1 ROUTING IN IP NETWORKS

Routing in IP networks has been a topic of great interest for the past two decades and has led to the emergence of several routing protocols. The main function of the routing protocol is to determine the "best" path to reach a destination according to various metrics and objective functions. For example, RIP [163] considers the best path as the path with a minimum number of hops, whereas the best path computed by OSPF [179] is the path with minimal cost where the path cost is the sum of all link costs along that path.

Routing tables are populated in routers and indicate the best next hop(s) for each reachable destination potentially along with other parameters. Upon receiving an IP packet, the router performs a routing lookup and forwards the packet to the best next hop according to the routing table until the destination is reached.

What seems fairly straightforward is not only quite sophisticated but has direct consequences on both the Quality of Service (QoS) provided by the network and the overall network reliability. Several routing protocols have been developed for intra-domain (e.g., RIP [163], IS-IS [131], OSPF [179], OLSR [41], AODV [194]) and inter-domain routing (e.g., BGP [212]). It is common for several routing protocols to coexist in the same network. For example, RIP can be used at the edge of the network to interconnect nodes organized in a (dual) star topology, OSPF, or IS-IS in the core of the network to provide a higher degree of connectivity (with route redistribution between the intra-domain routing protocols. Such routing protocols are also called Interior Gateway Protocols (IGPs) operating within an Autonomous System (AS) itself connected to the external world (either private or the public Internet) using routing protocols such as BGP.

5.1.1 IP Routing and QoS

QoS is the network's ability to meet certain criteria for the traffic such as network delays and jitter or packet drop probability. To provide differentiated QoS, according to traffic requirements, traffic must be marked at the edge of the network or at the source of the traffic and perform a number of tasks in the network as packets are forwarded from the source to the destination. Once the packet has been classified (colored) in a specific Class of Service (CoS), it will be processed according to its CoS along the forwarding path. The traffic may be "shaped" at the edge of the network, reservation could dynamically take place for a specific traffic for resource reservation, and should network congestion take place, resource allocation will be performed according to the traffic CoS using several

Interconnecting Smart Objects with IP. DOI: 10.1016/B978-0-12-375165-2.00005-3

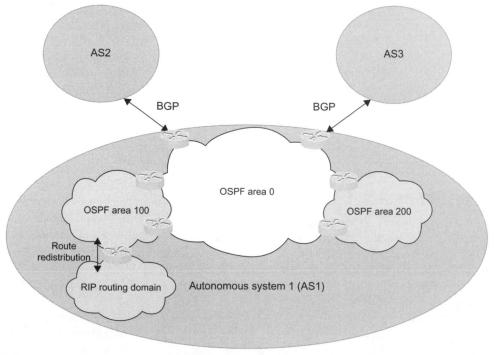

FIGURE 5.1

An example of the coexistence of intra- and inter-domain routing protocols.

sophisticated techniques such as congestion management and scheduling techniques. More details on QoS can be found in Chapter 15.

The role of the routing protocol is crucial to providing appropriate QoS to a traffic class, since most of time there are several paths between a source and a destination that may have very different characteristics such as delay, jitter, number of hops, and so forth. Thus it is the combination of the routing protocol and the QoS mechanisms along the forwarding path that determines the level of QoS provided to the traffic according to its CoS.

Path computation can either be performed using a centralized path computation element (also referred to as off-line) or a distributed routing protocol. In the former case, the path computation element (also called PCE) tries to optimize the traffic placement taking into account the network resources and topology and the (estimated) traffic matrix along with other parameters and objectives. Although the problem of finding an optimal solution is usually known as NP-complete, sophisticated heuristics have been developed to get relatively close to the optimal solution. In contrast, distributed routing protocols rely on a distributed control plane where routers exchange routing information (routes, topological data, etc.) to compute their routing tables. Off-line path computation is undoubtedly more expensive because of overhead (requires communication between all nodes and the PCE) and potentially in-band signaling protocols, and is less responsive to failures and more difficult to manage. The Internet Engineering Task Force (IETF) has formed a Working Group dedicated to this work (http://www.ietf.org/dyn/wg/charter/pce-charter.html). An alternative is to involve several PCEs in the computation of a path (referred to as distributed PCE path computation); for example, to find the best constrained shortest path in an inter-domain MPLS network. But the use of off-line path computation technique has been limited to specific situations requiring a high level of optimization that does not occur frequently in relatively small-to-medium scale networks (e.g., optical or multilayer networks). The vast majority of IP networks use distributed routing protocols where each router computes its own paths based on the routing information exchanged with the other routers in the network. The combination of off-line and distributed routing protocols could be an attractive option in some cases.

Routing in large-scale networks made of highly constrained smart objects brings several interesting technical challenges introduced in Section 5.2 and discussed in detail in Chapter 17.

5.1.2 **IP Routing and Network Reliability**

Most networks have some level of redundancy with more than one path between a source and a destination. It is the role of the routing protocol to find the best path according to metrics and objective functions. Several routing protocols are able to compute several equal cost paths toward a destination; this is called equal cost multiple path (ECMP). With ECMP routers distribute (load balance) the traffic among the paths of the same cost. This load balancing function may be on a "per packet" basis potentially unequally (X packets on path 1, Y packet on path 2) or sometimes called "per destination" based on traffic flows that are load balanced with all packets belonging to a traffic flow always following the same path (using a hash function) to avoid packet reordering.

A key function of the routing protocol is to find an alternate path in the presence of link or node failures. This is referred to as "rerouting." The time required to find an alternate path once a network element failure has been detected is called the "convergence time." The area usually called "fast convergence" is very important considering the constant need for network reliability improvement. This area has led to remarkable improvements and optimizations. New protocols and failure detection techniques have been designed such as the Bidirectional Forwarding Detection (BFD) protocol [144]. This is a fast keepalive mechanism used to quickly detect a failure or inter-layer failure signaling where the link layer sends an indication to upper layers upon detecting a failure at the link layer. Furthermore, a number of rerouting techniques have been developed to quickly find an alternate path upon detecting a network failure. Such alternate path(s) may be determined on the fly or pre-computed prior to the failure. Today's routing protocols typically offer rerouting times in a matter of milliseconds or hundreds of milliseconds depending on the routing protocol in use. [246] explores all of these techniques and optimizations in great detail.

The routing protocol may be coupled with lower layers protection restoration mechanisms. For example, an IP over optical network may rely on an optical restoration mechanism on top of which the routing protocol performs its own rerouting in the presence of failures. In this case, rerouting at multiple layers should be performed in a synchronized fashion.

Another well-known mechanism sometimes also used in smart object networks consists of duplicating the traffic and sending two copies of the same packet along two different (possibly diverse) paths. The challenge is then to compute diverse paths between a pair of nodes, which may or may not be fully diverse, as shown in Figure 5.2.

The paths A-B-E-H-J and A-D-C-F-I-J are said to be fully diverse. In contrast, the paths A-B-E-H-J and A-D-G-H-J are partially diverse (they share the node H and link H-J).

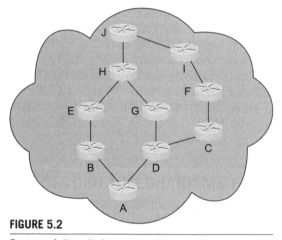

FIGURE 5.2

Degree of diversity in a network.

The computation of fully diverse paths in a network is quite challenging when using a distributed routing protocol. Link states routing protocols allow the computing engine to find diverse paths, but usually require an additional signaling mechanism to ensure the paths will stay diverse end to end. But ensuring end-to-end diverse paths with a distance vector routing protocol such as RPL (Routing for low-Power and Lossy networks, see [256]), the routing protocol for smart object networks, is significantly more difficult since the source cannot see the entire path. With RPL node A joins a set of parents along a directed acyclic graph (DAG) based on various criteria without knowing whether the path along those parents is diverse or not. Route recording techniques are possible but imply potentially costly overhead. These techniques consist of first setting up a path and recording the nodes along that path, then computing the second path avoiding the nodes traversed by the first path. Such a two-step diverse path computation cannot guarantee finding disjointed paths, even if they exist (the well-known "trapping" problem). RPL is described in great detail in Chapter 17.

The routing protocol strongly impacts the overall network reliability. Rerouting in Low-power and Lossy Networks (LLNs) is an interesting topic since both the characteristics of these networks and traffic requirements regarding the Service Level Agreement (SLA) significantly differ from traditional IP networks, as discussed in the next section.

5.2 SPECIFICS OF ROUTING IN LLNs

Networks made of smart objects significantly differ from "traditional" IP networks. Traditional IP networks are made of main-powered routers with several mega- or even gigabytes of memory (RAM) for high-end routers, extensive flash memory, and one or more powerful CPU interconnected by highly stable links. Everything is relative. Still, these networks may be constrained considering the amount of traffic they carry. IP core networks use 10 Gbits/s optical links (and more soon) and may be congested: we need to remember than their routing tables may be populated with more than hundreds of thousands of routes with intra- and inter-domain routes, not to mention the complex tasks that these routers perform.

The generic terms Low-power and Lossy Networks (LLNs) have been chosen to designate networks made of (highly) constrained smart objects interconnected by fairly unstable low-speed links, which unavoidably impose new constraints and challenges on the routing protocol of choice in LLNs.

As discussed in Chapter 17, the unique set of characteristics that make up LLNs led to the formation of a new IETF Working Group, called Routing Over Low-power and Lossy networks (ROLL; http://www.ietf.org/dyn/wg/charter/roll-charter.html). This group was chartered to design a routing protocol for such IP networks. The ROLL Working Group first produced a detailed set of

Routing for smart objects

Current Internet	Low-power and Lossy Networks (LLN)
Nodes are routers	Nodes are sensor/actuators and routers
IGP with typically few hundreds of nodes	An order of magnitude larger in terms of number of nodes
Links and nodes are stable	Links are highly unstable and nodes die much more often
Nodes constraints or link bandwidths are typically non-issues	Nodes/Links are highly constrained
Routing is not application-aware (MTR is a vanilla version of it)	Application-aware routing, in-band processing is a MUST

FIGURE 5.3

Routing in LLNs.

routing requirements for LLNs for various applications and conducted a survey studying the potential adequacy of existing IP routing protocols in light of these specific routing requirements. The ROLL Working Group quickly converged to define a new IP routing protocol, called RPL, which is described in greater detail in Chapter 17.

5.2.1 What Makes the Routing in LLNs Different?

Figure 5.3 is an overview of the main differences.

First, the devices and links used to interconnect smart objects are different.

The constrained nature of smart objects is discussed in length in Chapters 1 and 11. Existing routing protocols do not take into account the router characteristics in their routing decisions. There are very few exceptions to this rule, but in the majority of cases, routing protocols only consider the set of reachable destinations along with their cost (distance vector) or the entire network topology (link state). In most cases, node characteristics are not considered in existing routing protocols. Link state routing protocols only consider static link attributes and costs.

Using dynamic metrics: the idea of making the link metric dynamic (for example, based on the average queuing delay) was studied many years ago in the context of the ARPANET network, thus *some* form of dynamic node metric has been considered in the past. For a number of reasons (risk of route oscillation, especially in the presence of sudden congestion events, etc.) the use of dynamic metrics was abandoned.

Considering node characteristics when computing paths is a *must* in most LLNs. Routers may significantly differ from each other in several ways:

- Processing capability: Smart object resources can be equipped with a low-end, 8-bit microcontroller or more powerful dual 32-bit microcontrollers.
- Memory (and non-volatile memory, e.g., Flash) can vary from a few hundred bytes to a few dozen kilobytes.
- Energy is key in most LLNs. Whereas some nodes may be main-powered, battery-powered nodes must consume energy with extreme care to prolong the life of the network.

Considering the wide range of node capabilities, it is desirable and sometimes necessary for the routing protocol to compute paths that meet traffic requirements according to the limited network resources. For example, non-critical, pollution-monitoring data should preferably follow a non-optimal path but that traverse main-powered nodes, whereas more critical traffic flow must imperatively follow the path that provides minimal latency. Another example is the advantageous use of a traffic aggregator along the path to the destination. This is used to aggregate traffic and consequently free up network resources in the network. Another example would be to restrict the path to nodes that can perform traffic encryption, which may not be available on all nodes or link layers.

Furthermore, as discussed in Chapter 17, node constraints regarding memory, CPU power, and sometimes energy impose restrictions on the routing protocol design. Although the code size is usually not an issue on a typical router, it is imperative to design a lightweight routing protocol for LLNs that optimizes the code space and the number of states that must be maintained not only to reduce the memory and flash space requirements but also the energy required to run the protocol and power the memory needed to maintain routing states. Typically a lightweight IPv6 stack requires a few kilobytes to a few dozen kilobytes of RAM and a few dozen kilobytes of flash. The routing protocol must not dramatically exceed the amount of required resources.

Even more important, links in LLNs are also extremely different from SONET/SDH, fiber optics, Ethernet, and other media used in "traditional" IP networks. The bit error rate (BER) of an optical or Ethernet link is usually extremely low, detection and error correction are sometimes available, and protection/restoration techniques may be obtainable at these layers (e.g., with protected SONET/SDH VC, 1:1, and 1+1 optical protection, etc. making a link failure invisible to the IP layer). Links in LLNs are usually low speed (from a few Kbits/s to several MBits/s), but even more important is the variable quality, which is usually unpredictable because of a variety of environmental factors (interferences, floor noise, impedance variation in Powerline communication (PLC), etc.).

The link failure profile of a low-power link (wireless or PLC) significantly differs from the serial or optical link. As shown in Figure 5.4, large variations of the packet delivery ratio (PDR) on these links is common. Different link failure profiles require new mechanisms for the routing protocol to avoid route oscillations and lack of stability in the network: excessive control plane traffic also affects the network lifetime in the presence of battery-operated nodes.

Figure 5.4 shows the PDR variation of IEEE 802.15.4 links over time for several channels. More details can be found in the [254].

Note that lossy links are not limited to wireless links and most of the PLC links may also be fairly unstable because of impedance variation, various sources of interferences, floor noise, and so forth. Furthermore, PLC links play a critical role in LLN infrastructures such as Smart Grid networks as discussed in detail in Chapter 20.

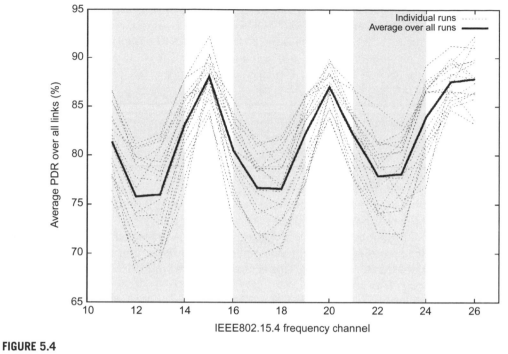

FIGURE 5.4

A wireless lossy link.

The use of lossy links has a direct implication on the routing protocol design: in most IP routing protocols, one of the most critical components is the convergence time (time to find/compute an alternate path around a failed network component). As soon as the failure is detected, the traffic is rerouted along an alternate path to mitigate the failure impact on traffic. Adopting a similar approach in the presence of lossy links may lead to routing instabilities and various types of oscillations and routing loops, which unavoidably occur with distributed routing protocols during transient failure (although recent improvements have considerably reduced the duration of such loops for "traditional" IP networks). The need for such a fast convergence time with routing protocols such as IS-IS and OSPF is also due to the type of traffic carried in these networks such as voice and video with very stringent traffic disruption requirements.

Routing in LLNs requires appropriate reactions during network-wide failures. Upon detecting the presence of a failure the traffic is locally redirected to an alternate next hop without immediately triggering a global recomputation of the paths in the network (a local routing protocol convergence also referred to as local repair). The failure may be transient and triggering a network-wide protocol convergence would not only be needless but would trigger the exchange of routing protocol messages. This leads to consuming energy and network resources, which is clearly undesirable in constrained environments. Furthermore, smart objects do not send a large amount of traffic, and it is likely that the node will only send a few packets, unlike voice and video traffic on IP high-speed networks.

Last but not least, scalability is of a different order of magnitude. The number of routers in an IP core network within a single administrative domain is a few hundred to a few thousand routers.

Although some LLNs are composed of a limited number of nodes for a foreseeable future (e.g., home automation), other types of LLNs are composed of hundreds of thousands of these routers (e.g., Smart Metering networks or Smart Cities). More details can be found in Part III of this book.

Most of these routers will be unattended so the routing protocol must be able to work autonomously and appropriately react to all situations in large-scale networks made of constrained devices interconnected by unstable links.

For the above-mentioned reasons, the new IP routing protocol RPL was designed to operate under the set of constraints described in Chapter 17.

5.3 LAYER 2 VERSUS LAYER 3 "ROUTING"

The discussion on whether routing in LLN should be performed at layer 2 (link layer) versus layer 3 (network layer: IP) has been a very sensitive topic.

Strictly speaking, routing implies protocols and mechanisms to compute paths in a multi-hop network at layer 3 (IP). It is possible to perform path computation at layer 2 in a multi-hop network using media access control (MAC) addresses. This is usually referred to as "mesh-under" in contrast with "router-over" (routing, thus at layer 3).

Beyond the terminology discussion, which is of minor importance, it is worthwhile to observe the consequences of adopting a multilayer routing architecture with routing processes operating independently at multiple layers.

Historically, the research community has been extremely active in routing in sensor networks. Many published papers make no assumptions about the protocol in use, instead focusing on the algorithmic aspects of routing and producing a large amount of interesting and useful work. Experiments have been conducted leading to the deployment of test beds usually deployed at a relatively small scale in real-life networks. In most cases, researchers implemented their protocols at layer 2 simply because their focus was more on algorithms than protocol architecture design.

With the extremely fast adoption rate of IP in LLNs for a number of applications (extensively discussed in Part III of the book), protocol architecture design is undoubtedly most important when looking at the global picture as opposed to each layer or component individually.

5.3.1 Where Should Path Computation Be Performed?

Until a few years ago, the number of low-power links available for LLNs was extremely limited and most people thought that IEEE 802.15.4 would be the only low-power link available (always a risky assumption). When a single link layer is in use, path computation can either take place at the link layer (layer 2) or IP layer (layer 3).

As clearly pointed out in Chapter 12, new low-power layer 2 technologies emerged thus reinforcing the use of a layered architecture such as IP. This guarantees layer independency and, in particular, layer 2 "agnosticism." Remember, the ability to use multiple link layers was one of the fundamental building blocks of the TCP/IP architecture design discussed in Chapter 2. It became apparent that a routing protocol (at layer 3) was a must, which led to the formation of the ROLL Working Group and the design of RPL.

Then the new question that emerged was whether or not it was desirable to adopt a multilayer routing architecture. Some paths computed by the link layer would then appear as IP links at layer 3 that would perform routing operation between IP links. Such a multilayer routing architecture is depicted in Figure 5.5.

At first, it was thought that such a multilayer approach could be designed and deployed. As discussed in Chapter 16, the 6LoWPAN Working Group even defined a mesh addressing header for its 6LowPAN adaptation layer that supported the "mesh-under" approach by encoding hops using IEEE 802.15.4 addresses since it operates at the link layer. Currently, there is no such link layer "routing" protocol designed.

This is probably one of those times where it is desirable to remember lessons learned, such as multilayer routing architectures, which have been studied in great detail and even partially deployed in specific contexts. IP over asynchronous transfer modes (ATM) is a notorious example with the ATM layer using PNNI [13] as a routing protocol to compute the paths of the virtual connections (VCs) in the ATM domain and IP. VCs are considered physical links and IP performs routing at layer 3, a routing "architecture" that has shown a number of drawbacks and limitations.

It is important to consider the consequences of such a *routing* "architecture":
Lack of visibility is one consequence. Since layer 3 considers the paths computed by layer 2 as IP links, the IP routing protocol has no visibility on the link layer path. This unavoidably leads to suboptimal routing. Indeed, the link layer "routing" protocol computes paths according to its own metrics and constraints and the resulting path properties are not communicated to the IP layer. Such links have static metrics usually independent or inconsistent with the IP metrics. Various studies and experiments dynamically updating the IP link costs according to the layer 2 path costs showed that such a

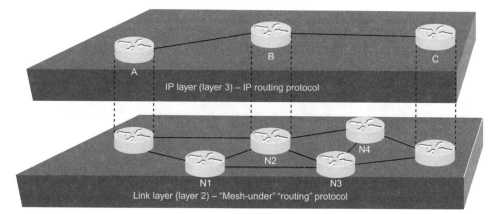

At the IP layers: Nodes perform IP routing function and do not "see" the nodes at the link layer. A and B have no visibility on some nodes at the link layer (N1, N3, and N4 in this example).

At the Link layer: Nodes performs "mesh-under" "routing" using MAC addresses to compute paths at the link layer. In this example, N1, N3, and N4 are link layer only nodes.

FIGURE 5.5

A multilayer routing architecture in LLNs.

strategy led to IP routing oscillations if great care was not given to the link layer routing strategy. This introduced a great deal of complexity in the network.

Such an issue is illustrated in Figure 5.6. In this example, domain 1 is a set of nodes (routers) interconnected by type 1 links (e.g., IEEE 802.15.4 links), whereas the nodes in domain 2 are interconnected type 2 links. Let's consider a computed path between node A in domain 1 and node C in domain 2. When both domains are interconnected with IP but each domain makes use of mesh-under routing, node A "sees" a two-hop path from itself to C (A-B-C). In reality, if the IP routing protocol is a distance vector routing protocol, it may not even know the details of the path (set of links along the path) but only the resulting path cost. The A-B-C path cost is computed according to the metric used by the IP routing protocol (e.g., metric reflecting the path latency). Now consider each link layer path. Within domain 1, the mesh-under routing protocol has computed the link layer path between node A and node B as A-N1-N4-N3-B according to the layer 2 metric, which may or may not be similar to the metric used by the IP routing protocol. The same reasoning applies to domain 2. This clearly shows that the use of multilayer routing leads to loose end-to-end path consistency, which may be a serious drawback. Even if similar metrics are used at both layers, the IP routing protocol still does not see the link layer path computed by the link layer. If there is a link failure at the link layer, the link layer path would be recomputed (with a potential new path cost), but the IP link (A-B) metric would not be updated, which leads to another source of suboptimal routing. Although technically feasible, in practice it is difficult to dynamically update the link layer path cost at the network layer and not in multilayer networks. Consider a link failure between the nodes N1 and N4. The link layer mesh-under routing protocol would recompute a new path (A-N1-N2-N3-B in our example) with a new cost that may not be reflected at the IP layer. This is illustrated in Figure 5.7. ⚠ Note: A

At the IP layers: Nodes perform IP routing function and do not "see" the nodes at the link layer. A and B have no visibility on the link layer topology (e.g., nodes N1, N2, N3, and N4 in this example).

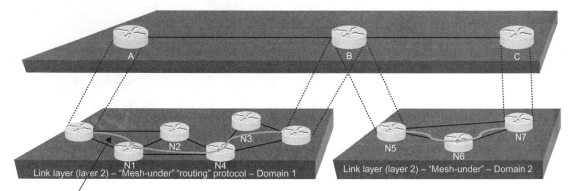

A-N1-N4-N3-B is the link layer path computed by the "mesh-under" "routing" protocol operating at the link layer in domain 1.

FIGURE 5.6

Interconnection of two IP routing domains, each using a mesh-under routing protocol.

very common misunderstanding of Multiprotocol Label Switching (MPLS) leads to the conclusion that it lies between the link layer and the IP routing layer with its own routing component. MPLS provides a mechanism that pushes a label used for forwarding, but the MPLS control plane (including routing and signaling) relies on IP. For example, the Traffic Engineering Label Switch Path (TE LSP) can be computed thanks to a traffic engineering database populated by IS-IS or OSPF. The signaling protocol used to signal TE LSP is RSVP-TE [14]. In other words, MPLS traffic engineering is not a multilayer routing architecture. Furthermore, IP routing does not "run" over MPLS TE LSPs. There are a few instances where a multilayer routing architecture is useful. For example, in IP over optical networks with Generalized Multiprotocol Label Switching (GMPLS) it might be efficient to use path computation elements (PCE) that would try to simultaneously optimize resources at both layers to determine the most optimal multilayer routing strategy, but such networks are extremely different from LLNs. By all means, this is not to say that PCE-based systems will not be applicable to LLNs, but this discussion applies to the use of multilayer routing.

Network Rerouting is another consequence. One of the main properties of a routing protocol is to find an alternate path in the network during network component failures (link or node). When such a failure occurs, it is likely that both layers detect the failure and trigger the recomputation of a new path around the failed network element. But this may not always be the case. There are failures detected by both layers (e.g., a link failure that lasts long enough for the routing protocol to lose a routing adjacency) and other failures that are only detected by one of the two layers. In the presence of routing protocol at both layers, the only viable solution is using a timer-based bottom-up approach to avoid concurrent rerouting at both layers. In other words, upon detection of the failure, layer 3 must wait until the expiration of a configurable timer before triggering a network reroute to give a

At the IP layers: Nodes perform IP routing function and do not "see" the
newly computed path at the link layer.

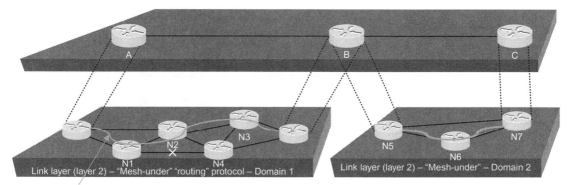

A-N1-N2-N3-B is the new path computed by the "mesh-under" "routing"
after the failure of the N1-N4 link.

FIGURE 5.7

Rerouting at the link layer.

chance to the lower layer to restore the link. The timer must be computed to be in the upper bounds of the layer 2 convergence time and is usually quite difficult to estimate. Furthermore, if the failure cannot be restored by the link layer and rerouting must take place at the IP layer, additional time will be needed to find a repair path. Such issues have been analyzed in detail in [246]. The fact that lossy links in LLNs have specific link layer profiles further adds to the level of complexity, since the simple use of timers is unlikely to be sufficient to coordinate rerouting in multiple layers.

Although such a multilayer routing architecture may be very appealing in IP over GMPLS networks where multilayer optimization is relevant, the level of additional complexity and issues inherent to multilayer routing is undoubtedly problematic for LLNs made of constrained and unattended nodes interconnected with lossy links and are at best no better than routing at the IP layer.

5.4 CONCLUSIONS

Routing is undoubtedly one of the key components of networking and has been a topic of great interest over the past two decades. A number of IP routing protocols have been successfully designed that support fast convergence, the ability to compute paths that meet specific QoS requirements in networks with hundreds or even thousands of nodes, and so forth.

But routing in low-power and constrained networks (LLNs) imposes a number of new restrictions: links are highly unstable compared to optical, SONET/SDH, or Ethernet links, constrained links and nodes must be considered (with dynamic metrics), and the routing protocol must have a small footprint while supporting hundreds and thousands of nodes requiring large scalability. Last but not least, there should be no overacting while routing in LLN in the presence of failures considering the potential high degree of instability and the need to bound the control traffic in these networks. These specific constraints led to a new routing protocol called RPL (discussed in great detail in Chapter 17).

Finally, with the emergence of multiple types of low-power link layers such as IEEE 802.15.4, WiFi, and PLC, it quickly became obvious that routing at the network layer (IP) was a must. Although routing at the link layer may be available with some link layers, trying to adopt a multilayer routing architecture in LLNs is clearly not a viable option considering the dramatic increase of network complexity and lack of efficiency.

Transport Protocols

In the IP stack, the transport protocols reside on top of the IP protocol. Applications do not use IP directly, but use the transport protocols to communicate with each other. In the IP protocol stack, there are two transport protocols that are by far the most widely used: the User Datagram Protocol (UDP), and the Transport Control Protocol (TCP). UDP is a best-effort delivery service, which does not add much on top of IP, whereas TCP is a reliable byte stream that adds a connection abstraction on top of the connectionless IP. Although there have been several other transport protocols defined, such as SCTP [229] and DCCP [152], they have as yet to be adopted by the mainstream.

Before we discuss other transport protocols, we must review the terminology used around the transport protocols in the IP suite. At the IP layer, the basic unit of transportation is called a packet. Although data from higher layers are transported in these packets, to avoid confusion other words are used to describe the unit of transportation. In UDP, the basic unit of transportation is called a *datagram*. When we discuss datagrams, we are referring to a UDP datagram. The TCP basic unit of transportation is called a *segment*. We use this terminology throughout this chapter.

6.1 UDP

UDP is the simplest protocol in the TCP/IP suite. This protocol is specified in the RFC768 document [202], which is exceptionally short; the full specification fits on two printed pages.

Many IP applications run over UDP. Simple request–response protocols such as Domain Name Service (DNS) lookups are implemented over UDP. Time-sensitive data such as real-time audio or video are also often transported over UDP.

For smart object networks, the simplicity and lightweight nature of UDP makes it a compelling choice for data that need to be quickly transported such as sensor data.

6.1.1 Best-effort Datagram Delivery

UDP provides a best-effort datagram delivery service. This mechanism is best-effort because the underlying IP network does its best to deliver the datagram, but does not guarantee that the datagrams are delivered at the destination. There are also no guarantees that the datagrams are delivered in the same order as they were sent.

UDP provides an extra layer of multiplexing on top of IP. Where IP provides addressing of a specific host in an Internet, UDP provides per-process addressing by the use of ports. The ports are

Interconnecting Smart Objects with IP. DOI: 10.1016/B978-0-12-375165-2.00006-5

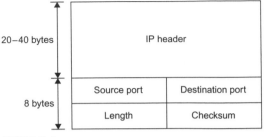

20–40 bytes

8 bytes

FIGURE 6.1

The UDP header consists of four fields: source port, destination port, a length field, and a checksum.

16-bit values used to distinguish between different senders and receivers at each end point. Each UDP datagram is addressed to a specific port at the end host and incoming UDP datagrams are demultiplexed between the recipients.

UDP also calculates a checksum over the datagram. The checksum covers the UDP header and data as well as a pseudo-header consisting of certain fields of the IP header, including the IP source and destination addresses. The checksum does not make UDP reliable; however, since UDP datagrams with a failing checksum are dropped without notifying the application process. Delivery of UDP datagrams is not guaranteed and UDP datagrams may arrive out of order and in any number of copies due to the nature of IP.

6.1.2 The UDP Header

The UDP header is small and consists of only 8 bytes. The size of the header is fixed: there are no variable-length fields.

The UDP header is shown in Figure 6.1. It contains four fields: the source port number, the destination port number, the length of the data portion of the datagram, and a checksum field. All fields are 16 bits.

- Source port: This 16-bit field contains the port number of the process that sent the datagram. This is used by the receiving process to know where to send a reply datagram. The source port field does not need to be filled in so it is set to zero.
- Destination port: This 16-bit field contains the port number of the process that is to receive the datagram. This field must always be filled in.
- Length: This contains the length, in bytes, of the data that follow the header.
- Checksum: This is a 16-bit Internet checksum of the data in the datagram, the UDP header, and the source and destination IP addresses from the IP header.

The source and destination port numbers are used when determining the destination of the datagram. Typically, the process can choose to listen for all incoming datagrams on a particular port, for datagrams that arrive on a port but have a specific source port number, or for datagrams that originate from a specific host.

The length field contains the length of the UDP header and the data in the datagram. The IP layer contains a length field, which contains the same information as the UDP header length field. Because the underlying IP layer may fragment packets, the UDP length field is a sanity check against packets that have been incorrectly reassembled [210,228].

6.2 TCP

Unlike the best-effort UDP, TCP [204] provides a reliable byte stream on top of the best-effort packet service provided by the IP layer. Reliability is achieved by buffering data combined with positive

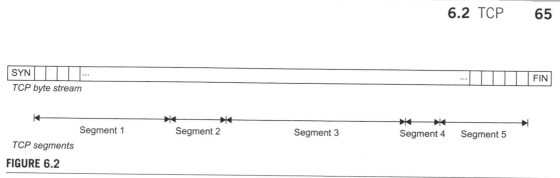

FIGURE 6.2

A segmented TCP byte stream.

acknowledgments (ACKs) and retransmissions. TCP hides the packet-oriented IP network beneath a virtual circuit abstraction, in which each virtual circuit is called a connection. Before any data are transported, the two connection end points must explicitly set up a connection. A connection is identified by the IP addresses and TCP port numbers of the end points.

TCP is the most common IP transport protocol. Many application layer protocols are defined over TCP, such as HTTP (Web), SMTP (e-mail), SNMP (network management), and XMPP (instant messaging).

For smart objects, the benefits of using TCP are both the reliable service that TCP provides, and the interoperability with existing protocols and systems.

Although TCP is more complex than UDP, the core functionality of TCP is lightweight. In this chapter, we first give an overview of TCP, then turn to focus on its core functionality.

6.2.1 Reliable Stream Transport

TCP provides a reliable stream transport service on top of the best-effort IP layer. TCP uses three mechanisms to achieve a byte-oriented reliable delivery:

- Acknowledgments and retransmissions: All data sent with TCP are acknowledged by the receiver. If the sender does not receive an acknowledgment within a given time interval, it retransmits the data.
- Sequence numbers: Every byte in the TCP byte stream is given a sequence number. The sequence numbers are used when matching acknowledgments with the corresponding data.
- Sliding window: The receiver advertises how many bytes it is currently able to receive and the sender sends only as much data as the receiver can receive. As the receiver receives the data, it is able to receive more data. This is known as a sliding window.

Each byte in the TCP byte stream is assigned a sequence number. The stream is partitioned into segments that may be arbitrarily sized as shown in Figure 6.2. A TCP sender will attempt to fill each segment with enough data so that the segment is as large as the maximum segment size of the connection, but this is not required.

Each segment is prepended with a TCP header and transmitted in separate IP packets. In theory, for each received segment the receiver produces an ACK. In practice, however, most TCP implementations send an ACK only on every other incoming segment to reduce ACK traffic. ACKs are also piggybacked on outgoing TCP segments. The ACK contains the next sequence number expected in the continuous stream of bytes. Thus, ACKs do not acknowledge the reception of any individual segment, but rather acknowledge the transmission of a continuous range of bytes.

If a TCP segment is lost, there is a gap in the byte stream. TCP provides a mechanism for receivers to fill in the gap. For example, consider a TCP receiver that has received all bytes up to and including sequence number χ, as well as the bytes $\chi + 20$ to $\chi + 40$ with a gap between $\chi + 1$ and $\chi + 19$ as seen in the top half of Figure 6.3. The ACK contains the sequence number $\chi + 1$, which is the next sequence number expected in the continuous stream. When the segment containing bytes $\chi + 1$ to $\chi + 19$ arrives, the next ACK contains the sequence number $\chi + 41$. This is shown in the lower half of Figure 6.3.

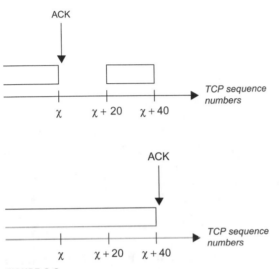

FIGURE 6.3

A TCP byte stream with a gap and the corresponding ACKs.

The sending side of a TCP connection keeps track of all segments sent that have not been acknowledged by the receiver. If an ACK is not received within a certain time, the segment is retransmitted. This process is referred to as a time-out and is depicted in Figure 6.4. Here we see a TCP sender sending segments to a TCP receiver. Segment 3 is lost in the network and the receiver will continue to reply with ACKs for the highest sequence number of the continuous stream of bytes that ended with segment 2. Eventually, the sender will conclude that segment 3 was lost since no ACK has been received for this segment and will retransmit segment 3. The receiver has now received all bytes up to and including segment 5 and will reply with an ACK for segment 5. Even though TCP ACKs are not for individual segments, it is sometimes convenient to discuss ACKs as belonging to specific segments.

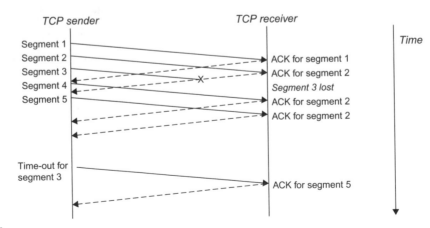

FIGURE 6.4

Loss of a TCP segment and the corresponding time-out.

6.2.2 The TCP Header

The TCP header is 20 bytes long and has room for a variable-sized option field between the header fields and the application data.

The TCP header, shown in Figure 6.5, consists of nine fixed fields:

- Source port: A 16-bit field that holds the port number of the sending process.
- Destination port: A 16-bit field that holds the port number of the receiving process.
- Sequence number: The 32-bit sequence number of the first byte of data contained in the segment.
- Acknowledgment number: If the acknowledgment flag is set in the flags field, the acknowledgment number field holds the 32-bit sequence number of the next byte that the receiver expects.
- Hlen: A 4-bit field that holds the length of the header, including options, divided by four.
- Flags: The 6-bit flag field contains the six flags FIN, SYN, RST, PSH, ACK, and URG.
- Window: The 16-bit window field holds the amount of bytes that the receiver is able to receive.
- Checksum: The 16-bit checksum is the Internet checksum of the data, the TCP header, and the IP destination and source addresses.
- Urgent pointer: If the URG flag is set, this 16-bit field points to a place in the byte stream that contains data that the application has defined to be urgent. The urgent pointer is rarely used.

The source and destination port numbers hold the TCP port numbers of the sending and receiving process for the TCP segment. Unlike UDP, where the source port number is optional, both the source and destination ports must be present in the TCP header.

The sequence and acknowledgment number fields are both 32-bit fields that hold TCP sequence numbers. The sequence number field contains the sequence number of the first byte of data in the TCP segment. If the segment contains a SYN or a FIN flag, which both occupy a position in the TCP byte sequence, the sequence number refers to the SYN or FIN. The acknowledgment number field holds the sequence number of the next byte the receiver is expecting on this connection. The acknowledgment number field is defined only if the ACK flag is set. In practice, most TCP segments, except for the initial SYN segment, have the ACK flag set.

The hlen field holds the length of the header, including options and padding, counted in 4-byte words. Since the size of the TCP header is always divisible by 4 to allow for operation on processor architectures that require 32-bit alignment of 32-bit memory accesses, the header length field can be efficiently represented using only 4 bits.

The flags field contains six flags: FIN, SYN, RST, PSH, ACK, and URG. The FIN flag is set in the final segment on a TCP connection and the SYN flag is set in the first segment. The RST flag terminates a connection, and is used both to abort an active TCP connection when, for example, the

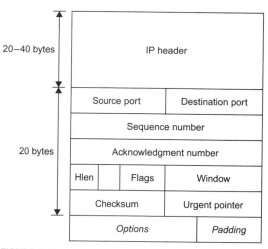

FIGURE 6.5

The TCP header consists of 20 bytes of header fields followed by options, if present. The options are padded so the packet header and options end on a 32-bit boundary.

controlling process has crashed, and to indicate that a TCP port is closed. The PSH flag is used to indicate that a TCP segment is the last in a sequence of segments sent by the application and that the receiving TCP should deliver these data directly to the application. The ACK flag is set in TCP segments where the acknowledgment sequence number field holds the next sequence number to be expected. The URG field, which is rarely used, indicates that an "urgent" data point will occur later in the byte stream.

The window field contains a 16-bit number that indicates how many bytes a TCP receiver is able to buffer. This is used in the TCP flow control mechanism described later. If the window field is zero, the TCP sender should not send any more data until it has received a TCP segment with a window larger than zero.

The checksum field contains a 16-bit Internet checksum that is computed over the entire TCP header including options and padding, the data portion of the segment, and the IP destination and source addresses.

The urgent pointer is a rarely used TCP feature that allows an application to specify that one byte in the byte stream is to be considered urgent. The urgent pointer is set only if the URG flag is set. If a TCP receiver sees an urgent byte, it notifies the application. The application may then choose to discard data that appear before the urgent data. If more than one urgent byte occurs in the byte stream, TCP only considers the last urgent byte.

6.2.3 TCP Options

TCP options provide additional control information. They reside between the TCP header and the data of a segment. Since the original specification of TCP [204], a number of additions have been defined as TCP options. These include the TCP selective acknowledgment (SACK) [170] and the TCP extensions for high-speed networks [136] that define TCP time stamps and window scaling options.

For smart objects, the arguably most important TCP option is the maximum segment size (MSS) option. The TCP MSS option specifies the largest TCP segment size that a TCP end point is able to accept. The MSS option is sent by both parties during the opening of a connection. The MSS option effectively limits the amount of data in each TCP segment. This is important for smart object networks, which typically can carry only small packets.

When opening a TCP connection, both the TCP sender and the TCP receiver indicate the MSS they can accept by placing the TCP MSS option in the SYN and the SYNACK segments. When receiving a TCP MSS option, a TCP end point must reduce the size of the segments it sends accordingly. This is useful for TCP end points with small amounts of memory, because it allows the end point to set a limit on the size of the packets it will receive.

6.2.4 Round-trip Time Estimation

A critical factor of any reliable protocol is the round-trip time estimation, since the round-trip time determines the time to wait for an ACK before retransmitting a segment. If the round-trip time estimate is much lower than the actual round-trip time of the connection, segments will be retransmitted before the original segment or its corresponding ACK has propagated through the network. If the round-trip time estimation is too high, time-outs will be longer than necessary, thus reducing performance.

TCP uses feedback provided by its acknowledgment mechanism to measure round-trip times. Round-trip time measurements are taken once per window, since it is assumed that all segments in one window's flight should have approximately the same round-trip time. Taking round-trip samples for every segment does not yield better measurements [7]. If a segment for which a round-trip time was measured is a retransmission, that round-trip time measurement is discarded [143]. This occurs because the ACK for the retransmitted segment may have been sent either in response to the original segment or to the retransmitted segment. Using the round-trip time estimate for a retransmitted segment would make the round-trip time estimation ambiguous.

6.2.5 Flow Control

The flow control mechanism in TCP assures that the sender will not overwhelm the receiver with data that the receiver is not ready to accept. Each outgoing TCP segment includes an indication of the size of the available buffer space, and the sender must not send more data than the receiver can accommodate. The available buffer space for a connection is referred to as the window of the connection. The window principle ensures proper operation even between two hosts with drastically different memory resources.

The TCP sender tries to have one receiver window's worth of data in the network at any given time provided the application wishes to send data at the appropriate rate (this is not entirely true; see the next section, Congestion Control). It does this by keeping track of the highest sequence number s ACKed by the receiver, and makes sure not to send data with a sequence number larger than $s + r$, where r is the size of the receiver's window.

Returning to Figure 6.4, we see that the TCP sender stopped sending segments after segment 5 had been sent. If we assume that the receiver's window was 1000 bytes and that the individual sizes of segments 3, 4, and 5 were exactly 1000 bytes, we can see that since the sender had not received any ACK for segments 3, 4, and 5, the sender refrained from sending any more segments. This is because the sequence number of segment 6 would be equal to the sum of the highest ACKed sequence number and the receiver's window.

6.2.6 Congestion Control

If flow control ignores that the buffer space will be overrun at the end points, the congestion control mechanisms [8,134] try to prevent the overrun of router buffer space. To achieve this TCP uses two separate methods:

- Slow start: Probes the available bandwidth when starting to send over a connection.
- Congestion avoidance: Constantly adapts the sending rate to the perceived bandwidth of the path between the sender and the receiver.

For smart object networks, which may have only limited amounts of data to send, TCP congestion control is rarely invoked. Yet we review it here for completeness.

The congestion control mechanism adds another constraint on the maximum number of outstanding, unacknowledged bytes in the network by maintaining a congestion window for each connection. The minimum of the congestion window and the receiver's window is used to determine the maximum number of unacknowledged bytes in the network.

TCP uses packet drops as a sign of congestion, because TCP was designed for wired networks where the main source of packet drops (>99%) is due to buffer overruns in routers. There are two ways for TCP to conclude that a packet was dropped: waiting for a time-out or counting the number of duplicate ACKs that are received. If two ACKs for the same sequence number are received, the packet was duplicated within the network (which can happen under certain conditions [193]). It could also mean that segments were reordered on their way to the receiver. However, if three duplicate ACKs are received for the same sequence number, there is a good chance that this indicates a lost segment. Three duplicate ACKs trigger a mechanism known as fast retransmit and the lost segment is retransmitted without waiting for its time-out.

During slow start, the congestion window is increased with one maximum segment size per received ACK, which leads to an exponential increase of the size of the congestion window. Despite its name, slow start opens the congestion window quite rapidly; the name was coined at a time when TCP senders started by sending the entire data of the receiver's window. When the congestion window reaches a threshold, known as the slow start threshold, the congestion avoidance phase is entered.

When in the congestion avoidance phase, the congestion window is increased linearly until a packet is dropped. The drop causes the congestion window to reset to one segment, the slow start threshold is set to half of the current window, and slow start is initiated. If the drop is indicated by three duplicate ACKs, the fast recovery mechanism is triggered. The fast recovery mechanism halves the congestion window and keeps TCP in the congestion avoidance phase, instead of falling back to slow start.

Increasing the congestion window linearly is harder than increasing the window exponentially, since a linear increase requires an increase of one segment per round-trip time rather than one segment per received ACK. Instead of using the round-trip time estimate and using a timer to increase the congestion window, many TCP implementations increase the congestion window by a fraction of a segment per received ACK.

6.2.7 TCP States

TCP not only provides a reliable stream transfer, but also a reliable way to set up and take down connections. This process is most often captured as a state diagram. The TCP state diagram is shown in Figure 6.6, where the boxes represent the TCP states and the arcs represent the state transitions with the actions taken as a result of the transitions. The boldface text shows the actions taken by the application program.

6.2.7.1 Opening a Connection

For a TCP connection to be established, one of the participating sides must act as a server and the other as a client. The server enters the LISTEN state and waits for an incoming connection request from a client. The client, in the CLOSED state, issues an **open**, which results in a TCP segment with the SYN flag set to be sent to the server and the client enters the SYN-SENT state. The server enters the SYN-RCVD state and responds to the client with a TCP segment with both the SYN and ACK flags set. As the client responds with an ACK both sides are in the ESTABLISHED state and can begin sending data.

This process is known as the TCP three-way handshake (Figure 6.7), and not only sets both sides of the connection in the ESTABLISHED state, but also synchronizes the sequence numbers for the connection.

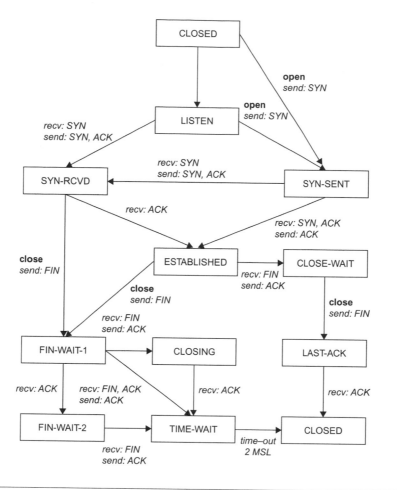

FIGURE 6.6

TCP state diagram.

Both the SYN and FIN segments occupy one byte position in the byte stream (refer back to Figure 6.2) and will reliably deliver to the other end point of the connection using the retransmission mechanism.

6.2.7.2 Closing a Connection

Closing a connection is more complicated than opening one because all segments must be reliably delivered before the connection can be fully closed. Also, the TCP close function will only close one end of the connection; both ends of the connection will have to close before the connection is completely terminated.

When a connection end point issues a close on the connection, the connection state on the closing side of the connection traverses the FIN-WAIT-1 and FIN-WAIT-2 states, optionally passing the CLOSING state, after which it ends up in the TIME-WAIT state. The connection is required to stay

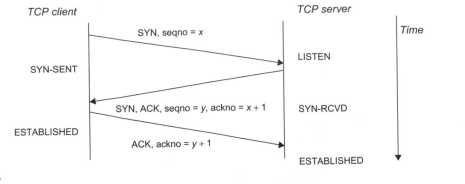

FIGURE 6.7

TCP three-way handshake.

in the TIME-WAIT state for twice the maximum segment lifetime (MSL) to account for duplicate copies of segments that might still be in the network. The remote end goes from the ESTABLISHED state to the CLOSE-WAIT state where it stays until the connection is closed by both sides. When the remote end issues a close, the connection passes the LAST-ACK state and the connection is removed at the remote end.

6.3 UDP FOR SMART OBJECTS

In the context of smart object networks, UDP has many benefits. First, UDP has a very low overhead for both header size and protocol logic. This means that both the packet transmissions and receptions consume less energy, and each packet has more room for application layer data. The simplicity and low complexity of the protocol logic may be advantageous for systems where memory footprint is at a premium. Since the protocol is simple, implementations typically have a very small code footprint.

The simplicity of UDP also fits well with many smart object applications. For example, in a smart object system for home automation, temperature sensors may periodically report data. The sensors can use UDP to send the data and to achieve low overhead. Since data are sent periodically, it does not matter that individual packets may be lost: a new temperature reading will be sent soon enough anyway. Generally, in smart object networks, UDP is well suited to traffic with low reliability demands. It is possible to provide reliability at the application layer, but this increases the complexity of the application.

UDP is also well suited to applications that require their own routing mechanisms. For these applications, routing can be implemented as an application overlay mechanism [67]. Finally, if applications want to use multicast delivery, UDP maps well onto the underlying multicast delivery mechanisms.

There are two drawbacks of UDP for smart object networks. First, they often lose packets in transit. UDP does not provide any recovery mechanism for lost packets. It is up to the application to recover from packet loss, which increases the complexity of applications that require reliability. Second, smart object networks often have small packet sizes and UDP does not provide any mechanism for applications to split their data into appropriately sized chunks for transmission. Thus the application must figure out what an appropriate packet size is and adjust its packets accordingly. Even if the IP layer provides support for packet fragmentation and reassembly, fragmentation at the IP layer is fragile, specifically in lossy networks [147]. Unlike UDP, TCP provides both reliability and a mechanism to automatically limit the packet sizes sent by applications.

6.4 TCP FOR SMART OBJECTS

For smart object networks, TCP has several compelling properties. Since many smart object networks operate over links where packets can be lost, many applications may want to use a reliable mechanism that automatically retransmits lost packets. Although TCP is known to have performance problems for high-throughput data when packets are lost over wireless links [15], for many smart object networks high throughput is not the primary objective, and reliable delivery of data is more important. Furthermore, since smart object networks often interoperate with existing systems where TCP is very widely adopted, the ability to directly communicate with existing systems speaks in favor of TCP.

The small packet sizes in many smart object networks require the packets to be kept small enough to fit, but large enough to effectively use available resources. The TCP MSS option is very useful both for memory-constrained systems and for systems that are constrained by a small packet size, such as systems running over wireless 802.15.4 networks. The TCP MSS option provides a way to set a small packet size for all TCP packets sent over the network. This is in contrast to UDP, where no mechanism for limiting the size of sent and received packets exists.

Even though the TCP specification and its related additions make TCP appear to be a complex protocol, the core of TCP is quite simple [64]. TCP was originally defined for data transport for general purpose computers, which require high throughput. Many of the complex mechanisms in TCP are intended to improve high-throughput performance. If high throughput is not a strict requirement, such as in most smart object networks, several mechanisms in TCP are not needed such as the sliding window algorithm and congestion control.

In Chapter 13, we discuss uIP, an implementation of TCP for memory-constrained smart objects. Our purpose is to show that TCP is simple enough to be implemented in resource-constrained smart objects.

TCP headers are large compared to UDP headers, but there are several ways a TCP header can be compressed [135]. TCP header compression methods have not yet been standardized for smart object networks, but this is likely to happen as the field grows.

Finally, many TCP implementations for smart objects are designed for severe resource constraints. As a result of the trade-off between memory footprint and throughput, such TCP implementations do not achieve as high a throughput as full-blown TCP stacks. There are two limiting factors. First, memory-constrained TCPs do not implement the sliding window mechanism. This means that a TCP sender cannot have more than one TCP packet for each active TCP connection in the network at any given time. Second, TCP delayed ACKs reduce the throughput.

The TCP delayed ACK mechanism is widely deployed by TCP [19,40]. It is intended to reduce the amount of acknowledgment packets sent over a TCP connection. With delayed ACKs, incoming TCP data are not acknowledged immediately. Instead, the host waits for a short time, usually 200 ms, before sending the acknowledgment. During this time, another TCP segment may arrive. If a second

TCP segment arrives, the ACK is sent immediately. If no TCP segment arrives, the ACK is sent after 200 ms. This effectively reduces the amount of ACKs by half for a busy TCP connection. For a constrained TCP sender, who only sends one TCP segment at a time, the delayed ACK mechanism may significantly reduce the throughput. By turning off the delayed ACK mechanism at the receiver, this problem is avoided.

6.5 CONCLUSIONS

The two most widely used transport protocols in the IP protocol suite are UDP and TCP. Transport protocols run over the best-effort IP layer to provide a mechanism for applications to communicate with each other without directly interacting with the IP layer. UDP provides a best-effort datagram service where applications must provide their own reliability and flow control, if needed. TCP provides a reliable byte stream and reduces the application complexity at the cost of a larger header size and more complex transport layer protocol logic.

For smart objects, there is still no standard transport protocol. UDP is lightweight and simple. The benefits of TCP are built-in reliability, control of the maximum size of its packets, and interoperability with existing systems. Application requirements thus dictate the choice of transport protocol.

Service Discovery

Service discovery is the process by which devices on a network learn what services are available. Without a mechanism for service discovery, new devices do not function properly as they have no way to discover services they may need, and no way to announce that they have services available. For example, in a smart object network deployed for building automation, a light switch device must use some form of service discovery to find the available lights. Similarly, the lights need to use some form of service discovery to locate nearby light switches. For smart objects, automatic service discovery is particularly important since most smart objects have very limited ways to interact with users.

Service discovery is especially important in deployments where several applications run simultaneously. Each application needs to discover its peer devices as well as devices to which they report or request data. Service discovery is important also for deployments with a single application that is hard-coded into the system. For example, in a temperature data collection network, the temperature collection application typically needs to locate the data sink — the place the sensor data should be sent. Locating this data sink is an act of service discovery.

Service discovery is important both for bootstrapping a network and for performing periodic service discovery of a network in steady state. In steady state, new devices enter and offer new services to the network. Also, the network may provide a new service that the devices can use.

Service discovery is closely related to autoconfiguration. Autoconfiguration is the process by which a device configures itself with network addresses and other information essential to its operation. Many service discovery frameworks contain an element of autoconfiguration. Autoconfiguration provides only network connectivity, however, and does not assist in configuring the application layer. It is the purpose of the service discovery mechanism to assist the application layer in configuring itself to perform its purpose.

As yet there is no standardized service discovery mechanism for IP-based smart objects. In this chapter, we review a set of existing available IP-based service discovery protocols and discuss their suitability for IP-based smart object networks. There are several ongoing efforts to find appropriate service discovery protocols for smart objects [190]. These efforts include using a compressed form of the Service Location Protocol (SLP) [230] and coupling service and neighbor discovery [166]. Some link layers provide mechanisms for a limited form of service discovery, such as IEEE 802.15.4, but it is not clear if these mechanisms can be efficiently mapped onto high-level service discovery mechanisms.

Interconnecting Smart Objects with IP. DOI: 10.1016/B978-0-12-375165-2.00007-7

7.1 SERVICE DISCOVERY IN IP NETWORKS

The IP architecture contains mechanisms for autoconfiguration of addresses, but it does not have any default service discovery framework. Address autoconfiguration is done either with a centralized protocol such as the Dynamic Host Configuration Protocol (DHCP) [60] or with a distributed mechanism such as IPv4 auto address configuration [36] or IPv6 stateless address configuration [235].

In general purpose IP-based networks, a common use for service discovery has been to find printers in the network. The printer provides a service for others to discover. Without service discovery, every computer attached to a network would have to be manually configured to recognize the printers on the network. The properties of all printers, such as if they support color printing, would also need to be manually or semi-manually configured on every computer. With service discovery, this process is automated so that computers are able to directly find the printers in the network. The printers announce not only their existence, but also their properties. No manual configuration of the individual computers is needed.

The IP protocol suite provides a number of different alternatives to service discovery. We review three: SLP, Zeroconf, and Universal Plug and Play (UPnP). These service discovery mechanisms are typically designed for traditional IP networks with general purpose computers and services such as printers. Their functionality is, however, generic enough to be used in a wide variety of situations.

In addition to the protocols discussed here, there are a number of different service discovery protocols for IP-based systems. The community that developed the concept of web services has devised a number of web service discovery protocols. The most common are the Universal Description Discovery and Integration (UDDI) mechanism and the WS-Discovery protocol. UDDI was envisioned to be a global service registry to which applications and organizations would register their online services. The protocol was based on XML, service descriptions annotated with the Web Service Description Language (WSDL), and messages encapsulated in Simple Object Access Protocol (SOAP) objects. The UDDI centralized service registry never took off, however, and is not used. WS-Discovery uses the same underlying protocols as UDDI, but unlike UDDI, the WS-Discovery protocol is not based on a centralized service registry.

The Device Profile for Web Services (DPWS) specification provides mechanisms for service discovery based on web services protocols and concepts. Although the mechanisms are often perceived as heavyweight, there is initial ongoing work to bring DPWS service discovery to smart objects [178].

7.2 SERVICE DISCOVERY PROTOCOLS

SLP, the Zeroconf protocol suite, and the UPnP protocol suite are all service discovery mechanisms. All three provide service discovery, but Zeroconf and UPnP additionally provide address autoconfiguration. SLP does not do address configuration by itself, instead it relies on the underlying IP layer to do it.

7.2.1 SLP

SLP is an Internet Engineering Task Force (IETF) standard protocol described in RFC2608 [101]. SLP is a lightweight service announcement and request protocol that allows devices to announce their services to other devices on the network and for devices to query the network for services.

In SLP, devices have three roles: service agent (SA), user agent (UA), or directory agent (DA). SAs are service providers. They announce their services and respond to service queries. UAs do not provide any services but query the network for services. DAs are aggregation points that keep a database of all available services and may act on behalf of SAs in answering service queries.

Services in SLP are represented by URLs. When a UA requests a service from the network, it indicates what type of service it is interested in by providing part of the URL that it expects for service responses. For example, a UA may query the network for a printer by submitting a service request with the URL *service:printer.* A printer that responds will have a URL that starts with *printer:* In addition to the URL, an SA provides a set of parameters that inform the UA of the configuration of the service. For example, a printer may indicate whether it can print in color or only in black and white.

SLP messages are sent either using UDP or TCP. Messages that are sent using multicast are always sent using UDP, whereas unicast messages can be sent with either UDP or TCP. If a message is too large to fit into a UDP packet, the message is sent over a TCP connection instead.

Figure 7.1 shows the behavior of a basic SLP service discovery operation. The process begins with the UA sending a service request message as a multicast to all SAs. In response to the service requests, the SAs send a service reply to the UA. The service replies are sent using unicast. To avoid overwhelming the UA, the SAs send their replies within a random time interval after receiving the service request. The time interval is configurable and is typically dependent on the speed of the underlying link layer. With a slow link layer, a longer time-out is configured to avoid overloading the link.

The behavior of SLP when DAs are introduced is different. DAs provide the network with a way to cache services so that the DA instead of the SA sends service replies. This reduces the total amount of network traffic because UAs direct all their service requests to the DAs instead of multicasting them to the entire network. Furthermore, the DA can combine multiple services into single replies, avoiding the overhead of sending individual SLP messages.

Figure 7.2 shows the behavior of an SLP network with a DA. The purpose of the DA is to keep track of all the services offered in the network and reply to service requests from UAs. Upon starting, SAs discover DAs by multicasting a special service request message that only DAs reply to. If a DA receives the message, the DA sends a service reply back to the SA, informing it about the availability of the DA.

SAs explicitly register their services with DAs. This is done through a special service registration message that is sent by the SAs to the DAs. Service registrations have a lifetime specified by the SA when it registers the service with the DA.

Before sending a service request, a UA always sends a special service request that looks for a DA. If a DA receives the request, the DA sends a service reply to the UA. The UA will then send its service request directly to the DA. The DA goes through its database of available services to find the one that matches the service request. Those services are then collected into a single service reply message that the DA sends to the UA.

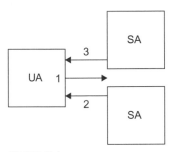

FIGURE 7.1

The basic SLP service discovery exchange: a UA sends a service request and two SAs send a service reply.

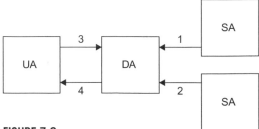

FIGURE 7.2

SLP service discovery with a DA. The SAs send their service announcements to the DA, which answers service requests from a UA.

For smart objects, SLP has several advantages over other IP-based service discovery protocol. First, the messages are lightweight in terms of overhead. Services are represented as URLs, which are specified by the participating parties. These URLs can therefore be compactly encoded without requiring any changes to the SLP mechanisms. Second, the use of DAs makes SLP scalable. This is a strong requirement for smart object networks, which may consist of thousands of nodes. Third, the SLP mechanisms are simple, which is important due to the limited memory and processing power of smart objects.

7.2.2 Zeroconf, Rendezvous, and Bonjour

Zeroconf is a set of IETF standard protocols for performing automatic address configuration, host-name resolution without the presence of a Domain Naming System (DNS) server, and service discovery using DNS. Apple's implementation of Zeroconf is shipped under the brand name Bonjour. Bonjour was initially named Rendezvous, but the name was already trademarked by another company so the name was changed in response to a lawsuit.

The address autoconfiguration part of Zeroconf is exactly the same as the automatic address configuration in IPv4 [36]. In fact, the IPv4 address autoconfiguration was initially developed as part of the Zeroconf effort and later fed back into IP.

Service discovery in Zeroconf is done using the standard IP DNS protocols, but with extensions to allow for dynamic operation without DNS servers. The protocol is called mDNS, or multicast DNS. mDNS works by hosts performing DNS queries over a multicast group. All nodes on the network are members of the multicast group and receive all DNS queries. If the incoming DNS query matches the name of the node, it replies to the originator of the query. Service discovery in Zeroconf is performed using multicast DNS queries. The service discovery protocol overloads the DNS names to encode service descriptions.

The multicast DNS and service discovery protocols in the Zeroconf suite are not standardized. Microsoft's implementation, called Link-Local Multicast Name Resolution (LLMNR) has been published as an informational RFC [3]. Apple's implementation is on its way to becoming published as an informational RFC, but was still in the draft stage in early 2010.

Zeroconf has several benefits for smart objects. The protocols are simple, which makes their implementation suitable for memory-constrained microcontrollers. The protocol message overhead is small, which makes the protocols suitable for low-power radio links. The one drawback is that the protocols require link-local multicast of all queries and that the architecture does not provide any caching agent, similar to the DA in SLP. Thus the scalability of the architecture could be a problem in large-scale smart object networks.

7.2.3 UPnP

UPnP is a full system configuration and service discovery protocol suite intended for both computers and devices. UPnP was originally developed by Microsoft, but the work is being continued by the UPnP forum. UPnP runs over IP and uses both standard IP protocols such as HTTP as well as extensions such as HTTP-over-UDP. UPnP uses the SOAP format for data encapsulation and the Extensible Message Language (XML) as its data format. UPnP is an international standard published by the International Standards Organization (ISO). Early versions of parts of the UPnP protocol suite were published within the IETF, but the final standardization took place in the ISO.

The UPnP protocol suite consists of service discovery as well as network address autoconfiguration, device control, and device presentation. With the device control mechanisms of UPnP, a system can send a request to a device to make it perform actions. With the device presentation mechanism, a user gets information about a device presented as a web page. This is useful for devices such as printers or cameras whose properties can be presented in a user-friendly manner.

For address autoconfiguration, UPnP uses the standard IP autoconfiguration features such as DHCP and stateless address autoconfiguration. For IPv6, stateless address autoconfiguration is part of the standard IPv6 features [235], whereas it is considered a separate but widely implemented standard for IPv4 [36].

UPnP uses a protocol called Simple Service Discovery Protocol (SSDP) to perform service discovery. Services are described by URLs. SSDP uses HTTP messages transported over best-effort UDP datagrams. The SSDP messages consist of an HTTP request with data consisting of a SOAP message that describes the service to be discovered. SSDP messages are sent using multicast to a specific multicast group. Nodes participating in the service discovery process join this group to receive messages.

SSDP supports both service announcements and service discovery. A system may repeatedly announce its presence and the services it provides to allow new devices to find it. New devices may also send out a request for all available services as it enters a network. By providing both announcement and discovery, SSDP reduces the overall load on the network as new devices join.

For smart objects, the UPnP architecture is not an ideal match due to the overhead inherent to the protocols used. Overhead includes implementation complexity and message overhead. Smart objects are limited in memory, bandwidth, and energy. The number of protocols in UPnP may be overwhelming to implement on a small microcontroller. The message overheads in the protocols have a negative impact on power consumption and bandwidth utilization.

Specifically, the SSDP protocol sends service data over UDP in the verbose XML format encapsulated in a SOAP envelope. Neither XML nor SOAP were designed to have compact data representations, because compactness often is not needed for high-speed, high-bandwidth networks. Thus the UPnP messages sent over UDP often are large and the specification requires that the entire message must be completely contained within a single UDP packet. When running over an IP-based smart object network, where the link layer maximum packet size is small, such packets must be broken into fragments that are sent separately. If one of the fragments is lost, all fragments must be discarded.

7.3 CONCLUSIONS

Service discovery is the process by which an application learns what services are available on the network, and also by which the network learns what services the application can provide. For smart object networks, service discovery is an important mechanism as it is the way smart objects learn about each other's presence and services.

For IP-based smart objects, a consensus around a standard protocol for service discovery has yet to emerge. The IP architecture provides a set of service discovery mechanisms. In this chapter, we reviewed three of them: SLP, Zeroconf, and UPnP. SLP is a promising mechanism for smart objects due to its low complexity and low overhead, as well as its ability to scale with large networks. Zeroconf also has a low complexity and overhead but its scalability is unclear. UPnP has a large overhead due to message overhead and implementation complexity, thus is not a good alternative for the requirements and constraints of smart object networks.

Security for Smart Objects

Security is important for smart objects because they are often deployed in important infrastructures such as the electrical power grid.

Smart object security is multifaceted, and in this chapter we focus on the communication aspects of smart object security. We discuss the basics of smart object security and encryption, and review the security mechanisms in the IP architecture. For an in-depth look, read Stajano's book on the subject [225].

In addition to communication security, smart objects also face other security-related problems. They are often deployed in places that make them amenable to intrusion attempts and in places where security breaches can be lethal. Smart objects deployed in people's homes can lead to intrusion attempts for economical benefit; for example, next generation electrical power meters can be tampered with to reduce the measured power consumption of households [183]. It has also been shown that the hardware configuration of smart objects makes it possible to sniff encryption keys [96]. Smart objects deployed in places where failure of operation may jeopardize lives are particularly important to protect. For example, it has been shown to be possible to remotely reprogram pacemakers installed in patients' hearts [87]. Physical security measures and tamper resistance are not specific to smart objects but have been studied in other contexts as well [6,12,109].

In general, security is defined as protecting the system from a determined adversary. This means that the adversary is not only actively trying to break into the system, but is determined to do so. Thus, the adversary should be expected to go to any length to try and find flaws or holes in our security model. Because we are dealing with a determined adversary, no part of the system can be left open to an attack. Just as a chain is no stronger than its weakest link, a system is no more secure than the weakest part, and a determined adversary *will* find the weakest spot.

Security is often confused with encryption. Although encryption is an important part of most security models, encryption alone is not a security model. Although strong encryption algorithms and keys do protect systems, most system breaches happen due to other problems than cryptographic failures [11]. Today's encryption algorithms are strong enough to withstand a significant amount of so-called brute force attacks. A brute force attack is when an attacker does not try to guess the secret encryption keys, but instead tries every possible combination of keys. Trying every key takes a significant amount of time, and a well-designed encryption algorithm ensures that the required time is long enough to ward off attackers. A strong encryption mechanism is, however, easily broken if the key is disclosed, for example, by a human operator.

Security models for smart objects are slightly different than those developed for general purpose computing systems. Smart objects typically have different threat models from general purpose computing systems because their applications are vastly different.

There is still no consensus about what should constitute a standard security architecture for IP-based smart object systems. In this chapter, we discuss smart object communication security concepts in general as well as the existing security mechanisms for IP architecture.

8.1 THE THREE PROPERTIES OF SECURITY

To explain security, we use a widely accepted security taxonomy that provides guidelines for what constitutes security [195]. Under this model, computer security consists of three parts: confidentiality, integrity, and availability:

- Confidentiality: Data should be confidential in the sense that only the right parties should be able to view it.
- Integrity: Data should not be tampered with or altered in any way.
- Availability: Data should be available at the right time for the right parties.

We use the term party to denote both individuals interacting with the smart objects and the smart objects themselves. Thus the parties can be either human or machine.

8.1.1 Confidentiality

Confidentiality is perhaps the most evident notion of security because it is understood in the real world. A piece of data is confidential only if the right parties can view it. If another party views the data, confidentiality is breached.

Confidentiality is not as easy to ensure as it may first seem. Before discussing how to implement confidentiality, two things must be decided: what it means to view data and what parties should have the right to view the data.

Smart object networks often communicate over wireless channels. Such channels are not protected by any physical security measures such as a protective casing. Because of this, every transmitted signal is easily overheard by attackers. Thus smart object confidentiality mechanisms must be prepared to deal with the lack of physical communication security.

Smart objects are physically distributed systems and are placed in physical locations where they may be tampered with. Thus the property of confidentiality must hold even for data stored on the smart object devices. For example, a smart object system used in the Smart Grid may require devices to be placed in homes where they could be potentially exposed to anyone such as the casually curious computer communications researcher, the investigative teenage hacker, or those with outright criminal intent.

Central to the concept of confidentiality is authentication. Authentication ensures that the identity of the sender is correct. There are several ways to achieve authentication. One example in general purpose computing systems is the password entry. Authentication is also necessary for automated node interactions.

Communication confidentiality can be achieved in various ways, most of which include encryption. Device data confidentiality is more difficult because it requires both logical and physical measures to protect against attackers.

8.1.2 **Integrity**

Data keep their integrity if they are sent through a system and are not altered or tampered with before they reach the rightful recipient. If the data are altered, integrity is breached. Even though integrity and confidentiality are related to each other, they are completely different concepts.

The integrity of a message does not imply confidentiality and confidentiality does not imply integrity. A message may be sent in the open for anyone to see, but still maintain its integrity. Conversely, a message may be sent encrypted, so that the confidentiality is maintained, but be altered in transit. The recipient will have no way of knowing that the data were altered.

For smart objects, integrity of the data is important for data originating from the smart objects and for data sent to the smart objects. The data originating in smart objects may be important for a decision-making process that is external to the smart object network. If the integrity cannot be ensured, wrong decisions may be taken. Likewise, data sent to the smart objects may contain important information such as reconfiguring the smart object. Again, it is important that data integrity is maintained.

8.1.3 **Availability**

Data should be available to the right party at the time they are needed. If availability is breached, the system is said to be suffering from a Denial of Service (DoS) attack.

For smart objects, which often use wireless radio communication, radio jamming is a threat to communication availability. This can be handled at the radio link layer and at higher layers [259]. Network rerouting and secure channel hopping are mechanisms available for a low-power radio to defend against jamming [192]. With secure channel hopping, the nodes switch the physical radio channel on which they communicate in a pseudo-random fashion. The pseudo-random sequence is generated to be cryptographically secure: only legitimate nodes know the sequence of channels to be used. Thus an attacker cannot guess what channels the nodes will communicate on, which makes jamming attacks more difficult.

8.2 **"SECURITY" BY OBSCURITY**

Before we go any further, a strong note about the concept of security of obscurity must be made.

The term security by obscurity is used to describe the erroneous notion that security can be achieved by keeping algorithms, architectures, and mechanisms secret. The idea is that as long as the secret is well kept, intruders and attackers cannot breach security. The problem with this model is that the moment the secret is out, the system is wide open to attacks. In many cases, it is impossible to keep such a secret for at least two reasons. First, anyone who works with the system knows about the secret and may leak it. Second, it may be possible to reverse-engineer the system so that the secret is exposed. In any case, secrecy cannot be relied upon.

The alternative to security by obscurity is to publicly publish the algorithms and protocols used to achieve security, and only keep information such as keys secret. This has two major advantages. First, it allows the algorithms and mechanisms to be scrutinized by a large number of security experts. This type of review is much better at detecting flaws than a single review by a small group of engineers. Second, if the designers of the system know that the algorithms and mechanisms are public, they know what the real secrets are — encryption keys.

Despite being known as a poor security model, security by obscurity has been used in a large number of systems, all of which have failed. The most striking example was the GSM mobile telephony system, which used a secret encryption algorithm to avert potential attackers. The algorithm was, however, reverse-engineered and the system became publicly known. Since the security of the system was designed with the assumption that certain parts of the algorithms would be kept secret, the system became insecure when the algorithms became public.

The concept of security by obscurity should not be confused with a legitimate need to keep secrets. Keeping the internal structure of a system a secret does improve security in many situations because it raises the bar for a potential attacker, which may discourage the casual attacker from attempting to break into the system. The problem of security by obscurity occurs when system designers begin to *rely* on the obscurity to provide security. The system designer should always work under the assumption that the entire structure of the system, including algorithms and protocols, is fully visible to would-be attackers. Only then can truly secure systems be built.

Even if the principle of security by obscurity is a known failure, it is important to repeat this message to help future system designers avoid the same trap.

8.3 ENCRYPTION

Encryption is a way to hide the meaning of a data message by running the message through an encryption mechanism. Encryption mechanisms, sometimes called ciphers, take the data to be encrypted (the plaintext) and an encryption key to form an encrypted form of the plaintext (the ciphertext). The ciphertext is decrypted by running it through a decryption mechanism. Like the encryption mechanism, the decryption mechanism also needs a key to be able to turn the ciphertext back into plaintext.

Encryption mechanisms can be divided into symmetric and asymmetric mechanisms. Symmetric mechanisms are considered symmetric because the same key used to encrypt the message can also be used to decrypt it (Figure 8.1). Two parties that use a symmetric cipher to ensure confidentiality of their communication thus require a shared key. There are a number of symmetric encryption algorithms available. The most common ones are the American Encryption Standard (AES) and the Digital Encryption Standard (DES).

Unlike symmetric encryption algorithms, asymmetric algorithms use different keys for encryption and decryption (Figure 8.2). Asymmetric algorithms allow two communicating parties to use non-shared keys when protecting the confidentiality of their communication. There are several asymmetric encryption algorithms. The most well-known example is the Rivest-Shamir-Adleman (RSA) algorithm.

Asymmetric algorithms are used in so-called public key encryption systems. In this system, every party keeps two keys: one private and one public. The public and private keys are used as encryption and decryption keys in an asymmetric encryption algorithm. Depending on how the messages are encrypted and decrypted, the private and public keys alternate as encryption and decryption keys.

As a simple example of how a public key mechanism encrypts data sent from two nodes, consider nodes A and B who want to securely send a message to each other. To encrypt a message between nodes A and B, node A first encrypts the message using its own private key. It then encrypts the message again, but with B's *public* key. The message is now encrypted twice. Node A now sends the message to node B. Node B now decrypts the message using its own private key, then with node A's public key. The message is now available in plaintext at node B. This may appear strange: How

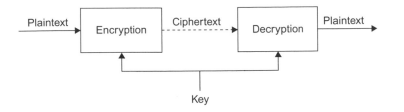

FIGURE 8.1

Symmetric encryption mechanisms use the same key for encryption and decryption.

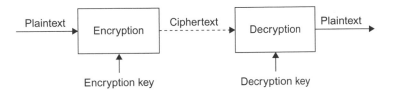

FIGURE 8.2

Asymmetric encryption mechanisms use different keys for encryption and decryption.

can node B decrypt the message without having access to the original encryption key with which A encrypted the message? This is the beauty of an asymmetric encryption system — it uses two different keys for encryption and decryption so the message can be decrypted without requiring the original encryption key.

The confidentiality of the message in the previous example depends on the nodes knowing the public keys. Before communication can commence, the nodes need to have these keys. This is done with a key distribution mechanism. With a public key mechanism, the public keys are not secret and can be distributed in plaintext across the network and stored in key repositories. Although the confidentiality of the messages are not affected by an attacker planting a forged public key (because the messages would be impossible to decrypt), the availability of the data is. With a false public key, the nodes would no longer be able to access the data from each other. Thus secure key distribution mechanisms are needed.

For symmetric encryption mechanisms, the key distribution mechanism clearly has to be secure because the keys are secret. Many security protocols use an asymmetric encryption mechanism to encrypt the secret, shared key for use in symmetric encryption mechanisms.

Symmetric and asymmetric encryption algorithms are built using very different types of mathematics. Symmetric encryption algorithms usually are defined using Boolean logic operations and bit substitutions that are computationally efficient and easy to implement in hardware. In contrast, asymmetric algorithms depend on the inherent complexity of certain mathematical functions and require significantly more processing time to encrypt and decrypt messages than symmetric algorithms. Moreover, asymmetric algorithms are not as efficient to implement as hardware as symmetric mechanisms. Because of this, many security protocols may use asymmetric algorithms to set up a shared key, which then is used with a symmetric algorithm during communication.

Cryptographic hash functions are another kind of cryptographic function. Hash functions are used to compute a value from a data message. This value can be used to maintain the data's integrity.

The hash function is defined in such a way that it is easy to compute, but it is very hard to compute what data were used to compute the hash value. Hash functions are used for ensuring integrity of messages. By computing a hash value of the data message and a secret key, and transmitting this hash value together with the message, the receiver can check the integrity of the message by computing the hash value with the same secret key. If the hash values match, the message integrity has not been breached. This use of a hash value is called a message authentication code (MAC). Note that this use of the MAC acronym is different from the Medium Access Control (MAC) that is used in other places in this book.

8.4 SECURITY MECHANISMS FOR SMART OBJECTS

Smart objects have a number of properties that set them apart from the general purpose computing systems for which typical computer security mechanisms have been developed. First, smart objects have limited computation abilities. For example, the microcontrollers used in low-power smart objects cannot execute asymmetric decryption operations within a reasonable time. For this reason, security mechanisms for smart objects must be based on computationally efficient encryption and decryption mechanisms such as symmetric encryption. Second, the physical environment in which smart objects operate is different from, and often more hostile than, that of a general purpose computing system.

In addition to the computation constraint, the power constraint of smart objects can also lead to security issues. To maintain low power consumption, wireless smart objects need to keep their radios switched off. An attacker can fool the smart object into keeping its radio on by sending bogus data to the device and depleting its battery, thus breaching the availability property. This attack is sometimes called a DoS attack or a sleep deprivation attack.

Stajano [225] presents a number of mechanisms that defend against sleep deprivation attacks. One example is to use a cryptographically secure channel hopping strategy. This makes it extremely difficult for an attacker to find the smart object's physical radio frequency, which makes it difficult to deplete its battery.

8.4.1 Security Policies for Smart Objects

Smart objects require different security policies than general purpose computer systems because of the widely differing applications, requirements, and physical appearance of smart objects

Authentication in smart object networks is a challenging topic because of the distributed nature of smart object systems. Not only are the devices physically distributed, but the system is also non-centralized. Because the system is non-centralized, there is no central server that can verify identities. Furthermore, since smart objects do not have the same user interface as a general purpose computer, password-based authentication schemes do not work.

With the understanding of the specific requirements and characteristics of smart object networks and ubiquitous computing, Stajano and Anderson developed a security model called the resurrecting duckling model [226].

The resurrecting duckling model is based on a real duckling and its mother duck. When a duckling is born, it is immediately imprinted with the physical appearance of its mother duck. From this

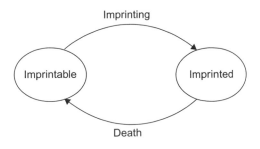

FIGURE 8.3

The resurrecting duckling model: devices are either imprintable or imprinted. After a device has been imprinted, only death can bring it back to the imprintable state.

point on, the duckling blindly follows its mother duck. The duckling accepts whatever it sees first as its mother duck, so it is possible to imprint the duckling with another duck that is not its biological mother. It is even possible to imprint the duckling with something completely different than a duck, such as a box.

The resurrecting duckling security model is illustrated in Figure 8.3. Devices are in one of two states: imprintable or imprinted. The imprintable state is equivalent to being unborn. In the imprinted state, only death can bring the device back to its imprintable state.

In the resurrecting duckling model, a node will be imprinted with the first encryption key it sees after manufacturing. The device will use this encryption key throughout its life. To recover the device from a faulty key, or to restore the device in case the key is compromised, the resurrected duckling model allows for the device to be "killed" and restored to life. After its resurrection, the device is able to receive a new key. The device can be killed either by its mother duck, by old age, or by the completion of a specific transaction. Stajano [225] illustrates how a device can be killed by using an example of a medical thermometer that may be killed every time it is disinfected.

The resurrected duckling model, and indeed any security model for smart objects, requires a way to securely transmit keys to the smart objects. Because smart objects do not have a user interface and often communicate using an insecure and easy-to-eavesdrop radio channel, key distribution is a challenge. But smart objects also have physical properties that can be leveraged for making efficient and secure key distribution.

Physical proximity can be leveraged to distribute keys. Keys can be sent using a short-range communication mechanism such as infrared (IR) light. An IR light can be configured to require perfect line-of-sight, which makes the key distribution more difficult to breach. Physical proximity can also be used for physical contact. During physical contact, keys can be securely transmitted.

8.4.2 Link Layer Encryption

Because smart objects often transmit information over insecure communication media, such as wireless radio, encryption is necessary to ensure confidentiality and integrity of the transmitted messages. For this reason, many radio communication standards for smart objects include encryption mechanisms. One example is the IEEE 802.15.4 low-power and low-data-rate radio standard that includes support for AES symmetric encryption for confidentiality and integrity of its messages. The AES mechanism can be used to encrypt the data sent across the wireless radio medium as well as to provide a MAC to the data.

To assist the implementation of security mechanisms for smart objects, several radio transceivers provide hardware functions for computing the necessary encryption functions. For example, the popular Texas Instruments CC2420 chip, which implements the IEEE 802.15.4 radio standard, includes an AES co-processor that encrypts and decrypts messages using AES so it can be used for encrypting over-the-air messages. In addition to encrypting messages, the co-processor can also be directly accessed from software, allowing the AES hardware to be used for other security processing as well. This includes security mechanisms such as the IP layer, which we discuss next.

The link layer encryption provided by the radio layer can only ensure confidentiality and integrity over a single hop. To provide security over a longer path, preferably across the entire end-to-end communication path, security at the IP layer and above is needed.

8.5 SECURITY MECHANISMS IN THE IP ARCHITECTURE

The IP architecture provides security mechanism at two layers of the IP stack: network and application. Both mechanisms are optional. These mechanisms provide different types of security operations ranging from fully encrypted end-to-end channels to end-to-end message authentication. In addition to the security mechanisms in the IP architecture, the architecture allows applications to implement their own security mechanisms on top of the IP stack.

Security in the IP architecture is provided by IPsec, which operates at the network layer, and transport layer security (TLS), which operates at the application layer. IPsec works on individual packets, whereas TLS works on an application stream of data over a TCP connection.

8.5.1 IPsec

IPsec is a network layer security suite that provides confidentiality and integrity at the IP layer. IPsec was originally developed for IPv6, but has been retrofitted to work for IPv4 as well. IPsec is defined in a number of RFC standards documents [118,145,148].

The IPsec architecture consists of two protocols: the Authentication Header (AH) and the Encapsulating Security Payload (ESP). AH provides integrity to messages and ESP provides confidentiality and integrity. Both mechanisms additionally authenticate messages.

Keys and other information, such as which encryption algorithms are used, are stored at the end points. A specific set of keys is called a security association (SA). Every packet belongs to a specific SA. Different SAs may use different encryption algorithms. To set up an SA, IPsec uses a key management protocol called Internet Key Exchange (IKE).

IPsec makes use of both symmetric and asymmetric encryption mechanisms. For smart objects, symmetric mechanisms are preferred because of their lower computational complexity. Specifically, for smart objects equipped with hardware AES acceleration, which is common in many IEEE 802.15.4 devices, it is possible to let IPsec take advantage of the AES acceleration. By using AES encryption as part of the IPsec SA, the smart object achieves a level of encryption performance that is impossible with software-only mechanisms.

8.5.2 **TLS**

TLS provides an end-to-end secure channel between two network end points. It provides confidentiality and integrity as well as mechanisms for authentication of the communication end points. TLS is defined by RFC5246 [56].

TLS was originally developed under the name Secure Sockets Layer (SSL) by Netscape Corporation for the Netscape web browser, but was later standardized by the IETF as TLS. Although the name is now officially TLS, it is still widely known as SSL. Many will recognize TLS from its use in web browsers, where the "https://" at the beginning of the URL signifies that the data were transported over a TLS connection.

TLS consists of several different layers and protocols. At the lowest layer, a symmetric encryption algorithm is used to provide confidentiality and integrity. To establish a key for use in the symmetric encryption algorithm, TLS first performs an authentication combined with a secure key exchange protocol. The authentication can be either unilateral, meaning that only one of the connection end points are authenticated, or bilateral, where both communication end points are authenticated. Unilateral authentication is used in the typical web browser to web server communication model, whereas bilateral authentication is used for secure transactions between two web servers, which is common in enterprise systems.

Before initiating the authentication phase, the TLS end points engage in a protocol negotiation phase. The end points use this phase to decide what encryption protocols to use for the remainder of the connection. TLS supports a number of different encryption protocols.

TLS was designed to perform the most expensive computations on the server side. In a web browsing scenario, this means that the web server will carry the largest burden, which leads to scalability problems for TLS-enabled web sites.

In the authentication phase, TLS makes extensive use of asymmetric cryptography. For low-end smart objects, this security mechanism is inappropriate. There are, however, ongoing efforts to provide more lightweight cryptographic algorithms to achieve end-to-end security for computationally constrained microprocessors [99,188].

8.6 **CONCLUSIONS**

Smart object security is important because smart objects are used in situations where a security breach can have potentially disastrous results, as systems ranging from critical infrastructures to on-body and in-body systems are equipped with smart objects.

Computer security consists of three properties: confidentiality, integrity, and availability. The purpose of a security architecture is to uphold all of these properties. To implement a security architecture, encryption is used to convert messages from plaintext into ciphertext, which is not readable by potential attackers.

Several mechanisms for smart object communication security exist. Security models such as the resurrected duckling model provide simple authentication and key distribution mechanisms. Hardware-assisted encryption implementations enable strong encryption support even for computationally constrained smart object microprocessors. There is still no consensus as to what the standard security model for IP-based smart objects should be, but work is ongoing in this area.

Web Services for Smart Objects

Thus far, we have discussed the use of the IP architecture as the means by which smart objects are connected. We have discussed how the IP architecture is built, how IP works with message routing, and how IPv6 fits the requirements for smart objects exceptionally well. But we have not yet discussed how these technologies are used to create smart object systems, and how smart objects can be integrated into existing IT systems. In this chapter, we take a look at web services — a technology by which smart objects can be efficiently integrated into existing IT and enterprise business systems.

Web services are a framework for building distributed applications. They have typically been used to build applications that either interact using a web browser, or are somehow related to the World Wide Web. But the technology that makes up web services is not tied to the World Wide Web or the particular technology that typically is associated with it, such as web browsers.

Web services are typically explained using examples from popular services that are used on the Web, such as flight travel booking systems, online book stores, or web searches. Even though those applications may sound removed from smart object systems, their inherent application properties are surprisingly similar to those in smart object systems. Web-style applications and smart object applications share many of the basic communication properties: they are composed of separate systems that exchange data.

Given the prevalence of the Web and its associated technologies, web services have seen a tremendous adoption in the general purpose IT world in the past couple of years. All major programming languages provide libraries tailored to build web-service-oriented applications. Hence, a large body of existing IT systems is built using web services. There are numerous online courses and other training material available to learn how to build web service applications.

Web services have traditionally been seen as a technology suitable for big servers, big datasets, and big systems. This technology has been used to couple database systems with each other in a framework that permits an expression of high-level concepts and dependencies, and yet is succinct enough to be standardized across a wide range of applications.

By using web service technology for smart object applications, existing web-service-oriented systems, programming libraries, and knowledge can be directly applied to the emerging field of smart object applications. This provides several benefits. For businesses, smart object applications can be directly integrated with existing business systems and use the same interfaces and systems existing business systems use. This makes it possible to integrate smart object applications into enterprise resource planning systems without any intermediaries, thus reducing the complexity of the system as a whole. For industries, smart object applications can be built using off-the-shelf technology without any customized interfaces or translators. Systems can be built without requiring smart object special-ists in every step of the project.

In this chapter, we discuss the use of web service technology for smart objects. Because of the expressiveness of the underlying principles, web services are highly suitable for smart objects. Despite the dominating belief that web services are a heavyweight concept, we demonstrate that they are indeed lightweight enough to be used for the resource-challenged environment in which smart objects exist. We do not discuss the details of web services in this chapter, however, as the concepts and the surrounding technology and its software are extensive and diverse. We keep the discussion at a relatively high level, and refer to more specialized publications for further details.

We examine the technology and principles behind web services, how they map onto smart object concepts, and how they can be efficiently implemented for smart objects. To ground the discussion, a concrete example of an existing web service for smart objects is provided: the Pachube service is a data-hosting service for smart-object-style applications where data are inserted and accessed using web service technology.

The performance of web services for smart objects has been questioned, because web services were initially used for large server systems. At the end of this chapter, we critically examine this by discussing the performance of published web service implementations for smart object systems. We find that the performance of web services for smart objects is indeed reasonable.

9.1   WEB SERVICE CONCEPTS

Web services are typically described as communication between business servers, typically ini-tiated by the interaction of a user through a web site. We make no exception to this, because this not only typifies the behavior of the web service technology, but also highlights the machine-to-machine communication aspects of web services.

Figure 9.1 is a canonical example of web service technology in action. In this figure a user is interacting with the web site of a travel agent through a web browser. Although this part uses the

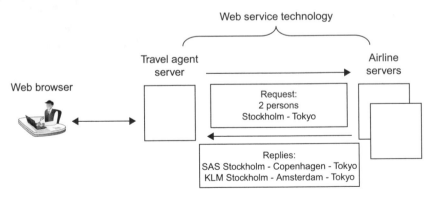

FIGURE 9.1

A traditional example of a web service transaction. A human user uses the travel agent's web site to look for flights. The travel agent server uses web service technology to query multiple airlines for possible routes and gets several results.

World Wide Web, it is not where web services are used. Rather, web services enter where the interaction between the user and the web site ends.

Web services are used as a communication mechanism between the travel agent's server and other servers that it communicates with to achieve its task. Neither the travel agent's server nor the airlines' servers are run by the same parties, so web services provide an intermediary that allows them to exchange data without in-between translation, since all servers adhere to the web services framework.

The travel agent's server sends a series of web service requests to a number of servers that belong to airline companies. The travel agent server receives replies from a number of them; in this case one from SAS and one from KLM. The travel agent server can then format these replies and present them to the user. The presentation of the data is independent of the format in which the data were sent between the airline servers and the agent server.

The example in Figure 9.1 illustrates how web services work, but not how they relate to smart objects. To shift the focus back to smart objects, Figure 9.2 shows an example of a smart object system realized through web services. In this example, a building automation server is connected to a network of temperature sensors and radiators. The sensors and radiators are located in a building and connected either to a wireless network or a wired in-house network. The particular communication technology used does not matter, because the system is built on IP.

The temperature sensors periodically post their temperature data to the building automation server using a web services framework. This allows the building automation server and the temperature sensors to be provided by different vendors since they both agree on a common communication mechanism and data format. The server may also query the sensors to get the current temperature value.

After the building automation server has received the temperature data from the house's temperature sensors, it uses this information to control the radiator. The radiator has a smart object with web service communication abilities, and the building automation server posts a configuration request to the radiator. The radiator updates its setting to match the value requested by the automation server.

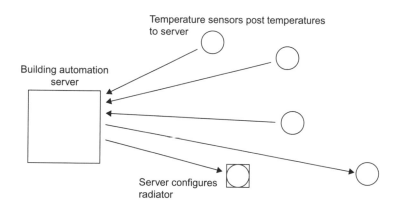

Temperature sensors post temperatures to server

Building automation server

Server configures radiator

FIGURE 9.2

A smart object system implemented with web services. Temperature sensors post temperature data to a building automation server. The building automation server configures a radiator based on the temperature data.

```
<xml>
  <sensors>
    <sensor>
      <name>Temperature</name>
      <value>27.1</value>
    </sensor>
  </sensors>
</xml>
```

FIGURE 9.3

An XML document.

9.1.1 Common Data Formats

Web services are a mechanism for exchanging data between disparate systems that are not developed by the same parties. The systems may be developed in different programming languages and run on vastly different hardware, but they still wish to exchange data in a system-independent way. For this reason, system-independent data formats are central to the web services framework.

The Extensible Markup Language (XML) is the most common data format associated with web services, but it is not the only data format available. In fact, the web services framework is not dependent on any particular data format, because it can operate across a range of data formats.

XML is a general purpose document format that provides a structured mechanism to encode machine-readable information. In addition to being machine-readable, XML documents are also human-readable, making them readily created and edited by humans as well as machines.

XML documents are composed of a set of tags, where each tag is shown as the name of the tag enclosed in the <and> characters. A tag consists of an open tag and a close tag. The close tag is the same as the open tag, but with the /character in front of the name. An example of a tag is <data>one</data>, where <data> opens the tag and </data> closes the tag. The value of the tag is the text between the open and close tag, which in this case is "one". Tags are nested to form a tree of tags.

An example of an XML document is shown in Figure 9.3. This XML document contains a temperature value from a fictional temperature sensor. The name of the sensor, "Temperature", is given in the <name> tag and the value is given in the <value> tag. The <sensor> tag contains information about one particular sensor. In this document, only a single sensor is present but more can be added following the closing of the <sensor> tag.

Because XML is a relatively verbose format, several ways to compress XML have been explored. The structured nature of XML makes XML possible to compress using source-specific techniques, and a number of variants of XML that use binary encodings rather than textual representations of the XML tags exist. There is, however, no standard for binary XML and none of the available formats have succeeded in achieving a de facto standard status.

An alternative to the verbose XML format is the JavaScript Object Notation (JSON) format. JSON is specified in RFC4627 [45] and provides a more lightweight markup than XML. Although JSON originally was designed to be easy to parse by JavaScript programs, the format is independent of any particular programming language. Libraries for parsing and constructing JSON messages are available for most programming languages.

An example of a JSON document is shown in Figure 9.4. This document contains the same information as the XML document in Figure 9.3, but is much more compact. The markup is more lightweight, but provides less means by which the document can be automatically translated between

```
{"sensors":
  [{"name": "Temperature", "value": 26.1}]
}
```

FIGURE 9.4

A JSON document.

different formats. Yet, the JSON format is a good match for smart object systems, where compactness of representation is important due to the inherent resource constraints.

9.1.2 Representational State Transfer

There are several ways to realize the web service concept. Some realizations are built on mechanisms that require significant processing power and communication bandwidth, whereas others are more lightweight. In this discussion, we do not go into detail about the web service mechanisms on the expensive side of the spectrum. Examples of mechanisms that we do not discuss are SOAP (originally defined as Simple Object Access Protocol, but is now known as only an acronym), the Web Services Description Language (WSDL), and the Universal Discovery Description and Integration mechanism (UDDI). For the description of those standards and mechanisms, please see the standards documents or the many online descriptions available.

The resource constraints inherent in smart objects regarding processing power, energy, and communication bandwidth necessitate the use of lightweight mechanisms. Despite a reputation as a heavyweight, web services have nothing inherent in their interaction models, communication mechanisms, or concepts that make them heavyweight.

Representational state transfer (REST) is a lightweight instantiation of the web services concept that is particularly well suited to the properties of smart objects. REST is not just a web service instantiation, but an architectural model for how distributed applications are built. Systems built around the REST architecture are said to be RESTful.

REST builds on three concepts: representation, state, and transfer:

- Representation: Data or resources are encoded as representations of the data or the resource. These representations are transferred between clients and servers. One example of a representation of a resource is a temperature value written as a decimal number, where the representation is the decimal number and the temperature is the resource.
- State: All of the necessary state needed to complete a request must be provided with the request. The clients and servers are inherently stateless. A client cannot rely on any state to be stored in the server, and the server cannot rely on any state stored in the client. This does not, however, pertain to the data stored by servers or clients, only to the connection state needed to complete transactions.
- Transfer: The representations and the state can be transferred between client and servers.

REST, as an architectural model, describes the interactions we have seen so far in this chapter. In the example of the travel agent (Figure 9.1), the request for a reservation between Stockholm and Tokyo was a representation as were the replies from the airline servers. Likewise, the building automation system illustrated in Figure 9.2 contains temperature data and radiator configurations as representations.

REST is an architectural model that can be efficiently implemented as a combination of the Hypertext Transfer Protocol (HTTP) [83] and TCP/IP. With this instantiation of REST, HTTP requests are used to transfer representations of resources between clients and servers. Uniform Resource Identifiers (URIs) are used to encode transaction states.

With this implementation of the REST architecture in mind, we return to the building automation example in Figure 9.2. In this example, the temperature sensors submit their temperature data to the building automation server using the HTTP PUT method. To query sensors, the server uses the HTTP GET method. The server then sends its configuration request to the radiator using the HTTP PUT method.

To make the discussion concrete, we turn to a detailed discussion of how a REST HTTP transaction for smart objects looks. Using the transaction from the building automation system in Figure 9.2, we focus on the server's request for temperature data from one of the sensors. This request is implemented by using the HTTP GET request, which is issued by the server to one of the sensors. The sensor responds with the temperature data of the sensor in JSON format.

The HTTP GET request sent by the server is shown in Figure 9.5. The HTTP request, which is human-readable, consists of two lines of text. The first line contains the HTTP GET verb, followed by the URI that represents the temperature sensor. In this case this is as simple as /sensors/temperature, but more complex URIs are possible. Ending the first line is the name and version of the HTTP protocol. HTTP 1.1 is the current version of the HTTP protocol.

The second line of the server's request contains the requested representation of the data that the client has to offer. This line contains the HTTP header "Content-type" followed by the type "application/json". This type is defined in the JSON specification as the content type to be used for JSON data [45].

The client's response to the server's request is shown in Figure 9.6. Again, this HTTP reply is in a human-readable format. The reply consists of two parts, the HTTP header and the HTTP body. The header is two lines long. The first line contains the HTTP/1.1 keyword, which again tells the receiver that this reply is in HTTP version 1.1 format. This keyword is followed by the HTTP status code 200,

```
GET /sensors/temperature HTTP/1.1
Content-type: application/json
```

FIGURE 9.5

An HTTP GET request for the data of a temperature sensor in JSON format. The server's response is shown in Figure 9.6.

```
HTTP/1.1 200 OK
Content-type: application/json

{"sensors":[{"name": "Temperature", "value": 26.1}]}
```

FIGURE 9.6

HTTP response for the HTTP request in Figure 9.5.

which tells the receiver that the HTTP request was successfully processed. The "OK" following the status code is a human-readable representation of the status code.

The HTTP reply contains the same "Content-type" header as the request, which tells the receiver that the data in the HTTP body are in JSON format. Following the HTTP header is a blank line that divides the header from the body.

The HTTP body contains the JSON data that represent the current temperature as sensed by the smart object's sensor.

This HTTP request is transported over a TCP connection, as discussed in Chapter 7. Armed with the knowledge of how TCP works, we can now construct a detailed picture of how the entire REST transaction between the building automation server and the smart object client looks.

Figure 9.7 shows the full REST transaction including all packets that are sent for the complete transaction. The transaction is divided into three phases: the TCP connection open phase, the REST data transfer phase, and the TCP connection close phase.

The transaction starts with the TCP connection phase. The TCP connection is opened by the exchange of the TCP SYN and TCP SYNACK segments between the server and the client. The server sends the TCP SYN to the client, and the client responds with the TCP SYNACK. When the server has received the TCP SYNACK segment, the connection enters the REST data transfer phase.

During the REST data transfer phase, the server sends the HTTP request from Figure 9.5 as one or more TCP segments to the client. The HTTP request may fit in a single TCP segment, if the segment size is large enough. The segment size for a connection is determined by the client and server during the setup of the TCP connection. In this case, however, the HTTP request is small enough to fit into most TCP segment sizes. All TCP segments are acknowledged by the receiver, and the

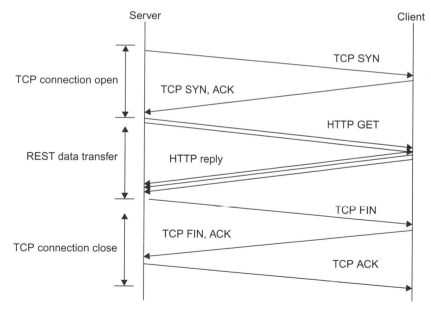

FIGURE 9.7

A full REST web service transfer over HTTP/TCP/IP with all packets indicated.

sender retransmits the segments if it does not receive the acknowledgments. In this case, however, the acknowledgments are piggybacked on the data packets sent in response to the reply.

The client responds to the request with the response from Figure 9.6. Again, this is sent as one or more TCP segments, depending on the size of the response and on the maximum segment size of the connection. The data packets are acknowledged. If the entire HTTP response fits in a single TCP segment, the acknowledgment for the data is piggybacked on the TCP FIN segment sent during the TCP connection close phase.

After the data transfer is complete, both the server and the client close the connection by sending a TCP FIN segment to the peer. This segment is acknowledged by a final TCP ACK segment, and the entire transaction is complete.

9.2 THE PERFORMANCE OF WEB SERVICES FOR SMART OBJECTS

The performance of web services for large-scale servers has been questioned on numerous occasions. Because of this, the performance of web services for smart objects has to be critically examined. Compared to the servers and networks on top of which large-scale web service applications run, smart object systems are severely constrained in both computational resources and bandwidth. Can smart objects maintain a good performance for web services?

In addition to the runtime performance of web services for smart objects, the constrained resources of the smart object nodes also require the implementation complexity of web services to be examined. Can a tiny smart object node bear the complexity of web services?

To answer these questions, we turn to the literature and find two independent studies of web services for smart objects: one by Priyantha et al. [207] from Microsoft Research and one by Yazar and Dunkels [260] from the Swedish Institute of Computer Science. Both studies implement a web services framework for smart objects, but the two studies focus on different aspects of the system. The study by Priyantha et al. investigates the use of XML transactions enclosed in SOAP messages sent over HTTP and TCP, whereas the study by Yazar and Dunkels uses REST transactions directly over HTTP. Both studies have implemented web services over the uIP TCP/IP stack [64], which is discussed in Chapter 13.

9.2.1 Implementation Complexity

For smart objects, their limited resources require a low software complexity. Smart objects are resource limited not only in energy and bandwidth, but also in memory. For web services to be a viable communication mechanism for smart objects, implementations of web services mechanisms must have a small footprint.

Web services for large-scale server systems have been criticized for being too complex even for large-scale systems, so it was not always clear that web services would be a viable alternative for smart objects. Recent implementations, such as those by Priyantha et al. and Yazar and Dunkels, have shown that web services are indeed a viable mechanism for resource-constrained smart object systems.

The web services implementation by Priyantha et al. [207] is a simplified variant of the SOAP-based web services that provide interoperable functionality with existing systems, but does not implement the full specification. Their system is implemented on top of the uIP TCP/IP stack [64], which is known for its small implementation complexity.

The code size and memory footprint for the web services implementation by Priyantha et al. is shown in Table 9.1. These data include both the size of the uIP TCP/IP stack and the simplified HTTP server and XML parser. The uIP code size includes the IP protocol (the part of the TCP protocol required for acting as a TCP server), but does not include the UDP protocol. The code size is measured for the MSP430 microprocessor and the code is compiled with the gcc C compiler.

The resulting code size is a few kilobytes, which is well suited for typical smart object systems. The system for which Priyantha et al. developed their web service implementation has 48 kB of code space available.

Similarly, the code size and data footprint of the implementation by Yazar and Dunkels [260] is presented in Tables 9.2 and 9.3. The two tables show the size of two different implementations of web services for smart objects: Table 9.2 illustrates the size of the implementation of REST-based web services for smart objects, and Table 9.3 illustrates the size of the implementation of SOAP-based web services for smart objects. The code size is for the MSP430 microprocessor and the code was compiled with the gcc C compiler.

Table 9.1 Memory Footprint for the Simplified SOAP Web Services Implementation[a]

Module	Code size	Data footprint
TCP/IP stack, uIP	2964	332
HTTP server + XML parser	2380	54

[a]Source: B. Priyantha, A. Kansal, M. Goraczko, and F. Zhao. Tiny Web Services: Design and Implementation of Interoperable and Evolvable Sensor Networks. In Proceedings of the 6th ACM conference on Embedded Network Sensory Systems (SenSys '08), pp. 253–266, Raleigh, NC, USA, 2008.

Table 9.2 Memory Footprint for the REST Web Services Implementation[a]

Module	Code size	Data footprint
TCP/IP stack, uIP	4274	412
HTTP server	3976	72
REST engine	692	4

[a]Source: D. Yazar and A. Dunkels. Efficient Application Integration in IP-Based Sensory Networks. In Proceedings of the ACM BuildSys 2009 workshop, in conjunction with ACM SenSys 2009, November 2009.

Table 9.3 Memory Footprint for the SOAP Web Services Implementation[a]

Module	Code size	Data footprint
TCP/IP stack, uIP	4274	412
HTTP server	3976	72
XML parser	5260	4
SOAP engine	2354	36

[a]Source: D. Yazar and A. Dunkels. Efficient Application Integration in IP-Based Sensory Networks. In Proceedings of the ACM BuildSys 2009 workshop, in conjunction with ACM SenSys 2009, November 2009.

Like the system by Priyantha et al., the system by Yazar and Dunkels uses the uIP TCP/IP stack as the underlying IP communication layer. Unlike the system by Priyantha et al., the system by Yazar and Dunkels includes the full uIP stack, including the full TCP and IP implementations as well as the UDP implementation. Thus the code size is larger. Furthermore, the Yazar and Dunkels implementation contains additional functionality over the implementation by Priyantha et al., making the code size for the HTTP server, the XML parser, and the SOAP engine larger.

Taken together, the two independent implementations by Priyantha et al. and Yazar and Dunkels show that the implementation complexity of web services is low. The results show that web services fit the memory constraints of smart object systems. Thus far, however, these data do not tell us whether the performance of web services is suitable for the bandwidth and power constraints of smart objects. We turn to this subject next.

9.2.2 Performance

Smart objects are severely limited not only in memory size, but also in bandwidth and energy. For example, the IEEE 802.15.4 low-power wireless communication standard, which is often used for smart object systems, has a maximum data rate of 250 Kbits/s. The limited bandwidth has implications for both data throughput and data latency. Furthermore, since communication consumes energy, it is imperative that the communication is efficient.

To examine the performance of web services for smart objects we again turn to the systems developed by Priyantha et al. and Yazar and Dunkels. Priyantha et al. present performance data at the TCP level, but do not provide any performance numbers for complete web services transfers. Yazar and Dunkels provide performance measurements for full REST transfers over HTTP and TCP/IP. Furthermore, Yazar and Dunkels have measured the energy overhead associated with a web services transfer on a smart object platform. Both studies are performed over an 802.15.4 low-power radio on an MSP430-equipped smart object platform.

Table 9.4 contains the measurements of the TCP processing overhead as measured by Priyantha et al. These data show that the processing overhead and the transmission of TCP are low. A full TCP transaction, with data sent from the server to the sensor and a reply sent back to the sensor, followed by a reply from the sensor to the server, is completed within 40 ms. These data were obtained after turning off the delayed acknowledgment mechanism in TCP, which is known to increase the round-trip time for single-segment TCP exchanges [64].

Yazar and Dunkels present measurements of the performance of web services requests over a network of smart objects where the smart objects route messages between each other, thereby extending the range of the network. Each hop of the network runs an IEEE 802.15.4 low-power wireless link. To save power, the radio runs a power-saving mechanism where the radio is switched off as often as possible, only to periodically wake up for a short while to check for a transmission from a neighboring node [25].

The completion times of a full REST transaction, including the TCP connection setup and closing phase, as measured by Yazar and Dunkels, are shown in Figure 9.8. The graph shows the completion time for three REST transfers with the number of network hops varied between one and four. The "dummy" transfer is a minimal REST transfer that contains only a few bytes of data, and the "temperature" transfer is a complete temperature request with temperature data sent in JSON format. The "sensors" transfer contains a full set of sensor data from the smart object, which in this case includes temperature, humidity, visible light, and UV light data.

Table 9.4 TCP Processing Overhead[a]

Time (ms)	Event	TCP action
0.00	Server Tx start	TCP data
6.19	Server Tx done	(74 byte request)
9.68	Sensor Rx done	
10.67	Packet processed	
10.68	Sensor Tx start	TCP ACK
11.71	Sensor Tx done	
29.29	Server Tx start	TCP data
33.35	Server Tx done	(27 byte request)
35.53	Sensor Rx done	
36.35	Packet processed	
36.36	Sensor Tx start	TCP data
37.78	Sensor Tx done	(37 byte reply)

[a]*Source: B. Priyantha, A. Kansal, M. Goraczko, and F. Zhao. Tiny Web Services: Design and Implementation of Interoperable and Evolvable Sensor Networks. In Proceedings of the 6th ACM conference on Embedded Network Sensory Systems (SenSys '08), pp. 253–266, Raleigh, NC, USA, 2008.*

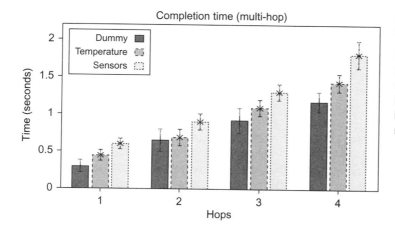

FIGURE 9.8

The completion time of full REST transfers over a multi-hop power-saving IEEE 802.15.4 network, from Yazar and Dunkels [260]. The y axis shows the time in seconds and the x axis the number of hops.

In addition to providing completion time data, the study by Yazar and Dunkels also measured the power consumption of a web services request. The findings show that the power consumption increases from 1 mW when the smart object is idle, to 4 mW for the "dummy" call and 5 mW for the "sensors" call.

By examining the results from the studies by Priyantha et al. and Yazar and Dunkels, it is clear that the web services are indeed reasonable for smart objects and that the performance is suitable for the constrained resources.

9.3 PACHUBE: A WEB SERVICE SYSTEM FOR SMART OBJECTS

To ground the discussion about web services and RESTful interfaces for smart objects, we investigate Pachube, one particular real-world instantiation of a RESTful interface for smart objects. Pachube is a web site, as shown in Figure 9.9, to which users can submit sensor data from sensor networks and upload and store the data on the Pachube server. The sensor data can later be retrieved and processed from the Pachube servers. The Pachube web site lists several ideas for which Pachube can be used such as electrical usage monitoring and management, real-time pollution monitoring, and home automation.

The developers of Pachube envision it as the fabric on which smart object systems and applications can be built. Smart objects, sensor networks, and telemetry systems submit data to the Pachube servers where the data are stored for later retrieval. The data can be retrieved by stand-alone applications that process the data to either visualize the data for human users, or to autonomously operate on the data. Examples of applications that may want to work on these data without a human in the loop are building automation systems or electricity savings systems. The input to such a system consists of

FIGURE 9.9

The Pachube web site. Data sources are marked on a world map.

temperature data and electricity readings from sensors that submit their data to Pachube. An excerpt of the Pachube web site that illustrates this concept is shown in Figure 9.10.

We use Pachube as an example because of its status as an emerging service provider in the ecosystem that is about to form around smart objects. Pachube provides an open Application Program Interface (API) based on the RESTful architectural model and allows remote sensors to send their data to the Pachube servers over an HTTP connection. Where many of the applications for smart objects target industrial applications, Pachube illustrates the possibility of a consumer-oriented service for smart objects.

Figure 9.11 shows how data stored on the Pachube server can be displayed directly in a web browser window, but this is only one of the many available alternatives for accessing the data. Since the data stored on the servers are opaque, the data can be retrieved and processed independent of the API.

Pachube provides an open API for accessing the sensor data stored on the servers over the Internet. It is intentionally simple and provides methods for uploading and downloading data. Application complexity is held outside of the system. Applications only query the Pachube servers for data, and any processing is performed on the application side.

Pachube data are divided into feeds. Roughly speaking, one feed corresponds to one instance of a particular application. For example, a building automation system built on Pachube may use one feed for the sensor data and control from one building.

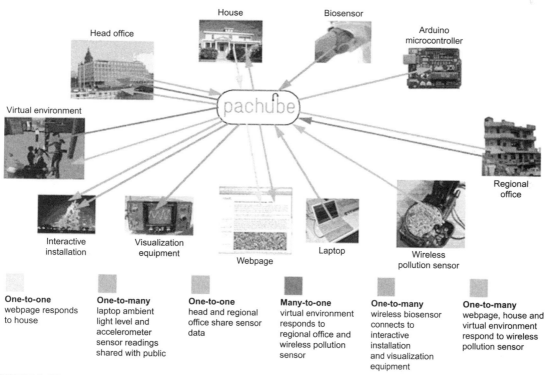

One-to-one	One-to-many	One-to-one	Many-to-one	One-to-many	One-to-many
webpage responds to house	laptop ambient light level and accelerometer sensor readings shared with public	head and regional office share sensor data	virtual environment responds to regional office and wireless pollution sensor	wireless biosensor connects to interactive installation and visualization equipment	webpage, house and virtual environment respond to wireless pollution sensor

FIGURE 9.10

Pachube is intended to be an intermediary for smart object applications.

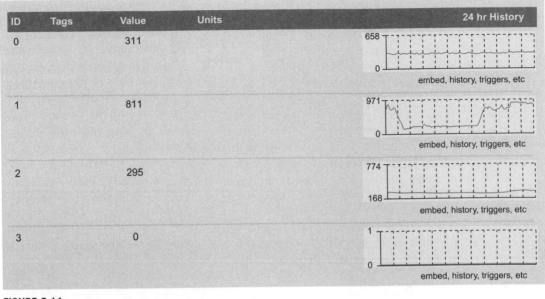

ID	Tags	Value	Units	24 hr History
0		311		embed, history, triggers, etc
1		811		embed, history, triggers, etc
2		295		embed, history, triggers, etc
3		0		embed, history, triggers, etc

FIGURE 9.11

A feed of sensor data from the Pachube web site.

Feeds are further subdivided into data streams. A data stream can come from one particular sensor or one particular physical location such as a room. Applications that work on the data can choose to collect data from one stream or many streams from the same feed, depending on the application.

Many of the sensors that serve their data to the Pachube servers are connected to the Internet via an external device such as a PC. As the field of smart objects continues to grow, we are likely to see IP-based smart objects that communicate directly with the Pachube server.

9.3.1 Interaction Model

The interaction model of the Pachube API is simple. Clients, either smart objects or sensors connected to an IP network through a PC, connect to the Pachube server using HTTP and send their data using the HTTP request. The server responds with a status code and an amount of data. The request may either provide new data to be stored on the Pachube servers or a request for data to be delivered from the same servers. Both types of requests are sent using HTTP.

When a client performs an HTTP request to a Pachube server, the client first sets up a TCP connection to the server. Once the TCP connection has been successfully opened, the client sends its request using the normal HTTP mechanism where the first line of data sent from the client contains the HTTP request verb, followed by additional lines of text that contain additional HTTP headers. If the request contains additional data, they follow after the HTTP headers.

The server responds in standard HTTP by sending the status code as the first data over the TCP connection. The status code is followed by the server's HTTP headers. If the request caused any data to be sent back from the server to the client, these data are sent after the HTTP headers.

When the HTTP interaction is complete, the TCP connection can either be closed directly or kept open in anticipation of another request at some later time. Whether the connection is closed or not is determined via a negotiation through the HTTP headers. If either the client or the server sends the connection close HTTP header, the connection is closed after the request has been completed. Otherwise the TCP connection is kept open in anticipation of another request between the client and the server.

9.3.2 Pachube Data Formats

Pachube supports several data formats for exchanging data between clients and servers. Providing different forms of exchanging data allows integration of different types of systems with the Pachube servers. A simple sensor that only wants to submit data to Pachube may choose to send its data in a simple format that requires low effort to construct and transport, whereas a visualization system that processes sensed data from the Pachube server to visualize it needs meta-information about the data such as where the data were sampled and when. In the Pachube system, the clients decide how they want their data to be formatted as part of the requests they pose to the Pachube servers. The responsibility for converting the data between the formats falls on the Pachube servers rather than the client, as the clients may be resource-constrained smart objects.

Not all data formats contain the same amount of information. The simplest formats contain sensor data values, whereas the more complex formats contain metadata such as where the sensor data were obtained and at what time the data were sampled. Pachube supports the following formats:

* Extended Environments Markup Language (EEML): A custom version of XML tailored to contain sensor data. The EEML format contains tags that specify the spatial location at which the sensor data were sampled, as well as meta-information about the sensor data such as the minimum and maximum values that the sensor data can reach, and the default unit in which the data are to be represented. An example of an EEML document is shown in Figure 9.12.

```
<eeml xsi:schemaLocation="http://www.eeml.org/xsd/005
http://www.eeml.org/xsd/005/005.xsd">
<environment>
<location exposure="indoor" domain="physical"
disposition="fixed">
  <name>My Room</name>
  <lat>32.4</lat>
  <lon>22.7</lon>
  <ele>0.2</ele>
</location>
<data id="0">
  <tag>temperature</tag>
  <value minValue="23.0" maxValue="48.0">36.2</value>
  <unit symbol="C" type="derivedSI">Celsius</unit>
</data>
</environment>
</eeml>
```

FIGURE 9.12

A document in EEML format that contains sensor data.

- JSON: The JSON format contains the same amount of information as the EEML representation, but formatted in JSON rather than EEML. The JSON format is more compact than the EEML format, and is also easier to parse for programs implemented in JavaScript.
- ATOM and RSS: The ATOM and RSS formats contain less information than the EEML and JSON formats. The ATOM and RSS formats contain sensor data, but include only a limited form of metadata such as the spatial location of the sensors as well as tags and titles of the sensors.
- Comma-separated value format (CSV): This is the most basic format. It also contains the least amount of meta-information: the data stream contains only the sensor data. The CSV format is suitable for use on tiny units with limited processing power where creation or parsing of the more complex formats is not suitable.

9.3.3 HTTP Requests

All Pachube requests between clients and servers are performed by using HTTP requests. As previously discussed, the REST architecture uses HTTP request types for different types of method invocations and Pachube is no different. Pachube uses four different HTTP request types for its operations: GET, PUT, POST, and DELETE. The different requests are used on different occasions:

GET: This request method is used to retrieve sensor data from a Pachube server. With a GET request, the URI provided as part of the request contains both the identity of the data feed and the client's data format. The URI contains information about the type of data the client wants to receive, the identity of the feed, and what data format the client wants. The identity of the data feed is given as the directory part of the HTTP URI, whereas the data format is provided as a file extension.

PUT: This method is used when submitting new sensor data to the Pachube server. Data to be submitted from the client to the server are provided in the data portion of the HTTP request, which follows the HTTP header. As with the GET request, the feed identity and the data format are included in the HTTP URI that is sent together with the HTTP request.

POST: This request method is used to create a feed and to create a new data stream within a previously established feed. The body of the HTTP request sent by the client contains the definition of the feed or the data stream. The definition is provided in EEML format. When establishing a stream, the server creates a stream into which the client may use the PUT method to insert data.

DELETE: This request method is used to delete a data feed or a data stream. The URI provided with the request contains the identifier of the feed or stream. Once a feed or stream has been deleted, it cannot be restored.

9.3.4 HTTP Return Codes

On every HTTP request the server responds to the client with a return code. The return code provides information about the request, such as if the request was successful or erroneous. If there was an error, the return code contains information about the cause of the error. HTTP return codes are represented as three-digit numbers. The basic HTTP return codes are specified in the base HTTP specification [83], but many HTTP servers have added their own codes.

The Pachube API uses HTTP return codes to inform the client about the state of the request. The return codes are sent to successful transactions as well as failed ones. For failed transactions, the return code provides insight into what caused the problem, and the HTTP body contains an XML document containing an error message.

The HTTP return codes used by the Pachube API are

- 200 OK: This code is returned when a request is completed successfully. Unlike the other return codes, this one does not indicate an error.
- 401 Not Authorized: This return code is sent in response to a client request that needed authentication, but where the authentication key was invalid or not present.
- 403 Forbidden: This error code is returned when the Pachube servers did not execute the request. The reason the server did not respond to the request is given in the body of the HTTP reply.
- 404 Not Found: The requested URI was not found. Either the feed it requested could not be found, or the method that the client invoked did not exist.
- 422 Unprocessable Entity: This return code is sent in response to client requests that contain EEML data. The return code tells the client that the EEML contained semantic errors, even if it was syntactically correct.
- 500 Internal Server Error: This return code is sent when there is an internal error with the Pachube servers.
- 503 No Server Error: This return code is sent when there are no Pachube servers available to complete a request.

9.3.5 Authentication and Security

To determine who can access what data, the Pachube system provides a simple form of authentication. The purpose of the Pachube authentication is to identify the client to the server, so that the server knows if it should trust requests from the client. Clients that are authenticated can insert data into a stream, create new streams within a feed, and retrieve data from a stream. Clients that cannot be authenticated are denied access to the data by the Pachube server.

The Pachube authentication mechanism is simple. With each HTTP request performed by the client, the client provides a secret key. The server checks the secret key with the pre-registered key for the feed that the client is trying to access. If the key supplied by the client matches the key stored on the server, the server allows the client access to the data.

The key for a particular data feed is created when the feed is created. When creating the feed, the client needs to remember the key that was created as part of the feed since the key is needed for future access to the feed.

The key is sent as part of each HTTP request performed by the client. The key can either be sent as part of the URI or as part of the HTTP headers. Since the authentication key is transmitted in clear text in every HTTP request, it is trivial for third parties to sniff the key as it traverses the network. The sniffed key can later be used not only to gain access to the data, but to delete the entire data feed, including the data history.

To make it harder for third parties to gain unauthorized access to the authorization key, Pachube provides a way to encrypt the data stream using transport layer security through the Secure Sockets Layer (SSL). With SSL, the entire HTTP transaction is protected by encryption so that third parties sniffing on the data cannot read the key or the data transaction.

```
[{
"trigger_type":"gt",
"stream_id":"0",
"environment_id":1233,
"user":"pachube",
"threshold_value":"20.0",
"url":"http:\/\/www.example.com\/notify",
"notified_at":"",
"id":13
}]
```

FIGURE 9.13

Pachube trigger function that triggers when the sensor data are greater than 20.0, expressed in JSON format.

9.3.6 Triggers

The synchronous API provided by Pachube works well for applications that periodically submit data to Pachube and periodically poll the servers for new data, but it does not allow fully reactive applications. Reactive applications react instantly to incoming data. One example of a reactive application is a burglar alarm that directly alerts the owner when the sensors detect a break-in.

To allow reactive applications, Pachube provides a mechanism called a trigger. A trigger is a small function that clients can upload to the server. Trigger functions are extremely simple and are only able to perform a threshold comparison on a data stream. If the data values in the data stream become greater than or less than the threshold provided in the trigger function, the trigger is executed.

When a trigger is executed, the Pachube server performs an HTTP GET request to a preprogrammed URI. The URI, which is provided by the client when configuring the trigger, points to an application hosted by the user on an external web server. The HTTP request sent by the Pachube server contains information about what feed and data stream caused the trigger to execute, as well as the current data value from the data stream. This permits reactive applications that do not need to poll the Pachube servers for data. After the trigger, the application may use the synchronous Pachube API to retrieve further information about the event that caused the trigger to execute.

Trigger functions can be represented either in XML or in JSON notation. An example trigger is shown in Figure 9.13. This trigger function is programmed to react when the data stream value exceeds 20.0. The "trigger_type" keyword is set to ">" (abbreviation for greater than). The stream ID is 0, the environment ID is 1233, and the user name is "Pachube". The threshold value is given by the "threshold_value" parameter and is set to 20.0. The "url" field contains the URI that the Pachube server will call when the trigger is executed. The URI must correspond to the RESTful API of the reactive application. The "notified_at" field is updated with the date and time the trigger was last executed. Finally, the "id" parameter contains the identity number of this particular trigger function.

9.4 CONCLUSIONS

Web services provide an established mechanism for exchanging data between disparate systems. They are widely used in general purpose IT systems and the integration benefits of running web services on smart objects are large. With web services for smart objects, smart object systems can be readily integrated in general purpose IT systems such as enterprise resource planning systems and business systems.

Web services can be implemented using the REST principles, which are an architectural model for distributed systems. The REST principles can be efficiently run on top of an HTTP connection, making it simple and compelling for the resource-constrained smart object devices.

Although the performance of web services has been criticized in the context of large-scale server systems, recent studies show that web services can be efficiently implemented on smart objects. Web services can be run over low-power radio networks with good results.

Taken together, the interoperability and integration benefits of web services for smart objects, combined with their low resource requirements and good performance, make them a compelling choice for smart object systems.

Connectivity Models for Smart Object Networks

10

10.1 INTRODUCTION

We conclude the first part of the book with a chapter exploring various connectivity models for IP-enabled smart object networks and the use of application layer overlay networks.

There are several potential connectivity models for IP smart objects ranging from the "true" Internet of Things where smart object networks are connected to the public Internet like any other network to autonomous smart object networks that are not connected to the public Internet. In between there are a myriad of models introduced in this chapter. One model consists of building an application layer overlay network that could be used to provide enhanced security, increase the scalability and efficiency of smart object networks thanks to in-network processing while still preserving the end-to-end principle of the Internet.

Smart object networks will undoubtedly play a central role in our day-to-day life in the near future, and the plethora of innovative applications that rely on these networks (several of them are discussed in Part III) will ineluctably contribute to the emergence of new deployment models and new architectures because of the remarkable flexibility of IP.

10.2 AUTONOMOUS SMART OBJECT NETWORKS MODEL

In this first deployment model, as shown in Figure 10.1, smart object networks are completely autonomous and not connected to the public Internet. Indeed, there are several use cases that do not require any connectivity with the public Internet. For example, *most* of the Smart Grid applications just do not require Internet connectivity for most use cases. As discussed in detail in Chapter 20, Smart Grid networks are made of a number of networks including power generation to substation automation and control, smart metering, and building/home energy management. The power grid automation does not require any connectivity to the public Internet, nor do the smart meter networks in most deployment models. Utilities may not want their network to see (at least some part of) their networks connected to the public Internet. On the other hand, connection to the Internet may be required for the power grid to send dynamic pricing and load shedding information for home energy management to home energy controllers, which could either be done via the smart meter network or the public Internet.

In other cases, such as industrial automation (e.g., nuclear power plant), the smart object network is in most cases completely disconnected from the public Internet. These networks use the IP protocol suite (they are IP smart object networks) but with no connection to the public Internet.

Interconnecting Smart Objects with IP. DOI: 10.1016/B978-0-12-375165-2.00010-7

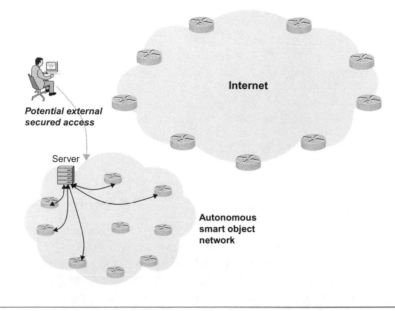

FIGURE 10.1

Autonomous smart object networks.

The lack of Internet connectivity leads to the question: Is IPv6 required in autonomous networks that do not require global addresses? The large address space provided by IPv6 is still a must in most cases, even if they are not used for global connectivity.

10.3 THE INTERNET OF THINGS

At the other extreme lies the Internet of Things, where smart object networks truly belong to the Internet just like any other network. There are applications that will be no different than e-mail and web services and should be accessible by the Internet community. Any Internet user will have access to the information provided by smart objects such as telemetry either directly accessing the device or by means of intermediate servers. There are already very simple forms of Internet access to smart objects and the number of these applications will continue to grow.

The connectivity model will likely have intermediate servers as shown in Figure 10.2. The servers will collect data from smart objects and the Internet will connect to these servers, as opposed to the smart object, to preserve scarce resources in smart object networks and increase scalability.

10.4 THE EXTENDED INTERNET

A myriad of new services and applications will be used in the near future to extend the Internet to the physical world. This is sometimes referred to as the "Physical Internet."

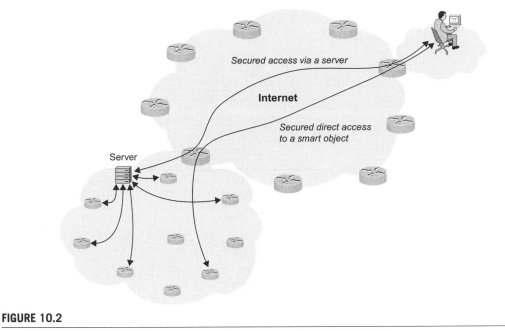

FIGURE 10.2

The Internet of Things.

Smart Cities will soon provide useful information to their citizens to improve their quality of life and help them make important daily decisions: environmental data such as air quality, real-time transportation information, emergency assistance, risk of attacks, and so forth. All of this valuable information can be provided to citizens via the public Internet. Other applications will provide data exploited by city departments to more efficiently manage the city such as street light management, water/gas leak detection, or traffic management. These data will be not be made available to citizens and may or may not go through the Internet.

The term "Extended Internet" refers to intermediate deployment models between the Internet of Things and "autonomous smart object networks": smart object networks are partially or completely connected to the Internet with the appropriate security protection. The notion of application layer overlay is getting some traction and is discussed in the next section. The basic idea consists of introducing in-band (in-network) data processing in the network while still preserving the notion of an end-to-end principle between application servers.

Let's consider Figure 10.3. The core IP infrastructure supports a myriad of applications and interconnects hundreds of thousands or even millions of smart object networks that are characterized by their constrained nature. All of these networks will make use of the IP protocol suite and the network may be connected to the Internet via a firewall in charge of securely controlling access to private IP networks from the public Internet.

In other words, such architecture prolongs the current Internet (thus the reference to the Extended Internet) just enough to provide access to smart objects that used to be isolated from the Internet.

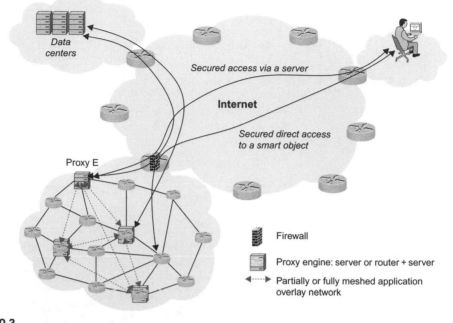

FIGURE 10.3

The Extended Internet.

Note that at best such networks used to be reachable from the Internet via complex and difficult to manage multiprotocol translation gateways: they are now using IP end to end.

10.4.1 The Role of Proxy Engines and the Application Overlay Networks

As shown in Figure 10.3, these architectures may require the use of "proxy engines." A proxy engine is a router/computer capable of performing a number of application-level processing tasks to improve the scalability of the Extended Internet.

The use of multiprotocol translation gateways has been discussed in detail in Chapter 3, and a number of arguments have been listed to illustrate why using these gateways is highly undesirable compared to a true IP end-to-end architecture. The Extended Internet model is a true IP end-to-end IP architecture with no protocol translation. If an application requires sending information to an actuator or receiving data from a sensor within the Low-power and Lossy Network (LLN), the IPv6 address is not converted along the data path. Furthermore, since IP is used end to end, the associated semantic is also preserved in support of Quality of Service (QoS), management, routing, security, and so forth. In other words, IP is truly used end to end.

But LLNs are not exactly comparable to "classic" IP networks due to their constrained nature and their large scale with potentially hundreds of millions of connected IP smart objects. Thus, it may be desirable in some situations to introduce proxy engines within LLNs to perform various tasks such as data collection and aggregation or even in-network data processing.

Consider the example of a Smart City equipped with hundreds of thousands of sensors and actuators to control environmental factors. One model may consist of collecting all data in a data center for further data mining and processing. Data analysis could then trigger a set of actions and commands that would be sent to actuators. Although fairly simple, such a model is suboptimal in many respects. First, the data flows and data traffic would significantly increase, as traffic gets closer to the sink/data center, which may affect the overall lifetime of the network. Traffic congestion would degrade the QoS, but even more important, it would increase energy consumption in the network, which is highly undesirable for battery-operated nodes. This is illustrated in Chapter 17 where it is observed that the traffic significantly increases closer to the sink thus leading to a number of challenges to solve. This is due to the multipoint-to-point nature of most (not all) of the flows in LLNs. Clearly such a simple and naïve model is not likely to scale and provide the level of required efficiency.

On the other hand, in-band data processing would help increase the overall scalability of the network by an order of magnitude. The idea of in-band data processing consists of introducing data processing modules (proxy engines) in the network that interpret the data and potentially trigger local actions. In other words, distribute the "intelligence" *in* the network. The network of proxy engines then forms an application overlay network embedded in smart object networks and in the Internet.

The degree of distribution would be determined by the application characteristics and requirements. Figure 10.3 shows an example of how such proxy engines could be used.

In this model, traffic flows are localized and processed by the network. Data processing engines are then responsible for interpreting the data and trigger a set of actions. For example, in its simplest form, the proxy engine could simply detect information duplicates to avoid unnecessary traffic to cross the network, but more complex tasks could also be performed such as data fusion, computing correlated data, performing data storage, or even triggering local actions on smart objects according to policy rules engines. This mode of operation is clearly in contrast with a purely centralized data model management that usually poorly scales and would be quite inefficient regarding network traffic, response times, and QoS.

A proxy engine is not necessarily an additional "box" in the network, but refers to network functionality. Modern routers already support this functionality. In addition to performing a myriad of networking tasks, the router hosts an application that performs in-band data processing. The router is thus one of the elements of the overlay application network.

Several projects are exploring the ability to dynamically configure the overlay network according to traffic observations. Nodes capable of hosting such applications could then join the network thus enabling in-network data processing where appropriate.

Furthermore, in addition to increasing network scalability and the overall network efficiency, the overlay network would help improve the application responsiveness. There are several applications that require immediate actions should an emergency be detected in the network. Instead of relaying the information up to the data center, a local proxy engine could trigger the appropriate action closer to the actuator reducing the overall reaction delays.

Finally, the use of in-band processing could be extremely useful in the presence of sleeping nodes. When the node is battery-operated, it is significantly more efficient not to wake up a node each time a request is issued by a central application. The proxy engine can then be used to cache requests and relay them when appropriate.

Does that "break" the end-to-end principle? Not at all. Proxy engines allow building overlay application layers to perform in-band network processing. In a sense, web caching is already a primitive form of application overlay networks. In this model the network does not interfere with traffic flows between end points. End points are simply moved within the network to increase its scalability. Manipulating data or adding complex states in the network in between the hosts would endanger the end-to-end principle. In this model, hosts communicate with other hosts (proxy engines) that communicate with data centers.

10.5 CONCLUSIONS

In this chapter several deployment models for smart object networks ranging from autonomous networks to the Internet of Things were explored. Models such as the Extended Internet involving (dynamic) application overlay networks will likely emerge allowing data processing and local action in the network to further increase the network and application efficiency as opposed to a naïve less efficient centralized model unlikely to provide the required level of scalability.

PART

The Technology

2

Smart Object Hardware and Software

11

Smart objects are defined both by their physical appearance (the hardware) and by their behavior (the software). In this chapter we discuss the typical hardware design of a smart object, the various ways that the software of the smart objects typically is designed, and the implications of software mechanisms on the power consumption of the smart objects.

11.1 HARDWARE

Smart objects contain a piece of hardware, which is a set of electrical circuits. The hardware consists of four main components, as shown in Figure 11.1:

- Communication device: This gives the smart object its communication capabilities. It is typically either a radio transceiver with an antenna or a wired connection.
- Microcontroller: This gives the smart object its behavior. It is a small microprocessor that runs the software of the smart object.
- Set of sensors or actuators: These give the smart object a way to interact with the physical world.
- Power source: This is needed because the smart object contains electrical circuits.

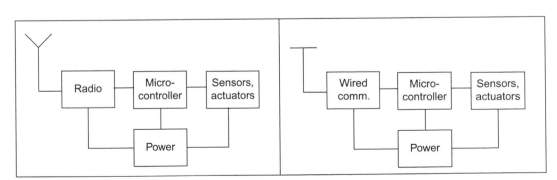

FIGURE 11.1

The hardware architecture of two smart objects: a radio-equipped, wireless smart object (left) and a smart object with wired communication (right).

Interconnecting Smart Objects with IP. DOI: 10.1016/B978-0-12-375165-2.00011-9

The communication device gives the smart object the ability to communicate. The microcontroller runs the software of the smart object and also is the central point that connects the communication device and the sensors. The microcontrollers used in smart objects are similar to the microprocessors used in general purpose computers, but smaller.

A power source is needed to provide the electrical circuitry with power. The most common power source is a battery, but there are other examples as well such as piezoelectric power sources, that provide power when a physical force is applied, or small solar cells, that provide power when light shines on them. The power source provides power for all components and is therefore connected to all of them.

The sensors and actuators give the smart objects a way to interact with the physical world. The sensors sense the environment and the actuators affect it. The canonical example of a sensor is a temperature sensor, but more complex sensors also exist such as cameras or devices for performing range-measurements using ultrasound. Like the sensors, the actuators can be very different ranging from a small LED indicator to relays for switching a high-voltage power source on and off.

Figure 11.2 highlights the components of a typical hardware platform, the MicaZ prototype board from Crossbow Technology. It shows the microcontroller, the power source, the radio transceiver, and an extension connector for connecting sensors or actuators. The power source is a battery pack consisting of two AAA cell batteries. The radio transceiver is mounted on the flip side of the board and cannot be seen. The system uses an external antenna attached to the side of the board. The board does not contain any sensors. Instead, sensors or actuators can be attached to the board through the extension connector. This allows the board to be used as a prototyping system for a wide range of different applications.

The previous example is a prototype board used when experimenting with smart object systems. For final products, the smart object hardware usually is tightly integrated with the product, making the hardware significantly smaller.

We now turn our attention to the different components that make up the hardware of a smart object: the communication device, the microcontroller, the sensors or actuators, and the power source.

Antenna

Microcontroller

Radio transceiver
(on flip side of the
board, not shown)

Extension connector
for sensor boards

Power source
(batteries)

FIGURE 11.2

A MicaZ prototype board with a microcontroller, power source, communication device, and sensor connectors.

Photo courtesy of Crossbow Technology.

11.1.1 Communication Device

The communication device gives the smart object its communication capabilities. For wireless smart objects, the communication device typically is a radio transceiver. The word transceiver is a portmanteau of the two words transmitted and receiver. As the name indicates, a radio transceiver is able to function both as a transmitter and receiver of radio messages. For a wired smart object, the communication device connects to a wired network connection such as Ethernet or Powerline communication (PLC). In this section, the focus is on radio transceivers, and the discussion of wired PLC connections can be found in Chapter 12.

Different types of radio transceivers have different amounts of built-in processing capabilities. The simplest radio transceivers only send and receive individual bits of information into the air, whereas more capable transceivers package the information into packets, form headers, and even encrypt and decrypt the data using secure encryption methods.

Of the hardware components of a smart object, the radio is usually the most power-consuming component. Compared to the power consumption of the microcontroller or the sensors, the radio transceiver often uses ten times as much power. This is due to the processing required for modulating and demodulating the radio signal. For low-power radios, only a small portion of the power consumption is used to send the radio signal into the air. The conclusion is that listening is as power consuming as sending.

Because the radio is the most power-consuming component, and because idle listening is as expensive as sending data, the radio must be switched off to conserve power. When the radio is switched off, however, it is not able to receive any data. To create multi-hop networks, the radios of all devices in the network must somehow be synchronized so they are able to receive data while conserving power. In Section 11.3, we look into a number of duty cycling mechanisms that keep the radio off for most of the time, while still allowing data to be exchanged between the nodes.

Figure 11.3 is an example of a Radiocrafts single-chip radio transceiver for smart objects. The Radiocrafts chip contains both a radio transceiver and a microcontroller. The radio transceiver, manufactured by Texas Instruments and called CC2430, is compatible with the IEEE 802.15.4 radio

FIGURE 11.3

Texas Instruments CC2430 single-chip radio transceiver with integrated 8051 microcontroller and on-board antenna manufactured by Radiocrafts. The size of the board is $1.2 \times 1.0 \, cm^2$.

Photos courtesy of Radiocrafts.

standard and capable of transmitting and receiving individual packets, rather than individual bits. The bit rate of the radio transceiver is 250 Kbits/s.

11.1.2 Microcontroller

The microcontroller gives smart objects their intelligence. It runs the software of the smart object and is also responsible for connecting the radio with the sensors and actuators. A microcontroller is a microprocessor with built-in memory, timers, and hardware for connecting external devices such as sensors, actuators, and radio transceivers. The microcontroller looks like a traditional microchip with a plastic casing and connectors of metal as seen in Figure 11.4.

Microcontrollers are widely used and are the most common type of microprocessor. Of the total number of microprocessors sold in 2002, over 90% had significantly smaller memory sizes than a modern PC [242]. Over 50% of all microprocessors were 8-bit processors, which typically can handle a maximum of 65536 bytes of memory.

Due to cost and power constraints, the microcontrollers used in smart objects are much smaller than the microprocessors used in general purpose PCs. Typically, a smart object microcontroller has a few kilobytes of on-chip memory and is run at a clock speed of a few megahertz. In comparison, modern PCs have several gigabytes of memory and run at several gigahertz. Table 11.1 shows four common microcontrollers used in smart objects: the MSP430 from Texas Instruments, the AVR ATMega128 from Atmel, the 8051 from Intel, and the PIC18 from Microchip.

The prices for the microcontrollers in Table 11.1 vary both with the amount of memory, I/O ports, and other hardware options as well as the quantity of the chips. Although the price may be

FIGURE 11.4

An Atmel ATTINY 2313 smart object microcontroller with 20 pins. The ATTINY 2313 has 2 kB of ROM and 128 bytes of RAM. This represents the low end of smart object microcontrollers.

Table 11.1 Microcontrollers Used in Smart Objects

Name	Manufacturer	RAM (kB)	ROM (kB)	Current consumption (active/sleep), mA
MSP430xF168	Texas Instruments	10	48	2/0.001
AVR ATmega128	Atmel	8	128	8/0.02
8051	Intel	0.5	32	30/0.005
PIC18	Microchip	4	128	2.2/0.001

Note: Each manufacturer has several models of each device. This table lists only one example from each manufacturer.

over $10 for individual components when bought as single units, for bulk sale of 10,000 units or more, the price is often significantly less.

Microcontrollers have two types of memory: Read-Only Memory (ROM) and Random Access Memory (RAM). ROM is used to store the program code that encodes the behavior of the device and RAM is used for temporary data the software needs to do its task. Temporary data include storage for program variables and buffer memory for handling radio traffic. The content of the ROM is burned into the device when it is manufactured and is typically not altered after the device has been deployed. Nevertheless, most modern microcontrollers provide a mechanism for rewriting the ROM, which is useful for in-field updates of software after the devices have been deployed.

The purpose of the microcontroller is to execute its software. The software is stored in the ROM of the microcontroller and is typically stored on the microcontroller by the manufacturer when the device is manufactured.

In addition to memory for storing program code and temporary variables, microcontrollers contain a set of timers and mechanisms for interacting with external devices such as communication devices, sensors, and actuators. The timers can be freely used by the software running on the microcontroller. External devices are physically connected to the pins of the microcontroller. The software communicates with the devices using mechanisms provided by the microcontroller, typically in the form of a serial port or a serial bus. Most microcontrollers provide a so-called Universal Synchronous/Asynchronous Receiver/Transmitter (USART) for communication with serial ports. Some USARTs can be configured to work as a Serial Peripheral Interface (SPI) bus for communicating with sensors and actuators.

11.1.3 Sensors and Actuators

Smart objects interact with the physical environment in which they are deployed by using sensors and actuators. Sensors are used to sense the environment and actuators are used to affect or change the environment.

The sensors and actuators attached to a smart object range from very simple to very complex. A smart object that measures the temperature needs only a simple temperature sensor. Conversely, a smart object used for surveillance or detection of people crossing a fence may need a set of sensors that include an ultrasonic range device or a camera.

Many sensors are simple, in both form and function. For example, most temperature sensors are a variable resistor where the resistance varies with the surrounding temperature. By applying a current over the temperature resistor, and by measuring the resulting voltage, the temperature can be measured. More precise temperature sensors use similar, but more complex, ways of determining the temperature.

11.1.4 Power Sources

A smart object is driven by electronics, and electronics need power. Therefore, every smart object needs a power source. Today, the most common power source is a battery, but there are several other possibilities for power, such as solar cells, piezoelectricity, radio-transmitted energy, and other forms of power scavenging. Smart objects located close to a power grid can also use power that is readily available. These are, however, the exception and not the norm.

Batteries are the most common power source for today's smart objects. They come in many forms and shapes. For smart objects, size typically is an issue, which limits both the amount of energy that can be stored in the battery, as well as the options for battery types. Lithium cell batteries are currently the most common. With low-power hardware and proper energy-management software, a smart object can have a lifetime of years on standard lithium cell batteries.

Rechargeable batteries, which are popular in many forms of electronics such as cell phones and laptop computers, are not particularly well-suited to smart objects. Unlike cell phones and laptops, which are human-operated, most smart objects are designed to operate without human control or human supervision. Furthermore, many smart objects are located in difficult to reach places, and many are embedded in other objects. Therefore, in most cases it is impractical to recharge the batteries used in smart objects. Nevertheless, a smart object may use rechargeable battery technology with some other form of energy scavenging to charge the batteries without a human in the loop.

Instead of using rechargeable batteries, battery-equipped smart objects are typically designed so a single battery should last the entire lifetime of the smart object. By using low-power electronics and power-saving software, a smart object can have a lifetime of many years on a single standard AA-size battery. When the battery is depleted, the smart object is simply replaced with another, newer, version of the system. In many cases, the expected lifetime of the battery may be longer than the expected lifetime of the system in which the smart object is used.

But batteries are not without problems. They are difficult to recycle and therefore are a burden to the environment. For large smart object systems, replacing depleted nodes may incur large costs. Batteries may fail prematurely due to unexpected conditions such as moisture or battery leakage. Due to these challenges, other power sources for smart objects are being explored.

Power scavenging is a technique that harvests power from the physical environment. Solar cells represent the most common form of power scavenging. They harvest their power from the ambient and direct light that hits the smart object. Piezoelectricity is another source for power scavenging. For this source, physical movement is converted into energy used to power the smart object. For example, EnOcean's smart light switches are completely driven by the energy harvested from the act of pressing the light switch.

The energy in radio waves can also be used as a power source. A well-known example of this are Radio Frequency Identification (RFID) tags that use radio energy to power a radio transceiver for a short while. The energy is emitted by an RFID reader device, which must be powered by an external power source. The reader transmits a directed radio beam with enough power to allow RFID tags to reflect the radio signal.

The RFID-style radio power technology can also be used to provide power to smart objects. The Intel WISP mote is a smart object platform that uses power from a nearby RFID reader to run a set of sensors, a microcontroller, and a radio transceiver [26]. The PowerCast RF-powered modules, as shown in Figure 11.5, are single-chip modules that provide electrical power harvested from radio signals. The module requires an external antenna that picks up the radio signals. A transmitter module transmits the radio signals that power the module.

A comparison of the different power sources is given in Table 11.2. It lists the maximum current draw and the typical charge capacity of a set of power sources for smart objects. The charge capacity determines how long the smart object can last with a given average current draw. A device with an average current draw of 0.1 mA can live for 30,000 hours, or about 3½ years, on a charge capacity of 3000 mAh. With 3 volts, a current draw of 0.1 mA equals a power consumption of 0.3 mW.

Regardless of the power source chosen for the smart object, power is a constrained resource. For battery-powered smart objects, the batteries typically cannot be recharged. For solar-powered smart

FIGURE 11.5

PowerCast P2100 module converts radio energy from the air into electricity that powers an electrical circuit. The module requires an external antenna to pick up the radio signals (not shown).

Photo courtesy of PowerCast Corporation.

Table 11.2 Different Power Sources for Smart Objects, Their Maximum Current Draw, and the Amount of Charge They Store

Power source	Typical maximum current (mA)	Typical charge (mAh)
CR2032 button cell	20	200
AA alkaline battery	20	3000
Solar cell	40	Limitless
RF power	25	Limitless

objects, and those powered by power scavenging, energy is difficult to store for extended periods of time. For this reason, both the hardware and the software of the smart object must be designed to meet stringent power requirements.

In Sections 11.2 and 11.3, we look at software techniques to reduce the power consumption of smart objects.

11.1.5 Outlook: Systems on a Chip, Printed Electronics, and Claytronics

The hardware technology used in today's smart objects may not be used in the future. There are several novel technologies that can be used for smart objects such as system-on-a-chip techniques, printed circuits, and even science-fiction-like technology such as Claytronics.

Systems on a chip are electrical circuits that provide more than one function, integrated as single chips. For smart objects, systems on a chip that combine the radio transceiver, the microcontroller, and a few sensors on a single chip have a promising future. Integrating such a system on a chip with

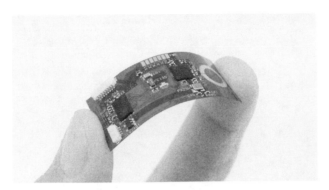

FIGURE 11.6

An ultra-thin, bendable circuit board.

Photo courtesy of IMEC.

an antenna on a single board, the resulting hardware is easily added onto ordinary objects and products turning them into smart objects. Traditionally, the engineering of the antenna onto a board is a problem due to the sophisticated planning of the board area required and because legal regulations of the radio spectrum have required hardware designs to be certified before use. By integrating a single-chip solution with an antenna, the design and certification procedure only needs to be done once simplifying the process.

The Texas Instruments CC2430 is an example of a system on a chip for smart objects (Figure 11.3). The CC2430 combines a radio transceiver with an 8051 microcontroller on a single chip. The on-chip 8051 microcontroller is programmed just like an ordinary microcontroller.

Ultra-thin technology allows entire hardware designs to be implemented on bendable soft boards. This technology is useful for developing smart objects integrated in clothes or worn attached to the body, such as sporting or medical equipment. With ultra-thin technology, the hardware components are not bendable, just the board on which they are soldered. Because the components are small, if the board can be bent, so can the smart object. Figure 11.6 shows an example of an ultra-thin, bendable circuit board.

Printed electronics is a technology that allows entire circuit designs to be printed out on ordinary paper with an ordinary printer, but with special ink as shown in Figure 11.7. The circuit boards can be quite complex and can include even simple microcontroller logic and sensors. Recent work has shown that simple batteries and displays can be printed. Printed electronics can result in drastically simplified smart object production processes and lower cost. The drawbacks are low electronics performance and large system size when compared to existing electronics.

Claytronics [95] is a futuristic idea for how smart objects should work, behave, and be designed. Claytronics are objects made of small, programmable particles that can form complex objects all by themselves. Each object consists of a large number of small particles that can attach to each other in any direction. The objects can be self-constructed by the programmed particles. Each particle runs a small program that tells it how it should attach to its neighbors. So far, the Claytronics team has built large-scale prototypes demonstrating the feasibility of the idea and of the programming models [51], but the realization of actual Claytronics is still several years away.

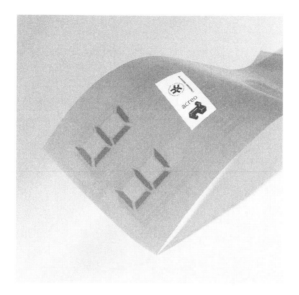

FIGURE 11.7

Printed electronics allow circuits and simple displays to be printed using a regular ink-jet printer.

Photo courtesy of Acreo AB.

11.2 SOFTWARE FOR SMART OBJECTS

The behavior of a smart object is defined by the software running on the microcontroller inside the smart object. The software inside the smart object is usually written similar to software for general purpose computers. The programs are written in a programming language, such as C, and compiled with a compiler to machine code for the microcontroller. The machine code is written to the ROM of the microcontroller when the smart object is manufactured. When the smart object is switched on, the microcontroller runs the software. This process is illustrated in Figure 11.8.

Although it is possible to program microcontrollers without using an operating system [173], most smart objects use operating systems. Because of the different requirements and constraints for a general purpose computer and a smart object, however, the operating systems for general purpose computers and smart objects are very different; smart object operating systems are much smaller and less resource-consuming. Because these operating systems are more specialized, they are also significantly less complex.

Because of power and cost constraints, smart objects have significantly less memory than general purpose computers. Memory size of a few kilobytes is common, compared to the many millions of kilobytes (gigabytes) of memory in today's PCs. See Table 11.1 for examples of typical memory configurations.

The memory constraints of smart objects make programming them a challenge. The memory footprint of the software must be small enough to run within the given limitations and the software must not use too much dynamic memory. In this section, we discuss three operating systems for smart objects and show how they deal with the challenges of smart object programming. We also

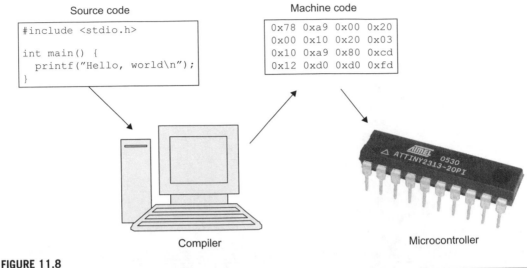

FIGURE 11.8

The process of software development for a smart object. Source code is compiled to machine code that is written to the ROM of the smart object microcontroller.

discuss the three programming models of smart objects: multi-threading, event-driven programming, and protothreads. Finally, we look at how the software manages the limited memory in smart object microcontrollers.

The smart object software must implement the communication protocols used by the smart objects. Because these protocols are designed in a layered style, where each layer is stacked on top of each other, communication protocols are typically known as a *stack*. The software that implements the protocol is also called a stack. Throughout this book, we use the term stack to mean both the communication protocols and their implementation.

11.2.1 Operating Systems for Smart Objects

Like general purpose computers, smart objects use operating systems. These operating systems are very different from general purpose operating systems used on PCs and mobile phones. The severe resource constraints regarding memory and processing power make a large-scale operating system such as Microsoft Windows, Mac OS X, or Linux impossible to use. Even scaled-down versions such as Microsoft Windows Mobile or the Linux-based Google Android are too large.

Operating systems for smart objects are tailored to the specific requirements of smart objects and to the specific constraints imposed by the hardware. The memory constraints make the programming model different from general purpose operating systems. The processing speed constraints require the use of low-level programming languages, such as the C programming language.

Smart object operating systems do not have a user interface like a general purpose operating system because no user directly interacts with the smart object operating system. Instead, the operating system is hidden deep within the microcontroller of the smart object. Usually, it is only the programmer of the smart object that comes in contact with the operating system.

In this section, we briefly look at three examples of operating systems for smart objects: Contiki, TinyOS, and FreeRTOS. In the next section, we look at the programming models used in those operating systems: event-driven programming, multi-threaded programming, and protothreads.

Contiki, TinyOS, and FreeRTOS are all open sources and their source code is available on the Web. Contiki is implemented in the C programming language and supports a range of different processors and hardware configurations. Contiki provides full IPv4 and IPv6 connectivity through the uIP [64] and uIPv6 [73] protocol stacks. uIPv6 is the only IPv6 stack for smart objects that has received the IPv6 Ready certification [73]. TinyOS is an operating system developed for research into sensor networks and smart objects. It provides implementations for a wide range of network and routing mechanisms. An adaptation of the uIP stack for TinyOS exists [37], and recent versions of TinyOS have basic IPv6 support. FreeRTOS provides IP communication capabilities through either the uIP stack or the lwIP stack [64].

11.2.1.1 *Contiki Operating System*

The Contiki operating system is an open source operating system for networked embedded systems in general, and smart objects in particular. The first version of Contiki was released in 2003. It is developed by a team of developers from the industry and academia. The Contiki project is lead by Adam Dunkels (one of the authors of this book).

Contiki provides mechanisms that assist the programmer when developing software for smart object applications as well as communication mechanisms that allow smart objects to communicate with each other and the surrounding world. Contiki provides libraries for memory allocation and linked list manipulation as well as communication abstractions and low-power radio networking mechanisms [71]. Contiki has a file system called Coffee that allows programs to use flash ROMs as a traditional file store [241]. Additionally, Contiki provides a set of simulators that simplify the development and experimentation with smart object networks [77,189].

Contiki was the first operating system for smart objects that provided IP communication with the uIP TCP/IP stack [64,67]. In 2008, the Contiki system incorporated uIPv6, the world's smallest IPv6 stack [73]. The footprints of the uIP and uIPv6 stacks are small: less than 5 kB for the uIP stack and approximately 11 kB for uIPv6. This makes them suitable for use in the constrained environment of a smart object.

Many components of Contiki are widely used in the industry. The uIP TCP/IP stack, and its larger cousin lwIP, is currently used by hundreds of companies in products ranging from car engines and airplanes to worldwide freighter container tracking systems and satellite systems. The protothread programming abstraction used in Contiki [70] is used in systems such as digital TV set-top boxes and high-performance server clusters.

Both the Contiki system and applications for the system are implemented in the C programming language. Because Contiki is implemented in C, it is highly portable. Contiki has been ported to more than twelve different microprocessor and microcontroller architectures.

Figure 11.9 shows a Contiki program waiting until a button is pressed and then sending a "Hello, world" message to the entire network. The program uses the trickle algorithm to reliably send the message to every node [159]. The trickle algorithm ensures that the message is delivered, even if

```
PROCESS_THREAD(example_trickle_process, ev, data)
{
  PROCESS_EXITHANDLER(trickle_close(&trickle);)
  PROCESS_BEGIN();

  trickle_open(&trickle, CLOCK_SECOND, 128,
               &trickle_call);
  button_sensor.activate();

  while(1) {
    PROCESS_WAIT_EVENT_UNTIL(ev == sensors_event &&
                             data == &button_sensor);

    packetbuf_copyfrom("Hello, world", 13);
    trickle_send(&trickle);

  }
  PROCESS_END();
}
```

FIGURE 11.9

Contiki program waiting until a button is pressed to send the message "Hello, world" to all nodes in a network using the trickle algorithm.

there are packet losses on the communication medium, by repeatedly transmitting messages until they are received.

Because Contiki contains an IP stack, it can directly communicate with other IP-based applications and web services, including Internet-based services. Figure 11.10 shows a Contiki program that posts a message to the Twitter microblogging service.

11.2.1.2 TinyOS Operating System

Like Contiki, TinyOS is an open source operating system for smart objects and sensor networks. It was originally created at the University of California, Berkeley [113], but is currently being worked on by a team from Stanford University [158]. The initial versions of TinyOS were released in 2000. It is primarily used for research into wireless sensor networks and has a large user base from academia. TinyOS focuses on networking and communication mechanisms for wireless sensor networks.

TinyOS is implemented in a TinyOS-specific programming language called nesC [90]. This language allows programs to be statically analyzed so certain types of race-condition bugs can be found at compile time. Recent work has also added the ability to detect bugs relating to memory safety at compile time [43].

Programs in TinyOS are written to resemble the way hardware is designed. This was originally intended to allow systems to be dynamically partitioned between software and hardware [113]. Programs are event-driven and consist of callback functions invoked in response to events, both external and internal.

TinyOS has been ported to a wide range of systems and prototyping boards.

```
int
send_twitter_message(struct twitter_state *s)
{
  PSOCK_BEGIN(&s->sout);

  /* Send POST header */
  PSOCK_SEND_STR(&s->sout,
          "POST/statuses/update.json HTTP/1.1\r\n");

  /* Send Authorization header */
  PSOCK_SEND_STR(&s->sout, "Authorization: Basic");
  PSOCK_SEND_STR(&s->sout, s->base64_username_password);
  PSOCK_SEND_STR(&s->sout, "\r\n");

  /* Send Agent header */
  PSOCK_SEND_STR(&s->sout, "User-Agent: Contiki 2.3\r\n");
  PSOCK_SEND_STR(&s->sout, "Host: twitter.com\r\n");
  PSOCK_SEND_STR(&s->sout, "Accept: */*\r\n");

  /* Send Content length header */
  PSOCK_SEND_STR(&s->sout, "Content-Length: ");
  snprintf(s->lengthstr, sizeof(s->lengthstr),
          "%d", strlen(s->message));
  PSOCK_SEND_STR(&s->sout, s->lengthstr);
  PSOCK_SEND_STR(&s->sout, "\r\n");

  /* Send Content type header */
  PSOCK_SEND_STR(&s->sout,
    "Content-Type: application/x-www-form-urlencoded\r\n\r\n");

  /* Send status message */
  PSOCK_SEND_STR(&s->sout, s->message);

  /* Close connection */
  PSOCK_CLOSE(&s->sout);
  PSOCK_EXIT(&s->sout);
  PSOCK_END(&s->sout);
}
```

FIGURE 11.10

Contiki program sending a message through the Twitter microblogging web service.

Figure 11.11 is an example of a TinyOS program. This program toggles an LED once every second. The program runs on any platform that provides an LED and a timer.

TinyOS has previously used uIP for IP communication [37], but has recently incorporated an independent IPv6 implementation [1].

11.2.1.3 The FreeRTOS Operating System

FreeRTOS is a small, open source operating system designed for embedded systems. Unlike Contiki and TinyOS, FreeRTOS provides real-time guarantees to applications. This means that applications running on top of FreeRTOS can schedule exactly when they want events in the system to occur.

```
implementation {

  command result_t StdControl.init() {
    call Leds.init();
    return SUCCESS;
  }

  command result_t StdControl.start() {
    return call Timer.start(TIMER_REPEAT, 1000);
  }

  command result_t StdControl.stop() {
    return call Timer.stop();
  }

  event result_t Timer.fired()
  {
    call Leds.redToggle();
    return SUCCESS;
  }
}
```

FIGURE 11.11

TinyOS program that blinks an LED every second.

This is important, for instance, in control applications where timing is of the essence. For example, an application that controls a robotic arm must be able to specify exactly when to turn the robot motor on and off or else the arm movements will be incorrect. FreeRTOS uses a preemptive, multi-threaded programming model.

FreeRTOS provides TCP/IP support through both the uIP and the lwIP stacks. The system designer chooses which stack to use depending on the application requirements and system constraints. For an application with high throughput demands, lwIP is chosen. For an application with less strong demands on throughput but with strong demands on memory size, uIP is chosen.

FreeRTOS has been ported to over 50 different microcontrollers and microprocessors, including the Texas Instruments MSP430 and the Atmel AVR.

11.2.2 Multi-threaded Versus Event-driven Programming

Multi-threading is a programming technique that allows multiple programs to run at the same time on a single processor. In multi-threaded programming, each program is given its own thread of control that runs alongside all other threads in the system. Each thread is given time to run on the microprocessor. To allow multiple programs to run at the same time, the operating system switches the threads so they each get their fair share of the microprocessor.

Multi-threaded programming is widely used in general purpose operating systems, where the threads are protected from each other so that one thread cannot reach another thread without going through well-specified interfaces. When threads are protected from each other, they are often called processes instead of threads.

For smart objects, the problem with multi-threading is that each thread requires its own piece of memory to hold the state of the thread, the so-called stack of the thread. The stacks contain local variables the thread uses and return values for the functions the thread calls, but also contains a comparatively large amount of unused memory. This memory must be allocated because it is unknown in advance how much stack memory each thread needs. Therefore the stack memory is typically over-provisioned.

Because of memory requirements, smart objects are often programmed differently. Event-driven programming is a memory-efficient way to write software for smart objects. With this type of programming, the software is expressed as event handlers: short sections of code that describe how the system responds to events. Examples of such events are an incoming radio packet from a neighboring node, a sensor reading from one of the sensors, and a timer. When the event occurs, the smart object responds by executing a part of its software.

Event-driven programming requires less memory than multi-threaded programming because there are no threads that require stack memory. The entire system can run as a single thread, which requires only one single stack.

The event-driven programming style is also a natural match for the event-driven nature of many smart objects. Because the object typically interacts with an event-driven environment, the programming model captures the observable behavior of the system.

The programming community has an ongoing debate about which of the two programming models (multi-threaded or event-driven) are best. Although it is possible to formally prove that the two models are equivalent [157], the programming model has implications on the structure and performance of the software running on top of the model. There are several ways to write software that take advantage of the specific properties of both programming models [4].

Protothreads [65,70] are one way to combine the advantages of the event-driven and the multi-threaded programming models. Protothreads are a programming mechanism developed for memory-constrained systems that combine the event-driven and multi-threaded programming models in a memory-efficient way. With protothreads, programs are sequentially structured, just like in the multi-threaded model, but use little memory similar to the event-driven model. Protothreads can be efficiently implemented in the C programming language without any assembly language or changes to the compiler. The drawback is that programmers must explicitly store variables when protothreads block. Because protothreads are implemented in C, they are very portable across different platforms. This has made them useful in other contexts as well [191,211].

Figure 11.12 shows an example of a program implemented with the multi-threaded programming model and the event-driven programming model. Figure 11.13 shows the same program implemented with protothreads. The difference between the models is not only how the code is structured, but also the length of the code. Although the event-driven code has more lines of code, it is more memory-efficient than the multi-threaded model.

Table 11.3 shows a qualitative comparison between multi-threaded programming, event-driven programming, and protothreads. It lists six important aspects of the programming model: memory requirements, control structures, debug stack retention, implicit locking, preemption, and automatic variables. As discussed, the memory requirements for multi-threaded programming are higher than for event-driven programming and protothreads. With multi-threaded programming, the programmer can combine control structures, such as *if* statements and *while* loops, with blocking statements. This is impossible in event-driven programming. With multi-threaded programming and protothreads, the

```
void                              enum {
radio_thread(void)                  ON,
{                                   OFF
  while(1) {                      } state;
    radio_on();
    timer_set(&t, T_AWAKE);       void
    wait_timer(&t);               timer_eventhandler()
    radio_off();                  {
    timer_set(&t, T_SLEEP);         switch(state) {
    wait_timer(&t);                 case OFF:
  }                                   if(timer_expired(&t)) {
}                                       radio_on();
                                        state = ON;
                                        timer_set(&t,
                                                  T_AWAKE);
                                      }
                                      break;
                                    case ON:
                                      if(timer_expired(&t)) {
                                        radio_off();
                                        state = OFF;
                                        timer_set(&t, T_SLEEP);
                                      }
                                      break;
                                  }
                                }
```

FIGURE 11.12

Examples of multi-threaded programming (left) and event-driven programming (middle).

```
int
radio_protothread(struct pt *pt)
{
  PT_BEGIN(pt);
  while(1) {
    radio_on();
    timer_set(&t, T_AWAKE);
    PT_WAIT_UNTIL(pt,
        timer_expired(&t));
    radio_off();
    timer_set(&t, T_SLEEP);
    PT_WAIT_UNTIL(pt,
          timer_expired(&t));
  }
  PT_END(pt);
}
```

FIGURE 11.13

Example of protothread-based programming.

Table 11.3 Qualitative Comparison Between Multi-threading, Event-driven Programming, and Protothreads

Property	Multi-threading	Event-driven programming	Protothreads
Memory requirements	Higher	Lower	Lower
Control structures	Yes	No	Yes
Debug stack retained	Yes	No	Yes
Implicit locking	No	Yes	Yes
Preemption	Yes	No	No
Automatic variables	Yes	No	No

Adapted from Dunkels et al. Protothreads: Simplifying event-driven programming of memory-constrained embedded systems. In Proceedings of the Fourth ACM Conference on Embedded Networked Sensory Systems (SenSys 2006), Boulder, CO, USA, November 2006.

history of the debug stack is retained when interrupting the program during debugging, which is not the case in event-driven programming where the back trace of calls is lost when each event handler has finished. Implicit locking is possible with both event-driven programming and protothreads, because it is certain that no called function will yield the thread. Preemption is, however, not possible with event-driven programming and protothreads. Automatic variables — variables located on the stack — are not retained in event-driven programming or with protothreads.

Each programming model has its benefits and drawbacks. Different programming problems are solved differently with each programming model. For example, programs that require high-level logic with multiple sequential steps may be better implemented with multi-threading or proto-threads, whereas low-level I/O behavior may be better implemented with event-driven programming. Ultimately, the choice of programming model is up to the software designer. For this reason, most smart object operating systems support a range of different programming models from which the system designer can choose.

11.2.3 Memory Management

Because of the restrictions put on power consumption, physical size, and cost of the microcontrollers used for smart objects, memory is constrained. Thus the available memory must be efficiently managed. There are several techniques to make the most of the constrained memory in a smart object. Unlike general purpose computers, where memory can be dynamically swapped to a hard drive, memory in a smart object microcontroller usually cannot be moved to secondary storage.

In smart object software, memory can be either statically allocated at compile time or dynamically allocated at runtime. Statically allocated memory allows the programmer to know beforehand if the program will fit in the memory of the microcontroller, but it does not allow the system to dynamically respond to the demands at runtime. Dynamic memory allocation, on the other hand, is able to respond to the actual memory load the system requires, but it is not possible to predict how the system will behave.

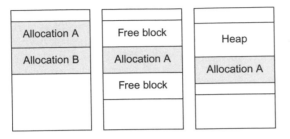

FIGURE 11.14

Static memory allocation (left), dynamic allocation from a static memory pool (middle), and dynamic allocation from a heap (right).

Because of the different advantages and drawbacks of the dynamic and static allocation methods, hybrid methods are often used. In this section, we take a look at three methods:

- Static allocation: All memory is allocated at compile time and no memory is allocated at runtime.
- Dynamic allocation from static memory pools: Memory can be dynamically allocated at runtime from a fixed set of static memory pools. The size of each allocation is predefined and cannot be changed at runtime.
- Dynamic heap allocation: Memory can be dynamically allocated at runtime and the size of each allocation can be determined at runtime.

Figure 11.14 shows how memory is allocated with static allocation, dynamic allocation from a static memory pool, and dynamic allocation from a heap. The figure shows memory allocations A and B allocated with the three different methods. With static allocation, the two allocations are present in memory from when the system boots up until the system is switched off. Memory is reserved for the two allocations and cannot be used for anything else.

With dynamic allocation, the memory for the allocations is not reserved for just those allocations, but can also be used by other allocations. When memory is allocated dynamically from a static memory pool, the memory pool has been statically allocated. This static allocation is then broken up into fixed-size segments. Memory can then be allocated from these fixed-size segments. After a segment has been allocated, it can only be used by the program that allocated it. When the program is done with the segment, the program returns the segment to the memory pool. The memory allocator marks the segment as free, and can give it out to another program that asks for it.

Dynamic allocation from a heap is more complex than dynamic allocation from a memory pool. With dynamic heap allocation, memory is allocated from a portion of the memory called the heap. Memory of any size can be allocated from the heap, as long as there are enough free consecutive bytes on the heap. Once a portion of the heap has been allocated, this portion of the memory cannot be moved or allocated by another program. When the program is done with its memory, it returns the memory to the heap.

The benefit of dynamic heap allocation is that memory segments of any size can be allocated. The price for this advantage is that the heap can become fragmented so that memory cannot be allocated from the heap, even if there are enough free bytes left. This is illustrated in Figure 11.15, where memory for allocation C cannot be allocated because there are not enough consecutive bytes left on the heap. Even if the number of free bytes on the heap is larger than the size of allocation C, the memory cannot be allocated due to fragmentation.

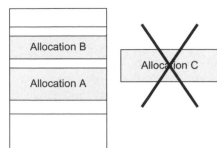

FIGURE 11.15

The problem with dynamic heap allocation: allocation C cannot be allocated, even if there is enough memory on the heap, because the memory has been fragmented.

Table **11.4** Properties of Three Memory Allocation Mechanisms: Static Allocation, Dynamic Allocation From a Memory Pool, and Dynamic Heap Allocation

Property	Static	Memory pool	Heap
Runtime allocation	No	Yes	Yes
Dynamic size	No	No	Yes
Fragmentation	No	No	Yes

Because of the problems of fragmentation in dynamic heap allocation, most smart objects use static allocation for most purposes and dynamic memory pool allocation when dynamic memory allocation is needed. Because smart objects are typically designed for a single task, static allocation provides a good baseline as a memory allocation strategy. But since the workload may vary, a certain amount of dynamic allocation is needed.

Table 11.4 summarizes the properties of the three different memory allocation mechanisms previously discussed.

11.2.4 Outlook: Macroprogramming, Java

So far, most smart objects are programmed as single nodes that possibly collaborate to achieve a common goal. This style of programming does not always allow high-level behavior to be cleanly expressed, but can require high-level application logic to be manually broken down into low-level actions. There has been research into the possibility of programming ensembles of smart object networks with a single program.

Macroprogramming [98,186] is a way to program a *network* of smart objects, as opposed to programming each individual node. With macroprogramming, the programmer writes the program to describe the behavior of the system and lets the underlying macroprogramming system partition the software on the nodes of the system. The programmer does not need to deal with low-level details such as how to send or receive radio packets, instead, he focuses on the application logic of the system to achieve the application goal. Program code is compiled into an intermediate format interpreted by the nodes. The nodes communicate between each other to form networks on top of which the program is executed. A prototype system of the macroprogramming mechanism has been developed.

Even though most smart objects are programmed in a low-level language such as C, there are several proposals to run high-level languages such as Java on them. The SunSpot nodes come with a Java virtual machine pre-installed [223], which allows them to directly run programs written in Java. The SunSpot hardware is, however, equipped with an ARM microprocessor, which is significantly larger, more power-consuming, and more expensive than microcontrollers in other smart objects. For the smaller microcontrollers, Java machines are also available [69,82,198], but these typically impose memory constraints on the programs running on them.

In the foreseeable future, however, smart objects will continue to be programmed on the node level in low-level languages such as C.

11.3 ENERGY MANAGEMENT

Smart objects must be careful about how they spend their energy. Energy is provided either by a battery or by scavenging energy from the environment. In either case, energy is a constrained resource. Power optimization must occur both at the hardware and the software level. Without power-efficient hardware, it is difficult to achieve low-power operation. Similarly, without power-efficient software, it is impossible to achieve the low-power operation of the hardware. To understand how to organize the software to optimize the power consumption of a smart object, we must first look at where energy is spent.

For radio-equipped smart objects, and indeed most low-power radio devices, the radio transceiver is the most power-consuming component. Figure 11.16 illustrates the power consumption breakdown for the Tmote Sky board [200]. It shows the power consumption of the microcontroller in sleep mode, the microcontroller in active mode, the radio transceiver in listen mode, and the radio transceiver in transmit mode. The power consumption of the microcontroller in sleep mode is very low. In fact, it is so low that it is not even visible on the graph. The radio transceiver consumes nearly ten times as much power as the microcontroller in active mode.

The most striking observation from Figure 11.16, however, is that the power consumption of the radio in listen mode is almost as high as the power consumption of the radio in transmit mode. This means that it costs almost as much energy to receive a packet as it does to transmit it. But most important, this means that the process of idle listening for radio traffic is very expensive.

Before going into the implications of expensive radio listening, we look into the radio transceiver to understand why the cost of listening and transmission are almost equal. Figure 11.17 is a schematic drawing of the internals of a radio transceiver as adapted from Wang and Sodini [252]. The figure shows the logical blocks of the transceiver: transmission circuitry (TX), reception circuitry (RX), local oscillator (LO), power amplifier (PA), and a filter for the incoming and outgoing signal. The antenna is outside of the box.

For a low-power radio, such as the IEEE 802.15.4, the output power delivered to the antenna is at most 1 mW. However, the device consumes 60 mW in total, as seen in Figure 11.16. Thus the

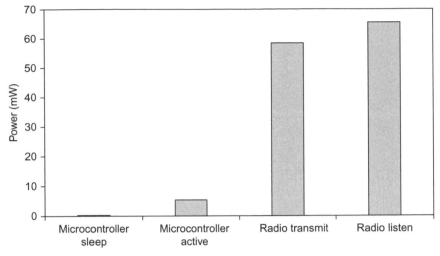

FIGURE 11.16

Power consumption of the microcontroller and the radio on the Tmote Sky smart object prototyping board. The power consumption of the microcontroller sleep mode is so low that it is not visible in the graph.

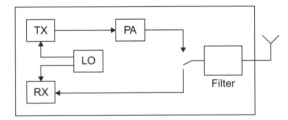

FIGURE 11.17

Schematic drawing of a radio transceiver.

additional 59 mW consumed by the transceiver is spent by the local oscillator and other parts of the transceiver circuitry. Because the reception and transmission circuitry are similar — they both modulate and demodulate the outgoing and incoming radio signal based on the clock coming from the local oscillator — it is clear that the power consumed by the power amplifier is not the primary power consumer in this low-power radio transceiver.

For a comparatively high-power radio, such as a WiFi 802.11 radio, the output power is much higher than 1 mW; therefore, the power spent on the power amplifier is much higher (up to 100 mW) [80]. Similarly, mobile telephony radios such as GSM have an output power of 1000 mW. For these radios, energy is conserved by avoiding transmissions, but this is not the case for low-power radios.

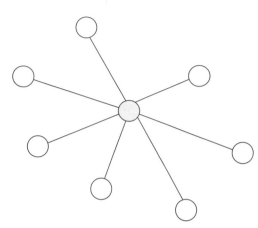

FIGURE 11.18

Star networks are the only types of networks possible if the devices never have the radio on to listen for transmissions from neighbors.

11.3.1 Radio Power Management Mechanisms

The observation that idle radio listening is expensive — as expensive as continuously transmitting packets — is important. This insight tells us that we cannot expect to save energy by avoiding transmissions, but that to conserve energy we must switch the radio off. When the radio is off we cannot hear transmissions from other nodes.

Not listening on the radio severely limits the type of network that can be constructed with smart objects. The only types of networks possible are the star networks, as shown in Figure 11.18. Star networks are given this name because their structure resembles a star consisting of a central node with connections to outside nodes. In a star network, the central node has its radio turned on all the time. This node has an external power source. All of the other battery-powered nodes keep their radios switched off to conserve energy. Only when the nodes have data to send do they switch on their radio to transmit a message. The only node they can transmit to is the central node because all of the other nodes have their radios switched off.

The star network approach is simple and useful, but it constrains the range of the smart object network to that of the physical transmission range of the radio transceivers. For some applications, this is good enough.

To allow the network range to be dynamically extended, the nodes must be able to receive transmissions from each other. With this ability, the network topology also can be constructed to provide redundant paths through the network, providing increased reliability. If a node goes down, the network can reroute the traffic around the failed node. This network structure is called a mesh network.

Figure 11.19 is an example of a mesh network. In a mesh network, all nodes can talk to each other and form a robust multi-hop network. The network can be dynamically extended as needed by adding more nodes. The new nodes automatically join the network and act as relay nodes that forward traffic.

To be able to form mesh networks, the radio transceivers of the nodes must be managed so that they are switched off when there is no traffic but switched on when neighbors want to communicate. Thus, the nodes must have a way to rendezvous so that two nodes who want to communicate can reach each other.

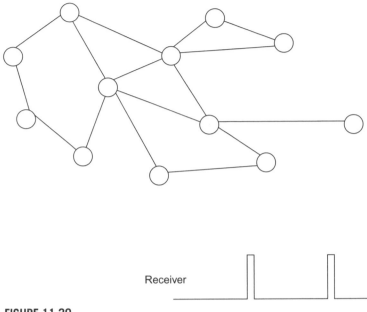

FIGURE 11.19

In a mesh network, all nodes can talk to each other, allowing the network range to be dynamically extended and enabling redundant network paths, which increase reliability.

Receiver

FIGURE 11.20

The radio duty cycling principle in LPL. The receiver keeps its radio off for most of the time, but switches it on for a short while to listen for a transmission from a neighbor.

Over the last ten years, several ways to synchronize the nodes so they can build mesh networks have been investigated [25,76,181,199,232,244,261,262]. Early work provided significant energy savings over an always-on radio. For example, the S-MAC mechanism reduced the average time the radio was turned on from 100% to 35% [261]. The WiseMAC protocol reduced this further to around 20% [76]. The B-MAC protocol showed an idle radio on-time of 1% [199]. Later developments even reduced the idle radio on-time even further.

In the remainder of this chapter, we look at two of these methods: the asynchronous low-power listening (LPL), as embodied in the X-MAC protocol [25] and the synchronous Time Synchronized Mesh Protocol (TSMP) [196].

11.3.2 Asynchronous Duty Cycling

LPL achieves low-power operation by switching the radio off most of the time and periodically switching it on for a short while. This procedure is called duty cycling. By keeping the radio on for a short while, the duty cycling mechanism makes it possible to receive transmissions from neighboring nodes. This process is illustrated in Figure 11.20. The time during which the radio is on and off is configurable. This configuration depends on the predicted traffic load of the network. Example configurations are an off-time of half a second and on-time of a few hundred microseconds. This is just enough to hear an incoming packet from a neighbor.

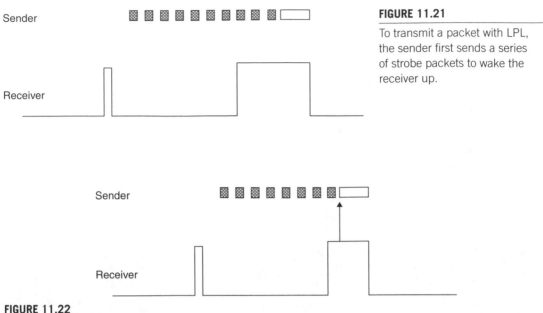

FIGURE 11.21

To transmit a packet with LPL, the sender first sends a series of strobe packets to wake the receiver up.

FIGURE 11.22

Strobe acknowledgment optimization in LPL. Each strobe contains the address of the receiver of the data packet. When the receiver hears a strobe, it sends a strobe acknowledgment packet to the sender who then immediately transmits the data packet.

To send a packet to a node, the sender first sends a train of short packets called strobes. When the receiver hears a strobe, the receiver switches its radio transceiver on in anticipation of the data packet. The strobe train must be long enough for all neighbors to listen at least once within the period. This is shown in Figure 11.21.

LPL reduces the power consumption in the network by switching the energy burden from the receivers to the senders. The receivers can have their radios switched off for most of the time, conserving power, at the cost of increased power consumption for the senders, who have to send more data on every transmission. This is a reasonable trade-off, however, since smart object networks are silent for most of the time. Thus it makes sense that the transmission is more costly if we can save energy for every other node.

The LPL procedure described thus far suffers from a number of problems. First, the strobes wake up every node, not only the one receiving the final packet. This wastes energy for all other receivers who must have their radios switched on but do not receive any useful data. Second, each packet transmission takes a considerable amount of time. If receivers are switched off for half a second, the strobe train must be sent during half a second.

To remedy these problems, each strobe is provided with the address of the recipient of the data packet. When another node hears the strobe, it determines that the packet is destined for another node and switches its radio off. When the node to which the data packet is addressed hears the strobe, it sends

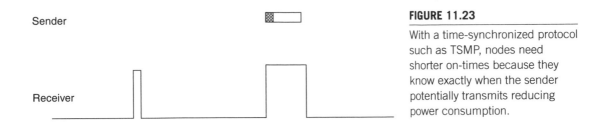

Sender

Receiver

FIGURE 11.23

With a time-synchronized protocol such as TSMP, nodes need shorter on-times because they know exactly when the sender potentially transmits reducing power consumption.

a short packet to the sender called a strobe acknowledgment packet. Because the sender knows that the receiver has its radio switched on, it immediately sends the data packet as shown in Figure 11.22.

As a further optimization, the sender can learn the duty cycle of its receivers. If the nodes have a constant duty cycle, the sender can start sending its strobes just before it expects the receiver to switch its radio on. This reduces both the power consumption of the sender, who does not need to send as many strobes, and the load on the network [76].

LPL is not explicitly synchronized. The sender and receiver do not need to be explicitly in synch with each other. Instead, the strobing process provides an implicit synchronization mechanism where the nodes synchronize on each data exchange.

11.3.3 Synchronous Duty Cycling

Although asynchronous, power-saving protocols such as LPL are useful in their simplicity, their performance can be improved by making them synchronous. Synchronous protocols are built on explicit time synchronization. Asynchronous, power-saving protocols implicitly synchronize themselves on every data transmission, but synchronous protocols explicitly synchronize themselves before sending any actual data packets. Several methods for time synchronization exist [167,216].

With time synchronization, a synchronous protocol can reduce the time that the protocol has to keep the radio switched on reducing the overall power consumption. One example of a time-synchronized, power-saving protocol is TSMP [196]. TSMP is the basis of the two industrial sensor network standards WirelessHART and ISA100a. In addition to providing a long lifetime by switching the radio off as often as possible, TSMP also achieves high reliability by constantly switching the physical radio frequency on which packets are sent. The network is centrally managed so that the entire network is scheduled by a network manager (a small server located next to the network). TSMP is designed for industrial use and is not intended to be suitable for people- or home-centric smart objects applications.

In TSMP, all nodes are time synchronized within $50\,\mu s$. Time is divided into slots that are 10 ms long. In every slot, a node is either listening, potentially transmitting (if the node has data to transmit), or sleeping. When listening, the node listens for a short while at the beginning of the 10 ms time slot. If a node is transmitting in the time slot, the transmission will start within $100\,\mu s$. Thus, the receiver does not need to keep its radio on for longer than $100\,\mu s$ every 10 ms in those time slots it is able to receive a packet.

The time-synchronized process is shown in Figure 11.23. The sender only needs to send a very short synchronization byte before sending its packet, because the receiver can quickly determine if there is a packet transmitted or not.

Table 11.5 Idle Radio On-time for Five Different Power-saving Mechanisms

Mechanism	Type of mechanism	Typical radio on-time (%)
X-MAC	Asynchronous	1.4
Arch Rock	Asynchronous	0.65
ContikiMAC	Asynchronous	0.45
TSMP	Synchronous	0.32
Dozer	Synchronous	0.16

11.3.4 Examples of Radio On-times

The primary purpose of the radio power-saving mechanisms presented in Table 11.5 is to reduce the power consumption by switching the radio off as often as possible. This is particularly important when the devices are idle or when there is no traffic flowing. Many smart object networks spend most of the time in idle mode.

Table 11.5 compares the idle radio on-time for five power-saving radio mechanisms: the X-MAC mechanism [25] as measured in the Contiki implementation, the Arch Rock mechanism as reported by Hui and Culler [125], the ContikiMAC mechanism as measured in its Contiki implementation, the TSMP mechanism as reported by Pister and Doherty [196], and the Dozer mechanism as reported by Burri et al. [27]. TSMP and Dozer are synchronous mechanisms whereas the others are asynchronous. The radio on-time depends on the system configuration and since different power saving mechanisms have different configurations, a direct comparison is not possible. The purpose of the table is to show that several existing mechanisms are able to keep the radio switched off for approximately 99% of the time.

Although the synchronous mechanisms are more efficient in reducing the idle radio on-time, this comes at the price of a higher network setup time. For example, with the TSMP protocol it may take several minutes for a node to join the network [196]. Additionally, the performance latency characteristics for the different methods vary. There are as yet no comparative studies that shed light on the typical system latency for the previously mentioned power-saving mechanisms.

11.4 CONCLUSIONS

In this chapter, we discussed the hardware and software for smart objects as well as the energy consumption of smart objects and how the hardware and software needs to cooperate to save power. The hardware typically consists of four parts: a radio transceiver, a microcontroller, a power source, and a set of sensors and actuators. The software, which runs on the microcontroller, consists of an operating system and the application programs that define the behavior of the smart object. Contiki, TinyOS, and FreeRTOS are three examples of such operating systems. Because of the power, size, and cost constraints of smart object hardware, there are severe memory constraints on smart object software.

The power consumption of a smart object is important because many smart objects have constrained power budgets. Smart objects either run on batteries, which are difficult to replace or recharge, or from environmental sources such as small solar cells. In either case, power is constrained. To provide a long lifetime, the smart object software must be smart about managing its energy consumption.

For many smart objects, the communication device consumes the most power, both for radio-equipped devices and for devices using other communication mechanisms. For radio-equipped systems, the radio consumes as much power when listening for radio traffic as it does when sending data. Therefore, radio energy management mechanisms must switch off the radio as often as possible. Because no communication can take place if the radio is switched off, the system must have a mechanism to synchronize nearby nodes so their radios are switched on simultaneously. Asynchronous, power-saving protocols, such as LPL, provide a high degree of power saving without requiring any explicit time synchronization between nodes. By adding explicit time synchronization, it is possible to achieve higher power effectiveness, at the cost of higher network setup time, as well as the additional complexity caused by the required time synchronization.

Communication Mechanisms for Smart Objects

12

Smart objects communicate with each other, but the choice of communication technology varies between different applications and different environments. In this chapter we look at the various ways in which communication between smart objects works. The communication principles behind smart object communication and how it differs from communication between traditional computers are also discussed. We then turn to three communication standards for smart objects: IEEE 802.15.4, IEEE 802.11 (WiFi), and Powerline communication (PLC).

12.1 COMMUNICATION PATTERNS FOR SMART OBJECTS

Smart object communication patterns can be divided into three categories: one-to-one, one-to-many, and many-to-one. Each communication pattern is used in different situations. Many applications use a combination of the patterns.

Smart objects have specific communication patterns based on their application. A person-centric smart object network used to measure bodily metrics of hospital patients differs greatly from an industrial smart object network used to monitor vibration of industrial robots. Yet, these diverse types of networks share many of the principles behind the communication within the network.

Smart objects often communicate over unreliable communication channels. The radio transmission of a smart object with a radio transceiver may be disturbed by other radio senders in the vicinity. Radio signals are also disturbed by physical obstacles between the sender and the receiver. Because low-power radios for smart objects use unlicensed radio frequency bands, where they coexist with other radio technologies, the risk of radio disturbance is even greater. For wired technologies, the risk of disturbance may be smaller, but is still a factor that the communication protocols must be prepared to deal with.

Because the communication channels are inherently unreliable, the communication protocols running on top of the communication channels often have mechanisms that provide reliability. Messages that are lost because of radio disturbance are retransmitted. Not all applications require strict reliability, however, and for such applications the underlying best-effort nature of the communication channel may provide enough reliability.

Radio is not only an unreliable medium, it is also a shared medium. When sending a message over radio, it is possible that another nearby node simultaneously sends a message. Because the medium is shared, the two messages collide in the air and a receiver may not be able to receive any of the sent messages. Communication protocols for radios must take this into account.

Interconnecting Smart Objects with IP. DOI: 10.1016/B978-0-12-375165-2.00012-0

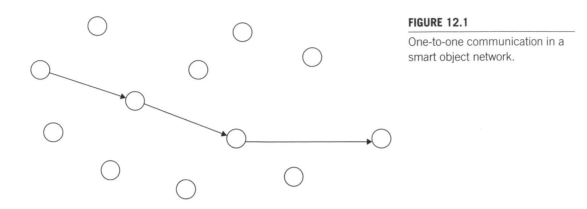

FIGURE 12.1

One-to-one communication in a smart object network.

Different smart object applications have different communication demands. Applications involving mobile objects, such as body-worn sensors, typically require rapid knowledge of the changing network topology around them. In contrast, highly static applications, such as industrial monitoring of stationary equipment, do not require rapid updates of the network topology because the topology rarely changes.

The power consumption of the radio transceiver affects network structures as well as possible communication patterns. Because the radio must be switched off to conserve power, networks with very low power budgets cannot expect to maintain complex communication patterns over extended periods of time.

Armed with a preliminary understanding of reliability concerns, the different application requirements, and the effect of power consumption, we turn to the three different types of communication patterns for smart objects: one-to-one communication, one-to-many communication, and many-to-one communication.

12.1.1 One-to-one Communication

The-one-to-one communication pattern occurs when one smart object communicates with another smart object. The communication may involve other smart objects, however, as the communication may be routed through a network of smart objects. In Figure 12.1, two smart objects communicate with each other, but two other smart objects are involved because they forward packets between the communication end points.

12.1.2 One-to-many Communication

The one-to-many communication pattern (Figure 12.2) is used for sending messages from one node to several other nodes and possibly all other nodes in the network. This can be used, for example, for sending a command to a set of nodes in the network.

There are several forms of one-to-many communication. Depending on the situation in which the communication pattern is used, the required reliability of the message delivery is different. If high reliability is required, the communication protocol must be able to retransmit the messages until every

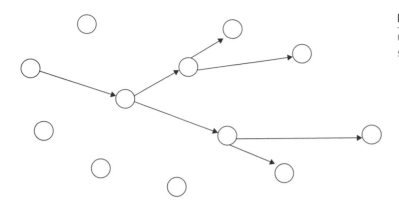

FIGURE 12.2

One-to-many communication in a smart object network.

receiver has successfully received it. If reliability is not a hard requirement, the protocol may not need to retransmit any messages: the protocol hopes that the underlying communication medium is reliable enough for the message to reach the receivers.

Many mechanisms and protocols have been designed to perform one-to-many communication in low-power radio networks. The simplest form of one-to-many communication is network flooding. This is done by having each node broadcast the message to be sent. When a node hears a broadcasted message from a neighbor, the node rebroadcasts the message to its own neighbors. To avoid cross-talk, each node waits for a random interval before rebroadcasting the message. The effect of this mechanism is that the message eventually reaches all nodes in the network, unless messages are lost because of radio disturbances or radio collisions.

Although a network flood may work well in many situations, it is not a reliable mechanism. There are no guarantees that messages sent with the mechanism reach their destinations. Messages that are lost due to disturbance or collisions are not retransmitted. To achieve reliable one-to-many communication, the communication protocol must detect lost messages and retransmit them.

Trickle [159] is a reliable one-to-many communication mechanism explicitly designed for low-power radio networks. It uses periodic retransmissions to ensure that lost messages are retransmitted. To avoid overloading the radio with too many transmissions, the protocol provides a mechanism to reduce the number of messages that are sent. By assigning each message a sequence number, the protocol knows which nodes have received a message. If a node is heard sending an old sequence number, any of its neighbors can retransmit its latest message to the node with the old sequence number, ensuring that the latest message is made known to all nodes.

One-to-many communication is also used in routing protocols to establish one-to-one communication paths. For example, the one-to-one AODV protocol [194] uses a one-to-many phase to find a path to the communication end point.

12.1.3 Many-to-one Communication

Many-to-one communication (Figure 12.3) occurs frequently in smart object networks that collect data from the nodes. In many-to-one communication, several nodes send data toward a single node. This node is often called a sink node.

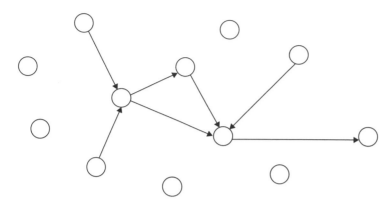

FIGURE 12.3

Many-to-one communication in a
smart object network.

Many-to-one communication can be used to collect sensor data, such as temperature data, from the nodes in the network, but it can also be used for network health status information. Nodes send periodic status reports to a sink node. The sink node then reports the overall performance of the network to an outside observer.

In many-to-one communication, there may be more than one sink inside the network. If the application does not specify a specific node to which the data are to be sent, the network may choose to send the data to the sink closest to the sender. This allows networks with multiple sinks to collect data with a higher efficiency than if all data had to be transported across the entire network.

To set up a many-to-one communication network, the nodes build a tree structure with its root at the sink. The sink announces its presence by sending repeated broadcast messages indicating that the sender is zero hops away from the sink node. Its neighbors hear the transmissions and transmit messages indicating they are one hop away from the sink. In turn, their neighbors will broadcast that they are two hops away from the sink, and so on. With this simple method, every node in the network will eventually know how many hops away they are from the sink and which of their neighbors is closer. When sending a packet, a node only has to send it to a node that is closer to the sink.

Although the hop-count-based routing path construction method is simple, it is not without problems. A node with a very short number of hops to the sink may be located where there is very bad radio coverage, while a node with more hops to the sink may be located where there is very good radio coverage. To reach the sink, it may be better to send to the node with better radio coverage but with more hops to the sink, because the packet has a higher chance of getting through without repeated retransmissions.

To account for radio quality in addition to hop count, several cost metrics for many-to-one routing exist. Woo et al. [258] explored several metrics and found that a metric based on how many transmissions are expected is a good choice. This metric, called expected transmissions (ETX) [50], computes an estimate of the amount of transmissions and retransmissions needed to reach the sink for a given path. When sending a packet, the node chooses the path with the smallest number of ETX. Others have corroborated this finding [85,94].

The idea of ETX is best explained with an example. Figure 12.4 shows a network of five nodes, A to E. Node A wants to send a message to node E: What path should be taken? The path A-B-E is two

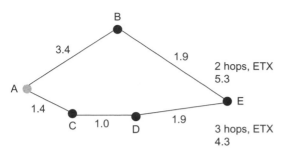

FIGURE 12.4

ETX in a five-node network.

hops, and the path A-C-D-E is three hops. If node A would use the hop count as a routing metric, path A-B-E would be chosen. An ETX-based routing metric takes the ETX of each path into consideration. The expected number of transmissions depends on the communication quality between two neighbors and can be estimated by sending probe packets between the neighbors and counting how many made it through. In the previous example, the ETX for each neighbor pair on the paths is already estimated. The routing protocol computes the sum of all ETX metrics for the paths to form a routing metric to the destination. In this case, the path A-B-E has an ETX of 5.3, which means that on average, a packet sent on this path requires 5.3 transmissions before it reaches its destination. The path A-C-D-E, on the other hand, has an ETX of 4.3, which is less than the path A-B-E. Thus the routing protocol chooses path A-C-D-E, which has a lower ETX, even if it has more hops than the path A-B-E.

The Collection Tree Protocol (CTP) is an example of a many-to-one protocol that uses ETX for setting up a tree network [94]. In CTP, each node periodically broadcasts its ETX toward the nearest sink node. To avoid overloading the network, the amount of broadcast is reduced through a suppression mechanism similar to that of Trickle [159].

12.2 PHYSICAL COMMUNICATION STANDARDS

Next, we discuss three different physical communication mechanisms for smart objects: two radio transmission mechanisms, IEEE 802.15.4 and IEEE 802.11, and PLC. The three mechanisms are different in many aspects, but similar in others. Both IEEE 802.15.4 and IEEE 802.11 are wireless radio mechanisms. PLC is inherently wired, as it uses physical power lines as its physical medium. Nevertheless, all three mechanisms operate over an unpredictable physical transmission medium and must be prepared to deal with data loss.

From a networking standpoint, the most important difference between the three mechanisms is the range of physical signals. IEEE 802.15.4 is a relatively short-range transmission mechanism with individual radio signals reaching only a few meters. IEEE 802.11 has a longer physical range, sometimes as much as several hundred meters. Finally, PLC has a physical transmission range determined by the length of the physical cables through which the signals are propagated and by the impedance of the loads connected to the wire.

The physical range has implications for network formation. In a PLC network, all nodes connected to the same physical network have the same connectivity to other nodes as long as no node is physically disconnected from the cable. In contrast, IEEE 802.15.4 nodes must be prepared for the network to dynamically change as nodes move or when the physical transmission environment changes. IEEE 802.11 has similar properties, but they are not as pronounced because of its longer physical range.

Because of its short range, IEEE 802.15.4 networks need a routing mechanism to provide a mesh network. Nodes must be prepared to relay traffic from neighbor nodes to other nodes in the network, because the nodes cannot directly reach all other nodes. In PLC, individual nodes do not need to route data to each other because all nodes reach each other directly, but nodes may need to route data to nodes on other networks. For 802.11, most 802.11 networks have access points that are connected to each other. Therefore, the nodes themselves do not have to relay data to each other, but can send data to nodes with which they have no direct connection to the nearest access point.

12.3 IEEE 802.15.4

IEEE 802.15.4 is a standard radio technology for low-power, low-data-rate applications [100]. The standard has been developed within the 802.15 personal area network (PAN) Working Group within the Institute of Electrical and Electronics Engineers (IEEE). IEEE 802.15.4 has a maximum data rate of 250,000 bits/s and a maximum output power of 1 mW. IEEE 802.15.4 devices have a nominal range on the order of a few tens of meters. The focus of the IEEE 802.15.4 specification is to allow low-cost and low-complexity transceivers, which has made IEEE 802.15.4 popular for smart objects. Many companies manufacture IEEE 802.15.4-compliant devices.

Because of the ubiquity of IEEE 802.15.4 and of the availability of IEEE 802.15.4-compliant radio transceivers, many of the recently developed low-power radio stacks are built on IEEE 802.15.4: WirelessHART, ISA100a, IPv6, and ZigBee.

The IEEE 802.15.4 standard specifies two layers:

• Physical: Specifies how messages are transmitted and received over the physical radio medium.
• Media access control (MAC): Specifies how messages coming from the physical layer are handled.

Although the IEEE 802.15.4 standard specifies several mechanisms in the physical and MAC layers, not all parts of the specification are widely used. For example, the WirelessHART standard uses the physical layer specification and the MAC layer packet header format, but not the full MAC behavior. Instead, WirelessHART adds its own logic on top of the MAC format.

The maximum packet size in 802.15.4 is 127 bytes. Packets are small because IEEE 802.15.4 is intended for devices with low data rates. Because the MAC layer adds a header to each packet, the available amount of data for an upper layer protocol or application is between 86 and 116 bytes. Upper layer protocols, therefore, often add mechanisms to fragment larger data portions into multiple 802.15.4 frames [176].

IEEE 802.15.4 is typically implemented in a combination of hardware and software. The low-level parts — the physical layer and parts of the MAC processing — are implemented in hardware, whereas the higher-level parts such as the MAC layer logic are implemented in software. Several implementations of the standard exist.

IEEE 802.15.4 networks are divided into PANs as shown in Figure 12.5. Each PAN has a PAN coordinator and a set of PAN members. Packets sent over a PAN carry a 16-bit PAN identifier that specifies to what PAN the packet is destined. A device can participate in one PAN as the PAN coordinator and simultaneously participate as a PAN member in another PAN.

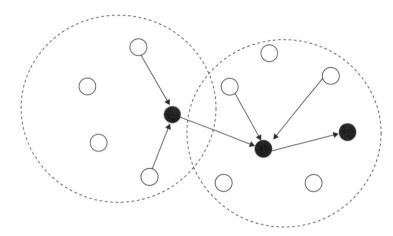

FIGURE 12.5

An IEEE 802.15.4 network with FFDs shown as dark dots and RFDs shown as hollow dots. Two of the FFDs are PAN coordinators in the two PANs, shown as dotted circles. The right PAN contains two FFDs, but only one is the PAN coordinator.

The IEEE 802.15.4 standard specifies two types of devices: fully functional devices (FFDs) and reduced function devices (RFDs). FFDs are more capable than RFDs, and can act as PAN coordinators. RFDs are simpler devices intended to be easier to implement, making them less costly to manufacture. RFDs can only communicate with FFDs. FFDs can communicate with both FFDs and RFDs.

Although the 802.15.4 specification defines three types of network structures that 802.15.4 supports — star topology, mesh topology, and cluster tree topology — most of the protocols that operate on top of 802.15.4 do not use the 802.15.4 topologies. Instead, they build their own network topologies on top of the 802.15.4 MAC layer. For that reason, we do not go into detail into the network topologies defined by 802.15.4.

12.3.1 **802.15.4 Addresses**

Each node in an 802.15.4 network has a 64-bit address that uniquely identifies the device. Because of the limited packet size in 802.15.4, however, the length of the 64-bit addresses is prohibitive. Therefore, 802.15.4 allows nodes to use short addresses that are 16 bits long. Short addresses are assigned by the PAN coordinator and are valid only within the context of a PAN. Nodes may choose to send packets using either of the two address formats.

Addresses are written as hexadecimal digits separated by colons. An example of a long 802.15.4 address is 00:12:75:00:11:6e:cd:fb. Figure 12.6 is an example of two 802.15.4 addresses, one long and one short.

Long addresses are globally unique and each 802.15.4 device is assigned an address when manufactured. Each manufacturer requests a 24-bit, unique organizational unique identifier (OUI) from the IEEE. For this, the requesting organization pays a one-time fee of $1650 to the IEEE. The OUI is used as the first 24 bits of the address of the device. The remaining 40 bits are assigned by the manufacturer and must be unique for each device.

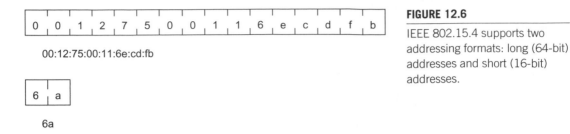

FIGURE 12.6

IEEE 802.15.4 supports two addressing formats: long (64-bit) addresses and short (16-bit) addresses.

Short addresses are assigned at runtime by the PAN coordinator. A short address is valid only within the PAN in which it was assigned. Nevertheless, it is possible for a device with a short address to communicate with devices outside of its own PAN by including the 16-bit PAN identifiers of its own PAN and the PAN of the device with which it communicates in each message. The IEEE 802.15.4 standard does not specify any particular algorithm to be used by a PAN coordinator when assigning unique short addresses within the PAN.

12.3.2 The 802.15.4 Physical Layer

The physical layer determines the physical radio frequency at which the radio operates, the radio modulation, and the encoding of the signal. IEEE 802.15.4 operates on three, license-free radio frequency bands. Because of local radio regulations, the exact frequency is different in different parts of the world. In the United States, IEEE 802.15.4 uses the 902–928 MHz band. In Europe, 802.15.4 uses the 868–868.8 MHz band. In the rest of the world, 802.15.4 uses the 2400–2483.5 MHz band.

IEEE 802.15.4 defines 26 different operational channels. Within each frequency band, there are several channels defined, as shown in Figure 12.7. Channel 0 is defined only in Europe, and resides on the 868 MHz band. Channels 1 to 10 are defined only in the United States on the 902–982 MHz band. The channel spacing is 2 MHz.

Channels 11 to 26 are defined on the 2.4 GHz band, which makes them available everywhere. The channels are defined with 5 MHz channel spacing.

IEEE 802.15.4 uses two types of radio modulation, depending on the channel frequency. Channels 0 to 10 use binary phase-shift keying (BPSK), whereas channels 11 to 26 use quadrature phase-shift keying (QPSK). On all channels, IEEE 802.15.4 uses direct-sequence spread spectrum (DSSS) modulation.

Like the modulation technique, the bit rate is dependent on the radio channel. The bit rate of channel 0 is 20,000 bits/s. For channels 1 to 10, the bit rate is 40,000 bits/s, and for channels 11 to 26 the bit rate is 250,000 bits/s.

The IEEE 802.15.4 radio channels in the 2.4 GHz band share their radio frequency with 802.11 (WiFi) and have a considerable overlap with the 802.11 channels. Because 802.11 has a significantly higher output power, 802.11 disturbs 802.15.4 traffic. Figure 12.8 shows the overlap between 802.15.4 and 802.11. All 802.15.4 channels except channels 25 and 26 are covered by 802.11 channels. When the non-overlapping 802.11 channels 1, 6, and 11 are used, there are two additional 802.15.4 channels (15 and 20) that do not

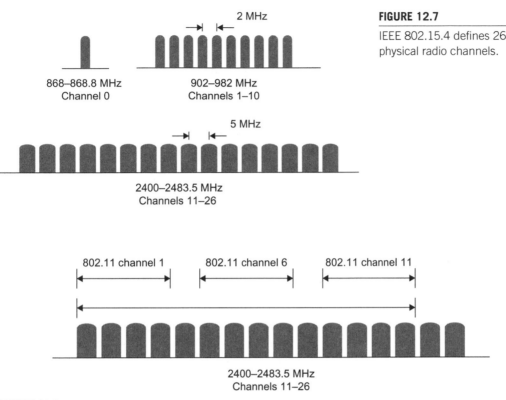

FIGURE 12.7

IEEE 802.15.4 defines 26
physical radio channels.

2 MHz

868–868.8 MHz
Channel 0

902–982 MHz
Channels 1–10

5 MHz

2400–2483.5 MHz
Channels 11–26

802.11 channel 1

802.11 channel 6

802.11 channel 11

2400–2483.5 MHz
Channels 11–26

FIGURE 12.8

IEEE 802.15.4 channels 11–24 overlap the 802.11 channels. Channels 25 and 26 are not covered by 802.11 channels. When the non-overlapping 802.11 channels 1, 6, and 11 are used, two additional 802.15.4 channels are undisturbed by 802.11.

see interference from 802.11 traffic. Channel assignments are, however, subject to variations within different jurisdictions and may change over time.

The physical layer also provides mechanisms to measure the radio energy for a given radio channel. This is used by the MAC layer to determine if another node may be transmitting on a particular channel, and by the MAC coordinator to scan for available channels with a low idle energy level. A low idle energy level is an indication of low interference from other radio sources on the frequency of the channel.

The radio energy detection mechanism is also used to provide a clear channel assessment (CCA) mechanism, where the physical layer can assess if another node is currently transmitting over the radio. This is done in one of three ways: by measuring the radio energy and comparing it with a predefined energy threshold, by demodulating the incoming radio signal to see if it is a valid 802.15.4 signal, or by a combination of the radio energy detection method and the signal modulation method. The CCA is used by the MAC layer to control access to the radio medium.

12.3.3 MAC Layer

The purpose of the MAC layer is to control access to the radio medium. Because the radio medium is shared between all senders and receivers in the vicinity of each other, the MAC layer provides mechanisms for the nodes to determine when the medium is idle and when it is safe to send messages.

The IEEE 802.15.4 MAC layer provides channel access management, validation of incoming frames, and acknowledgment of frame reception. Additionally, the 802.15.4 MAC provides optional mechanisms for a time-division multiple access (TDMA) mechanism for medium access where the PAN coordinator assigns time slots to PAN devices and enforces a schedule through the transmission of beacon messages. This beacon mode is, however, not widely used by the protocols running on top of 802.15.4, therefore, it warrants no further discussion.

Channel access management is done by using the CCA mechanism provided by the physical layer. Before sending a packet, the MAC layer asks the physical layer to perform a CCA check. If the CCA indicates that another node is currently transmitting, the MAC layer refrains from sending its own packet. Instead, the MAC layer waits for a specified time and later retries sending the packet.

The MAC layer performs validation of incoming frames by computing a 16-bit cyclic redundancy check (CRC) of the entire frame [132]. The CRC is used to check for transmission errors in the frame and is computed by the sender of the frame as the frame is sent. It is added to the transmitted packets. If the CRC computed by the receiver does not match the CRC in the frame footer, the receiver discards the frame.

The MAC layer provides a mechanism for automatic acknowledgment of received frames. If an incoming frame has the acknowledgment bit set, the MAC layer sends an acknowledgment frame into the air. The acknowledgment frame is sent only if the destination address of the incoming frame is the same as the address of the device, and if the CRC of the incoming frame is valid. The acknowledgment frame is not explicitly addressed to the sender of the data frame, but is broadcast to all nodes. Because of this, many of the upper layer protocols running on top of 802.15.4 implement their own acknowledgment mechanisms.

12.3.4 The 802.15.4 Frame Format

Communication protocols specify a common packet format so that all nodes know how to construct and parse packets from others. Packet formats consist of three parts: a header, a data portion, and a footer. The header contains control data such as addresses, sequence numbers, and flags. The data portion contains the upper layer data. Therefore, the structure of the data portion is typically unspecified, but left to the upper layer protocols for specification. The footer, if specified, usually contains checksums or cryptographic signatures. Such data can often be computed while the packet is transmitted. The footer is then sent after the rest of the packet has been sent.

IEEE 802.15.4 defines a common packet format for all packet transmissions. The packet format consists of both a physical layer part and a MAC layer part. The physical layer adds a synchronization header and the MAC layer adds a header and a footer. The header format is shown in Figure 12.9.

The header added by the physical layer consists of a preamble, a start of frame delimiter (SFD), and a length field. The preamble is used to synchronize the sender and the receiver so the receiver is able to correctly receive the packet that follows. The SFD indicates to the receiver that the preamble ends and that the frame begins. The single-byte length field tells the receiver how many bytes will follow. The maximum length of the packet that follows is 127 bytes.

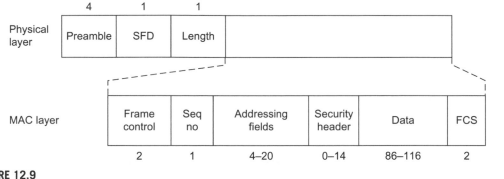

FIGURE 12.9

The IEEE 802.15.4 physical layer and MAC layer header formats.

The MAC layer header follows directly after the physical layer header. The MAC layer header contains two control bytes, called the frame control, that contain flags that tell the receiver how to interpret the rest of the header as well as flags to indicate whether or not the frame should be acknowledged. Following the frame control bytes is a single-byte sequence number. The sequence number is used to associate acknowledgments with the data packet they acknowledge. The acknowledgment carries the same sequence number as the data packet.

After the frame control and sequence number bytes are the addressing fields. They contain the address of the sender of the packet and the address of the receiver of the packet as well as identifiers of the sending and receiving PAN. All addressing fields are optional. Their presence is indicated by flags in the frame control field. The addressing fields are used by a receiver to determine if a received packet is destined for itself or not. The addressing field is followed by an optional security field that contains data for security processing, such as an optional cryptographic message integrity check (MIC) field.

The data follow the MAC layer header, and can be between 86 and 116 bytes long. The maximum size of the data is determined by how many optional MAC layer fields are used. The structure of the data portion of the 802.15.4 frame is not specified by the 802.15.4 standard, but defined by the protocols or applications running on top of 802.15.4.

At the end of the 802.15.4 packet is the frame check sequence (FCS) footer, which contains the CRC that the MAC layer uses to check if incoming packets should be discarded due to bit errors.

12.3.5 Power Consumption

The power consumption of IEEE 802.15.4 is determined by the current draw of the electrical circuits that implement the physical communication layer, and by the amount of time during which the radio is turned on. As shown in Chapter 11, there are several ways a radio can be switched off while maintaining communication abilities. Figure 12.10 shows the power consumption of the electrical circuitry of the CC2420 IEEE 802.15.4 transceiver, as reported by the CC2420 data sheet. It shows that the idle power consumption is significantly lower than both the listen and the transmit power consumption. In the idle mode, however, the transceiver is not able to receive any data. The power consumption in the transmit modes is lower than the power consumption in listen mode. The power consumption of the transmit mode depends on the output power, which is configurable via software on a per-packet basis.

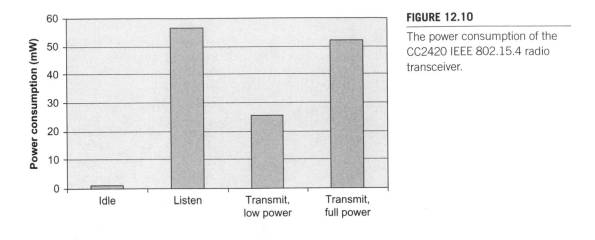

FIGURE 12.10

The power consumption of the CC2420 IEEE 802.15.4 radio transceiver.

12.4 IEEE 802.11 AND WIFI

IEEE 802.11 is a wireless communication standard originally designed as a high-speed, short-range communication mechanism for laptops and general purpose PCs. IEEE 802.11 was introduced in the late 1990s and several versions of the standard have been released since its inception. Each new version of the standard has enabled a higher transmission rate. The first version of the standard, which was released in 1997, has a maximum transmission rate of 1 Mbit/s. The latest version of the standard, 802.11g, has a maximum transmission rate of 54 Mbits/s.

WiFi is a brand name of the WiFi Alliance. The purpose of the WiFi brand is to identify equipment and software that is compatible with other WiFi and 802.11 systems. With early 802.11 equipment, it was not certain that this equipment from different vendors would interoperate with each other. With the WiFi brand, this is no longer an issue. In this book, we use the name 802.11 to distinguish that we are discussing the underlying technology and not the interoperability aspects.

IEEE 802.11 and WiFi are used in many homes and offices to provide wireless Internet connectivity. Today's laptops have integrated 802.11 circuits. 802.11 base stations are low cost and available worldwide. Many home broadband routers and DSL modems contain an 802.11 base station. Smartphones such as the iPhone contain 802.11 transceivers. It has been estimated that the number of 802.11 devices worldwide by 2012 will be counted in billions.

For smart objects, 802.11 has many positive aspects. The widespread adoption of 802.11 makes deployment of smart objects easy. In locations where an 802.11 network exists, no additional infrastructure is needed to support an 802.11 smart object network. Also, the availability of 802.11 chipsets, routers, and network access cards reduces the cost of hardware for 802.11-enabled smart objects. Furthermore, the widespread adoption and availability of 802.11 has led to a widespread knowledge and understanding of 802.11. For smart object businesses, this provides a large market of skilled network architects and engineers.

Because 802.11 was designed for high-speed transport for laptops and PCs, it has had a reputation for being power-hungry. Compared to 802.15.4 transceivers, 802.11 transceivers typically have an order of magnitude higher power consumption.

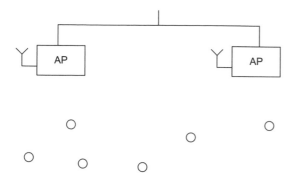

A network topology of 802.11 in access point mode. Each 802.11 transceiver is associated with an access point. A network may be served by more than one access point. The access points typically have wired network access.

For smart objects, power consumption is a critical issue. Traditionally, 802.11 has been seen as a power-hungry technology and therefore not deemed useful for smart objects. Recently, however, a new generation of low-power 802.11 transceivers has emerged. They are optimized for systems that, like smart objects, spend most of their time in sleep mode. By providing significantly lower power consumption in sleep mode, these transceivers extend the life of standard AA cell batteries.

12.4.1 Network Topology and Formation

IEEE 802.11 supports two modes of network topology: infrastructure and ad hoc, also called independent (IBSS) mode. In infrastructure mode, all 802.11 transceivers are in the direct range of an access point that handles all nodes within its range. In ad hoc mode, 802.11 transceivers can communicate directly with each other, without the need for an access point in range. Although most 802.11 transceivers support the ad hoc mode, infrastructure mode is mostly used.

Figure 12.11 is an example topology of an 802.11 network in access point mode. The network has two access points connected to a wired backbone network. The access point is connected to mains power. Every 802.11 transceiver is associated with one of the access points. Communication between nodes goes through the access points or directly over the radio medium. If nodes are in range of each other, they directly communicate with each other; otherwise, they communicate by sending their packets to the access point to which they are associated. Communication with outside networks always goes through the access point.

Before communication takes place in an infrastructure mode network, the nodes must associate themselves with the access point. A set of nodes and their access point are called a basic service set (BSS). If more than one access point is involved, the set of nodes and access points are called an extended service set (ESS). A service set has a service set identifier (SSID) associated with it. The SSID is typically a human-readable textual string. The string is typically called the network name or the network ID.

To join a network, a node first probes for available SSIDs. The scan can be either active or passive. With an active scan, the node broadcasts a probe request packet. The probe request can contain an SSID, in case the node wants to join a particular network, or it can contain a blank SSID, in case the node wants to probe any available network. The access points reply to the node with a probe

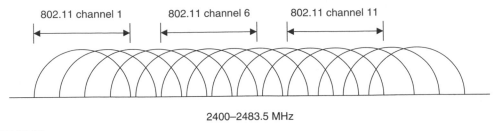

FIGURE 12.12

IEEE 802.11 operates on 14 different channels in the 2.4 GHz band. Channels 1, 6, and 11 do not overlap. Channels 12, 13, and 14 are not available in every country due to radio frequency licensing restrictions.

response packet. It contains the configuration parameters for the network, such as what channels the network uses. When a node has found a suitable network with which to associate, the node first must authenticate itself to the network. If the authentication request is accepted by the access point, the node sends an association request frame to it. The access point replies with an association reply frame, and the node is associated with the network.

12.4.2 Physical Layer

Most IEEE 802.11 networks use the license-free 2.4 GHz band, but other radio frequencies are defined by the standards. The original 802.11 specification, first published in 1997, provided two versions of the radio layer: one for frequency hopping and one for DSSS. Later, other physical layers emerged such as 802.11a, 802.11b, and 802.11g, which use more elaborate modulation mechanisms and achieve higher speeds.

In the 2.4 GHz band, IEEE 802.11 operates on 14 different physical radio channels as shown in Figure 12.12. Channels 12, 13, and 14 are not available in every country, most notably Japan, because a larger part of the 2.4 GHz band is available due to radio frequency licensing. The 14 channels are not completely separated, but have considerable overlaps. Channels 1, 6, and 11 are non-overlapping and current best practice for 802.11 networks says that those channels should be used whenever possible.

Several bit rates are supported by 802.11. Each 802.11 packet is sent with a fixed bit rate, but the bit rate may differ between packets. Transmitter–receiver pairs with a good physical connection may negotiate a higher bit rate when sending packets between each other. To be compatible with older versions of the standard, broadcast packets are sent with a lower bit rate than packets addressed to a specific host. This ensures that even older transceivers are able to participate in a network of 802.11 devices, but also allows newer devices to make use of the higher speed of newer transceivers.

12.4.3 MAC Layer

The purpose of the 802.11 MAC layer is to control access to the radio medium to ensure that transmissions from different nodes do not interfere with each other. The 802.11 MAC layer is based on a carrier sense multiple access with collision avoidance (CSMA/CA) scheme. Before sending a packet, each node listens for transmissions from other nodes. If a transmission from another node is heard, the node defers its own transmission for a random period to allow the transmitting node to complete its transmission.

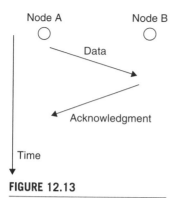

FIGURE 12.13

The IEEE 802.11 MAC layer uses acknowledgment packets that inform the sender that a packet was successfully received by the receiver.

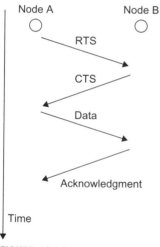

FIGURE 12.14

The RTS/CTS mechanism of the 802.11 MAC layer. To send a packet, a node first sends an RTS packet. If the access point grants the request, it sends a CTS packet and the node can send its packet.

The 802.11 MAC layer uses positive acknowledgments: a node that receives a packet from another node must reply with the transmission of an acknowledgment packet. The purpose of the acknowledgment packet is to let the sending node know that the packet was received. If the sending node does not receive the acknowledgment packet, the data packet is perceived to be lost. Even if the data packet was successfully received, but the acknowledgment packet was lost, the data packet is deemed lost. The acknowledgment process is shown in Figure 12.13.

In wireless communication, the so-called hidden node problem occurs when a node is in range of two other nodes, but the two other nodes are not in range of each other. Because of this, these nodes may unknowingly interfere with communication of the first node.

To avoid the hidden node problem, the 802.11 MAC layer offers a request to send/clear to send (RTS/CTS) mechanism. When a node is about to send a packet, it broadcasts a request to send (RTS) message. The RTS message contains the address of the node to which the data packet is to be sent. When the receiving node hears this message, it replies with a clear to send (CTS) message, if it currently is possible for the node to send its packet. If the node knows that another transmission is about to take place, the node does not send its CTS message. The sending node sends its data packet only after hearing a CTS message. This process is illustrated in Figure 12.14.

The RTS message serves a dual purpose. First, it is used as a request to the receiver to check if the medium is clear to use. Second, it tells all nearby nodes that a message transmission is about to take place, and they should not try to send any packet before this transmission has ended.

12.4.4 Low-power WiFi

The widespread adoption and the low cost of 802.11 equipment and modules make 802.11 a compelling choice for smart objects. Until recently, however, the power consumption of 802.11 components has been prohibitive. Because 802.11 was designed for laptops and general purpose PCs, where the power budget is less restrictive than for a smart object, existing 802.11 modules have required too much power to be usable in battery-powered smart objects.

Recently, however, a number of low-power 802.11 circuits have emerged that enable battery-operated 802.11 devices. The low-power consumption of these devices adds several years of operation to traditional AA cell batteries.

Low-power 802.11 devices not only improve the power consumption of data transmission and reception, but more important, they significantly improve the power consumption of the 802.11 device in sleep mode. Since smart objects spend most of their time in sleep mode, even a small improvement to the sleep mode power consumption means a longer battery life.

In addition to reducing the power consumption of existing modes of the 802.11 module, low-power 802.11 modules also add a low-power mode that is not available in existing 802.11 modules. This mode allows the device to switch most of its parts off, but still be able to quickly resume operation when needed.

Figure 12.15 compares the power consumption of a conventional 802.11 module and a low-power 802.11 module. Although there are significant savings regarding transmission and reception power, the most important reduction in power consumption is during sleep mode. Table 12.1 compares the power consumption of the standby and sleep modes of a conventional 802.11 transceiver and a low-power 802.11 transceiver. This comparison shows that the power consumption in sleep mode is one order of magnitude lower than that of a conventional 802.11 transceiver. In addition to the sleep node, the low-power 802.11 transceiver also has a standby mode where the transceiver uses one tenth of the power it does in sleep mode.

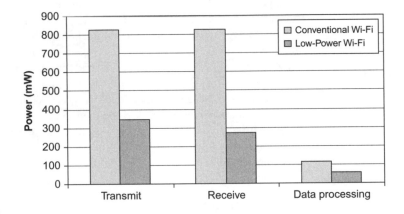

FIGURE 12.15

Comparison of power consumption in transmit, receive, and processing mode for conventional 802.11 and low-power 802.11.

Table 12.1 Power Consumption of Standby and Sleep Modes of a Conventional 802.11 Transceiver and of a Low-power 802.11 Transceiver

	Conventional 802.11 (mW)	Low-power 802.11 (mW)
Standby mode	N/A	0.018
Sleep mode	13	0.2

Note: Conventional 802.11 transceivers do not have a standby mode.

The difference between the sleep mode and the standby mode is how fast the transceiver is able to wake up. In standby mode, most of the transceiver is switched off. The only circuitry that is switched on is the wake-up module and the rest of the transceiver is switched off, consuming no power.

12.5 PLC

Smart objects do not necessarily need to communicate over radio. When a wired infrastructure is available, it can also be used for smart object communication. Even though a wireless system has many benefits regarding extendibility, range, and ease of deployment, a fixed wired infrastructure can be more economical. This is particularly true if the fixed infrastructure is already in place.

PLC is a way to send data over power lines. It has many uses ranging from long-range, high-speed broadband provisioning to homes and offices to home automation. For smart objects, PLC is an attractive communication technology because of the widespread availability of power lines. Moreover, because smart objects need power to function, PLC has the potential to provide the smart objects with power and communication.

Figure 12.16 shows how a home is connected with PLC over its power lines. Each device connected to the same power line can also use the power line for data communication. A home automation system can use the network to switch house lights on and off and to send a message to the home owner if the stove is turned on for an unusual amount of time. The TV can use the network to download movies from the computer.

With PLC, data are transported across the 50 or 60 Hz electrical distribution network. Because the electrical distribution network was not designed to carry high-frequency data signals, the electrical equipment may add significant amounts of noise to any data signals transported across the network. Thus PLC transceivers and protocols must be able to manage data loss.

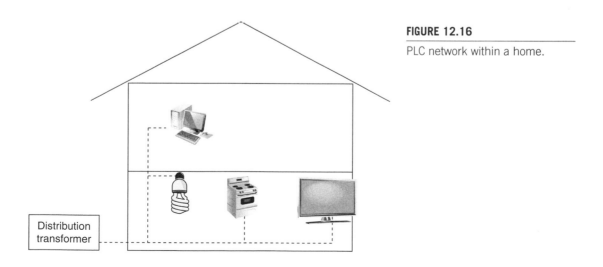

FIGURE 12.16

PLC network within a home.

PLC can be used to send data over long haul links such as for providing broadband to homes, or over shorter distances, such as within a home or an office building. Additionally, PLC has been used for automated meter reading of power meters in homes. PLC can also be used to control street lights and other large-scale electrical networks. PLC for short-range communication is designed only to communicate within one electrical domain such as a home or an office building, because the modulated data signal cannot traverse the electrical voltage transformers outside the electrical domain.

There are several specifications and standards for PLC, both for broadband connectivity and for smart object applications. Homeplug [234] is a specification for PLC specifically targeted to home environments. It provides a 15 Mbits/s data rate. The resulting transmission rate is similar to that of 10 Mbits/s 802.11 [234].

X10 [227] is an older home automation mechanism that uses power lines for communication. It was developed in 1975 and today there are many types of X10 devices available ranging from light bulbs and power outlets to automated vacuum cleaners and burglar alarms. X10 devices communicate with a transmission rate of 100–120 bits/s and a resulting data rate of 20 bits/s. Bits are sent during the zero-crossings of the current on the alternating current (AC) power lines. The X10 protocol consists of short commands that can switch devices on and off, dim lights, and do slightly more complex processing such as timer-based commands. Because of its low data rate, however, X10 is not a viable communication mechanism for general smart object networks.

12.5.1 Physical Layer

PLC uses the copper wire in the power lines as its physical medium. Because the copper wires are also used to carry a high-power AC signal, they are noisy for a physical medium for communication. To make matters worse, other devices, such as lamps, household appliances, computers, and TV sets, that are attached to the same power distribution network interfere in unpredictable ways.

Because the underlying physical medium is unreliable, the physical layer in PLC communication stacks must provide a substantial amount of reliability. Most PLC standards use combinations of error-robust modulation, strong error-detection mechanisms, and automatic packet loss detection and retransmission schemes.

Different PLC standards use different forms of modulation and carrier frequencies depending on the desirable data rate. Subsequently, data rates vary from hundreds of bits per second to millions of bits per second. Higher data rates typically imply shorter distances.

12.5.2 MAC Layer

Even though PLC is a wired technology, the PLC MAC layer has more in common with wireless MAC layers than with wired MAC layers. Wired MAC layers such as Ethernet often use CSMA/CD where packet collisions are detected and handled via a back-off mechanism. Such collision detection builds on the fact that Ethernet transceivers are able to listen to incoming signals while transmitting their own signal.

PLC transceivers are similar to wireless radio transceivers in that they cannot listen for incoming signals while transmitting their own signals. Therefore, PLC uses CSMA/CA, which is similar to IEEE 802.15.4 and IEEE 802.11. The RPL MAC layer also provides automatic repeat request (ARQ) mechanisms.

12.5.3 **Power Consumption**

PLC networks always have access to power because they are connected to a power source. Thus power consumption of the devices is not of the same concern as for wireless radio devices. Nevertheless, achieving low-power consumption is still important for several reasons. First, low-power consumption means low heat emissions. A PLC chip embedded in a device should not heat up the surrounding system. Second, and more important, many of the applications for PLC and smart object technology reduce power consumption of other devices. An example of this is Smart Grid applications, where smart object technology is used to lower the electricity consumption of homes, offices, and industrial settings. In such applications, it is important that the power consumed by the smart object devices is so low that the power savings incurred by the smart object technology significantly outweighs the power consumed by the smart object devices themselves.

Modern PLC chipsets have a power consumption on the same order of magnitude as wireless low-power radios. For example, the Watteco WPC PLC modem chip has an average power consumption of less than 10 mW, which is similar to 802.15.4 transceivers and lower than low-power 802.11 transceivers.

12.6 **CONCLUSIONS**

Smart objects communicate with each other, but the choice of communication technology varies between different applications and different environments. PLC is a viable communication technology for smart objects deployed in environments where power lines are present, such as homes, and where the smart objects can be directly connected to the power lines. For smart objects deployed in environments without a fixed infrastructure of network links or power lines, low-power radios are the most convenient technology.

Both radio communication and PLC suffer from communication channels of varying and unpredictable quality. Communication protocols running on top of such channels must be able to repair lost packets through retransmissions. Smart object communication can be divided into three patterns: one-to-one, one-to-many, and many-to-one. Communication protocols may employ a combination of patterns.

IEEE 802.15.4 is a low-power radio standard designed for low-data-rate applications such as smart objects. It has a maximum data rate of 250,000 bits/s and operates over a set of license-free radio bands in the 868 MHz, 918 MHz, and 2.4 GHz ranges. Packets have a maximum size of 127 bytes. Many emerging standards and specifications are built on top of 802.15.4 including WirelessHART, ISA100a, 6LoWPAN, and ZigBee. There are several implementations of 802.15.4 available, both in hardware and as a combination of hardware and software.

Low-power WiFi is emerging as a contender to IEEE 802.15.4 for smart objects. The advantage of WiFi is the abundant availability of infrastructure. Traditionally, power consumption has been an issue for WiFi, but with the latest low-power chipsets, the power consumption of the sleep mode is significantly reduced. By applying mechanisms for radio duty cycling, the power consumption of WiFi may soon be in low enough for smart object applications.

PLC allows data to be transported over a fixed power line infrastructure. It has several applications ranging from long haul broadband connectivity for homes to home automation. Many PLC standards exist, with data rates varying from a few bits per second to multi-megabit per second transmissions. For smart objects, PLC is a promising technology when smart objects are deployed in homes, offices, and other places where a fixed power line infrastructure is present.

uIP — A Lightweight IP Stack

13

IP was long believed to be too complex and heavyweight to be usable in smart objects. The micro-controllers used in smart objects are constrained regarding memory size and processing power. In this chapter, we dispel the myth that the IPs are heavyweight by studying the open source uIP IP stack, the first IP stack for smart objects.

To communicate using the IP, a device needs an IP stack. This is a software system that implements the IP protocols enabling IP communication. Every computer on the Internet runs an IP stack. They are part of all general purpose operating systems such as Microsoft Windows, Linux, and Mac OS. Smart objects are, however, severely memory-constrained and the IP stacks in general purpose computers require comparatively large amounts of memory. For example, the IP stack in Linux requires at least one megabyte of memory to maintain memory buffers for incoming and outgoing data. In contrast, as we discuss in Chapter 11, a smart object typically has only a few kilobytes of memory available.

At a high level, the activities of the IP stack are simple: it sends and receives packets from the communication device driver. Applications communicate with the IP stack either through the operating system or directly with the IP stack. When a packet arrives from the communication device driver, the IP stack parses the packet headers in the packet, extracts any application data from the packet, and sends the data up to the application. When an application wants to send data, the application sends its data to the IP stack. The IP stack puts the application data into a packet, creates the necessary packet headers, and sends the packet to the communication device driver for transmission over the communication device. In addition to responding to direct requests from the application and to incoming packets, the IP stack also deals with periodic protocol processing such as performing retransmissions.

The uIP TCP/IP stack is an implementation of the IP stack specifically designed to meet the strict memory requirements of smart objects and other networked embedded systems [64]. The first version of uIP was released in September 2001. It was released under a permissive open source license that allows the software to be used freely in commercial and non-commercial systems. Since its first release, the uIP stack has seen a significant industrial adoption, and the software is now used in systems and products such as oil pipeline monitoring systems, global container tracking systems, car engines, and pico satellites.

uIP is the principal IP communication component of the Contiki operating system. Although the uIP stack can be used as a stand-alone software package, and often is used this way, its continued development is done within Contiki.

Interconnecting Smart Objects with IP. DOI: 10.1016/B978-0-12-375165-2.00013-2

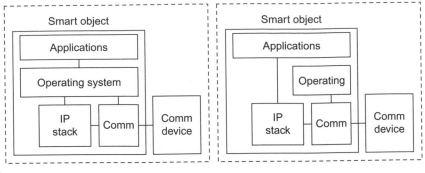

FIGURE 13.1

The IP stack takes care of the communication. Applications can either use the IP stack through the operating system (left) or directly interface with the IP stack (right). The IP stack sends and receives packets from the communication device driver.

uIP has very low memory requirements. In its default configuration, it requires only about one kilobyte of RAM and a few kilobytes of ROM. This includes the IP, ICMP, UDP, and TCP protocols. The specific code size depends on the processor on which the uIP is used. It is possible to reduce the RAM footprint further, but at the expense of standard compliancy. The smallest configuration requires only about 100 bytes of RAM, but such a configuration is not necessarily standard compliant. Also, the size of the memory footprint affects the achievable data throughput. For many applications, however, a low memory footprint is more important than a high throughput.

The uIP stack was developed about one year after the release of the lwIP stack [64]. The lwIP stack is designed for slightly larger systems than uIP and requires a larger amount of memory both for buffering and for storing the executable code. An lwIP installation typically requires about 40 kB of RAM and 20 kB of ROM. The benefit of the lwIP stack is the higher performance it achieves when compared to the uIP stack.

The uIP stack was originally designed to be used both with and without an operating system, as shown in Figure 13.1. Today, many operating systems use the uIP stack for IP communication. The most prominent example is the Contiki operating system, which is also the current development platform for uIP. FreeRTOS provides a choice of either the uIP stack or its larger cousin lwIP. TinyOS uses uIP for IPv4 communication, but recently has included a stand-alone implementation for IPv6.

The uIP stack implements the network and transport layer protocols of the IP protocol family: IP, ICMP, UDP, and TCP. It was the first IP stack for embedded systems to fully implement the TCP protocol in a way that makes it fully compatible with the standards.

The first versions of the uIP stack featured only IPv4 communication, but in 2008 Cisco Systems extended uIP with IPv6 capabilities. It was developed by Julien Abeillé and Mathilde Durvy. The uIPv6 stack was the first stack to comply with all the IPv6 requirements, which enabled it to use the IPv6 Ready logo, as shown in Figure 13.2 [73]. The uIPv6 extensions were also released as open source software and added to the Contiki operating system, making it widely available.

uIP uses three methods to reduce code size and memory usage: an event-driven programming interface, an intentionally simple buffer management scheme, and a memory-efficient TCP implementation. We return to these mechanisms after looking at how uIP processes incoming and outgoing packets.

13.1 PRINCIPLES OF OPERATION

The principle of operation for the uIP stack is simple, as shown in Figure 13.3. The uIP stack does three things: it processes packets that arrive from the communication device driver, it processes requests from the application, and it does periodic processing. The uIP forwarding module is responsible for relaying traffic to other nodes. The forwarding module queries a routing protocol module to find out to where packets should be relayed.

Input processing starts when the communication device driver has received a packet. The driver calls the input processing function of uIP, which processes the headers of the incoming packet, determines if the packet contains application data, and if so passes the data to the application. The application may produce a reply to the incoming data, which then is handled by the output processing part of uIP.

FIGURE 13.2

uIP was the first IPv6 stack for smart objects to be certified under the IPv6 Ready program. Because it is certified as IPv6 Ready, it may use the IPv6 Ready logo.

Output processing is simple. Output processing occurs after the application has been called from uIP, and only when the application has produced data for the uIP stack to send. The output processing code adds protocol headers to the packet that is to be sent and hands the packet over to the communication device for transmission.

Periodic processing is done to perform timer-based actions such as retransmissions. The periodic processing mechanisms in uIP are intentionally simple. The uIP periodic processing function is invoked regularly to check if there are any retransmissions needed. If so, it produces the packet to be retransmitted and gives it to the communication device driver which sends it out.

Forwarding and routing are done separately. Forwarding is the process of resending a received packet to a neighbor, whereas routing is the process of determining to which neighbors packets should be forwarded. The uIP forwarding module maintains a table of destinations and addresses of the next-hop neighbor. Routing protocols, which typically are implemented on top of either UDP or TCP, populate the forwarding table based on data received from the routing protocol.

13.1.1 Input Processing

When the communication device driver receives a packet from the network, it calls the uIP input processing function to deliver the packet to uIP. The uIP input processing code parses the packet headers and determines if the application should be called. If so, uIP delivers the application data to the application.

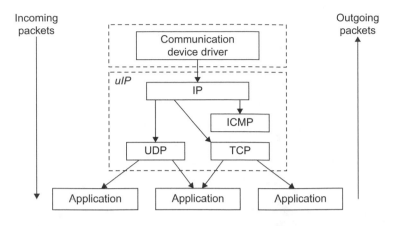

FIGURE 13.3

The principle of operation for uIP. Incoming packets are passed to uIP from the communication device driver. After uIP has finished processing the data, if any, the packet is passed to the corresponding application. Outgoing data pass through uIP, which adds protocol headers, before the packet is passed to the communication device driver for transmission.

The uIP input processing starts at the IP header. The flow of the input processing functionality is shown in Figure 13.4. Packet headers are parsed from top to bottom, starting with the IP header. The uIP input processing code first checks the first byte of the IP header to make sure that the incoming packet is an IP packet and that the version of the IP protocol matches one that uIP can handle. uIP can currently handle both IPv4 and IPv6 data, but can only handle one of them at a time.

After making sure that the packet has the right IP version header, uIP checks the validity of the IP header. It checks the length that is reported in the IP header with the length of the packet it received from the underlying layer. If the length in the IP header is longer than the packet in the buffer, the packet is deemed to be malformed and is discarded. If the length of the packet in the buffer is longer than reported in the IP header, the packet is assumed to be well formed, but with garbage data in the end, and uIP continues to process the packet anyway. For IPv4, the fragment flag of the IPv4 header is checked. If the packet is an IP fragment, it is copied into the defragmentation buffer. If the fragment buffer contains a full IP packet because of the incoming fragment, the reassembled IP packet is seen as the incoming IP packet and the input processing continues. For IPv6, IP fragment reassembly is performed as part of the extension header processing.

Next, the source and destination addresses of the packet are inspected. Packets with an illegal IP source address are dropped. Examples are packets where the source address is a broadcast or multicast address. Packets with a destination IP address that does not match any of the IP addresses of the node are either discarded or delivered to the uIP packet-forwarding module. The uIP packet-forwarding module may choose to forward the packets to a next-hop neighbor, depending on the destination IP address.

Packets with a destination IP address that matches one of the IP addresses of the node are processed further. Here, the processing code differs between IPv4 and IPv6. For IPv4, the IP header checksum is computed to make sure that it matches. For IPv6, no header checksum is defined. For IPv6 packets, uIP checks the packet for the existence of any extension headers and processes them.

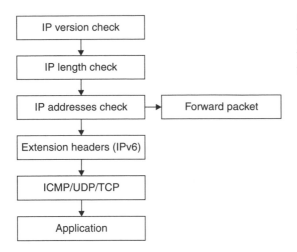

FIGURE 13.4

Input processing in uIP. All incoming packets pass through the IP and transport layers before reaching the application.

If uIP found errors in the IPv6 extension headers, an ICMPv6 error message is generated and sent back to the sender.

When uIP has verified that the IP header is correct, that the length of the packet is correct, and that the destination address matches the address of the node, the packet is given to the correct transport layer protocol. uIP supports three such protocols: ICMP, UDP, and TCP. ICMP is, strictly speaking, not a transport layer protocol but it is implemented as such in uIP.

The packet is processed differently depending on its upper layer protocol. TCP is the most complex of the protocols that uIP implements. UDP processing is very simple. ICMP processing is very simple for IPv4 but slightly more complex for IPv6.

13.1.1.1 ICMP Input Processing

For IPv4, the ICMP processing consists of a single piece of functionality — to respond to incoming ICMP echo messages. When a node receives an ICMP echo message, it responds by sending an ICMP echo reply. The reply message contains a copy of the data in the ICMP echo message. ICMP echo messages are sent by the "ping" program present in most general purpose operating systems. The ping utility sends ICMP echo messages to check if a particular IP node is alive and for measuring the round-trip time to the node. When the ping program receives an ICMP echo reply that matches the ICMP echo message it previously sent, the program prints out the round-trip time to the screen.

ICMP processing for IPv6 is more complex than IPv4 because ICMP has a more significant role in IPv6 than in IPv4. In addition to the echo functionality, ICMP in IPv6 is used for neighbor discovery (ND), router discovery, duplicate address detection, and other mechanisms. uIP supports ICMP neighbor solicitation messages, neighbor advertisement messages, router solicitation messages, and router advertisement messages. In IPv6, ICMP neighbor solicitation messages are also used to perform duplicate address detection, which is supported by uIP.

13.1.1.2 UDP Input Processing

UDP input processing in uIP is simple. The input processing code first recalculates the UDP checksum to make sure that the packet is valid. Then, it uses the UDP port numbers in the packet to find the application to which the packet data should be delivered. uIP maintains a list of applications and what UDP port numbers they use. An application may specify the remote end point by providing the IP address and UDP port number of the remote peer, or it could leave them blank. Applications with blank remote IP address and UDP port numbers receive all packets that arrive for the application's UDP port. Otherwise, only packets from the specific IP address and UDP port number are delivered to the application.

13.1.1.3 TCP Input Processing

The most complex protocol implementation in uIP is TCP. Still, the implementation is significantly simpler than the TCP implementations in other IP stacks such as the BSD UNIX stack [172]. This occurs because the uIP TCP performs only the necessary mechanisms needed for standards compliance and host-to-host interoperability. Because uIP is optimized for a small memory footprint and not for high performance, the uIP TCP implementation refrains from implementing a number of performance-optimizing mechanisms that are present in other IP stacks. We return to this later in the chapter in Section 13.4.2.

TCP processing begins by validating the TCP checksum. The TCP checksum is computed over the TCP header, the application data, and parts of the IP header. After validating the checksum, the TCP port numbers of the packet are checked against the list of active TCP connections. If the packet does not match any of the current connections, uIP checks the list of listening TCP ports, but only if the incoming packet has the TCP SYN flag set. If the packet is not for an active connection or is not a TCP SYN packet for a listening port, uIP sends a TCP RST packet to the IP address that sent the packet.

If the incoming packet was a TCP SYN packet for a listening connection, uIP creates a new entry in the table of active TCP connections and fills in the correct TCP sequence number from the incoming TCP SYN packet. If the TCP SYN packet contains a TCP maximum segment size (MSS) option, uIP remembers the MSS it can send over this connection. Next, uIP produces a TCP SYN packet with the ACK flag set and sends it back to the remote peer.

If the incoming packet was destined for an active connection, uIP first ensures that the TCP sequence number of the incoming segment is what uIP expects. If the sequence number is higher than expected, it indicates that a packet has been lost. If so, uIP discards the packet, knowing that the remote end will retransmit the packet some time later. Although it would be possible for uIP to buffer the incoming packet so that it would be immediately available once the missing packet has been retransmitted, this would require buffer memory unavailable in the memory-constrained systems for which uIP is designed.

After verifying the TCP sequence number, uIP performs a round-trip time (RTT) estimation mechanism. The purpose of the RTT estimation is for uIP to have a suitable value for the retransmission timer. For a TCP connection with a long RTT, the retransmission timer must be set to a high value, and conversely, a TCP connection with a short RTT requires a low value on the retransmission timer. uIP performs RTT estimation by keeping a counter for each TCP connection. The counter is incremented as part of the periodic uIP processing. When a TCP packet arrives, uIP uses the value of the counter as an estimate for the RTT of the packet. An averaging filter is used to provide a smoothed RTT estimate for the TCP connection [134].

Next, uIP takes different actions depending on the state of the TCP connection. If the TCP connection is established, the application is invoked and passes the application data present in the incoming

TCP packet. The application consumes the data and may produce a reply and uIP sends it back to the remote peer. If the TCP connection for which the incoming packet is destined is in a state where it is about to be opened or closed, the TCP connection switches states as described in the TCP specification [204].

When a TCP connection is opened or closed, uIP informs the application of the event by calling it. Depending on the state of the TCP connection, the application may choose to send data in response to the event. The packet then makes its way through the output processing code of uIP.

13.1.2 Output Processing

Output processing in uIP is simpler than input processing. Output processing starts when uIP calls the application. When called by uIP, the application can choose to produce a packet. uIP adds the necessary packet headers and passes the packet, with headers, to the communication device driver for transmission. The structure of the uIP output processing is shown in Figure 13.5.

For TCP connections, an application cannot send data unsolicited, but must wait for uIP to call the application. uIP calls the application not only when new data arrive on the connection, but also as part of the periodic processing. This gives the application the opportunity to send data even when no data are arriving on the connection. Applications that use UDP may choose to send data at any time and do not need to wait for uIP to call them.

TCP output processing starts when the application has been called either as part of the input processing or during periodic processing. If called as part of the input processing, uIP either delivers a packet to the application or informs the application that a connection is opened or closed. In either case, the application may want to send data to the remote host. If so, uIP updates the connection state for the TCP connection, adds the necessary headers to the data, computes the necessary checksums, and sends the packet. The state of the connection needs to be updated because the application data will increase the TCP sequence number for the connection. The application may also want to close or abort the connection, and uIP will respond accordingly.

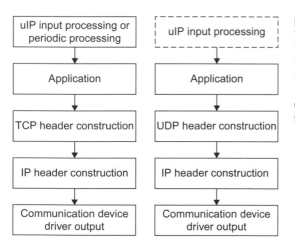

FIGURE 13.5

uIP output processing is simpler than input processing. For TCP connections (left), all output processing starts with uIP calling the application. For UDP connections (right), applications may send UDP data directly but can also send data when called from the uIP input processing code.

UDP output processing may start either when uIP has called an application because of incoming data, or because the application calls uIP directly. uIP adds the UDP header to the application data, with the necessary UDP port numbers, and computes the UDP checksum before passing the packet to the IP layer to add the IP header. The IP layer adds its header and computes the IP checksum. The packet is then sent by the communication device driver.

13.1.3 Periodic Processing

The purpose of the uIP periodic processing is to update timer-based counters, perform retransmissions, and remove connections that have timed out. Periodic processing is typically invoked once or twice every second, depending on the configuration of the system in which uIP runs.

Periodic processing starts with updating the status of the IP fragment reassembly buffer. If a packet is waiting to be reassembled, the periodic code updates the counter that keeps track of the age of the packet. If the packet is older than 30 seconds, the packet is removed from the reassembly buffer.

Next, the periodic processing code goes through every active TCP connection to check if there are any packets that should be retransmitted. If there is a pending retransmission, and if the retransmission includes application data, uIP calls the application to reproduce the data it previously produced for the original transmission of the packet. The application, or an application library provided by uIP, may have buffered the packet in an external memory buffer in preparation for a retransmission, in which case the application can copy the buffered packet back to uIP. To save memory, however, the application may have chosen not to buffer the packet, but to regenerate it instead. The contents of the packet may, for example, have originated in a ROM buffer from which it can be quickly copied into the retransmission packet, or the contents of the packet are easily regenerated. In either case, once the application has produced its packet, uIP constructs the necessary headers and sends out the retransmission. uIP also updates the retransmission timer by doubling its value, the so-called exponential back-off procedure of TCP.

The periodic TCP code also checks for connections that should be timed out. Connections that have retransmitted too many packets without receiving an acknowledgment are examples of this. Such connections are discarded by uIP.

13.1.4 Packet Forwarding

Packet forwarding is done when uIP receives a packet that has a destination IP address that does not match any of the IP addresses of the node. A node typically has multiple addresses: one or more unicast addresses and at least one broadcast or multicast address. Packets that do not match the addresses should be forwarded to a neighboring node, either because the address matches that of the neighbor or because the neighbor has a route to the destination address.

Packet forwarding occurs only when uIP has been configured to be a router. The packet forwarding mechanism is then invoked as part of the output processing.

The packet forwarding mechanism is modular and does not specify any particular routing mechanism to be used. Rather, a routing mechanism will register itself with the forwarding module upon startup. For every packet, the forwarding mechanism asks the routing module to look up the destination IP address and return the address to the next-hop neighbor. The routing module may implement this any way it wants by using a table of destination addresses, a table of network prefixes, a hash table of addresses, a cache of the recently used routes, or any other way it finds suitable. The routing protocol may perform a route discovery for each address not found in its cache.

By separating packet forwarding and packet routing, uIP can adapt a wide range of requirements such as routing performance and memory requirements, as well as take advantage of future development in routing protocols. A system with strict memory requirements and low routing performance requirements may use a cache configuration that prompts frequent network route discoveries, whereas a system with strict requirements on routing performance but lax memory requirements may choose a larger cache setting.

13.2 uIP MEMORY BUFFER MANAGEMENT

Buffer management is a critical operation in any protocol stack. Incoming and outgoing data packets are buffered in memory and the buffer management system ensures that there is enough memory available for the data packets. In a general purpose protocol stack, poor buffer management strategy can lead to suboptimal performance. In a smart object, where the memory requirements are exceptionally strict, buffer management has a critical function in ensuring that the protocol stack is able to function even when memory is scarce.

To provide high throughput, traditional IP stacks use buffer management strategies of varying complexity [172]. Buffers need to be allocated and deallocated quickly to keep up with the large amounts of data coming from the network and sent by applications. For smart objects, where data rates typically are much lower than for general purpose computers, the buffer management strategy does not need to be optimized for high throughput. Instead, memory is a scarce resource so the buffer management mechanism must work efficiently with small amounts of memory.

The buffer management strategy of uIP is intentionally simple. To keep memory size and code complexity down, all packets in uIP are kept in a single memory buffer. Incoming packets are copied to this buffer when the communication device driver has received them. Outgoing packets are created directly into the same buffer.

Using a single memory buffer has several advantages. First, there is no need for any complex buffer management mechanisms to be implemented. Such mechanisms require code space and buffer memory, both of which are at a premium in a memory-constrained system. Second, the protocol implementations become simpler when they do not need to deal with multiple buffers. Third, because the buffer is at a single place in memory and does not move, the C compiler is often able to make better optimizations at the machine code level, which leads to more efficient use of the scarce code memory.

The packet buffer is large enough to contain one packet of maximum size. When a packet arrives from the network, the device driver places it in the global buffer and calls the uIP input processing code. If the packet contains application data, uIP calls the corresponding application with the application data in the packet buffer. Because the data in the buffer will be overwritten by the next incoming packet, the application will either have to act immediately on the data or copy the data into a secondary buffer for later processing. The packet buffer will not be overwritten by new packets before the application has finished processing the data.

To ensure that the packet buffer is not overwritten while uIP is processing a packet, uIP does not allow the communication device driver to write directly into the buffer, except when uIP explicitly asks it to do so. If a packet arrives when uIP is processing data in the buffer, the packet is queued either in the hardware of the communication device or by the communication device driver. Most communication devices have a hardware-implemented buffer memory in which they store incoming packets as they arrive.

The size of the packet buffer is configurable at compile time. The total amount of memory usage for uIP depends on the applications of the particular system in which the implementations are to be run. The memory configuration determines both the amount of traffic the system should be able to handle and the maximum amount of simultaneous connections. A system sending and receiving large amounts of data to multiple simultaneous clients typically is configured to use more memory than a system that occasionally sends a few bytes. It is possible to run the uIP with as little as 100 bytes of RAM, but such a configuration provides extremely low throughput and only allows a small number of simultaneous connections.

13.3 uIP APPLICATION PROGRAM INTERFACE

The Application Program Interface (API) defines the way the application program interacts with the TCP/IP stack. The most common API for IP stacks is the BSD socket API. The BSD socket API is used in most UNIX systems and has heavily influenced the Microsoft Windows WinSock API. The socket API is, however, designed around a multi-threaded programming model. This model incurs a memory overhead, which is not ideal for smart objects and their constrained memory.

Instead of the multi-threaded socket API, uIP provides an event-driven API. Having an event-driven API has several advantages in the context of smart objects. First, event-driven mechanisms have a lower memory overhead than multi-threaded mechanisms. Second, the event-driven API does not need to use additional buffers between the uIP stack and the application, something that a traditional BSD socket API requires. This further reduces the memory requirements. Third, the event-driven API has a higher execution time efficiency than a multi-threaded API, which is beneficial because of the low processor speeds used in smart objects. Because applications are able to act immediately on incoming data and connection requests, low response times can be achieved even in low-end systems.

The event-driven API is used primarily for TCP connections, even though UDP-based applications can also use it. The use of an event-driven API for TCP has later been used by other IP stacks for smart objects [1].

Although the event-driven API works well for many applications, there are applications that benefit from a sequential API. Therefore, uIP optionally provides a sequential BSD socket-like API based on protothreads. The sequential API is called protosockets and allows programs to be written in a top-down fashion. The protosockets' API also provides buffers for retransmissions, relieving the programmer of the potential burden of regenerating data for retransmission at the price of higher memory requirements.

13.3.1 The Event-driven API

The event-driven uIP API uses an event-driven interface where the application is invoked in response to events that occur on TCP connections. uIP calls applications when data are received, when data have been successfully delivered to the other end of the connection, when a new connection has been set up, or when data have to be retransmitted. The application is also periodically polled for new data.

Applications provide a callback function to uIP. uIP calls the callback function for every event that occurs on a TCP connection. When invoked, the callback function must return quickly to uIP, and if the callback function blocks, uIP cannot respond to incoming packets.

To reduce the memory size, uIP requires applications to participate in the process of retransmitting. IP stacks for general purpose computers or high-end servers buffer the transmitted data in memory until the data are known to be successfully delivered to the remote end of the connection. If the data need to be retransmitted, the stack takes care of the retransmission without notifying the application. With this approach, the data have to be buffered in memory while waiting for an acknowledgment even if the application might be able to quickly regenerate the data if a retransmission has to be made.

When the application callback function is invoked, uIP passes it a number of flags that tell the application why it was invoked. Each event has a corresponding test function used to distinguish between different events. The functions evaluate to either zero or non-zero, depending on what event has occurred. Some events happen in conjunction with each other and the application must test for the existence of each such event separately. For example, new data can arrive at the same time as data are acknowledged.

Applications are informed by the reception of data using a reception event. If the uIP test function uip_newdata() is non-zero, the remote host of the connection has sent new data. The application data are placed in the packet buffer. After the application invocation, the data are not retained by uIP, but are overwritten after the application function returns, and the application has to either act directly on the incoming data or copy the incoming data into a buffer for later processing.

Sending data is done during an application invocation by copying the data into the packet buffer before returning to uIP. uIP adjusts the length of the data sent by the application according to the available buffer space and the current TCP window advertised by the receiver. The amount of buffer space is dictated by the memory configuration and by the current MSS used over the connection. Applications can send only one packet of data at a time and must wait for the data to be successfully acknowledged by the remote peer before sending the next packet.

When a connection is idle, uIP invokes the application function as part of the uIP periodic processing with the poll flag set. The application tests for the poll flag to check if it was invoked due to periodic processing.

Polling has two purposes. The first is to let the application periodically know that a connection is idle, which allows the application to close connections that have been idle for too long. The other purpose is to let the application send new data that have been produced. The application can only send data when invoked by uIP, therefore polling is the only way to send data on an otherwise idle connection.

13.3.1.1 Retransmitting Data

Retransmissions are driven by the periodic TCP timer. Every time the periodic timer is invoked, the retransmission timer for each connection is decremented. If the timer reaches zero, a retransmission should be made. As uIP does not keep track of packet contents after they have been sent by the device driver, uIP requires that the application takes an active part in performing the retransmission. When uIP decides that a segment should be retransmitted, the application function is called with the retransmission flag set, indicating that a retransmission is required.

The application checks the retransmission flag and produces the same data that were previously sent. From the application's standpoint, performing a retransmission is no different from how the data were originally sent. Therefore, the application can be written in such a way that the same code is used both for sending and retransmitting data. Even though the actual retransmission operation is carried out by the application, it is the responsibility of the stack to know when the retransmission should be made. Thus the complexity of the application does not necessarily increase because it takes an active part in retransmitting.

13.3.1.2 Closing Connections
The application closes the current connection by calling the uIP TCP close function during an application invocation. This causes the connection to be cleanly closed. To indicate a fatal error, the application might want to abort the connection and does so by calling the uIP TCP abort function.

If the connection has been closed by the remote end, the application is invoked with the closed flag set. The application may then do any necessary cleanups, such as freeing memory that was allocated as part of the TCP connection.

13.3.1.3 Reporting Errors
There are two fatal errors that can happen to a connection: the connection is aborted by the remote host, or the connection retransmitted the last data too many times and has been aborted. uIP reports this by invoking the application function with either the aborted or the timed out flag set. The application checks for the existence of these flags to find out if a connection was aborted or timed out.

13.3.1.4 Listening Ports
uIP maintains a list of listening TCP ports. A new port is opened for listening with the uip_listen() function. When a connection request arrives on a listening port, uIP creates a new connection and calls the application function. The test function uip_connected() is true if the application was invoked because a new connection was created.

The application can check the lport field in the uip_conn structure to check to which port the new connection was connected.

13.3.1.5 Opening Connections
New connections can be opened from within uIP by the function uip_connect(). This function allocates a new connection and sets a flag in the connection state that opens a TCP connection to the specified IP address and port the next time the connection is polled by uIP. The uip_connect() function returns a pointer to the uip_conn structure for the new connection. If there are no free connection slots, the function returns NULL.

The function uip_ipaddr() may be used to pack an IP address into the two-element, 16-bit array used by uIP to represent IP addresses.

13.4 uIP PROTOCOL IMPLEMENTATIONS

To optimize memory and code space, the protocol implementations in uIP implement only the necessary mechanisms for compliance with the standards and interoperability. Many of the mechanisms in the TCP/IP protocol suite were designed to improve protocol performance. In general, uIP does not implement such mechanisms that provide a better performance at the expense of higher memory requirements.

13.4.1 **IP Fragment Reassembly**

IP fragment reassembly is implemented using a separate buffer that holds the packet to be reassembled. An incoming fragment is copied into the right place in the buffer and a bit map is used to keep track of which fragments have been received. Because the first byte of an IP fragment is aligned on an 8-byte boundary, the bit map requires a small amount of memory. When all fragments have been reassembled, the resulting IP packet is passed to the transport layer. If all fragments have not been received within a specified time frame, the packet is dropped.

uIP maintains a single buffer for holding packets to be reassembled. The buffer is separate from the packet buffer used by the test of uIP to avoid being overwritten by other packets. Because uIP only maintains a single buffer for reassembling fragments, uIP does not support simultaneous reassembly of more than one packet. The reason for this design decision is that IP fragments are relatively uncommon in today's networks.

13.4.2 **TCP**

The TCP implementation in uIP is designed to be as simple as possible without removing any of the required TCP mechanisms. There are several mechanisms in TCP intended to provide a high throughput. Many of these mechanisms are not needed in a system that has only small amounts of data to be sent. uIP therefore makes the trade-off that memory efficiency is more important than high data throughput. If high data throughput is required, then uIP is not a suitable choice.

The TCP implementation in uIP is driven by incoming packets and the periodic processing. Incoming packets are parsed by TCP and if the packet contains data to be delivered to the application, the application is invoked by the application function call. If the incoming packet acknowledges previously sent data, the connection state is updated and the application is informed, allowing it to send out new data.

TCP allows a connection to listen for incoming connection requests. In uIP, a listening connection is identified by the 16-bit port number and incoming connection requests are checked against the list of listening connections. This list of listening connections is dynamic and can be altered by the applications in the system.

13.4.2.1 *Sliding Window*

Most TCP implementations use a sliding window mechanism when sending data. Multiple data segments are sent in succession without waiting for an acknowledgment for each segment. This is intended to provide a high throughput because the entire network pipe between the sender and the receiver can be filled with packets without waiting for the receiver to acknowledge the reception of the packets.

An implementation of the sliding window mechanism uses a significant amount of 32-bit additions and subtractions because of the 32-bit sequence numbers used by TCP. Because 32-bit arithmetic is expensive regarding code size on many 8- and 16-bit microcontrollers, uIP does not implement the sliding window mechanism. Also, uIP does not buffer sent packets and a sliding window implementation that does not buffer sent packets will have to be supported by a complex application layer. Instead, uIP allows only a single TCP segment per connection to be unacknowledged at any given time.

It is important to note that even though most TCP implementations use the sliding window algorithm, it is not required by TCP specifications. Removing the sliding window mechanism does not affect interoperability or standards compliance in any way.

13.4.2.2 Retransmissions and RTT Estimation

Retransmissions are driven by the periodic TCP timer. Every time the periodic timer is invoked, the retransmission timer for each connection is decremented. If the timer reaches zero, a retransmission should be made.

To find a suitable value for the retransmission time-out, TCP continuously estimates the current RTT of every active connection. The RTT estimation in uIP is implemented using TCP's periodic timer. Each time the periodic timer fires, it increments a counter for each connection that has unacknowledged data in the network. When an acknowledgment is received, the current value of the counter is used as a sample of the RTT. This sample is used together with Van Jacobson's standard TCP RTT estimation function to calculate an estimate of the RTT [134]. The Karn and Partridge algorithm is used to ensure that retransmissions do not skew the estimates [143].

13.4.2.3 Flow Control

The purpose of the TCP flow control mechanisms is to allow communication between hosts with wildly varying memory dimensions. In each TCP segment, the sender of the segment indicates its available buffer space. A TCP sender must not send more data than the buffer space indicated by the receiver.

In uIP, the application cannot send more data than the receiving host can buffer, and an application cannot send more data than the amount of bytes it is allowed to send by the receiving host. If the remote host cannot accept any data at all, the stack initiates the zero-window probing mechanism.

13.4.2.4 Congestion Control

The congestion control mechanisms limit the number of simultaneous TCP segments in the network. From the outset, the algorithms used for congestion control are designed to be simple to implement and their implementation requires only a few lines of code [134].

Since uIP only handles one in-flight TCP segment per connection, the amount of simultaneous segments cannot be further limited, thus the TCP congestion control mechanisms are not needed.

13.4.2.5 Urgent Data

TCP's urgent data mechanism provides an application-to-application notification mechanism, which can be used by an application to mark parts of the data stream as more urgent than the normal stream. It is up to the receiving application to interpret the meaning of the urgent data.

In many TCP implementations, including the BSD implementation, the urgent data feature increases the complexity of the implementation because it requires an asynchronous notification mechanism in an otherwise synchronous API. As uIP already uses an asynchronous event-based API, the implementation of the urgent data feature does not lead to increased complexity.

13.4.3 Checksum Calculations

The TCP and IP protocols implement a checksum that covers the data and header portions of the TCP and IP packets. Since the calculation of this checksum is made over all bytes in every packet sent and received, it is important that the function that calculates the checksum is efficient. Most often, this means that the checksum calculation must be fine-tuned for the particular architecture on which the uIP stack runs.

Table 13.1 Memory Footprint of the Individual Functions
in the uIPv6 Stack

Function	ROM	RAM
IPv6 ND input/output	4800	20
IPv6 ND structures	2128	238
IPv6 network interface management	1348	118
IPv6 address autoconfiguration	372	16
IPv6 input processing	1434	44
Packet buffer	0	1296
UDP	1345	0
TCP	4192	240
Total	**15,619**	**1972**

*Note: The data are given in bytes. As a comparison, the memory footprint
IP stack in a modern general purpose operating system is several
hundreds of thousands of bytes.*

While uIP includes a generic checksum function, it is also open to an architecture-specific implementation of the two functions uip_ipchksum() and uip_tcpchksum(). The checksum calculations in those functions can be written in highly optimized assembler rather than generic C code.

13.5 MEMORY FOOTPRINT

The memory footprint of uIP is very small compared to existing IP stacks for general purpose computers. The IP stack in Linux, for example, requires several hundred thousand bytes of memory. For the memory-constrained microcontrollers used in smart objects, such an IP stack does not fit.

The code footprint of uIP is a few kilobytes and the memory footprint is less than 2 kB. The code footprint is slightly higher for IPv6 than for IPv4. Table 13.1 shows the breakdown in code and memory footprint for the different functions in uIPv6. The footprint is measured for the Atmel ATmega128 processor and the code is compiled with the gcc C compiler [73].

As shown in Table 13.1 about half of the code footprint is used by the IPv6 and the rest by TCP and UDP. For IPv6, the ND is the largest part, whereas the IPv6 input processing is small.

13.6 CONCLUSIONS

A common belief has been that the IP stack is too complex to efficiently implement for the microcontrollers used in smart objects. This belief has been shown to be false by several memory-efficient implementations of the IP stack. In this chapter, we investigated the widely used open source uIP stack, the first IP stack for smart objects, to see how it achieves its low code and memory footprint. uIP was first released in 2001. In 2008, uIP was the first IP stack for smart objects to be certified under the IPv6 Ready program.

uIP implements the most important protocols in the IP stack: IP, ICMP, UDP, and TCP. It contains both an IPv4 and an IPv6 implementation. Application layer protocols such as HTTP and SNMP are implemented on top of uIP.

The code and memory footprint of uIP is very small compared to that of IP stacks for general purpose operating systems. uIP requires only a few kilobytes of code to implement a full IPv6 stack. To achieve such a small footprint, the design of uIP is intentionally simple. Packets are processed in sequence, the buffer management mechanism is simple, and the application API is event-driven. The uIP stack is not unique in its efficient memory. The mechanisms from uIP have been adopted by several other IP stacks for smart objects.

Standardization

14

14.1 INTRODUCTION

Standardization is in many ways synonymous with openness and interoperability. It is also because IP has always been an open standard with no royalties that a plethora of new applications emerged in the past few decades while ensuring interoperability between devices from different manufacturers. Standardization is not used just to produce documents that define protocol specifications, but rather to ensure that implementers will be able to develop systems that smoothly interoperate.

Conversely, the lack of standardization has many undesirable effects. Over the past 15 years, a plethora of proprietary technologies and architectures have been developed to address the requirements of Low-power and Lossy Networks (LLNs) for highly specific environments. At first such an approach may satisfy the specific requirements for that application and is supposedly "optimized" for that environment, but proprietary solutions suffer from severe limitations:

- Limited evolution and innovation: There are very few examples of proprietary solutions that have survived. This means that proprietary solutions are tied to a particular organization, thus limiting the chances for other organizations and individuals to contribute new innovative ideas. The evolution of the solution is driven by the business priorities of that organization, not the willingness to design innovative applications and solutions.
- Absence of interoperability: More important is the lack of interoperability with non-proprietary solutions. Although the proprietary solution may not require interoperability with the rest of the world at first, such a situation rarely lasts for a long period of time and it quickly becomes necessary to connect that proprietary "island" with other standardized networks. As discussed in length in Part I, connecting the two "worlds" by a gateway is not only technically challenging but usually an expensive and difficult "solution" to manage. This also means that the overall architecture is now based on the least common denominator, thus reinforcing the lack of flexibility and evolution.

The world of "smart objects" (sometimes also called "sensor networks") is not an exception and has been remarkably driven by proprietary solutions until a few years ago. Dozens of proprietary solutions have been developed. The lack of standardization explains the limited scope of deployment in light of the unlimited number of opportunities.

The use of an open standard such as IP for smart objects is crucial and a *must* to build a scalable architecture for the next Internet and other private IP networks. IP has largely demonstrated its flexibility and ability to evolve to support new applications.

Interconnecting Smart Objects with IP. DOI: 10.1016/B978-0-12-375165-2.00014-4

It must be noted that although IP is used in the Internet, its use is not limited to the Internet and has been deployed in networks with no relation to the Internet. The standardization body in charge of IP is the Internet Engineering Task Force (IETF).

14.2 THE IETF

The IETF is the international open standardization body in charge of specifying the IP protocol suite. It was formed in 1986 and is exclusively made of individuals, not companies. The IETF motto (quote by David Clark in 1992) "We reject kings, presidents and voting. We believe in rough consensus and running code" has been driving the IETF and has led to the specification of a number of IP-based protocols over the past two decades.

The first IETF meeting took place in January 1986 in San Diego, California, with 21 attendees. The IETF now meets three times a year with several thousands of attendees from all continents (see Figure 14.1).

14.2.1 The IETF Mission

The mission of the IETF, as referenced in [10] is "to produce high quality, relevant technical and engineering documents that influence the way people design, use, and manage the Internet in such a way as to make the Internet work better."

Documents are produced in the form of RFCs (request for comments) by Working Groups (see the section IETF Organization for more details on the IETF process).

The number of published RFCs has significantly grown over the past 20 years as shown in Figure 14.2. The IETF is governed by these fundamental principles:

- Open process: Anyone is free to participate in the IETF with no conditions (e.g., no fees) via Working Group mailing lists and IETF meetings organized three times a year.
- Technical competence: The IETF only works on technical issues in which it has the required competence and is willing to receive input from any technically competent sources.

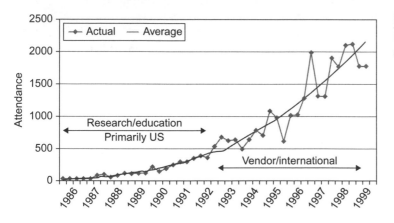

FIGURE 14.1

Evolution of the IETF attendance over the past 20 years.

- Volunteer core: Each participant and leader volunteers in the IETF to make the Internet better.
- Rough consensus and running code: This is one of the fundamental rules of operation of the IETF. Standards are produced based on the combined engineering judgment of its participants and real-life experience of implementations. There is no formal voting or counting and no requirement of unanimity. This helps when there is no unanimity but still a rough consensus determined by the Working Group chairs.

Each Working Group has a bounded scope defined in its charter.

14.2.2 The IETF Organization

The IETF is made up of Working Groups encompassing the following areas:

- Applications (APP): Protocols seen by user programs, such as e-mail and the Web. Examples include application layer optimization, Calendaring and Scheduling Standards Simplification, Hypertext Transfer Protocol Bis, and Internationalized Domain Names in Applications (Revised).
- General (GEN): Catch-all for Working Groups that do not fit in other areas (there are very few).
- Internet (INT): Different ways of moving IP packets and DNS information. Examples include IP over IEEE 802.16 Networks, IPv6 over Low-power WPAN, IPv6 Maintenance, DNS Extensions, Dynamic Host Configuration, Network Time Protocol, Timing over IP Connection and Transfer of Clock, Mobility EXTensions for IPv6, Mobility for IPv4, and so forth.
- Operations and Management (OPS): Operational aspects, network monitoring, and configuration. Examples include Benchmarking Methodology, Global Routing Operations, IP Flow Information Export, MBONE Deployment, Performance Metrics for Other Layers, RADIUS EXTensions, and so forth.
- Real-time applications and infrastructure (RAI): Delay-sensitive interpersonal communications. Examples include audio/video transport, telephone number mapping, basic level of interoperability for SIP Services, SIP for instant messaging and presence leveraging extensions, and so forth.

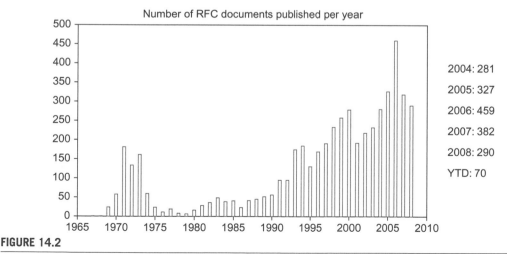

FIGURE 14.2

Number of published RFC since 1970, RFC Editor, IETF-74.

- Routing (RTG): Getting packets to their destinations. Examples include Multiprotocol Label Switching (MPLS), Open Shortest Path First IGP, IS-IS for IP Internets, Path Computation Element (PCE), routing over Low-power and Lossy Networks, and so forth.
- Security (SEC): Authentication and privacy. Examples include IP security maintenance and extensions, provisioning of symmetric keys, multicast security, and transport layer security.
- Transport (TSV): Special services for special packets. Examples include Datagram Congestion Control Protocol, congestion and pre-congestion notification, robust header compression, Transport Area Working Group, TCP maintenance and minor extensions, and so forth.

The Internet Engineering Steering Group (IESG) is responsible for the direct operation of the IETF and the overall quality of the work it produces. A detailed description of its charter can be found in [9]. The IESG is composed of the IETF chair and all of the area directors. The Internet Architecture Board (IAB) chair and the IETF executive director are also part of the IAB as ex-officio members of the IESG.

14.2.3 **IETF Standard Tracks**

When working on standardization it is necessary to have a good understanding of the Internet standard process described in [22]. Producing a high-quality standard is not an easy task. The goals of the standardization process are

- Technical excellence
- Prior implementation and testing
- Clear, concise, and easily understood documentation
- Openness and fairness (a cardinal principle of the IETF)
- Timeliness

Finding the right compromise between technical excellence, prior implementation and testing, giving a chance for all interested parties to comment and contribute, and timeliness in the fast moving world of high technology is somewhat challenging.

Internet standard specifications fall into one of these two categories:

- Technical specification (TS): Technical description of a protocol, services, procedure, convention, or format.
- Applicability statement (AS): As mentioned in [22], "An applicability statement specifies how, and under what circumstances, one or more TSs may be applied to support a particular Internet capability." For example, an AS may specify the circumstances under which one or more technical specifications may (or may not) be utilized or parameterized (e.g., timer values, activation of a particular subfunction). An AS may have different requirement levels:
  - Required: Implementation of the referenced TS as specified in the AS is a *must* to be conformant to the standard.
  - Recommended: Although the implementation of the referenced TS is not a must for conformity, it is desirable in the domain of applicability of the AS. In other words, vendors are strongly encouraged to implement the referenced TS in their products and omission should be carefully justified.
  - Elective: Implementation of the TS is optional.

- Limited use: Use of the TS is appropriate under very specific circumstances. A good example is the use of a TS in the experimental track, which should be limited to those involved in the experiment.
- Not recommended: When a TS is considered as inappropriate for general use.

Note that each TS and AS is conceptually separate and could be combined in a single document. In other cases it is preferable to have separate documents. For example, the Routing Over Low-power and Lossy networks (ROLL) Working Group in charge of the routing issues in LLNs chose to develop a generic routing protocol (TS) that contains some AS but is also accompanied by a series of AS to provide recommendations on the use of the TS in specific environments (e.g., parameterization).

The IETF standardization defines several categories of specification: standard track, experimental, and informational.

Let's first focus on the standard track. Each document that follows the standard track can have three levels of maturity.

14.2.3.1 Level of Maturity of Standard Track Documents

The first level of maturity is known as the Proposed Standard (PS). A TS reaches this level of maturity when the specification is stable and has been extensively reviewed by the community, and known design choices have been resolved and are well understood. Although it is not required to have implementations to reach this maturity level, it is highly encouraged to get implementations for a TS to become a PS. This may also be required by the IESG when the protocol affects the core of the Internet. PSs are subject to changes based on experience if issues are found.

The second level of maturity is called Draft Standard and is reached when at least two independent and interoperable implementations exist (from different code bases) that have demonstrated sufficient and successful operational experience. Note that this applies to all of the options and features specified by the specification.

The last level of maturity is the Internet Standard. A specification may be elevated to this level when significant implementations and successful operation have been obtained and the specification has reached a high level of maturity.

There are about 80 Full Standards, 90 Draft Standards, and 1532 Proposed Standards. Unlike other standardization bodies, the IETF considers a specification to be deployable when it reaches the PS maturity level.

14.2.3.2 Non-standard Track Specifications

There are other categories (non-standard track) for documents that are not intended or ready to become standards.

- Experimental track: This is used for specification resulting from research or development efforts. It is not uncommon for some specification to move to the standard track once more experience in the field has been acquired.
- Informational: This type of RFC is a documentation made available to the general community that does not represent an Internet community consensus or recommendation. Requirement documents for the specification of a protocol are usually published as informational and used to provide some guidance during the protocol specification cycle. For example (as discussed in Chapter 17), the ROLL Working Group has produced four application-specific requirement documents that have been used to design a routing protocol.

Informational and experimental specification may either be submitted directly to the RFC editor (in which case the RFC editor will consult the IESG for review) or may be the product of a Working Group.

Note that some specifications may be marked as *historic* when they are considered obsolete or have been superseded by a more recent specification. For example, the RFC1863 (a BGP/IDRP Route Server alternative to a full mesh routing) has been reclassified as historic since implementations of RFC1863 route servers do not exist and are not used as an alternative to full mesh routing. The current technologies are the BGP route reflectors, BGP confederations, or private autonomous systems (AS) numbers.

14.2.3.3 The Best Current Practice Series

The best current practice (BCP) series is used to standardize practices and is the result of community deliberation. Note that BCPs do not follow the three-stage standard track process and once approved are published. BCPs are useful in many ways, both for implementers and end users.

14.2.4 The IETF Standard Process

The first stage of the life cycle is the posting of an individual submission document in the IETF directory. Note that this process is open to anyone and does not require any approval. The name of the document should be of the form draft-X-rev.txt where X is generally the author name followed by a concise description of the document content (e.g., draft-johnson-dns-extensions-multicast-00.txt) and rev is a number corresponding to the revision number of the document.

It is very common to follow the document name by the targeted Working Group where the document will be discussed.

Note that each document (except once recommended by the IESG for publication) automatically expires after six months and can be simply refreshed by reposting the document after having incremented the revision number.

As shown in Figure 14.3, at this stage the document is being discussed in the appropriate Working Group. If the document addresses one of the Working Group items listed in its charter and there is a Working Group consensus to adopt the document as a Working Group document, then the document becomes "officially" adopted by the Working Group. Some documents may directly be elected to the status of Working Group documents.

Following our previous example, the document name becomes draft-ietf-dns-extensions-multicast-00. txt and effectively becomes the "property" of the Working Group. All changes and evolutions of the document must then be discussed and agreed upon by the community involved in the Working Group. Once the document comes through a number of iterations and is considered mature and stable, a Working Group Last Call is issued by the Working Group chairs. All comments received during that period must be addressed by the authors, at which point a publication request is sent to the Area Director by a Working Group chair.

Note that the process is different for an individual submission that is not the product of the Working Group. In this case, the document is discussed with the RFC editor and the IESG that reviews it.

The IESG determines whether or not the document satisfies the applicable criteria for recommendation action and also decides whether or not the technical quality and clarity is consistent with the required maturity level to which the specification is recommended. In some cases the IESG may issue

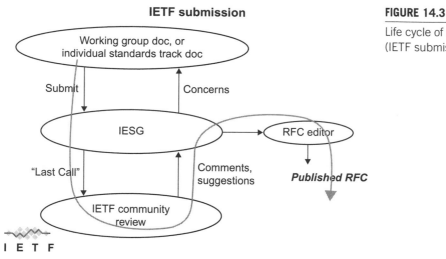

IETF submission

FIGURE 14.3

Life cycle of an IETF document (IETF submission).

a general IETF last call period (between two and four weeks) during which anybody can send comments. The IESG may decide to change the publication category. During review, IESG members may send comments on the specification or "DISCUSS" positions. The DISCUSS position identifies one or more issues with the document that must be addressed by the authors in coordination with the Working Group chairs and (if needed) reviewed by the Working Group. A DISCUSS is a "blocking" position that prevents the publication of the document until resolved. It may be stated for a number of reasons: specification impossible to implement due to technical or lack of clarity issues, technical flaws in the protocol design, likelihood that multiple implementations will not interoperate due to lack of clarity of the specification, risk of damaging the Internet if the specification was widely deployed, existence of security holes in the specification, a normative reference necessary to implement the document has been omitted, and so forth. DISCUSS must be resolved by the authors of the specification with the help of the Working Chairs and potentially the Working Group. Once each DISCUSS is resolved the IESG approves the publication of the specification.

If approved for publication, a notification is sent to the IETF and the RFC editor.

14.2.5 The IAB

The IAB (http://www.iab.org/) is made up of twelve sitting members and the IETF chair who serve as individuals and not representatives of companies. Six of the twelve members are appointed each year for a period of two years.

The IAB is chartered to perform the following tasks:

- IESG appointment: The IAB reviews IESG candidates consenting to some, all, or none of the candidates provided by the IETF nominating candidates (Nomcom) for vacant IESG seats.
- Architectural oversight: This is undoubtedly a key mission of the IAB. The IAB pays particular attention to the long-term issues of the Internet. Such issues are brought to the attention of the groups that address them, when the groups are already in place. IAB members also participate in "Birds of Feather" (BOF) and help the IESG determine whether a new IETF Working Group

or IRTG Research Group should be formed. The IAB also reviews the charter of newly formed Working Groups for review of the architectural consistency and integrity. IAB also organizes the Internet Research Task Force (IRTF) and is involved in the formation of new Research Groups. The IAB also convenes workshops on specific topics. For example, workshops have been organized in the past on "Internet Information Infrastructure" (October 1994), "Routing and Addressing" (October 2006), "Unwanted Traffic" (March 2006), "Social Networking" (June 2008), and so forth. The IAB is free to invite any relevant parties of the IETF or other organizations; the outcome of such workshops is a report destined for the IETF community and IESG.

- The IAB also provides oversight of the process used to produce Internet Standards. Appeals to handle complaints of improper execution of standards processes are also handled by the IAB.
- The IAB is the representative of the IETF community for technical liaisons with other organizations. Such liaisons are as informal as possible with the objective of improving the quality of the IETF standards. Examples of liaisons with other standardization bodies include: ISO (http://www .iso.org/iso/home.htm), ITU (http://www.itu.int/net/home/index.aspx), IEEE (http://www.ieee.org/ portal/site), 3GPP (http://www.3gpp.org/), and IP/MPLS Forum (http://www.ipmplsforum.org/).
- The IAB also approves the appointment of an organization to act as RFC editor (in charge of the editorial management of RFCs) and an organization to act as the Internet Assigned Numbers Authority (IANA) that is responsible for the assignment of the various protocol parameters specified by the IETF.

More details can be found in [33].

14.2.5.1 IRTF

The mission of the IRTF is to "to promote research of importance to the evolution of the future Internet by creating focused, long-term and small Research Groups working on topics related to Internet protocols, applications, architecture and technology."

The IRTF is organized into Research Groups (RGs) to focus on various topics related to protocols, application architecture, and technologies. Similar to the IETF, IRTF members are individual contributors as opposed to company representatives. RGs are expected to have long-term membership to promote the development of research collaboration and teams for research-related topics.

The IRTF is managed by the IRTF chair (appointed by the IAB) in consultation with the Internet Research Steering Group (IRSG), which includes the IRTF chairs, the RG chairs (appointed by the IRTF chairs in consultation with the IRSG and approval of the IAB), and potential individuals from the research community.

There are twelve RGs:

- Anti-Spam Research Group (ASRG)
- Routing Research Group (RRG)
- Delay-Tolerant Networking Research Group (DTNRG)
- Peer-to-Peer Research Group (P2PRG)
- Host Identity Protocol (HIP) Research Group (HIPRG)
- IP Mobility Optimizations (Mob Opts) Research Group (MOBOPTS)
- Network Management Research Group Charter (NMRG)
- Transport Modeling Research Group (TMRG)
- Scalable Adaptive Multicast Research Group (SAMRG)
- Crypto Forum Research Group (CFRG)

- End-to-End Research Group Charter (END2END)
- Internet Congestion Control Research Group (ICCRG)

More details on the IRTF can be found in [255].

14.3 IETF WORKING GROUPS RELATED TO IP FOR SMART OBJECTS

Until 2007 the IETF had not paid any particular attention to the world of smart objects. It was extremely important to quickly stop the emergence of proprietary protocols and pay the required level of attention and energy to specify IP-based protocols for smart objects. A presentation was made during the Routing Area Plenary session during the IETF-69 in Chicago on July 2007 to highlight the need for specific work in this area (see Figure 14.4).

The intent has always been to reuse existing IP protocols whenever possible with a strong incentive to not "reinvent the wheel." The world of smart objects is not an exception. Many of the existing IP protocols can be reused without change such as the UDP (User Datagram Protocol; see [202]) or TCP (Transport Connection Protocol; see [204]).

There were other areas that required specific solutions. The use of IPv6 over IEEE 802.15.4 handled by the 6LoWPAN Working Group requires protocol enhancement and some protocol adaptations to optimize the transport of IPv6 packets in an IEEE 802.15.4 frame. Another example is routing.

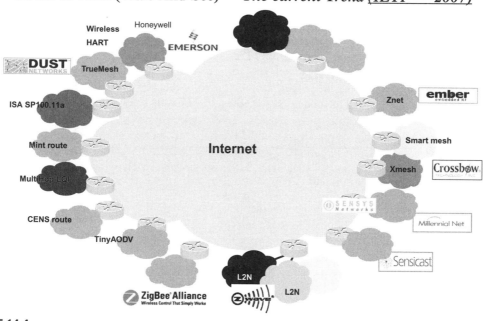

FIGURE 14.4

Presentation during the Routing Plenary Session IETF 2007.

This section provides a description of the two IETF Working Groups (so far) that are focusing on issues specific to IP-based smart objects: 6LoWPAN and ROLL. New IETF Working Groups devoted to smart objects are likely to emerge.

14.3.1 The IPv6 over Low-power WPAN Working Group

The IPv6 over Low-power WPAN (6LowWPAN) Working Group was formed in 2004 to work on protocol specifications to optimize the operation of IPv6 over networks made of IEEE 802.15.4 [129] links in LoWPAN (Low-power Wireless Personal Area Networks). The 6LoWPAN Working Group belongs to the Internet area (INT) of the IETF.

Note that the 6LoWPAN Working Group uses the term LoWPAN whereas the ROLL Working Group prefers the more generic term Low-power and Lossy Networks (LLNs). The two terms are somewhat equivalent when referring to networks made of constrained devices regarding CPU, memory, or energy (some of these nodes, especially when battery-operated, may be in sleep mode for long periods of time) and usually interconnected by means of unstable links (qualified as "lossy" links). Furthermore, these networks may be deployed on a large scale. As discussed in Chapter 2, the major distinction, though, is that LLNs are not restricted to IEEE 802.15.4 links but also occur in other low-power links such as WiFi, Powerline communication (PLC), and so forth. In other words, a LoWPAN is an LLN where devices are interconnected by IEEE 802.15.4-compliant links.

The key characteristics of LoWPANs include:

- Small packet size imposed by the IEEE 802.15.4 standard: The maximum packet size at the physical layer is 127 bytes minus a maximum of control fields of 25 bytes, which leaves 102 bytes available at the media access control (MAC) layer. Depending on the security mechanism in place, this only leaves 81 bytes available (21 octets of overhead in the AES-CCM-128 case, 9 octets for AES-CCM-32, and 13 octets for AES-CCM-64), which is far below the minimum maximum transmission unit (MTU) size of the IPv6 packet imposed by [53]. According to [53], "IPv6 requires that every link in the Internet have an MTU of 1280 octets or greater." Consequently, this requires a fragmentation and reassembly adaptation layer. The second consequence is the need for compression header techniques considering the header size of an IPv6 packet (40 bytes). Both the fragmentation/reassembly and compression techniques specified by the 6LoWPAN Working Group are detailed in Chapter 16.
- Support of both the 16-bit short address and the IEEE 64-bit extended MAC addresses.
- As in most LLNs, links are inherently "low" bandwidth: 250, 40, and 20 kbps for each of the currently defined physical layers (2.4 GHz, 915 MHz, and 868 MHz, respectively) of the IEEE 802.15.4 standard.

[156] provides a 6LoWPAN problem statement and lists some of the goals of the Working Group such as fragmentation and reassembly, header compression, address autoconfiguration (a key requirement for LoWPAN and LLNs in general), network management, implementation considerations, and security.

The 6LoWPAN Working Group was re-chartered in 2008 to work on the following items:

- 6LoWPAN bootstrapping and 6LoWPAN IPv6 ND Optimizations: The objective is to define minor extensions to the IPv6 ND process defined in [185] for the specific environments of LoWPAN. This document is still in progress (proposed standard track).

- Produce 6LoWPAN header compression techniques that are improved forms of those defined in [176] known as HC1 and HC2; furthermore, the document will describe compression of non-link local addresses. This document will be a proposed standard likely to deprecate some of the mechanisms defined in RFC4944.
- Produce a 6LoWPAN architecture: This document will help design and implement 6LoWPAN networks and it will be informational.
- Use cases for 6LoWPAN: This document will show several application scenarios and the list of dominant parameters of each scenario regarding deployment, mobility, network size, power (battery- or main-powered nodes), security level, routing connectivity, criticality to support differentiated Quality of Service (QoS), and typical traffic patterns (point-to-point, point-to-multipoint, multipoint-to-point, etc.). This document will be informational.
- 6LoWPAN security analysis defining the thread model of 6LoWPAN: This document discusses the suitability of key management mechanisms as well as bootstrapping, installation, commissioning, and setup issues. It will be informational.
- The final Working Group item is related to routing requirements that are 6LoWPAN specific. This document will be informational.
- ⚠ Confusion between LLNs and 6LoWPAN networks: 6LoWPAN has sometimes been used as a generic term for LLN or sensor networks. 6LoWPAN is the work devoted to IPv6 optimization techniques and protocol adaptation for smart objects interconnected by IEEE 802.15.4 links. LLNs are made of a variety of links that are not limited to IEEE 802.15.4 and where the techniques for header compression and ND defined by the 6LoWPAN Working Group may not apply at all.

14.3.2 The ROLL Working Group

Routing has always been a central component of networking and several IP routing protocols have been defined over the past two decades, both Interior Gateway Protocols (IGPs) such as IS-IS [30] and OSPF [179], for use within an Autonomous System (AS) or Exterior Gateway Protocols (EGPs) such as BGP [212] between AS.

Several of these protocols in their early stages were designed for routers with very limited resources supporting low-speed interfaces with capabilities similar to smart objects, but the properties of these networks differed significantly from LLNs. Most of the main differences are highlighted in Figure 14.5.

- Scalability: Although some LLNs may only have a few dozen nodes (e.g., in a home), there are environments that may have hundreds of thousands of nodes. As further discussed in Part III, some urban or Smart Grid networks will undoubtedly reach such numbers so scalability is very important. Large enterprises or service provider networks using OSPF or IS-IS as IGPs rarely exceed a few thousand nodes in a single area/level. The number of nodes in large LLNs does exceed the size of current IP-based networks by an order of magnitude.
- Network stability: This is another difficult challenge for routing in LLNs. Both nodes and links in the Internet and private IP-based networks are extremely stable. Not only have modern routers became extremely powerful regarding number of interfaces and software richness, but their reliability has also remarkably increased. Furthermore, modern routers are equipped with a high level of redundancy and support-enhanced software allowing for fast recovery in case of hardware or software failure. It is now possible on these routers to perform in service software upgrades (ISSUs), and many control plane protocols are capable of failure recovery with no impact on traffic

Routing for smart objects

Current Internet	Low-power and Lossy Networks (LLN)
Nodes are routers	Nodes are sensor/actuators and routers
IGP with typically few hundreds of nodes	An order of magnitude larger in terms of number of nodes
Links and nodes are stable	Links are highly unstable and nodes die much more often
Nodes constraints or link bandwidths are typically non-issues	Nodes/Links are highly constrained
Routing is not application-aware (MTR is a vanilla version of it)	Application-aware routing, in-band processing is a MUST

FIGURE 14.5

Routing in the Internet versus LLNs.

forwarding. Unfortunately, such mechanisms often require node resources not always available on smart objects that usually have no redundancy and a failure rate significantly higher than Internet routers. In some cases, they simply "die" without being replaced and redundancy is in the network itself. Alternatively, some nodes may not be operational for a period of time (e.g., battery-operated devices that ran out of energy). But the most critical factor of network instability in LLNs is ineluctably due to link error rates and "flaps." In the Internet optical fibers provide very low bit error rates (BER) of the order of 10^{-8}, but low-power links such as IEEE 802.15.4, low-power WiFi, or PLC are characterized by high error rates and link instability. It is not uncommon for a link to "flap" because of various kinds of interferences. Several examples are provided in Chapter 17.

- Link and node instability in LLNs: This is difficult for routing protocols to overcome. The usual trade-off between network stability and convergence time is particularly challenging. In any routing protocol design, it is desirable to support fast convergence (ability to find an alternate path after a network failure). This implies quick detection of the failures and recomputing alternate paths around the failed network component. Unfortunately, there is a serious risk of network instability, oscillations, and routing loops in the presence of frequent failures, especially with distributed routing protocols. This is why the compromise between fast failure recovery (convergence time) and network stability is quite challenging in LLNs. Such issues are discussed in great detail in Chapters 5 and 17.
- Degree of constraints: Routers in IP networks are typically not constrained. Core routers have several gigabytes of RAM and powerful CPUs. As explained in detail in Chapter 1, although smart objects are now equipped with a reasonable amount of memory and CPU power, these are an order of magnitude more constrained that routers in "traditional" IP networks. Another critical and very common node constraint is energy. It is fairly common for nodes in LLNs to be battery-operated, in which case energy consumption is a major constraint. Some of these constraints can be used for constraint-based routing or as a metric (see Chapter 17).

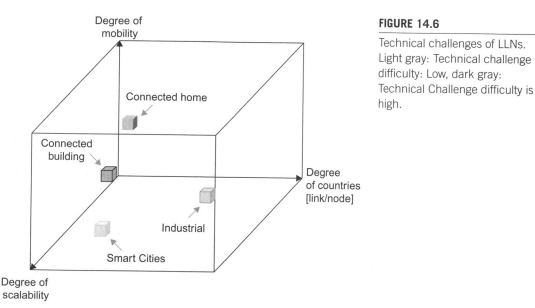

FIGURE 14.6

Technical challenges of LLNs. Light gray: Technical challenge difficulty: Low, dark gray: Technical Challenge difficulty is high.

- Application aware routing: IP packets are routed in the Internet according to their destination and IGPs are responsible for computing shortest paths according to fixed metrics. QoS allows packet coloring to assign different priorities to traffic flows. In the presence of congestion, packet processing is handled by sophisticated queuing algorithms according to the traffic priority to provide the required Service Level Agreement (SLA). Multi-topology routing (MTR) has been introduced to support multiple virtual topologies over a given physical topology. The traffic can then be forwarded on a specific virtual topology according to its class of service. Not only does the routing protocol for LLN require the support of MTR and QoS routing in the network, but it may also be necessary to support application aware routing, which is the ability to route the traffic according to the packet content. This must not be performed at each hop since it would require deep packet inspection and would also imply "layer violation," but it could be done either at the edge of the network (by the source) or along the path (on data traffic concentrators/aggregators). The packet content (application) could then be abstracted using the Diffserv Code Point (DCP) or Flow Label field of the IPv6 packet to avoid packet inspection along the path (refer to Chapter 15 for an IPv6 Technology overview). A specific capability of a node that could act as a data aggregator could be advertised by the routing protocol, which would then directly influence the routing decision.
- Technical challenges: Routing in LLN is extremely challenging because of the high degree of network constraints (constrained links and devices, instability, scalability, etc.), but also because of the remarkable diversity of the requirements and environments where LLNs are deployed. The design of a routing solution addressing all requirements is a truly multidimensional issue. Three dimensions are presented in Figure 14.6 highlighting the diversity of the requirements and constraints in each dimension for several applications. In a connected home network, the degree of link/node constraint is relatively low (reasonably low level of interference, most devices are

main-powered, just a few devices are mobile nodes). At the other end of the spectrum industrial environments are significantly more constrained: most of the devices are battery-operated, their number can be relatively large, and such networks are usually deployed in harsh environments.

There are many environments with "middle ground"-level constraints in all dimensions. Narrowing the scope to the four applications previously mentioned (industrial, urban networks, home and building automation) was meant to avoid a too disparate set of constraint levels. One approach when designing a protocol that must address such a wide set of constraints is to simply consider the superset of all requirements driven by all of these constraint dimensions. Although satisfactory in its functionality, this would unavoidably lead to a routing protocol not optimized for any of the environments and certainly too "heavy" for the constrained devices deployed in these networks. The approach taken by the designers of the routing protocol for LLN (as discussed in Chapter 17) was to adopt a modular approach that consisted of a defining a core of basic functionalities satisfying the set of common requirements augmented with optional capabilities activated when and where needed. This is where applicability statement documents come into play.

14.3.2.1 The Formation of a New Working Group: ROLL

The unique characteristics of the LLNs justified the formation of the ROLL Working Group. It was formed in March 2008 and belongs to the Routing Area Group (RTG). Detailed information about ROLL can be found at http://www.ietf.org/html.charters/roll-charter.html.

ROLL was initially chartered to produce detailed routing requirements and evaluate whether or not existing routing protocols already defined by other IETF Working Groups would meet its unique set of requirements.

The set of applications of LLNs is vast: Smart Cities, transportation, assets tracking, home automation, healthcare, building automation, industrial automation, energy savings, Smart Grids, military applications, environmental studies, agriculture, and so forth. To stay focused and avoid building a routing solution that could not accommodate all requirements, the decision was made to limit the scope of the requirements to four main applications: industrial automation, urban networks, and home and building automation. The superset of all of the requirements driven by the aforementioned applications also covers many of the other areas previously mentioned. Furthermore, the goal was not to exclude any other area but rather to focus on some of the applications, knowing that these applications would also cover the requirements of many other ones.

The ROLL Working Group has produced four corresponding application-specific routing requirements documents: Urban WSNs Routing Requirements in Low-Power and Lossy Networks, Industrial Routing Requirements in Low-Power and Lossy Networks, Home Automation Routing Requirements in Low-Power and Lossy Networks, and Building Automation Routing Requirements in Low-Power and Lossy Networks.

The most recent versions of the requirement documents can be found at http://www.ietf.org/html.charters/roll-charter.html.

The ROLL Working Group extensively discussed whether or not an existing protocol (with no change) could satisfy the specific routing requirements. To that end, several criteria were selected to evaluate whether or not existing protocols would satisfy the requirements of ROLL:

- Routing state: Scalability of the protocol regarding required states and the number of links and nodes in the network

- Loss response: That criteria was used to study the impact of link churn (fairly common in LLN) on the routing protocol to make sure of local response without triggering global re-optimization
- Control cost: Ability for the routing protocol to limit the control cost (routing control plane "overhead") by the data rate plus a small constant
- Link and node cost: Requirement for the routing protocol to consider link and node metrics/constraints in route computation

The criteria previously listed have been studied in a series of existing protocols; namely OSPF (Open Shortest Path First; [179]), IS-IS (Intermediate System to Intermediate System; [131] and [238]), OLSR [41], TBRPF (Topology Dissemination Based on Reverse Path Forwarding; [187]), RIP (Routing Information Protocol; [163]), AODV (Ad-hoc On Demand Vector Routing; [194]), DYMO (Dynamic Mobile On-Demand routing), and DSR (Dynamic Source Routing; [141]). After six months, the Working Group reached a consensus that no existing protocol could satisfy the routing requirements spelled out in the series of application-specific routing requirements previously listed. Consequently, the ROLL Working Group was successfully re-chartered to specify a routing solution to finalize the protocol specification by February 2010. Here are the ROLL Working Group items:

- Protocol work: The Working Group will either specify a new routing protocol or extend an existing routing protocol that satisfies the list of requirements listed in the application-specific routing requirement documents.[1]
- Routing metrics: Those specified for IGPs such as OSPF and IS-IS are fairly straightforward and can be used by the network administrator to reflect bandwidth, delays, cost, or any combination. Other RFCs such as [249] have introduced the ability to specify new link attributes (e.g., link protected by a fast reroute mechanism). Technologies such as MPLS Traffic Engineering introduced a new set of link metrics such as Affinities (administrative flag), Reservable Bandwidth, and so forth. But LLNs have other specific characteristics that require the specification of new link and node routing metrics/constraints. Producing a set of routing metrics/constraints for the routing protocol of ROLL is a key Working Group item.
- Security: This is critical for a majority of the applications supported by LLNs. ROLL is producing a security framework for that purpose. Security requirements have been covered in detail in the routing requirement documents and special attention is given to security in the routing protocol design.
- Management: Most LLNs are made of nodes that must support minimal configuration (such networks are usually installed by non-IT experts). Furthermore, the number of nodes can be very large. It is thus paramount to support 0-config setup mode of operation where the nodes can be installed in the field without requiring any complex (if any) configuration tasks.
- Architectural framework: The Working Group will produce an architecture document for routing and path selection in LLN whether to use a distributed versus centralized routing, use of routing hierarchy, and so forth.
- Applicability statements: The Working Group will also produce several application statement documents. An applicability statement documents the use of protocols and mechanisms specified by the Working Group in a particular context (e.g., how to use the routing protocol in an urban network with battery-operated devices under certain conditions of traffic pattern).

---

[1] The ROLL Working Group chose to specify a new routing protocol discussed in detail in Chapter 17.

14.4 CONCLUSIONS

As stated in the Introduction, standardization is absolutely critical and synonymous of openness and interoperability. IP is by excellence an open standardized technology. Anybody willing to contribute to IP standardization is free to participate in the IETF. The IETF has produced an impressive number of extremely high-quality standards over the past few decades ensuring interoperability between billions of devices. As IP networks (private IP networks and the Internet) continue to grow interconnecting several billions and most likely trillions of smart objects, standardization will continue to be crucial to ensure interoperability, manageability, and innovation while continuing to lower the cost of these networks in contrast with proprietary solutions.

This chapter provided a fairly detailed description of the IETF, IAB, and IRTF regarding organization and mode of operation. It was shown that the IETF continues to quickly evolve and form new Working Groups standardizing new IP protocols for smart objects. New Working Groups are formed when needed since most of the existing IP protocols can be used in smart object networks. IETF will undoubtedly continue to be a fast moving and central standardization body for IP smart objects for years to come.

IPv6 for Smart Object Networks — A Technology Refresher

15

15.1 IPv6 FOR SMART OBJECT NETWORKS?

A number of books have been published on IPv6. This chapter provides a technology refresher to show how IPv6 is used for IP smart objects. More details on IPv6 that are less applicable to Low-power and Lossy Networks (LLNs) are not covered in this chapter. For more information the reader is referred to [104], [49], [201], [17], [243], [164], and the IPv6 RFCs produced by the Internet Engineering Task Force (IETF) for more details.

As discussed in Part I, IPv6 plays a fundamental role in the "Internet of Things/IP smart objects" for many reasons that are briefly examined in this chapter. By reviewing the key motivations for IPv6 contained in [53], the choice of IPv6 for smart object networks will become quite obvious.

IPv6 strictly follows the fundamental architectural principles of IP, it is just the next revision of IP solving several limitations of IPv4. Even with these limitations, IPv4 has been a tremendous success and is still in operation after 25 years. IPv4 will undoubtedly remain in operation for years to come, and the IPv6 designers have developed a plethora of mechanisms allowing for a smooth transition to IPv6; for example, to interconnect native IPv6 clouds over an IPv4 core network to support the transition to IPv6.

Let's now briefly focus on some key functionalities of IPv6.

- Larger address space required for large-scale networks: Although some LLNs such as home automation networks may only consist of a few dozen nodes, in many other cases, the number of these nodes may be an order of magnitude larger than in conventional IP networks. This will be discussed in great detail in Part III, but urban networks, Smart Grids, and industrial automation networks are examples where IP smart object networks will potentially comprise hundreds of thousands of nodes. With the IPv4 address depletion at the horizon of 2012, IPv6 is the obvious choice. By extending the address space from 32 to 128 bits, there are a significantly larger number of addressable nodes as well as many more levels of addressing hierarchy (key for routing table efficiency) and autoconfiguration features. Note that the scalability of multicast has been enhanced due to a new scope field and the notion of anycast address will be introduced later in Section 15.3.1 of this chapter. Scoped addresses allow better support of ad hoc networking and are also discussed in Section 15.3.3 of this chapter. But these are not the only reasons for choosing IPv6.
- Autoconfiguration: With networks of very large scale, management at large (provisioning, configuration, management of faults, inventory, performance analysis) quickly becomes very challenging.

Interconnecting Smart Objects with IP. DOI: 10.1016/B978-0-12-375165-2.00015-6

Thus, the set of autoconfiguration features natively supported by IPv6 is another reason to use it in smart object networks.

- Header change: Several unused IPv4 header fields have been removed (e.g., fragmentation, checksum, etc.) and a simpler structure with a fixed header potentially augmented with optional daisy-chained extended headers has been adopted. New fields have also been added (e.g., flow label).
- Authentication and privacy: Extensions have been defined in support of authentication, data integrity, and (potentially) confidentiality.
- Security: IPSec (optional in IPv4) is mandatory in IPv6.

15.2 THE IPv6 PACKET HEADERS

15.2.1 IPv6 Fixed Header

A good way to start learning a protocol is to first observe the packet header field. The IPv6 packet header format is shown in Figure 15.1.

Description of the fields include:

- Version (4 bits): IP versions number = 6.
- Traffic class (8 bits): 8-bit field used to indicate the Class of Service (CoS) of the packet. Quality of Service (QoS) is discussed in Section 15.9.
- Flow label (20 bits): A label may be used by a source node to refer to a sequence of packets identifying a flow that requires specific handling of the packet by routers along the path to its destination. The flow label should be randomly generated to help with hash key function implementation on the intervening router. It is expected that the source node does not use the same flow label value for two different flows at any time. Note that the use of this field is still mostly experimental.
- Payload length (16 bits): This field indicates the length of the payload (excluding the packet header). Note that the length of the extended headers (described in Section 15.2.2) is included in the payload length.
- Next header (8 bits): This field identifies the header that follows the IPv6 packet header. This provides a very flexible way to add optional headers using a daisy chain.
- Hop limit (8 bits): This field is decremented each time the packet is forwarded by a node. When the hop limit field is equal to 0, the packet is discarded.

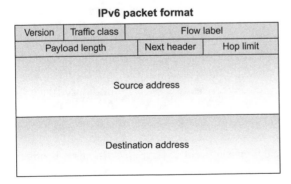

IPv6 packet format

Version	Traffic class	Flow label	
Payload length		Next header	Hop limit
Source address			
Destination address			

FIGURE 15.1

IPv6 packet header format.

- Source address: 128-bit IPv6 source address of the packet.
- Destination address: 128-bit IPv6 destination address of the packet.

This leads to the observation that the fixed IPv6 header (with no option) is 40 bytes long compared to the 20-byte header of an IPv4 packet. Such extra overhead may be an issue for LLNs composed of low-speed links, especially when the link layer maximum transmission unit (MTU) and the data payload are small (a fairly common situation in LLNs). That is precisely the case of the IEEE 802.15.4 links described in Chapter 12, a fairly popular link in LLN. This is why the 6LoWPAN Working Group specified various header compression schemas to reduce the header overhead. These mechanisms are described in detail in Chapter 16.

In contrast with IPv4, there is no checksum in the IPv6 header. Thus all the transport layer protocols are required to compute a checksum taking into account the IPv6 header. This is also true for UDP. Thus, the UDP checksum (optional in IPv4) is mandatory in IPv6 and all higher-level protocols that use the 32-bit IPv4 address to compute their checksum. They must be modified to use the 128-bits IPv6 addresses.

15.2.2 Extended Headers

IPv6 has a fixed header optionally followed by a daisy chain of headers called extended headers. Optional headers follow the fixed header and precede the transport header.

The next header value simply identifies the type of the following header. Consider Figure 15.2. In the first example, the next header value is equal to 6, thus identifying a TCP header (there is no extended header in this case and the transport packet data unit (PDU) immediately follows the fixed header). In the third example, there is a series of three extended headers following the fixed IPv6 that are daisy-chained. The IPv6 next header value is equal to 43, indicating that the next header (first extended header is a routing header) is composed of a next header field with a value of 51 that indicates the presence of an authentication header. The transport header is specified by the value of 6

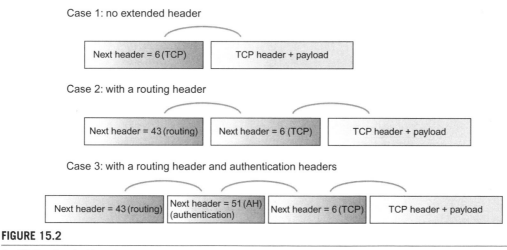

FIGURE 15.2

An IPv6 extended header.

(referring to a TCP) in the next header field of the authentication header. This provides a very flexible architecture, adding header only when needed.

Note that headers *must* appear in a specific order and are not processed by intermediate routers along the data path except the hop-by-hop option header. Indeed, the hop-by-hop header is the only header that must be processed by all the routers along the path including the source and the destination, which is why, when present, it must immediately follow the fixed header (its presence is indicated by a value of 0 in the next header field of the fixed header).

As specified in [53], all IPv6 implementation must support the following extended headers:

- Hop-by-hop options [53]
- Routing (type 0) [53]
- Fragment [53]
- Destination options [53]
- Authentication (specified in [146] and [155])
- Encapsulating security payload (specified in [145])

[53], [145], [146], and [155] define each of the extended headers including the format, processing rules, error handling, and so on. Since the objective of this chapter is not to be an IPv6 reference book, a brief description of the extended headers relevant to LLNs is provided and implementers should refer to the RFCs for implementation details.

Options in headers: there are two extension headers (hop-by-hop options header and the destination options header) that carry a variable number of type-length-values (TLVs) that allow specification of a number of options for the header. The option type identifier (T value) defines the option type and the two higher order bits specify what the node is expected to do if the option is not recognized such as ignore, silently discard, discard and send an Internet Control Message Protocol (ICMP) packet, and so forth. The third higher order bit specifies whether or not the option data can be changed en route along the data path.

15.2.3 The Hop-by-hop Option Header

The hop-by-hop option header is used to carry extra information and must be processed by all routers along the data path including the source and destination of the IP packet. Its structure is depicted in Figure 15.3, which shows the first 8-bit identifying the next header, followed by an 8-bit field specifying the payload length not including the first 8 bits, followed by the payload of variable length carrying the set of TLVs.

15.2.4 The Routing Header

The routing header is used to identify a set of nodes that must be traversed by the packet along its path to the destination, also known as "source routing." This does not require listing all the nodes along the paths: a subset of some nodes along the path can be listed as opposed to all nodes (a source routing technique referred to as loose source routing).

The first two fields are identical to the first two fields of the hop-by-hop option header. The routing option is a routing variant and the segment left field indicates the number of remaining route segments before reaching the destination. The type-specific data field is a variable length field of a type defined by the routing type field value.

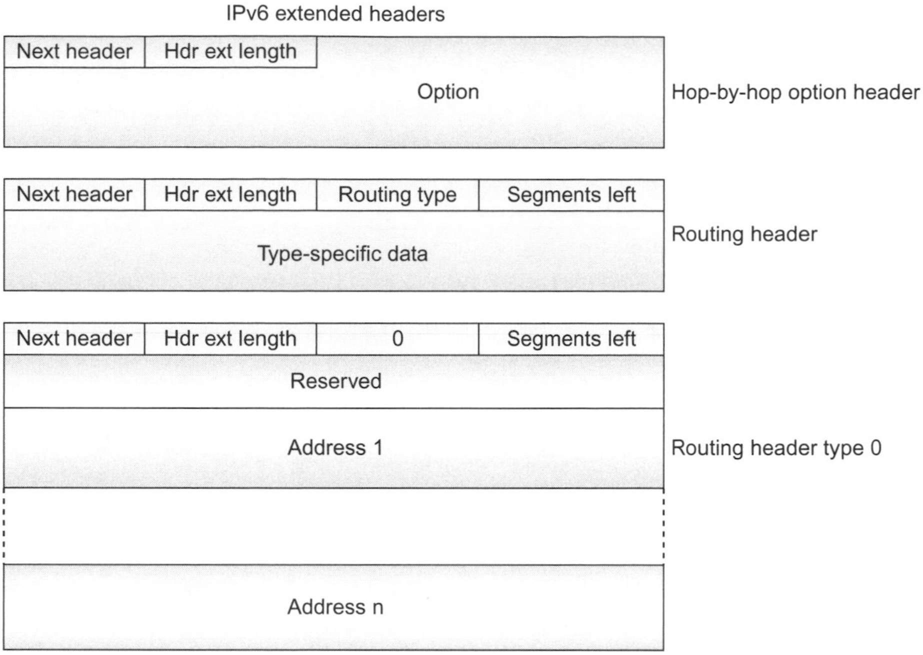

IPv6 extended headers

Next header	Hdr ext length		
Option			

Hop-by-hop option header

Next header	Hdr ext length	Routing type	Segments left
Type-specific data			

Routing header

Next header	Hdr ext length	0	Segments left
Reserved			
Address 1			
Address n			

Routing header type 0

FIGURE 15.3

Hop-by-hop and routing headers.

For example, a particular instantiation of the routing header is shown in Figure 15.3 for the routing header of type 0. The routing header is type 0 and only carries unicast addresses.

The processing of the routing header is interesting because it is used not only to list the set of nodes that must be traversed but also to record the set of nodes that have been traversed.

Next is an important note on security. When a node needs to reply to a packet that was received with a routing header, the response packet must not include a routing header that was automatically computed by reversing the route specified in the routing header of the received packet unless the integrity and the authenticity of the received source address and routing header have been verified.

A drawback to routing header subtype 0 (RH0) is the introduction of security issues that have been documented in [2] that lead to its deprecation. Indeed, a single RH0 may contain multiple intermediate routers/hosts and it is legal to include the same address more than once. This means that a single packet may circle and be processed multiple times by the same routers/hosts, leading to a Denial of Service (DoS) attack. Note that the same attack exists with IPv4 but is exemplified in the case of IPv6 since many addresses could be listed in the header.

Consequently, other routing header subtypes have been used. Routing header subtype 1 has been experimented with and routing header subtype 2 is defined for IPv6 Mobility in [140] (see Figure 15.4).

15.2.5 The Fragment Header

In contrast with IPv4, the routers along the data path never perform any form of fragmentation. IPv6 mandates that each link must be able to carry 1280-byte packets, which is not always the case in LLN.

IPv6 routing header subtype 2

Next header	Hdr ext length = 2	Routing type = 2	Segments left = 1
Reserved			
Home address			

FIGURE 15.4

Routing header subtype 2.

In particular, the MTU of IEEE 802.15.4 links is equal to 127 bytes. In this case, it is required to handle packet fragmentation and reassembly at the link layer. This is specified in [176] and [124] as a result of a work item from the 6LoWPAN Working Group. These mechanisms are described in Chapter 16.

This implies that IPv6 should support mechanisms to discover the minimum MTU supported on each link along the path to the destination. This is performed using a procedure called path maximum transmission discovery (PMTU) defined in [171]. It uses a sequence of ICMP packets along the path until it discovers the minimum MTU along the path. This value is then cached on the host in a table on a per-destination basis and must be rediscovered on a regular basis since IP paths may change due to rerouting from network element failures. An implementation not supporting PMTU may simply decide to send packets no larger than 1280 octets.

An IPv6 source node fragments a packet each time its size is larger than the minimum MTU along the path to the destination.

The format of the fragment header is shown in Figure 15.5. The fragment header is identified by the value 44 present in the next header field of the previous header (which could either be the IPv6 fixed header or the routing header, if present). The next header value is identical to the original next header type of the fragmented packet. The fragment offset simply indicates the offset of the fragment (in 8-octet units) relative to the start of the fragmentable part of the original packet. The identification field is a 32-bit encoded value chosen by the source node to identify the fragmented packet that will be reassembled by the destination node. Each time a source node fragments a packet it uses a different identification number for each fragmented packet destined to a specific node. The source is expected to use an identification number different from any already sent packet for the expected lifetime of a packet. A simple wraparound counter considering the 32-bit encoding scheme for the identification number is assumed to be perfectly reasonable. The 2-bit "reserved" field is set to 0 and the M-bit is used to indicate whether the fragment is the last one (1: more fragment, 0: last fragment).

Now let's illustrate the fragmentation process of a packet. The original packet has an unfragmentable part made of the original header and any extended header that must be processed by the nodes along the path to the destination (all headers up to and including the routing header if present). The rest of the packet makes the fragmentable part of the packet.

The format of each fragment is shown in Figure 15.5. Each fragment is made of the unfragmentable part of the original packet, the fragment header, and the payload of the fragment. Note that the unfragmentable part of each packet has a payload size equal to the size of the fragment excluding the length of the IPv6 header. The next header field of the last header of the unfragmentable part is set to 44. Now looking at the fragment header, it contains a next header value that identifies the first header of the fragmentable part of the original packet.

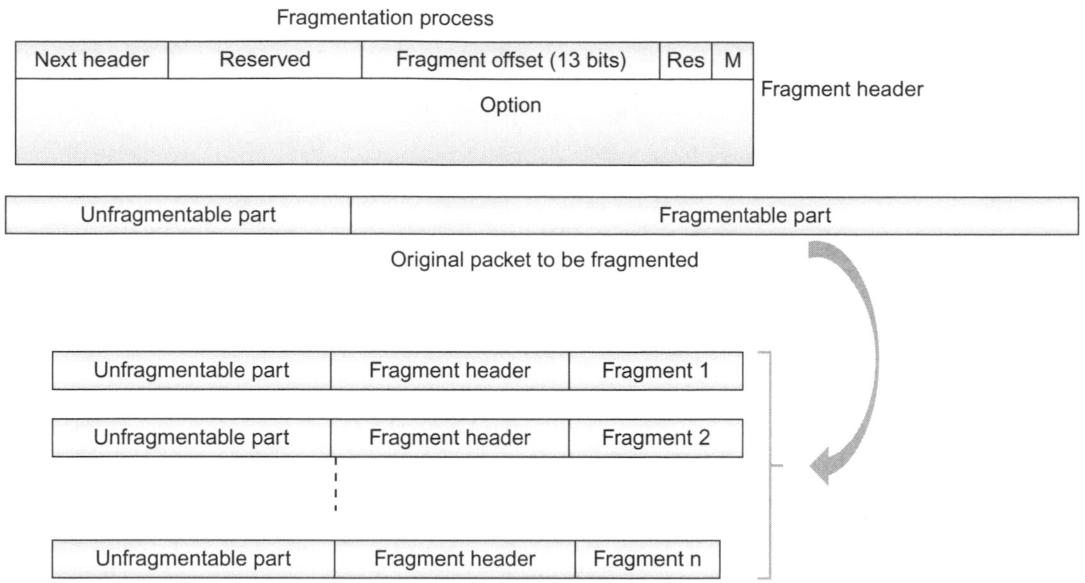

Fragmentation process

Next header	Reserved	Fragment offset (13 bits)	Res	M	
Option					Fragment header

Unfragmentable part	Fragmentable part

Original packet to be fragmented

Unfragmentable part	Fragment header	Fragment 1

Unfragmentable part	Fragment header	Fragment 2

Unfragmentable part	Fragment header	Fragment n

FIGURE 15.5

Fragment headers.

Fragments may be lost, especially in LLNs where bit error ratios (BERs) are fairly high and links are potentially quite unstable. IPv6 mandates that all fragments are to be received within 60 seconds after the reception of the first fragment (which may or may not be fragment number 1). After the time expires, and not all fragments have been received, the procedure is simply stopped and all fragments are discarded. An ICMP error message is then sent to the source of the packet. Other error cases (e.g., incorrect packet length, etc.) are also covered and illustrated in [53].

15.2.6 The Destination Option Header

The destination option header is used to carry optional information processed by the destination node, and is identified in the next header field of the previous header by a value of 60. The format of the destination option header is quite straightforward: an 8-bit next header field followed by an 8-bit header extension length field indicating the length of the header in 8-octet units, excluding the first 8 octets. The payload contains one or more TLVs.

Optional information is encoded in two different ways: (1) by using a TLV carried within the destination option header or (2) by defining a new extended header. The highest two order bits are used to indicate the expected behavior of the destination that does not recognize the option.

15.2.7 The No Next Header

This header (value = 59) is used to indicate that nothing follows this header.

15.3 IPv6 ADDRESSING ARCHITECTURE

Needless to say, IPv6 addressing deserves a chapter on its own.

Its addressing architecture is described in [116].

This section will help understand Chapter 16 where header compression mechanisms specified by the 6LoWPAN Working Group for IPv6 over IEEE 802.15.4 and the routing operation in general will be discussed. This is not a data format, but a true addressing architecture instead.

128-bit addresses allow $3.4\ 10^{38}$ addresses, in other words, $4.8\ 10^{23}$ addresses per person on earth or $6.6\ 10^{23}$ addresses per square meter, which should leave enough addresses for years to come.

15.3.1 Notion of Unicast, Anycast, and Multicast

A unicast address uniquely identifies a single interface by its address. An interface can have multiple unicast addresses and must have at least one link-local address. A link-local address is an address used on a link between two nodes. In some cases, link-local addresses are sufficient if the node does not need to send packets beyond a local link. Note that a node may assign a unicast address (or a set of unicast addresses) to more than one interface if and only if it treats them as one interface when presenting to the network layer. This could be useful to load balance traffic over a set of physical interfaces.

An anycast address is an identifier for a set of interfaces: a packet sent to an anycast address is only delivered to one of the interfaces of the set, typically the closest one according to routing metrics.

In contrast, a packet sent to a multicast address is delivered to all interfaces identified by the multicast address. There is no broadcast in IPv6, so multicast addresses are used. For example, routing control packets in IPv4 use broadcast addresses whereas specific multicast addresses are used in IPv6.

15.3.2 Representation of IPv6 Addresses

32-bit IPv4 addresses are represented in the following form: x.y.z.t (e.g., 124.4.12.3). A portion of the address represents the network part and the rest of the address represents the host part.

128-bit IPv6 addresses are usually represented in the form x:x:x:x:x:x:x:x where each x is a hexadecimal value (thus representing 16 bits); for example, 2020:CA28:0000:0000:0023:0222:0000:2900.

Since these addresses can be rather long, there is a way to simplify text representation. For example, 0000 can be represented as 0 or even nothing. A sequence of 16 bits all equal to 0 can be represented as ::, which can only be present once in an address.

Back to the previous examples, the address can be represented as 2020:CA28::23:222:0:29.

The ::1 address represents the loopback address (the equivalent of the 127.0.0.1 address for IPv4 addresses) and :: is the unspecified address. This must not be addressed to any node and simply specifies an absence of address; for example, :: can be used as the source address of the node that has not yet learned its own unicast address, and must not be used as a destination address or in the routing header.

IPv6 does not impose any specific boundary for the network part similarly to classless inter-domain routing (CIDR) used in IPv4.

In a mixed environment (IPv4 and IPv6) it is sometimes convenient to use the following format: 2020:CA28::222:124.4.12.3 (see Table 15.1).

Table 15.1 Initial Allocation of Prefix Ranges

Allocation	Prefix (binary)	Fraction of address space
Reserved	0000 0000	1/256
Unassigned	0000 0001	1/256
Reserved for NSAP allocation	0000 001	1/128
Reserved for IPX allocation	0000 010	1/128
Unassigned	0000 011	1/128
Unassigned	0000 1	1/32
Unassigned	0001	1/16
Aggregatable global unicast addresses	001x xxxx	1/8
Unassigned	010x xxxx	1/8
Unassigned	011x xxxx	1/8
Unassigned	100x xxxx	1/8
Unassigned	101x xxxx	1/8
Unassigned	110x xxxx	1/8
Unassigned	1110 xxxx	1/16
Unassigned	1111 0xxx	1/32
Unassigned	1111 10xx	1/64
Unassigned	1111 110x	1/128
Unassigned	1111 1110 0	1/512
Link-local unicast addresses	1111 1110 10	1/1024
Site-local unicast addresses	1111 1110 11	1/1024
Multicast addresses	1111 1111	1/256

Table 15.1 shows the initial allocation of prefix range. The IPv6 address type is conditioned by the values of the leading bits of the address. For example, multicast addresses always start with 11111111 (FF). Anycast addresses are part of the unicast address space.

15.3.3 Unicast Addresses

A unicast address is made of a subnet prefix and an interface identifier (interface ID). Interface IDs are used to identify an interface on a link and thus must be unique on that link; it is very common for the interface ID to be identical to the link layer address of the interface. As discussed in Chapter 16, this interesting property is exploited for header compression when carrying IPv6 packets over IEEE 802.15.4 links.

15.3.3.1 Global Unicast IPv6 Addresses

As shown in Table 15.1, global unicast addresses have their three leftmost bits set to 001. Consequently, a global unicast address belongs to the 2000:: to 3FFF:FFFF:FFFF:FFFF:FFFF:FFFF:FFFF:FFFF range. In most cases, the leftmost 64 bits are used to identify the network portion of the address (thus implying a /64 prefix length) and the rightmost 64 bits are used to identify the host portion of the address.

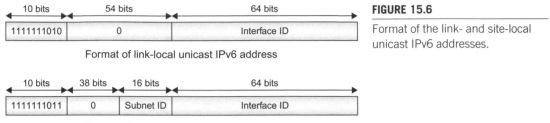

FIGURE 15.6

Format of link-local unicast IPv6 address

Format of site-local unicast IPv6 address

Format of the link- and site-local unicast IPv6 addresses.

To allow for address aggregation to reduce routing table sizes in the Internet, IPv6 mandates using addresses provided by Service Providers. The network portion of the address is subdivided into a

- 48-bit field corresponding to the prefix provided by the Service Provider
- 16-bit field used by the network administrator to allocate subnets within a site (thus resulting in 2^{16} available subnets)
- 64-bit field corresponding to the host part (the interface ID); that large a field allows for embedding the 48-bit media access control (MAC) address, which is extremely convenient for address autoconfiguration as explained in Section 15.7

The process of building the interface ID is detailed in Section 15.7.

15.3.3.2 Local Unicast IPv6 Addresses
There are two types of local unicast IPv6 addresses: link-local and site-local.

Link-local unicast addresses are used on a single link for autoconfiguration, neighbor discovery, or in the absence of router. Since the scope is local, packets with link-local scope are never forwarded by the router beyond the scope of the link.

The site-local address was initially introduced in [114]. The site-local address is an address forwarded within a site that does not need to reach in the Internet (thus no need for a global routable prefix). Consequently, packets with such addresses were not forwarded by routers outside of the site. Site-local addresses have been deprecated by [127] and must no longer be supported by new implementations. New implementations must treat site-local addresses as global unicast addresses.

The format of the link- and site-local unicast IPv6 addresses is depicted in Figure 15.6.

Thus a link-local scope unicast address always starts with FE80:0:0:0 followed by the interface ID.

15.3.3.2.1 Unique Local Unicast Addresses
[117] defines the concept of unique local addresses that are globally unique and intended for local communication (not routable in the Internet).

A unique local unicast address has the format shown in Figure 15.7.

By default, the scope of unique local unicast addresses is global. These addresses may be used within a site or even between sites, although they are not routable in the Internet.

The choice was made to choose a 7-bit prefix length providing about 2.2 trillion addresses while only using 0.781% of the IPv6 addressing space. The allocation of the Global ID must use a pseudo-random

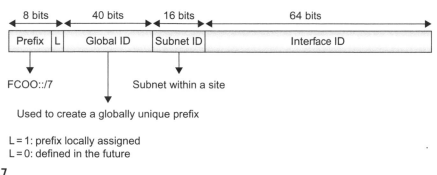

Format of an IPv6 unique local address

FIGURE 15.7

Format of the unique local unicast addresses.

algorithm consistent with [75]. Assignments are self-generated with an extremely high probability of uniqueness. [117] proposes the use of the following pseudo-random algorithm:

1. Obtain the current time of day in 64-bit Network Time Protocol (NTP) format (see [175] for the specification).
2. Obtain an EUI-64 identifier from the system running this algorithm. If an EUI-64 does not exist, one can be created from a 48-bit MAC address as specified in Section 15.7.1. If an EUI-64 cannot be obtained or created, a suitably unique identifier, local to the node, should be used (e.g., system serial number).
3. Concatenate the time of day with the system-specific identifier to create a key.
4. Compute an SHA-1 digest on the key as specified in [74,79]; the resulting value is 160 bits.
5. Use the least significant 40 bits as the Global ID.
6. Concatenate FC00::/7, the L bit set to 1, and the 40-bit Global ID to create a local IPv6 address prefix.

Collisions still exist but with an extremely low probability. Good approximations give a probability of collision of $1.81 \ 10^{-12}$ for 2 connections, $4.54 \ 10^{-9}$ for 100 connections, and $4.54 \ 10^{-5}$ for 10,000 connections.

15.3.4 Anycast Addresses

An anycast address is an address allocated to a set of interfaces that typically belong to different routers. When a packet is destined to an anycast address, it is delivered to the closest interface that has this anycast address, where the term "closest" is determined by the routing protocol. An anycast address must be assigned to a router not a host and cannot be used as a source address.

Since anycast addresses are unicast addresses, when an interface is configured with an anycast address it must be explicitly configured on the router owning that interface. This is done because anycast addresses cannot be distinguished from any other unicast addresses.

One example of an anycast address is the subnet-router anycast address. This address format is formed by a subnet prefix of n bits that identifies a specific link followed by 128-n bits all set to 0.

So in this example, a packet sent to the subnet-router anycast address is delivered to one of the routers on that subnet link.

15.3.5 Multicast Addresses

Multicast addresses are used in many contexts and are very important (remember that IPv6 does not use broadcast addresses). A multicast address identifies a group of nodes called a multicast group and must not be used as a source address or in a routing header. The format of a multicast address is shown in Figure 15.8.

All multicast addresses start with FF (first 8 bits of the address), followed by a 4-bit flag field, a 4-bit scope field, and a 112-bit group ID.

15.3.5.1 Flags

The R flag is used to embed a rendezvous point in the address (see [219]). The P flag identifies a unicast prefix-based multicast address, as defined in [103]. The T flag determines whether the multicast address is permanent (T = 0) and assigned by the Internet Assigned Numbers Authority (IANA; what is considered a well-known address) or a transient address (T = 1). Then a second 4-bit field identifies the scope of the multicast address (e.g., link-local, node-local, site-local, etc.).

Some multicast addresses are reserved such as FF00:0:0:0:0:0:0:0, FF01:0:0:0:0:0:0:0, FF02:0:0:0:0:0:0:0, FF03:0:0:0:0:0:0:0, FF03:0:0:0:0:0:0:0, FF05:0:0:0:0:0:0:0, FF06:0:0:0:0:0:0:0, FF07:0:0:

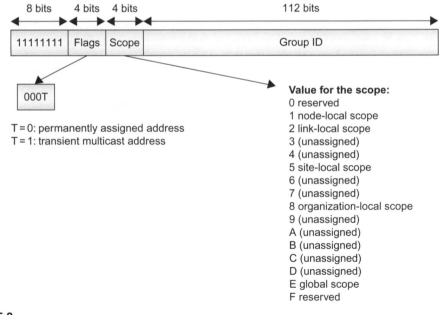

FIGURE 15.8

Format of an IPv6 multicast address.

0:0:0:0:0, FF08:0:0:0:0:0:0:0, FF09:0:0:0:0:0:0:0, FF0A:0:0:0:0:0:0:0, FF0B:0:0:0:0:0:0:0, FF0C:0:0:
0:0:0:0:0, FF0D:0:0:0:0:0:0:0, FF0E:0:0:0:0:0:0:0, and FF0F:0:0:0:0:0:0:0.

Other predefined addresses that are used often include:

- Multicast address for all node-local (scope restricted to the node) IPv6 nodes: FF01:0:0:0:0:0:0:1
- Multicast address for all link-local IPv6 nodes: FF02:0:0:0:0:0:0:1
- Multicast address for all node-local IPv6 routers: FF01:0:0:0:0:0:0:2
- Multicast address for all link-local IPv6 routers: FF02:0:0:0:0:0:0:2
- Multicast address for all site-local IPv6 routers: FF05:0:0:0:0:0:0:2

Well-known multicast addresses have also been defined for routing protocols:

- Multicast address for all link-local RIP routers: FF02:0:0:0:0:0:0:9
- Multicast address for all link-local OSPF routers: FF02:0:0:0:0:0:0:5
- Multicast address for all link-local OSPF DR routers: FF02:0:0:0:0:0:0:6
- Multicast address for all link-local PIM routers: FF02:0:0:0:0:0:0:D

The solicited-node address is a multicast address that has the format FF02:0:0:0:0:1:FFXX:XXXX and is computed from the node's unicast and anycast addresses. The 24 lower order bits of the unicast or anycast address are appended to the prefix FF02:0:0:0:0:1:FF00::/104.

Each node must compute and join (to use multicast terminology) the solicited-node address for each of its unicast and anycast addresses, thus making the node listen and process packets sent to that multicast address.

The solicited node address is used during the address resolution procedure detailed later in Section 15.5.1. In IPv4, when a node needs to obtain the link layer address (MAC address) of a node it uses a procedure known as Address Resolution Protocol (ARP), which sends a broadcast message on the link that disturbs all of the nodes including the ones that do not run IPv4. With IPv6 one could use a link-local all-node multicast address but a further optimization consists of using the solicited-node address instead in the neighbor solicitation message.

15.4 THE ICMP FOR IPv6

ICMP has been used in the Internet for a long time for error reporting and diagnostics, supporting a variety of features such as echo request/reply, notification of various errors (TTL exceeded, destination unreachable, etc.), redirection, and so forth.

ICMPv6 is a key component of the IPv6 architecture and not only supports most of the features available with IPv4 but was also augmented with several features supported by other non-ICMP protocols such as ARP and the Internet Group Membership Protocol (IGMP) as well as new key functionalities used in support of useful IPv6 features such as autoconfiguration (see Section 15.7). RPL, the routing protocol for smart objects (discussed in great detail in Chapter 17), also makes use of ICMPv6. ICMPv6 is identified by a new protocol type (type 58) specified in the immediately preceding header field.

Most of the ICMPv6 features are specified in [42], but some have been defined in other RFCs.

ICMPv6 specifies two categories of messages: error and informational.

Each ICMP message has the following structure:

- 8-bit type field: Indicates the type of message (and thus the format of the remaining data).
- 8-bit code field: Used to provide additional granularity for a given ICMP message type.
- 16-bit checksum: The reason for adding a checksum is that (by contrast with IPv4) the IPv6 header does not have any checksum. The checksum is the 16-bit complement sum of the entire ICMPv6 message starting with the ICMPv6 message type field prepended with a pseudo-header of IPv6 header field.
- Variable length data field.

[42] specifies the rules used to determine the source address for the ICMP message. For example, if the message is a response to a message sent to a unicast address the node belongs to, the source must be this address. If the message is a response to an error (e.g., the forwarding failed), even if the original message was sent to an address that does not belong to the node, the source must be a unicast address belonging to the node. It must follow standard source address selection rules unless another unicast address belonging to the node can give more information about the destination. For example, the node can use a source address in the reply message that can be useful for diagnostics.

Refer to [42] for a detailed set of messages and processing rules.

15.4.1 **ICMPv6 Error Messages**

The type field of error messages is a value between 0 and 127.

Table 15.2 lists ICMPv6 informational messages defined in [42] with a short description.

All packets received with an error in the IPv6 header or an extended header must be discarded and an ICMP error message sent. Some firewalls do not send ICMP error messages to dissimulate their presence, which can be an issue for troubleshooting or protocols such as PMTU.

15.4.2 **ICMP Informational Messages**

The type field of informational messages is a value between 128 and 255.

Table 15.3 lists some of the ICMPv6 error messages with a short description.

As IPv6 continues to evolve, new functionalities are added and additional ICMP codes are specified.

RS, RA, NS, and NA ICMPv6 messages are very important for autoconfiguration and described in great details in Section 15.7.

A number of other ICMPv6 messages were defined in other RFCs. For instance, major protocols such as multicast listener discovery (MLD; [92]) and Mobile IPv6 [140] make extensive use of existing and new ICMPv6 messages.

15.5 **NEIGHBOR DISCOVERY PROTOCOL**

The Neighbor Discovery Protocol (ND; specified in [185]) provides a set of key autoconfiguration features for IPv6 such as the discovery of the presence of neighbors on a link, discovery of routers on the link that provide important information like the network prefix, discovery of link layer addresses, or maintenance of reachability information about paths to active neighbors.

Table 15.2 ICMPv6 Error Messages

	Type	Code	Description
Destination unreachable	1	0	No route to destination (no routing entry for the packet). This does not include packet drop error due to congestion.
		1	Communication with destination administratively prohibited (e.g., case of a firewall that cannot forward the packet because of filtering action triggered by policy).
		3	Address unreachable for other reasons than the reasons listed above.
		4	Port unreachable.
Packet too big	2	0	The packet size exceeds the MTU of the outgoing link (used by the PMTU discovery process).
Time exceeded	3	0	Sent when the hop limit field (after being decremented) is equal to 0 or the received packet has a hop limit field equal to 0.
Parameter problem (problem with the field of the IPv6 header or extended headers)	4	0	Erroneous header field encountered.
		1	Unrecognized next header type encountered.
		2	Unrecognized IPv6 option encountered.

Needless to say, ND plays an important role in IP smart object networks.
ND offers a number of services that include:

- Router discovery: Discovery of a router capable of forwarding packets destined to off-link addresses.
- Prefix discovery: Discovery of the set of addresses that are on-link for the attached link using the network prefix.
- Parameter discovery: Discovery of MTU, hop limits, and so forth.
- Address autoconfiguration: Process by which the node can compute its unique global address.
- Address resolution: Discovery of the link layer address. ARP is used in IPv4 to discover the link layer address for a node knowing its IPv4 address. In IPv6, such function is performed by the ND, which is also used to detect if a node has a new link layer address.
- Next-hop determination: Algorithm to find the IP next hop to use to forward a packet for a specific destination.
- Neighbor unreachability detection (NUD): Process by which a router determines that a neighbor is no longer reachable.
- Duplicate address detection (DAD): Verification process ensuring that the address a node is intending to use is not already in use by another node.
- Redirect: Process allowing a node to find a better next hop to reach a specific destination.

Table 15.3 ICMPv6 Informational Messages

	Type	Code	Description
Echo request	128	0	
Echo reply	129	0	
Router solicitation (RS)	133		See Section 15.5.4
Router advertisement (RA)	134		See Section 15.5.3
Neighbor solicitation (NS)	135		See Section 15.5.1
Neighbor advertisement (NA)	136		See Section 15.5.2
Redirect	137		

ND specifies five new ICMP message types. The following sections describe a packet format type and describe the processing rules for each packet along with the associated services.

The ND protocols define a series of options that may appear in the ND messages such as the source/target link layer address option, the prefix information option, and redirect header or the MTU option. In this section we provide more details on the prefix information option since this option plays an important role in the stateless autoconfiguration feature described later in Section 15.7 of this chapter.

15.5.1 The Neighbor Solicitation Message

The format of the neighbor solicitation (NS) message is shown in Figure 15.9.

The NS message is used for address resolution, neighbor unreachability detection (NUD), and DAD. An NS message is sent by a node to obtain or confirm the link layer address of a neighbor for which it knows the IP address. The NS messages are multicast packets using the solicited-node multicast address of the target address for the destination address and an address of the requesting node or the unspecified address during the DAD process for the source address. Upon receiving the NS packet, the target replies with a neighbor advertisement (NA) message, if appropriate. The choice of source and destination addresses depends on the service performed and will be detailed later.

NS may include a link layer address option. It allows the receiver to learn the link layer address of the sender without having to perform address resolution. The receiver will still be required to perform NUD if he wants to confirm the reachability of the initial sender of the NS message. The presence of this option is not always allowed, for instance, a node performing DAD procedure must not include it in an NS message.

Finally, NS messages are also used to detect that a neighbor is unreachable.

15.5.2 The NA Message

The neighbor advertisement (NA) is used to provide the link layer address to a requesting node or to inform of a link layer address change. NA messages are used for address resolution, NUD, and DAD procedures in response to an NS message, but they may also be used for other purposes, usually in such as an unsolicited way for instance to inform of relate an address change or a mobility event.

The source address is the address of the sender. The destination address is the address of the requester present in the received NS message. If the source address of the NS message is an unspecified

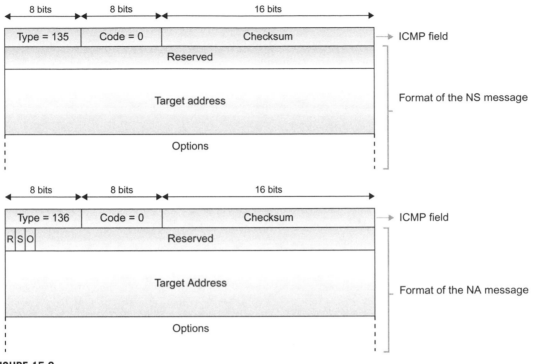

FIGURE 15.9

Format of the neighbor solicitation (NS) and neighbor advertisement (NA) messages.

address, then the destination address is the all-nodes multicast address. As shown in Figure 15.9, the format of the NA message is very similar to the format of the NS message with the addition of three bits:

- R-bit: When set, this indicates that the sender is a router. This is used to detect, via the unreachability process, that a router changes to a host.
- S-bit: When set, the solicited flag indicates that the advertisement was sent in response to the reception of an NS message. This bit is used as a reachability confirmation for NUD.
- O-bit: The override flag is set to indicate that the advertisement should override an existing cache entry.

Note that the target address is the target address present in the NS message.

If there is an unsolicited message, the target address corresponds to the IP address of the node for which the link layer address has changed. In this case, the destination address is the all-nodes multicast address.

NA messages typically carry a target link layer address option.

15.5.3 The Router Advertisement Messages

Router advertisement (RA) messages are periodically sent by routers and serve multiple purposes: they are used by routers to advertise their presence in addition to various link and Internet parameters, including the network prefix information used by the host to configure their unicast global address.

RA messages can either be sent by routers unsolicited (periodically) as well as solicited in response to an RS message sent by a host that does not want to wait for the reception of an unsolicited RA message (e.g., especially useful for mobile nodes). With periodic timers they are slightly randomized to avoid global synchronization of all routers on the link.

RA messages contain information about prefixes used for on-link determination and/or autonomous address configuration. RA messages also inform nodes whether they should use a stateful (DHCP) and/or stateless autonomous address configuration (see Section 15.7).

Figure 15.10 shows the format of the RA message.

Next is a description of the various fields of an RA message.

IP fields:

- Source address: Local-link address assigned to the interface from which the packet is sent.
- Destination address: Typically the source address of the sender of the RS message (solicited message) or the all-nodes multicast address (FF02::1;unsolicited message). In the case of a solicited message, when the source address is not provided in the RS message, the RA message is also sent using the all-nodes multicast address.

RA message:

- Current hop limit: The default value that should be used in the hop count field of an IPv6 header for outgoing IP packets.

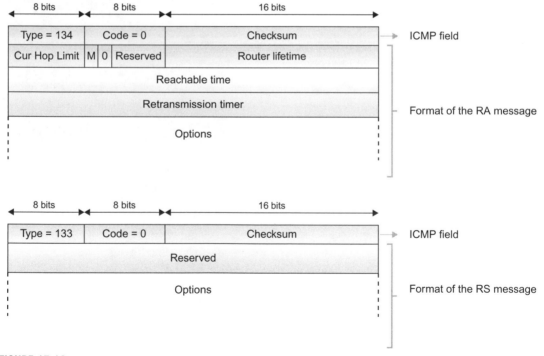

FIGURE 15.10

Format of the RA and RS messages.

- The M-bit or managed address configuration bit: When set, this indicates to the host that it must use the administered stateful protocol for address autoconfiguration in addition to the stateless address autoconfiguration mode.
- The O-bit (other stateful configuration) flag: Indicates whether configuration information other than addresses can be obtained via DHCPv6.
- Router lifetime: This field indicates the lifetime of the associated default route in seconds. When set to 0, the router should not be considered a default router.
- Reachable time: This value is used by the NUD process and indicates in milliseconds the time that a node assumes a neighbor is reachable after having received reachability confirmation.
- Retransmission timer: Time in milliseconds between the retransmission of NS messages. This timer is used by the address resolution and the NUD processes.

The most notable options that a RA message may contain are

- Source link layer address: This field indicates the link layer address of the interface from which the RA message was sent. The router may omit this option if load balancing across a set of link layer addresses is desired.
- MTU: Maximum transmission unit on the link.
- Prefix information: This important optional field indicates the list of prefixes used for on-link determination and autoconfiguration. The router should provide all of its on-link prefixes (for multi-homed hosts).
- DNSS: Provides the address of a recursive DNS server available on the network.

15.5.3.1 Options Prefixes Advertised in the RA Messages

The prefix information is used in RA messages to provide hosts with on-link prefixes and prefixes for address autoconfiguration. The format of the prefix information option is shown in Figure 15.11.

Description of the prefix information option fields:

- Prefix length: Number of leading bits in the prefix that are valid (from 0 to 128 bits).
- L-flag: When set, this indicates that the prefix can be used for on-link determination. Conversely, when the L-flag is cleared, no statement can be made on whether the prefix is on- or off-link.

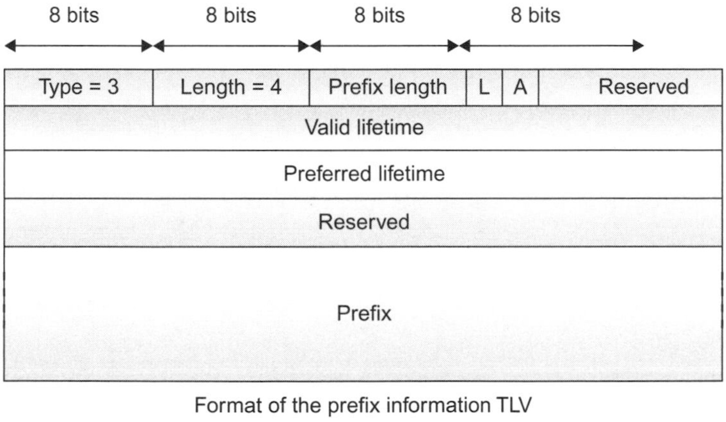

FIGURE 15.11

Prefix information option.

Format of the prefix information TLV

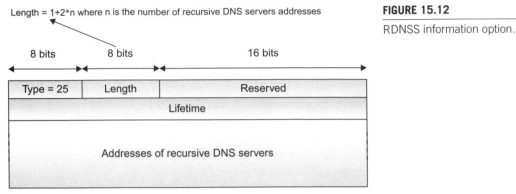

Length = 1+2*n where n is the number of recursive DNS servers addresses

FIGURE 15.12

RDNSS information option.

Format of the RDNSS option TLV

- A-flag (autonomous): When set, this indicates that this prefix can be used for autonomous address configuration.
- Valid lifetime: This indicates in seconds the length of time that the prefix is valid.
- Preferred lifetime: Length of time in seconds that the address generated from the prefix via stateless autoconfiguration remains in the "preferred" state.

The notion of valid and preferred lifetimes offers an efficient mechanism for smooth renumbering, which may happen, for example, when migrating from one Service Provider to another. The valid lifetime is simply the lifetime of a prefix, where the preferred lifetime indicates the period of time during which a host should use the prefix. After the expiration of the preferred lifetime, if the valid lifetime has not expired, a host only uses the address for already established communications.

15.5.3.2 Recursive DNSS Option Advertised in the RA Messages

[138] specifies an RA option allowing a router to advertise recursive DNS server (RDNSS) addresses in RA messages. This provides a useful alternative to DHCP to locate DNS servers. This is particularly interesting for smart objects using stateless autoconfiguration that retrieves DNS information processing the unique RA message, thus saving potentially scarce energy resources.

The RDNSS option (see Figure 15.12) uses the regular ND messages such as RA and RS previously described.

All addresses share the same lifetime value that indicates the maximum time in seconds over which a node can use the RDNSS address for name resolution. A node may send an RS message to refresh the state before the expiration of that time. It is recommended to set the lifetime values between MaxRtrAdvInterval and 2* MaxRtrAdvInterval where MaxRtrAdvInterval is defined as the maximum time in seconds allowed between sending unsolicited multicast RA messages from the interface. A value of 0xFFFFFFFF represents infinity, and a value of 0 indicates that the addresses must no longer be used.

15.5.4 The Router Solicitation Message

The router solicitation (RS) message is sent by a host to get an RA message in reply (if at least one router is present on the link) without having to wait for the expiration of the RA periodic timer.

The RS message structure is very simple (a 32-bit field set to 0). The IP fields are:

- Source address: IP address of the interface used to send the RS message or unspecified address during autoconfiguration (see Section 15.7).
- Destination address: Typical all-routers multicast address (FF02::2).

The ICMP type is equal to 10.

15.5.5 The Redirect Message

Redirect packets are sent by routers to inform a host of a better first node on the path to the destination.

15.5.6 Neighbor Unreachability Detection (NUD)

NUD is a powerful mechanism used for unicast destination allowing a node (a host or a router) to verify the reachability of a neighbor. When the path to the neighbor seems to fail, if the destination is the ultimate destination, the address resolution should be performed again. On the other hand, if the neighbor is a router, it might be appropriate to select another router. The procedure used in this case is the next-hop determination (the neighbor cache entry is then deleted).

First, how does a node determine whether a neighbor is reachable? Positive confirmation that a neighbor is reachable can either be the receipt of an NA message in response to an NS message or a hint from the upper layer (e.g., receipt of a TCP ACK or new non-duplicate data from the peer via the neighbor). When the transport protocol cannot provide a hint (e.g., UDP), then the node sends a probe to the neighbor (solicited unicast NS message). Receipt of an unsolicited message such as an RA or NA message with the "solicited" flag set to 0 cannot be used for a neighbor reachability confirmation (only confirms one way path integrity).

Neighbor cache entries are found in various states. For example, if no reachability confirmation has been received from a neighbor after Reachabletime milliseconds (configuration timer), the neighbor cache entry is flagged as "stale." If the node must send a packet to that neighbor, it starts another timer after the expiration. If no neighbor reachability has been received, it starts an active probing procedure. The probing procedure (at this stage the cache entry is in the PROBE state) consists of sending a unicast NS message to the neighbor using the cached link layer address of that neighbor. NS messages are retransmitted every RetransTimer millisecond until an NA message in received in response. If after sending MAX_UNICAST_SOLICIT messages no NA message has been received, the cache entry is deleted.

Link layer information reporting link failures can be used to trigger the cache entry deletion, but the indication that the link layer is operational cannot serve as a neighbor reachability confirmation (the link layer may be operational, although the neighbor is not reachable).

15.6 LOAD BALANCING

There are several circumstances where it is useful for a router to make use of input load balancing (reception of traffic from different interfaces that share the same IPv6 address).

This is achieved by not including any link layer addresses in the RA messages. Consequently, this forces the host to send NS messages to get the router link layer address to which the router will reply with NA messages using different link layer addresses, depending on which host issued the NS message.

15.7 IPv6 AUTOCONFIGURATION

The ability for a node to support autoconfiguration is very important, especially when the number of nodes is extremely large and the nodes are unattended, which is precisely the case in smart object networks. In these networks, for example, in a city where the number of smart objects can easily be on the order of hundreds of thousands or even millions, one cannot expect each node to be manually configured. In several requirement documents the term 0-config was even mentioned. This is why the set of autoconfiguration features supported by IPv6 is particularly well suited to smart object networks. Although some of these features were supported with IPv4, several new features have been added to IPv6 that are particularly useful for smart objects.

15.7.1 Building the Link-local Address

When an interface is first initialized the node builds its link-local address by prepending the well-known link-local prefix FE80::0/10 (the first 10 leftmost bits are 1111 1110 10) followed by 54 bits set to 0 and the interface ID. Note that the interface ID may be of any length (less than 118 bits, otherwise the autoconfiguration process fails), but generally 64-bit addresses (EUI-64 identifier) are used.

Let's take a node with a 48-bit MAC address to illustrate how such an address is converted into an EUI-64 address to build the interface ID (see Figure 15.13).

The process is fairly straightforward: the 16 bits (FFFE) are simply inserted in the middle of the 48-bit MAC address to produce the 64-bit EUI-64 format address. The interface ID is then created from the EUI-64 address by complementing the universal/local bit in the EUI-64 address, which is the next to lowest order bit of the first octet of EUI-64.

The link-local address has an infinite preferred and valid lifetime and never times out.

In our previous example the link-local address would be FE:80:0:0:0:0:0:0:14:B1:FF:FE:CA:8 E:47. At this stage, the node can communicate with any other node on the same link. These packets will not be forwarded by routers on other links.

15.7.2 The Stateless Autoconfiguration Process

The autoconfiguration process consists of several steps:

- Creation of a link-local address and uniqueness on a link
- Determination of what should be autoconfigured
- Determination of whether addresses should be obtained using a stateless or a stateful procedure

The stateless autoconfiguration process (described in [235]) allows a node to generate its link-local, site-local, and global addresses using a combination of local information and information

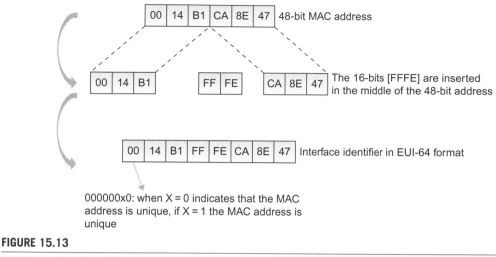

FIGURE 15.13

Building an interface ID.

advertised by routers with no configuration on the host, minimal (if any) configuration on the router, and no external server (in contrast with stateful configuration). Both stateless and stateful autoconfiguration mechanisms may be combined and complement each other. As discussed in Section 15.5.3, the M-bit of the RA message indicates whether to use a stateless or a stateful autoconfiguration mechanism.

Autoconfiguration is only supported on multicast capable links (and links that emulate multicast).

15.7.2.1 *Building Unicast IPv6 Addresses*

As discussed earlier, a global address is obtained by concatenating the prefix information with the interface ID. The stateless mechanism is used by hosts only and not routers, with the exception of the link-local address that is generated by a router and the support of the DAD mechanism, which is also supported by routers.

The first step of the process is building the link-local address by prepending the interface ID with FE80:0:0:0. The link-local address allows local communication between all nodes residing on the local link.

Before assigning a unicast address (link-local or global), the node must first verify the uniqueness of the address with the DAD procedure. This does not apply to anycast addresses. The DAD procedure uses the NS and NA messages, and if the address is already in use by another node, the procedure stops and a new interface ID must be configured on the node. DAD is not completely reliable so it is possible that duplicate addresses exist. All packets received before the completion of the DAD process destined to the address under verification must be silently discarded.

15.7.2.2 *DAD Process*

The DAD process verifies the uniqueness of an address prior to assigning it to an interface. This process must be used regardless of the address allocation technique (stateless, stateful, or manual configuration).

The node first starts by computing the EUI-64 address if needed. It then assigns the all-nodes multicast address to the interface and the solicited-node multicast address of the tentative address. To verify the uniqueness of the address, the node sends a (configurable) number of NS messages (see Section 5.1 of [235]). NS messages must be separated by RetransTimer milliseconds. This parameter is advertised in the RA messages sent by the routers. The target address present in the NS message must be equal to the address checked. In this case, the IP source of the NS message is sent to the unspecified address, and the destination address is sent to the solicited-node multicast address of the target address. The DAD mechanism allows for jittering when NS messages are first sent to avoid the race condition should a set of nodes try to simultaneously run the procedure — for example, after a power outage.

When a node receives an NS message, it does the following:

- If the target address has already been assigned to the node, this is a duplicate address (therefore it cannot be used).
- If the target address is in a "tentative" state (the receiving node is also trying to assign that same address to itself) and the source address is unicast, then the sending node is not trying to run the DAD procedure but is in fact trying to obtain the link layer address. In this case, the NS message should simply be discarded. On the other hand, if the source address of the NS message is not unicast but is equal to the unspecified address, the NS message is from a node running the DAD procedure that is trying to assign the same address to one of its interfaces (this address cannot be used).

If an NS message for a tentative address is received prior to having sent an NS for the same address, the tentative address is a duplicate (it is about to start DAD for an address that another node is also trying to use). This occurs when two nodes are trying to run the DAD procedure for the same address, but one of them has sent the NS message before the other (by using random timers). There is also a mechanism that covers the case of an NS message sent approximately at the same time.

In short, if the node does not receive an NA for the target address, it is free to assign it to the interface, otherwise there is a duplicate and the address cannot be used. When this happens the DAD process is stopped and an error message must be generated. The DAD process is not entirely reliable; for example, when a packet drops because of some unreliable links (pretty common in lossy environments) or if the links were partitioned when the DAD process took place.

15.7.2.3 Optimistic DAD
[177] has defined a modification to the DAD procedure called "optimistic DAD" to reduce the address configuration delays in the successful cases while reducing disruption in the failure cases. [183] introduces addresses called "optimistic" assigned to an address that is available for use, but whose DAD procedure has not yet been completed. In a nutshell, an optimistic address is equivalent to a deprecated address because it is available for use but should not be used if another suitable address is available. Note that optimistic DAD should be used for addresses based on unique identifiers (e.g., typically not for manually configured addresses).

15.7.2.4 Creation of the Unicast Global and Site-local Addresses
Building the unicast global and site-local addresses requires obtaining the prefix information from the RA messages sent by routers. The node may either wait until it received a periodic RA message or may send an RS message to the all-routers address to receive a solicited RA message. If no RA message is received, the node must attempt to use stateful autoconfiguration.

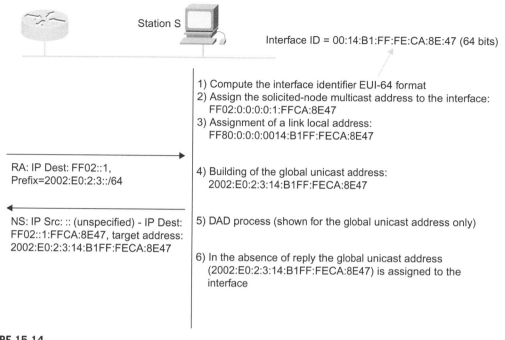

Station S

Interface ID = 00:14:B1:FF:FE:CA:8E:47 (64 bits)

1) Compute the interface identifier EUI-64 format
2) Assign the solicited-node multicast address to the interface:
   FF02:0:0:0:0:1:FFCA:8E47
3) Assignment of a link local address:
   FF80:0:0:0:0014:B1FF:FECA:8E47

RA: IP Dest: FF02::1,
Prefix=2002:E0:2:3::/64

4) Building of the global unicast address:
   2002:E0:2:3:14:B1FF:FECA:8E47

NS: IP Src: :: (unspecified) - IP Dest:
FF02::1:FFCA:8E47, target address:
2002:E0:2:3:14:B1FF:FECA:8E47

5) DAD process (shown for the global unicast address only)

6) In the absence of reply the global unicast address
   (2002:E0:2:3:14:B1FF:FECA:8E47) is assigned to the
   interface

FIGURE 15.14

Stateless autoconfiguration.

Once the set of prefixes has been received, the node assigns these addresses to the interfaces after completing the DAD process previously detailed. Figure 15.14 provides an example of stateless auto configuration process.

15.7.3 Privacy Extensions for Stateless Address Autoconfiguration in IPv6

[184] specifies extensions for autoconfigured stateless addresses derived from non-changing addresses (typically IEEE addresses). This may be an issue if privacy must be preserved; indeed, a packet sniffer could infer the host activity fairly easily. Thus changing the address of a host over time could help preserve privacy. This may be of particular interest for strategic smart objects reporting sensitive data. An eavesdropper may be able to track the movement of a mobile smart object because of its address (a case where encryption would not help since the address is not encrypted).

Even with DHCP IPv4 addresses would not change that often. The issue becomes more apparent with IPv6 since the interface ID would never change (with permanent link layer address use) even if the node joins another network thus inheriting a new prefix ID.

[184] proposes a set of mechanisms in order to create additional global scope addresses based on a randomly generated interface identifier. It must be noted that the stateless address autoconfiguration mechanisms remain unchanged. These addresses are only used for outgoing sessions and would be used for short periods of time (hours to days) before being deprecated. The actual value of the randomized identifier changes over time, but a unique identifier can be used to generate more than one address.

Two approaches are proposed for the generation of randomized IDs depending on whether stable storage is available on the node. In this case, historical data can be recorded and used as input for the algorithm after a system restart.

When stable storage is available, the algorithm assumes that a 64-bit "history value" is available. The very first time the system boots up, a pseudo-random algorithm such as [75] can be used to generate the history value. The history value changes as new random identifiers are generated. Here are the proposed algorithms specified in [184]:

1. Take the history value from the previous iteration of this algorithm (or a random value if there is no previous value) and append the interface identifier generated to it.
2. Compute the MD5 message digest [215] over the quantity created in the previous step.
3. Take the leftmost 64 bits of the MD5 digest and set bit 6 (the leftmost bit is numbered 0) to zero. This creates an interface identifier with the universal/local bit indicating local significance only. Save the generated identifier as the associated randomized interface identifier.
4. Take the rightmost 64 bits of the MD5 digest computed in step 2 and save them in stable storage as the history value to be used in the next iteration of the algorithm.

Without stable storage there is no history value and pseudo-random algorithms such as [75] can be used.

The DAD procedure must be triggered for the newly computed temporary address.

One drawback of using randomized temporary addresses is the increased complexity when troubleshooting.

15.8 DHCPv6

15.8.1 Stateful Autoconfiguration

DHCPv6 specified in [62] and DHCP for IPv4 provide similar services: a *centralized* mechanism to configure node addresses (including the host part of the node address) and obtain other useful information such as DNS addresses. Compared to its IPv4 counterpart some changes have been made in IPv6 (some message types have been removed, others have been added, the ability to request more than one address has been added, etc.).

As discussed in Section 15.5.3, if the M-bit (managed configuration flag of the RA message) is set, the requesting node must use the administered stateful protocol for address autoconfiguration (DHCP) in addition to the stateless address autoconfiguration mode.

The discovery process of the DHCP server consists of sending a message to the well-known link-local address (FF02::1:2) used to address all DHCP agents on the local link in contrast with DHCPv4 that uses broadcast addresses. If it turns out that the DCHP server is not located on the same link, routers can be configured to relay these messages or to send a direct reply to the requesting node if the router knows the DCHP address. When relaying the request, the relaying routers use all DHCP address site-local multicast addresses: FF05::1:3.

Once the DHCP server has been located, messages are exchanged between the requesting node and the DHCP server to gather the requested data.

Another mechanism known as prefix delegation and specified in [240] can be used in some cases to automate the delegation of IPv6 using DHCP. Prefix delegation is typically used by Service

Providers: the customer router acts as a DHCP client requesting prefixes to the Service Provider router that acts as a DHCP server (and does not have to know the topology of a customer's network).

15.8.2 Stateless DHCP

Once the IPv6 global address has been obtained by manual configuration or the stateless autoconfiguration process previously described, stateless DHCPv6 services (specified in [61]) allow a node to obtain various information such as DNS recursive name servers or SIP servers. In contrast with stateful DHCP, stateless DHCP does not perform address assignment but is limited to providing configuration information. Such a stateless DHCP server does not maintain any dynamic state for DHCP clients.

Stateless DHCP servers only support a subset of the DHCP messages specified in [63]. The DHCP client uses a DHCP information-request message to obtain configuration information to which the stateless DHCP server replies with a reply message that carries configuration information such as DNS recursive name servers or SIP servers.

The simplicity of stateless DHCP makes it a very appealing functionality for smart object networks.

15.9 IPv6 QoS

This section does not provide a complete description of the wide set of mechanisms and protocols designed over the past decade to provide QoS in IP networks, but rather highlights the fact that QoS in IPv6 is very similar to QoS in IPv4. This is excellent news considering the number of mechanisms and protocols that have been successfully designed for IPv4 to provide very tight Service Level Agreements (SLAs) to IP traffic. As a reminder, IP networks do carry traffic such as voice and high-definition video that are very sensitive to delays, jitter, and packet loss.

QoS is undoubtedly a key architectural component of IP networks and has been approached in many ways. The first and most simple approach is to throw more bandwidth in the network, increasing the network capacity by using higher speed links and/or new links to avoid any potential congestion. As traffic increases, upon crossing some link utilization thresholds, the network is upgraded to "try" to avoid congestion in the network and minimize queuing delays and jitter. Although very effective, such an approach (usually referred to as an over-provisioning policy) may be very expensive, especially when SLAs must be maintained in the presence of link and/or node failures. This topic is discussed in great detail in [246].

In most cases, congestion cannot be avoided and may occasionally take place for a period of time in parts of the network because of a burst of traffic, a network element failure, and so forth.

The objective of QoS mechanisms is to assign different priorities to the traffic, consequently, providing a differentiated treatment to packets according to their Class of Service (CoS). QoS does not create bandwidth but does provide a preferential treatment to the most important or sensitive traffic, where the notion of "most important" is defined by the user according to configurable parameters.

15.9.1 The Diffserv Model

Diffserv, specified in [16], basically relies on the ability to mark traffic (usually at the edge of the network) and uses a per-hop behavior (PHB) on each node along the path where resources are appropriately assigned to a limited number of CoS identified by the packet marking.

The first step, "classification/marking," is usually performed at the edge of the network and consists of "coloring" the packets according to user-specified rules. Coloring (marking) refers to setting the traffic class (TC) field of the IPv6 header (or the ToS field with IPv4). Such rules are based on the source/destination address, higher-level protocol, nature of the applications, or other sophisticated rules. Some routers can even support deep packet inspection techniques to perform on-the-fly classification (typically not available on a smart object, at least for now).

The TC field is divided in two subfields:

- Diffserv Code Point (DCP) — 6 bits identifies the PHB. Several of them have been standardized including best effort, expedited forwarding (EF, specified in [137]), and assured forwarding (AF, specified in [112] and [97]) with several levels of drop preference.
- The Explicit Congestion Notification (ECN) specified in [208] explicitly notifies the presence of a congestion instead of the implicit notification by dropping packets. Although initially targeted for TCP, the ECN could be used by other transport protocols including future transport protocols under investigation for smart object networks.

Once the packet has been marked with the appropriate CoS, each router along the path can process the packet accordingly using a PHB defined for its CoS. This basically involves two categories of mechanisms:

- Traffic management: This refers to the use of queuing mechanisms. A plethora of queuing mechanisms have been defined, implemented, and deployed over the past decade that can be used to provide very fine-grained QoS according to the CoS.
- Congestion avoidance: When queues are getting full, instead of simply dropping packets, several mechanisms can be used to start dropping packets using a probabilistic approach when the queue length crosses specified thresholds. The rate at which packets are dropped can be a function of the CoS within the same queue, should multiple CoS share a queue. The most common congestion avoidance mechanism is the "weighted random early detection" algorithm called WRED (see [84]).

Queuing mechanisms are usually fairly simplistic on smart objects considering the memory and CPU constraints, but the mechanisms are supported by IPv6.

15.9.2 The IntServ Model

The integrated service (IntServ) model was defined in 1994 ([20]) to support real-time and non-real-time services. It relies on resources reservation mechanisms to effectively reserve resources in the network for critical flows. Resources reservation is performed using the RSVP protocol [21].

IntServ has not been as popular as Diffserv in core networks mainly because of its limited scalability, but it is being used more often at the edge of the network for call admission control (CAC).

The use of the IntServ model in smart object networks is not likely to take place in the near future, because it requires non-negligible control plane overhead and state maintenance, unless a lightweight version is designed that could be combined with the routing functions.

15.10 IPv6 over an IPv4 Backbone Network   227

15.10 IPv6 OVER AN IPv4 BACKBONE NETWORK

Although most networks will likely migrate to IPv6 in the next 3 to 5 years, IPv4 will undoubtedly be used in many networks for decades to come. This raises the legitimate question: How should IPv6 "islands" of smart objects be interconnected if the backbone network is not natively supporting IPv6? Indeed, a Service Provider, a city, or large enterprise may want to deploy an IPv6 smart object network without having to immediately migrate its IPv4 backbone network to IPv6. This is achievable because of tunneling mechanisms that have been in used in the Internet for many purposes for a long time. These tunneling mechanisms are convenient but require some extra configuration on the edge routers supporting the tunnels and may not always offer the most optimal path in the network. Still, they are useful mechanisms to enable an IPv4 network with IPv6 capabilities.

One solution may be to run dual stacks on routers and hosts in the network, thus supporting native IPv6 and IPv4 for the applications that have not yet migrated to IPv6 [91]. But let's focus on the situation where the backbone network does not support IPv6 natively.

Several mechanisms have been defined. This section provides a brief overview of a mechanism referred to as 6to4 and specified in [34]. If the network is MPLS enabled, other approaches such as 6PE (IPv6 Provider Edge) can be used where the customer PE-CE (Provider Edge–Customer Edge) links are IPv6 enabled and the core-facing interface of the PE routers is IP/MPLS enabled. Details on this technology and deployments can be found in [247].

6to4 uses *dynamic* tunnels to interconnect IPv6 islands over an IPv4 core network, effectively making the IPv4 network a collection of link layer point-to-point links.

Figure 15.15 illustrates the 6to4 router to router, but 6to4 host-to-host tunneling also exists, although it is much less relevant to smart objects.

This is how the site prefix (/48) is formed:

- IANA assigns a permanent 13-bit top-level aggregator equal to 0x0002 under the IPv6 format prefix 001 for 6to4. Thus the first 16 bits of the address are 2002.
- The next 32 bits correspond to the IPv4 address of the relay router (R1 in as depicted in Figure 15.15).
- The next 16 bits are the SLA ID (site level aggregation identifier).
- The next 64 bits of the address correspond to the interface ID.

Let's consider the example in Figure 15.15.

- The IPv4 addresses of R1 and R2 used for the 6to4 tunnel are, respectively, 192.100.1.1 and 192.100.2.2.
- The IPv6 prefix address for site 1 is 2002: <IPv4 address of R1>/48 or 2002:c064:101 in hexadecimal notation.
- The IPv6 prefix address of site 2 is 2002: <IPv4 address of R2>/48 or 2002:c064:202.
- S is an IPv6 sensor sending an IPv6 packet to a host H. The IPv6 address of S is 2002:c064:101:10::10.
- H is a host collecting sensor data. The IPv6 address of H is 2002:c064:202:20::20.

Now let's consider the process of sending a packet from S (2002:c064:101:10::10) to H (2002:c064:202:20::20). Upon receiving the packet, R1 extracts the IPv4 tunnel end point, which is c064:202=192.100.2.2. Then it adds an IPv4 packet header to the IPv6 packet (tunneling) where the

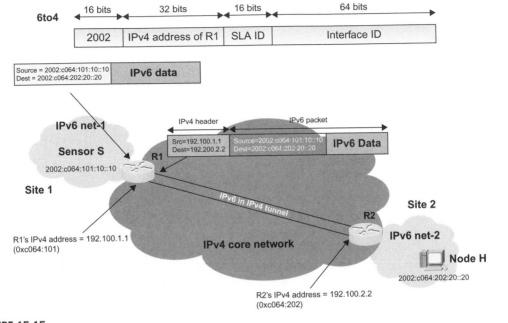

FIGURE 15.15

6to4 tunnels.

IPv4 source and destination address are, respectively, 192.100.1.1 and 192.100.2.2. Upon receiving the packet R2 performs a similar operation and forwards the corresponding IPv6 packet to H.

This shows a simple and dynamic mechanism to interconnect two IPv6 islands across an IPv4 core network. There are more complex scenarios when the destination site does not have a router supporting this mechanism. In this case, it is also possible to use relays that can be autodiscovered.

15.11 IPv6 MULTICAST

IP multicast is a key functionality of IP. In the past two decades, many protocols and features have been developed to support multicast services, and a number of applications used in the Internet and private IP networks make use of IP multicast (e.g., content distribution, video, etc.) to save network resources and avoid traffic duplication when sending a flow to a number of recipients.

Smart object networks consisting of a sink sending data to a number of sensors or actuators is another example where multicast can be used to send commands to a set of devices or perform a software upgrade while avoiding unnecessary traffic duplication.

IPv6 has greatly benefited from the IPv4 past experience: many of the IPv4 multicast features and protocols have been reused with minimal changes other than the addressing scheme and some IPv4 multicast protocols have been not been adopted for IPv6, while other ones have been redesigned.

As previously discussed, multicast is used by IPv6 by the ND protocol (e.g., unsolicited RA messages are sent to all-nodes multicast address FF02::1) and for IPv6 autoconfiguration. Beyond link-local scope, IP multicast supports the building of multicast distribution trees (MDT) using various routing protocols and a protocol for multicast group management.

IPv6 uses MLD (multicast listener discovery) for multicast group management in order to discover local multicast listeners and which multicast addresses are of interest on the local link. The information is then provided to the multicast routing protocol to ensure that the multicast traffic of interest is distributed to links with interested multicast listeners. MLD is in many ways similar to IGMPv2 [81] used for IPv4. MLD is specified in [92]. A second version called MLDv2 [251] is equivalent to IGMPv3 for IPv4 [29].

The main difference between MLD and IGMP is that MLD uses ICMP (the next header field value of the preceding header is equal to 58), whereas IGMP packets are encapsulated in IP packets (Protocol Number 2).

MLD packets are sent using the local link address as the source address with a hop limit field equal to 1, since they are not forwarded by routers beyond the local link. All MLD messages are sent with an IPv6 Router Alert option in a hop-by-hop option header to make sure that routers examine the messages even if they are sent to a multicast group that is of no interest to the routers.

Routers connected to multicast-enabled links listen packets sent to the all link layer multicast address (e.g., addresses that start with 0x3333 on Ethernet links).

Three types of MLD messages are defined:

- Multicast listener report: These are messages sent by a node expressing its interest in joining a multicast group. The report message is sent to the multicast address of interest. If the router already receives traffic for that multicast group, it only resets a timer, otherwise it joins the relevant MDT. Reports are sent periodically by each interested listener (note that a listener does not resend a report if another node has sent a similar report since the router is only interested in knowing that there is at least one interested listener for that multicast group).
- Multicast listener done: These messages are sent to the link-local all-routers address to inform routers that the node is no longer interested by a multicast group.
- Multicast listener query (with two subtypes, known as general query and multicast-address-specific query): Queries are sent by routers requesting multicast listeners to send reports. This happens when a Done message is received in order to know if there is still at least one listener interested by a specific multicast group. If no report for this multicast group is received, the router knows that it no longer needs to forward multicast traffic for that group. The general query messages are periodically sent to all nodes on the local link (IP address link-local all-routers FF02::2) requesting them to report all multicast groups they are interested in.

MLD makes use of an elected router, which is the only router sending queries. This is only to minimize the number of queries. Since all MLD packets are sent to multicast addresses, they are received by all routers on the link, not just the elected router.

A number of multicast routing protocols have been designed for IPv4: Distance Vector Multicast Protocol (DVMRP), Multicast OSPF (MOSPF), Protocol Independent Multicast (PIM), Core Based Trees (CBT), Pragmatic General Multicast (PGM), and so forth.

Learning from deployment experience, IPv6 chose to only keep a few variants of PIM and the IPv6 implementation is very similar to the IPv4 version:

- PIM-SM (PIM Sparse Mode) [78]
- PIM-SSM (PIM Source Specific Multicast) [119]
- PIM-Bidir (Birectional) [106]

15.11.1 **IPv6 Multicast Addressing**

IPv6 addressing and multicast addressing were discussed in Section 15.3. [102] provides multicast allocation guidelines for permanent and dynamic multicast addresses.

The general approach consists of mapping the low order 32 bits of the IPv6 multicast address (called the group ID) into a link layer destination address: [102] specifies how the group IDs are assigned.

There are several types of multicast addresses: permanent IPv6 multicast addresses, permanent IPv6 multicast group IDs, and dynamic IPv6 multicast addresses.

The permanent IPv6 multicast addresses are assigned with group IDs in the range of 0x00000001 to 0x3FFFFFFF (see [115] for examples).

Permanent group IDs are allocated in the range 0x40000000 to 0x7FFFFFFF.

Dynamic addresses can either be allocated by a server or by the host and must have their T-bit set (see Figure 15.8). Allocation servers use the group ID range 0x80000000 to 0xFFFFFFFF. When allocated by a host, the generated group ID must also belong to the 0x80000000 to 0xFFFFFFFF range and a pseudo-random algorithm must be used to generate that number.

15.12 **CONCLUSIONS**

As discussed in the beginning of the chapter, a number of reference books have been released and the aim of this chapter was to provide a technology refresher needed to better understand the key functionalities of IPv6 in smart object networks. A particular focus was made on the IPv6 addressing architecture (key for smart object networks) and the auto configuration features provided by IPv6 for auto configuration, which are much needed to manage a large number of (unattended) smart objects. The number of enhancements provided by IPv6 made it the natural protocol of choice for IP smart object networks.

The 6LoWPAN Adaptation Layer

16.1 TERMINOLOGY

Before digging into the IP protocols developed for smart object networks, several terms that may be confusing need to be defined. According to [156] a LoWPAN is Low-power Wireless Personal Area Networks (LoWPANs) composed of devices conforming to the IEEE 802.15.4-2003 standard defined by the IEEE [129]. IEEE 802.15.4 devices are characterized by short range, low bit rate, low power, and low cost.

IEEE 80.15.4 networks have the following characteristics:

- Small packet size (the maximum transmission unit or MTU on IEEE 802.15.4 links is 127 bytes), which provides even less room for data when including other headers (as discussed in detail in Section 16.2).
- Support for both 16-bit short or IEEE 64-bit extended media access control (MAC) addresses.
- Low data rates; the IEEE 802.15.4 specification allows various data rates from 20 Kbits/s (868 MHz) to 250 Kbits/s (2.45 GHz).
- Support of star and mesh topologies.
- Constrained devices regarding power (e.g., battery-operated devices), memory, and CPU. Most of the time these devices are low cost.
- Large number of deployed devices in the network requiring scalable technologies.
- IEEE 802.15.4 networks are usually ad hoc networks since their location is usually not predetermined. Furthermore, some locations (e.g., mobile smart objects used for asset tracking, wearable sensors) may be moving devices.
- The nodes within a LoWPAN are interconnected by IEEE 802.15.4 links, which are usually unreliable, especially when compared to wired links such as Ethernet or fiber-optic links. This key aspect of such smart object networks has been discussed in Chapter 12.
- It is very common for nodes to be in sleep mode for long periods of time. Depending on the device, it can be in various sleep mode states that have a different impact on the energy consumption while in sleep mode and the speed at which the node can wake up (see Chapter 11 for more details).

A LoWPAN is a Low-power and Lossy Network (LLN) where the links interconnecting the nodes are IEEE 802.15.4 links. When the Internet Engineering Task Force (IETF) 6LoWPAN Working Group was formed, it was decided to exclusively work on the required IPv6 protocol extensions for

Interconnecting Smart Objects with IP. DOI: 10.1016/B978-0-12-375165-2.00016-8

LoWPAN (such as fragmentation and reassembly, header compression, neighbor discovery adaptation, etc.) where the nodes were exclusively interconnected by IEEE 802.15.4 links.

Then the Routing Over Low-power and Lossy network (ROLL) Working Group was formed to deal with routing issues in networks with similar characteristics at the IP layer thus alleviating the restriction of using IEEE 802.15.4 links, since by definition routing operates at the network layer. This led to the use of the more generic term Low-power and Lossy Network (LLN).

Note that the terms "nodes," "routers" (when discussing a routing-related item), and even "devices" (since most smart objects performing sensing or actuating are usually routers) are used interchangeably.

16.2 THE 6LoWPAN ADAPTATION LAYER

Since IPv6 mandates supporting links with an MTU (Maximum Transmission Unit) of 1280 bytes, it was necessary for IEEE 802.15.4 links that have an MTU of 127 bytes to specify an adaptation layer below IP responsible for handling packet fragmentation and reassembly.

The MTU size of IEEE 802.15.4 links was purposely small to cope with limited buffering capabilities and to limit the packet error rate since the bit error rate (BER) is relatively high. Various header compression techniques have been added to the adaptation layer that are specified in [176] and [124]. The compression header techniques originally specified in [176] were improved in [124] in many ways: individual compression on the traffic class (TC) and flow label field, use of share contexts that is particularly useful when using non-link-local addresses, and optimizations for multicast addresses.

The IEEE 802.15.4 frame MTU is 127 bytes minus a set of protocol fields:

- Maximum MAC frame overhead: Frame control (2 bytes) + sequence number (1 byte) + addressing field (up to 20 bytes with the source and destination PAN ID and the source and destination 64-bit extended addresses) + FCS (2 bytes) = 25 bytes.
- MAC security header: 21 bytes (AES-CCM-128), 13 bytes (AES-CCM-64), and 9 bytes (AES-CCM-32).

In the worst case this only leaves 81 bytes (127 bytes − 25 − 21 = 81) for the data payload (IPv6 packets). After removing the size of the IPv6 header (40 bytes), there are 41 bytes left. Next, we must deduct the transport layer protocol header (8 bytes for UDP and 20 bytes for TCP), thus leading to a very short payload for the application layer.

This shows that an adaptation layer is needed to comply with the IPv6 requirement to support a minimum MTU size of 1280 bytes as well as to support compression techniques to reduce protocol overhead.

The 6LoWPAN adaptation layer provides three main services:

- Packet fragmentation and reassembly
- Header compression
- Link layer (layer 2) forwarding when multi-hop is used by the link layer

In most cases the use of efficient compression techniques allows most applications to send their data within a single IPv6 packet.

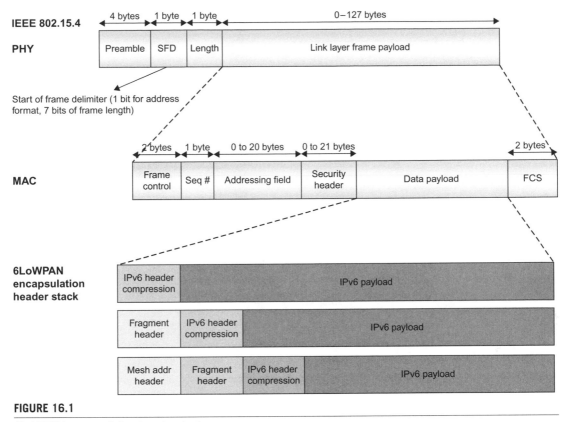

FIGURE 16.1

6LoWPAN encapsulation header stack.

As previously discussed in Chapter 12, IEEE 802.15.4 frames support the use of 16-bit short addresses (temporary addresses allocated by the personal area network or PAN coordinator or 64-bit long addresses (24 bits are used for the organizational unique identifier; OUI + 40 bits assigned by the chipset manufacturer).

Similar to IPv6, the 6LoWPAN adaptation layer makes use of header stacking (headers are added only when needed).

The 6LoWPAN adaptation currently supports three headers: a mesh addressing header, the fragment header, and the IPv6 header compression header (they must appear in that order when present).

The 6LoWPAN adaptation layer defines what is called the "encapsulation header stack," which precedes each IPv6 datagram. The encapsulation header stack is shown in Figure 16.1.

As shown in Figure 16.2, the first byte of the encapsulation header identifies the next header. For example, if the first 2 bits are equal to 11, the next header is a fragmentation header.

If the first 8 bits are equal to 01000001, what follows is an IPv6 *uncompressed* packet. In contrast, a value of 01000010 indicates that what follows is a header related to a compressed header using HC1 compression (see Section 16.2.3 for details on 6LoWPAN header compression techniques).

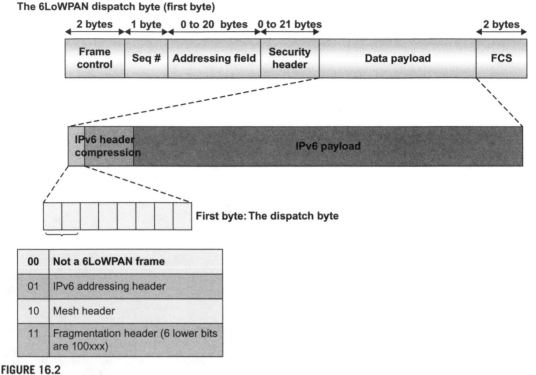

FIGURE 16.2

Dispatch byte of the IPv6 header compression header.

16.2.1 The Mesh Addressing Header

The mesh addressing header is used in conjunction with a mesh-under "routing" approach where nodes that are not in direct communication make use of multi-hop "routing" at the link layer using link layer addresses. According to IEEE 802.15.4, only full function devices (FFDs) perform mesh-under operation. Reduced function devices (RFDs) systematically send all of their traffic to FFDs.

The source and destination nodes are then referred to as the originator and final destination, respectively.

As shown in Figure 16.2, the first 2 bits of the dispatch byte identify the presence of a mesh-header and are equal to 10.

Figure 16.4 shows the various bits of mesh addressing type and header:

- Bit 2 (V, Very first bit):
  0: The originator address is an IEEE extended 64-bit address (EUI-64).
  1: The originator address is a short 16-bit address.

The 6LoWPAN dispatch byte (first byte)

First byte: The dispatch byte

Pattern	Header type
00 xxxxxx	NALP - not a LoWPAN frame
01 000001	IPv6 - uncompressed IPv6 addresses
01 000010	LOWPAN_HC1-LOWPAN_HC1 compressed IPv6
01 000011	reserved - reserved for future use
...	reserved - reserved for future use
01 001111	reserved - reserved for future use
01 010000	LOWPAN_BCO - LOWPAN_BCO broadcast
01 010001	reserved - reserved for future use
...	reserved - reserved for future use
01 111110	reserved - reserved for future use
01 111111	ESC - additional dispatch byte follows
10 xxxxxx	MESH - Mesh header
11 000xxx	FRAG1 - fragmentation header (first)
11 001000	reserved - reserved for future use
...	reserved - reserved for future use
11 011111	reserved - reserved for future use
11 100xxx	FRAGN - fragmentation header (subsequent)
11 101000	reserved - reserved for future use
...	reserved - reserved for future use
11 111111	reserved - reserved for future use

FIGURE 16.3

Value of the 6LoWPAN dispatch byte.

- Bit 3 (F, Final destination):
  0: The final address is an IEEE extended 64-bit address (EUI-64).
  1: The final address is a short 16-bit address.
- Bits 4 through 7 (HopLeft): The HopLeft field value is decremented by each node before sending the packet to its next hop. When the HopLeft field reaches the value of 0, the packet is simply discarded. When equal to 15, an additional byte (called the deep hops left) immediately follows when forwarding along a path with more than 14 hops is needed.
- The originator and final link layer address fields then follow (16 or 64 bits).

It is possible to use short 16-bit addresses for broadcast and 64-bit addresses as a source address since the V and F permit the use of different link layer address formats.

With mesh-under routing it is necessary to provide the originator and final destination as well as the hop-by-hop source and destination addresses.

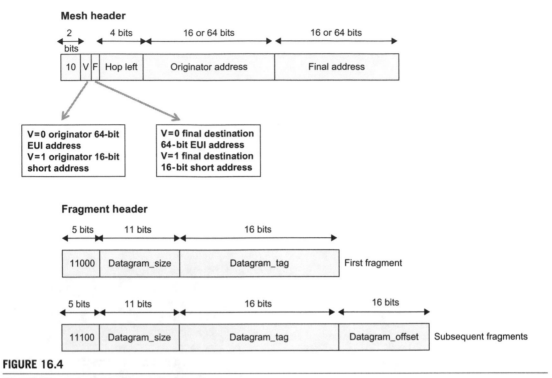

FIGURE 16.4

6LoWPAN mesh and fragmentation headers.

Thus the set of link layer addresses is as follows. When a node A sends a frame to a final destination C via the node B:

- The originator address of the mesh header is set to the link layer address of A.
- The final destination address of the mesh header is set to the link layer address of C.
- The source address of the IEEE 802.15.4 frame is the address of the node sending the frame (A).

The destination address of the IEEE 802.15.4 frame is the link layer address of the next-hop node as determined by the mesh-under routing protocol (B in this example). Upon receiving the frame, B performs the following process:

- The hop left field is decremented.
- If the hop left field is not equal to 0 (if equal to 0, the frame is discarded), then B determines that the next hop is C.
- The originator and final destination address of the mesh header are unchanged.
- The source address of the IEEE 802.15.4 frame is set to the link layer address of B.
- The destination address of the IEEE 802.15.4 frame is set to the link layer address of C.

This is similar to the mode of operation with IP routing over a link layer where the source and destination addresses of the IP packet are never changed, and the source and destination addresses present in the link layer frame correspond to the address of two adjacent nodes (connected by a common link layer).

As previously discussed, there is no mesh-under protocol defined. For further discussion about routing at multiple layers see Chapter 5.

16.2.2 **Fragmentation**

Fragmentation may be required at the 6LoWPAN adaptation layer when the IPv6 payload cannot be carried within a single IEEE 802.15.4 frame because it exceeds the MTU size. In this case, the link frame is broken into multiple link fragments using the fragment header shown in Figure 16.4. All fragment sizes are expressed in units of 8 bytes. The first fragment does not contain a datagram offset, which makes it slightly different from the subsequent fragment.

Description of the fragment fields (see Figure 16.4):

- datagram_size: This 11-bit field is used to indicate the size in 8-byte units of the original IPv6 packet (or IPv6 fragmentation also taking place at the IP layer). Link layer fragmentation supports a 1280-byte packet as mandated by the IPv6 specification [51]. The datagram_size may only be needed in the first link fragment and then elided in other link fragments. The drawback of this approach is that subsequent link fragments (other than the first link fragment) may arrive first, especially in the presence of multi-hop routing. In this case the receiver would not know how much memory should be allocated for the entire frame.
- datagram_tag: This field is used in conjunction with the IEEE 802.15.4 source address (or originator address if a mesh header is present), the IEEE 802.15.4 destination address (or the final destination address if a mesh header is present), and the datagram_size to uniquely identify the fragmented frame and must be identical for all link fragments. It is recommended to increment the datagram_tag for successive fragmented frames.
- datagram_offset: The 8-bit datagram_offset field is present in all link fragments except the first fragment and indicates the offset in 8-byte units from the beginning of the payload datagram.

[176] specifies the use of a reassembly timer that is started when receiving the first link fragment and upon the expiration of which, if not all link fragments have been received, all fragments must be discarded. The maximum value of the reassembly timer is 60 seconds.

16.2.3 **6LoWPAN Header Compression**

16.2.3.1 *Header Compression Using LOWPAN_HC1 and LOWPAN_HC2*

A plethora of IP compression techniques have been designed over the past decade (e.g., ROHC, see [18]). These techniques rely on stateful flow-based compression optimized for long-lived flows. The basis of this principle consists of suppressing common values within a long-lived flow, which is a very efficient approach for long-lived flow between two nodes. Unfortunately these compression techniques are less suited to 6LoWPAN networks with typically short-lived flows (often these devices send a few packets and then go back into sleep mode with the exception of infrequent firmware upgrades that may require large flows to be exchanged). Thus the whole idea of header stateless compression techniques in 6LoWPAN consists of avoiding information redundancy across layers as opposed to between IP packets that belong to the same long-lived flow as ROCH.

The general idea of the 6LoWPAN header compression is to derive the IP address from link layer addresses to avoid needless information duplication and suppression of IPv6 headers that have common values (typically elide the fields that have a value of 0). Furthermore, the use of shared contexts such as the use of a common network prefix for the LoWPAN allows address compression of IPv6 global addresses.

6LoWPAN header compression can either be stateless or stateful and is flow independent. Several of the IPv6 headers have common values and are easily compressed; for example, the IP version (v6), the flow label, TC, and so on. Furthermore, information such as the IPv6 interface ID can be derived from the link layer frame when using extended 64-bit 802.15.4 addresses.

[176] first focused on highly optimizing the compression unicast link-local addresses. A new encoding technique (IPHC) was then introduced in [124] to cope with multicast addresses and non-link-local addresses along with other optimizations such as the individual compression of the IPv6 flow label and TC field.

⚠ More than likely, the header compression part of [176] will be deprecated at some point to only support one header compression technique such as IPHC. There has been no decision to deprecate the header compression defined in [176], so both header compression techniques are described in the following section.

16.2.3.1.1 The HC1 Compression Technique
The HC1 compression technique relies on the following observations:

- IP version is always 6.
- Since HC1 is optimized for link-local addresses, the IPv6 interface ID (bottom 64 bits of the IPv6 address) can be inferred from the link layer MAC address.
- The packet length can be inferred from the frame length field of the IEEE 802.15.4 frame (or from the datagram size field of the fragment header when present).
- Common value for the TC and flow label is 0 (as shown later in Section 16.2.3.3, IPHC allows for individual compression of these fields).
- Next header is UDP, TCP, or ICMP.

These observations allow a considerable reduction of the protocol overhead. The only IPv6 header field that cannot be compressed and must be carried in full is the 1-byte hop limit field. This leads to only 3 bytes instead of the 40-byte IPv6 header: 1 byte for the dispatch byte (equal to 01000010), followed by a 1-byte HC1 byte, and 1 byte for the hop limit field, as shown in Figure 16.5.

When set, bit 7 of the HC1 byte allows for the compression of the next header of the original IPv6 header.

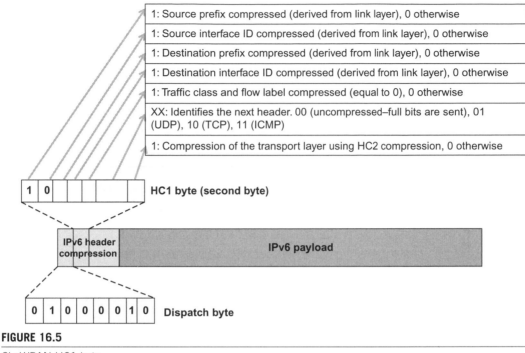

1: Source prefix compressed (derived from link layer), 0 otherwise

1: Source interface ID compressed (derived from link layer), 0 otherwise

1: Destination prefix compressed (derived from link layer), 0 otherwise

1: Destination interface ID compressed (derived from link layer), 0 otherwise

1: Traffic class and flow label compressed (equal to 0), 0 otherwise

XX: Identifies the next header. 00 (uncompressed–full bits are sent), 01 (UDP), 10 (TCP), 11 (ICMP)

1: Compression of the transport layer using HC2 compression, 0 otherwise

| 1 | 0 | | | | | | | **HC1 byte (second byte)** |

IPv6 header compression | IPv6 payload

| 0 | 1 | 0 | 0 | 0 | 0 | 1 | 0 | **Dispatch byte** |

FIGURE 16.5

6LoWPAN HC1 byte.

The non-compressed fields must follow the HC1 byte in this particular order: source address prefix (64 bits) and/or interface ID (64 bits), destination address prefix (64 bits) and/or interface ID (64 bits), TC (8 bits), flow label (20 bits), and next header (8 bits).

16.2.3.2 The HC_UDP Compression Technique (HC2 Byte)

When bit 7 of the HC1 byte is set, it indicates more header compression according to the HC2 encoding format. If bits 5 and 6 of the HC1 byte are equal to 0 and 1, respectively, this indicates the compression of the UDP header (called HC_UDP encoding). In this case, the HC2 byte immediately follows the HC1 byte (thus before the IP hop limit field) and provides information on the UDP header compression scheme. The HC_UDP compression technique allows compression of the UDP header to various degrees. When non-compressed, the UDP fields must appear in the same order as the original UDP header (source port, destination port, length, and checksum).

HC_UDP encoding allows compression of the source and destination UDP ports in addition to the length field. The length field can be inferred from the length field of the IEEE 802.15.4 frame. According to [176], the UDP checksum is never compressed and always carried in full, but improvements have been added to allow UDP checksum compression [124] and are described later in Section 16.2.3.6.

The main idea for compressing the source and destination UDP port uses a short_value 4-bit field instead of the original 16-bit field. The original 16-bit field is simply obtained by the formula short_value+61616 (0xF0B0).

Bit values of the HC2 byte:

- Bit 0 (UDP source port): When cleared, this indicates that the UDP source port is not compressed and thus carried in full. Conversely, when set, the compressed short_value is carried in line.
- Bit 1 (UDP destination port): When cleared, this indicates that the UDP destination port is not compressed and thus carried in full. Conversely, when set, the compressed short_value is carried in line.
- Bit 2 (length): When cleared this indicates that the length field of the UDP header is carried in line. Conversely, when set, the length is computed from the IPv6 header (this can be derived from the IEEE 802.15.4 frame). The value of the UDP length field in this case is equal to the payload length of the IPv6 field minus the length of all headers present between the IPv6 header and the UDP header.
- Bits 3 through 7 are reserved.

Figures 16.6, 16.7 and 16.8 provide different examples of header compression. As shown in Figure 16.8, HC1+HC2 header compression allows a very efficient compression technique for reducing the header size from 40 bytes (IPv6 header) + 8 bytes (UDP header) down to 7 bytes.

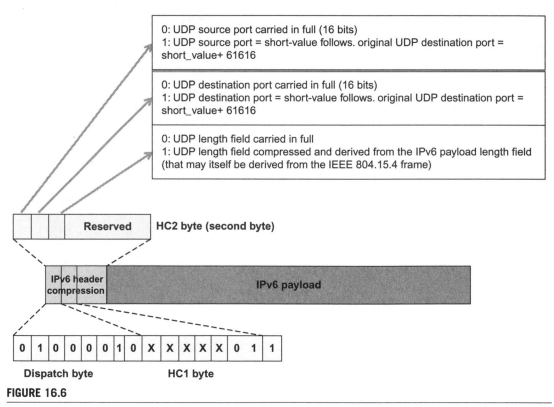

FIGURE 16.6

Header compression using HC1 and HC2 bytes.

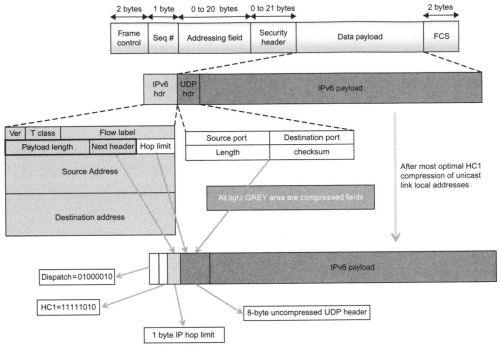

FIGURE 16.7

Compression of the IPv6 HC1 link-local IPv6 addresses without UDP header compression.

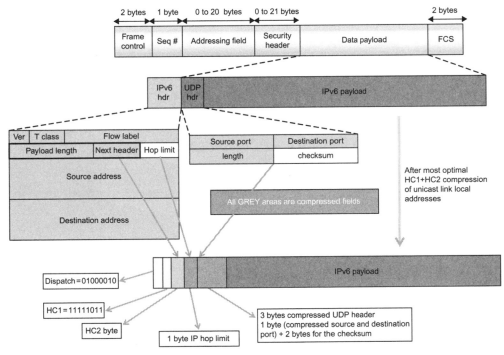

FIGURE 16.8

Maximized compression of IPv6 and UDP headers using HC1 and HC2 with link-local IPv6 addresses.

16.2.3.3 The 6LoWPAN Improved Compression Technique and Stateful Shared Context-based Compression

The compression techniques defined in [176] are quite efficient for unicast link-local addresses (used in many circumstances such as ND, DHCP, and other local protocols as discussed in Chapter 15), but have a very limited effect on global and multicast addresses. Efficient compression techniques for global IPv6 addresses are needed for communication between nodes residing in different IP subnetworks (typically nodes in different PANs in the context of IEEE 802.15.4 networks), where routable addresses are required. In this case the HC1 compression technique requires carrying the sources and destination IPv6 addresses in-line (non-compressed).

Improvements defined in [124] are presented in this section, specifically new compression techniques referred to as LOWPAN_IPHC and LOWPAN_NHC (called IPHC and NHC for simplicity). As already discussed, IPHC will more than likely become *the* header compression technique used by the 6LoWPAN adaptation layer and HC1 and HC2 will undoubtedly be deprecated.

The IPHC encoding is depicted in Figure 16.9. IPHC requires 13 bits, 5 bits of which are taken from the rightmost part of the dispatch byte and an optional additional byte is added.

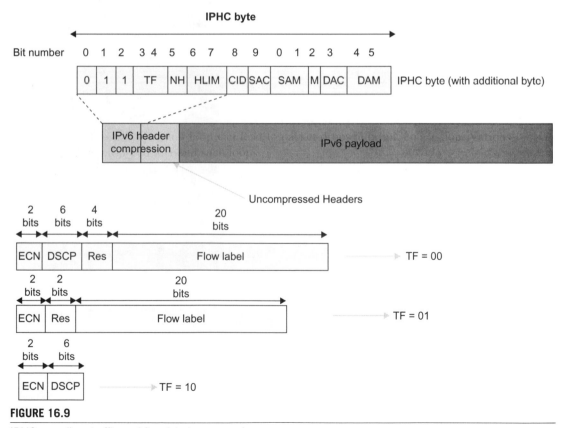

FIGURE 16.9

IPHC encoding: traffic and flow label compression.

All non-compressed header fields always appear in the same order as the non-compressed IPv6 header as specified in [53]. The version field is always elided and the IPv6 payload length field is inferred from the length field of the IEEE 802.15.4 field or from the 6LoWPAN fragmentation header when present.

Description of the IPHC byte includes:

- Bits 3 and 4 (TF: Traffic Class): These bits allow for more granular compression of the TC and flow label IPv6 header fields.

  00: Both the TC and flow label fields are carried in line as shown in Figure 16.9. Note that 4 bits have been added for byte alignment.

  01: The TC field is compressed to 2 bits (ECN), as defined in [209] and the flow label field is uncompressed. Since the ECN bits are encoded using 2 bits and the flow label field is uncompressed, this leads to 22 bits to which 2 bits of padding are added for byte alignment.

  10: The flow label field is compressed (fully elided) and the TC field is carried in-line.

  11: The TC and flow label fields are compressed.

- Bit 5 (next header):

  0: The full 8-bit header of the next header is carried in-line.

  1: The IPv6 next header field is elided and another encoding mechanism (called next header coding; NHC) defined later is added.

- Bits 6 and 7 (HLIM, hop limit): In contrast with the HC1 compression technique, IPHC allows compression of the hop limit field of the IPv6 header.

  00: The hop limit field of the IPv6 packet is carried in-line.

  01: The hop limit field is elided and the hop limit is equal to 1.

  10: The hop limit field is elided and the hop limit is equal to 64.

  11: The hop limit field is elided and the hop limit is equal to 255.

- Bit 8 (context identifier extension; CID).

  0: There is no use of additional context information.

  1: An additional 1-byte CID is added that immediately follows the destination address mode (DAM) field.

- Bit 9 (source address compression; SAD).

  0: Address compression is stateless.

  1: Address compression is stateful based on context.

- Bits 10 and 11 (source address mode; SAM).

  If SAC=0

    00: The full 128-bit address is carried in-line.

    01: The first 64 bits of the IPv6 address are elided and the value of the 64 bits is the link-local prefix, padded with zeros. The remaining 64 bits are carried in-line.

    10: The first 112 bits of the IPv6 address are elided and the value of those bits is the link-local prefix, padded with zeros. The remaining 16 bits are carried in-line.

    11: The address is fully elided. The first 64 bits are the link-local prefix. The remaining 64 bits are inferred from the IEEE 802.15.4 frame, similarly to HC1.

  If SAC=1

    00: The address is the unspecified address (::).

    01: 64 bits. The 64-bit prefix address is derived from the context information (see Section 16.2.3.4) and the remaining 64 bits are carried in-line.

10: 16-bits. The 64-bit prefix address is derived from the context information (see Section 16.2.3.4) and the remaining 16 bits are carried in-line.

11: 0 bits. The address is derived from the context information and potentially the link layer and no bits are carried in-line.

- Bit 12 (multicast compression; M).

  0: The destination address is not a multicast address.

  1: The destination address is a multicast address.

- Bit 13 (destination address compression; DAC).

  0: The compression of the destination address is stateless.

  1: The compression of the destination address is stateful, based on the context.

- Bits 14 and 15 (DAM).

  If DAC=0

  00: 128 bits. The full 128-bit address is carried in-line.

  01: 64 bits. The first 64 bits of the IPv6 address are elided and the value of the 64 bits is the link-local prefix, padded with zeros. The remaining 64 bits are carried in-line.

  10: 16 bits. The first 112 bits of the IPv6 address are elided and the value of the 112 bits is the link-local prefix, padded with zeros. The remaining 16 bits are carried in-line.

  11: The address is fully elided. The first 64 bits are the link-local prefix and the remaining 64 bits are inferred from the IEEE 802.15.4 frame, similarly to HC1.

  If DAC=1

  00: Reserved.

  01: 64 bits. The prefix address is derived from the context information and the 64 bits are carried in-line.

  10: 16 bits. The prefix address is derived from the context information and the 16 bits are carried in-line.

  11: The address is derived from the context information and potentially the link layer and no bits are carried in-line.

  If M=1 and DAC=0

  00: 128 bits. The full address is carried in-line.

  01: 48 bits. The address is coded using 48 bits and has the form FFXX::00XX:XXXX: XXXX.

  10: 32 bits. The address is coded using 32 bits and has the form FFXX::00XX:XXXX.

  11: 8 bits. The address is coded using 8 bits and has the form FF02::00XX.

  If M=1 and DAC=1

  00: 48 bits. The address is coded using 48 bits and has the form FFXX::XXLL:PPPP:PPPP: PPPP:PPPP:XXXX:XXXX. X denotes nibbles carried in-line, P denotes nibbles to encode the prefix (i.e., given by the specific context), and L denotes nibbles used to encode the prefix length. The prefix information P and L is derived from the context itself. This format is compliant with the unicast-prefix-based IPv6 multicast addresses defined in [103] and [219].

  01: Reserved

  10: Reserved

  11: Reserved

16.2.3.4 The Context Identifier (CID)

IPHC relies on the notion of shared context between the sending node compressing the IPv6 packet and the receiving node expanding the received packet. The current specification does not describe how contexts are shared or maintained. At some point there might be protocol extensions or a new protocol for dynamic setup and negotiation of shared contexts. As indicated previously, the CID field in the LOWPAN_IPHC encoding indicates that an additional bit is added that follows the IPHC byte and precedes the IP header fields that are carried in-line.

That byte is used to identify the context used to identify the source and destination, respectively (the first 4 bits called the source context identifier or SCI is used for the source address and the following 4 bits called the destination context identifier or DCI is used for the destination address). Since 4 bits are used to identify the context, up to 16 contexts are allowed.

16.2.3.5 The IPv6 Next Header Compression

As seen in Chapter 15, IPv6 makes use of stacked headers where the next header field is used to indicate the header type that immediately follows. Similar to HC1 where the next header information is encoded in the HC1 byte (bits 5 and 6), IPHC specifies a compression mechanism to elide the IPv6 next header field. IPv6 next header compression is indicated by setting bit 5 of the IPHC byte and by adding a new byte called the LOWPAN_NHC byte. This immediately follows the non-compressed (carried in-line) IPv6 header field, as show in Figure 16.10.

The NHC byte is of variable length depending on the next header type, which allows a more efficient and flexible compression technique. As shown in Figure 16.10, the first 7 bits of the NHC byte

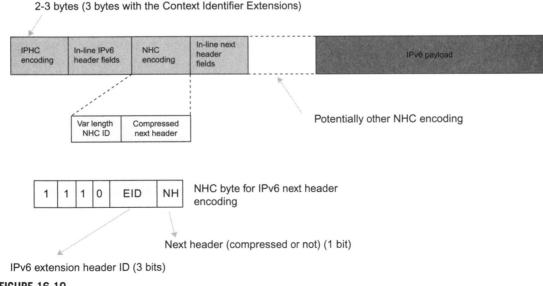

FIGURE 16.10

IPv6 packet using LOWPAN_IPHC and LOWPAN_NHC compression.

are used to identify the next header that follows. The extension header ID (EID) field indicates which extended IPv6 header immediately follows.

- 0: IPv6 hop-by-hop options
- 1: IPv6 routing
- 2: IPv6 fragment
- 3: IPv6 destination options
- 4: IPv6 mobility header (defined in [140])
- 5: Reserved
- 6: Reserved
- 7: IPv6 header

The hop-by-hop option header, routing header, fragment header, and destination option header are described in Chapter 15.

The last bit of the NHC byte is used to indicate whether the next header is compressed using the LOWPAN-NHC technique (bit set) or whether the next header is carried in full (bit cleared).

When using the NHC compression technique, the IPv6 extended header is kept unchanged with two exceptions:

- The next header field is simply elided when the NH field of the NHC byte is set (to avoid redundancy of the information).
- The length field of an extended IPv6 header such as the hop-by-hop option or routing header (see Chapter 15) is used to indicate the length of the IPv6 extension header not including the LOWPAN_ NHC byte.

16.2.3.6 Compression of the UDP Header Using LOWPAN_NHC

Section 16.2.3.2 described the use of the HC_UDP byte to compress the UDP source port, destination port, and length field headers. The compression technique indicates a 4-bit short value that is used to extract the original UDP port using the formula 61616 (0xF0B0) + short_value.

NHC introduces another UDP header compression technique with several improvements.

A range of 16 contiguous well-known ports is specified in the form 0xF0Bx, thus identical to the HC_UDP compression technique for UDP ports. This introduces compatibility issues with applications already using these ports. This is why the specification recommends using the Transport Layer Security Message Integrity Check (TLS MIC; see [55]) to validate the content and its integrity.

Although [53] mandates the use of UDP checksum, the [124] specification allows bypassing this rule if and only if the upper layer permits. Although the [124] specification allows an intermediate node to elide the UDP checksum even if the received packet has the UDP checksum in-line, it also clearly states that this should not be done without the confirmation that the operation is authorized by the sender. Conversely, an intermediate node may decide to insert a UDP checksum after receiving a packet without a UDP checksum after having computed its value according to the rules specified in [202] and [53].

Figure 16.11 shows the format of the NHC byte for the UDP header.

- Bit 5 (Checksum; C).
  0: The 16-bit UDP checksum field is not compressed and carried in-line.
  1: The 16-bit UDP checksum is elided and recovered and recomputed by the 6LoWPAN termination point.

Example of IPHC + NHC for extended IPv6 option (fragment) and for UDP compression

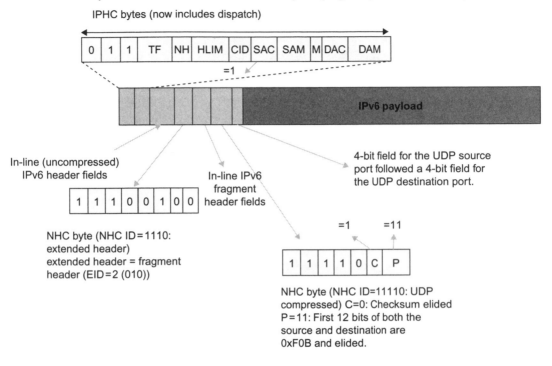

FIGURE 16.11

IPv6 packet using LOWPAN_IPHC and LOWPAN_NHC compression for extended IPv6 header compression and UDP header compression.

- Bits 6 and 7 (Ports; P).
  00: Both the source and destination 16-bit ports are carried in-line.
  01: The 16 bits of the source port are not compressed and carried in-line. The first 8 bits of the destination port are elided (and equal to F0) and the remaining 8 bits are carried in-line.
  10: The first 8 bits of the source port are elided (and equal to F0) and the remaining 8 bits are carried in-line. The 16 bits of the destination port are not compressed and carried in-line.
  11: The first 12 bits of the source and destination ports are elided and equal to 0xF0B0. The remaining 4 bits of both ports are carried in-line.

Figure 16.11 shows a complete example where:

- IPHC is used for header compression.
- NHC is used to compress an extended IPv6 fragment header.

NHC is used to compress the UDP header with maximum level of compression (the checksum is elided and both the source and destination ports are compressed).

So in the very best case

- With link-local unicast address, HC1 encoding allows compression of the IPv6 header to two octets (the dispatch byte + the HC1 byte). When routing over multiple hops, the compression still performs quite well compressing the IPv6 header to 7 octets (the dispatch byte + the HC1 byte + 1 byte for the IP hop limit field + 2 bytes for the sources address + 2 bytes for the destination address).
- With the use of global addresses, the IPv6 header can be compressed to 4 bytes (2 bytes for the IPHC encoding + 1 byte for context identifier extension + 1 byte for the IP hop limit field + 0 bytes for the source and destination addresses with the interface IDs derived from the IEEE 802.15.4 link layer address). When using Context 0, the 1 byte for the context identifier is not needed. Potentially, additional bytes may be added if the TC and flow label field of the IPv6 field are not compressed.

In the best case, the compressed UDP header only requires 2 bytes (1 byte for the NHC header + 1 byte for the compressed source and destination UDP ports) when the UDP checksum field is elided.

16.2.3.7 Header Compression of Multicast Address

The LOWPAN_HC1 encoding technique specified in [176] does not allow compression of multicast addresses, consequently, 128-bit multicast addresses must be carried in-line, uncompressed. [124] specifies an encoding technique for efficient compression of IPv6 multicast addresses using shared contexts.

The first mode of operation is based on stateless compression. The M-bit and the DAC bit of the IPHC bytes must be set to 1 and 0, respectively.

As a reminder, each node is assigned a solicited multicast address used in IPv6 ND messages during the duplicated address detection (DAD) process. The solicited-node address has the form FF02::1:FFXX:XXXX and is computed from the node's unicast and anycast address. The 24 lower order bits of the unicast or anycast address are appended to the prefix FF02::1:FF00::/104.

The multicast stateless compression supports the compression of the solicited-node multicast address in addition to any IPv6 multicast address where the upper bits of the multicast group identifier are zeros. The least significant bits identify the multicast group and the multicast scope in-line. The flag bits are carried in-line except when the DAM flag is set (address in the form FF0X::0XXX) in which case the flags are not carried in-line. Figure 16.12 shows the format of the compression multicast address.

The second mode is based on a stateful context-based address compression. In this case both the M-bit and the SAC bit of the IPHC bytes are set. The SAM is set to 01, which indicates that the address is derived using context information and the 64 bits identifying the multicast group are carried in-line for unicast-prefix-based IPv6 multicast addresses. The prefix length and network prefix are derived from the context. In contrast with the IPv6 multicast addressing architecture defined in [54], [103] specifies a multicast address format that carries unicast prefix information in the IPv6 multicast address: the 112-bit field is replaced by an 8-bit reserved field + an 8-bit flag field + a 64-bit prefix information field (identifying the network prefix of the unicast subnet that owns the multicast address) + a 32-bit group ID.

Thus, for a unicast-prefix-based IPv6 multicast address the IPHC encoding only requires 6 bytes: 4 bits for the flags, 4 bits for the scope, an 8-bit reserved field, and the 32-bit group identifier.

Stateless address compression

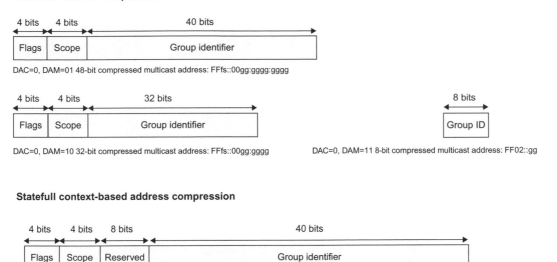

DAC=0, DAM=01 48-bit compressed multicast address: FFfs::00gg:gggg:gggg

DAC=0, DAM=10 32-bit compressed multicast address: FFfs::00gg:gggg   DAC=0, DAM=11 8-bit compressed multicast address: FF02::gg

Statefull context-based address compression

DAC=1, DAM=00 Unicast-prefix-based IPv6 multicast address compression

FIGURE 16.12

Stateless and stateful multicast address compression.

As specified in [219], the address of the rendezvous point can be encoded in the IP multicast group address to simplify the deployment of intra-domain multicast configuration and help in the inter-domain case. The reserved field is then used to encode the Rendezvous Point Interface ID (RIID).

16.2.4 Stateless Configuration

As explained in Chapter 15, the IPv6 interface ID may be derived from the EIU-64 that is computed by converting a 48-bit MAC address. In IEEE 802.15.4, all devices have a 64-bit EUI address, but the use of short 16-bit addresses is also allowed. When using a short address, a pseudo 48-bit address is computed using the following algorithm:

- The first 16 bits correspond to the PAN ID.
- The next 16 bits are all zeros.
- The remaining 16 bits correspond to the short address.

This 48-bit address is then used according to the "IPv6 over Ethernet" encapsulation technique [44].

Note: Multicast IPv6 packets are transmitted as broadcast IEEE 802.15.4 frames (IPv6 only supports multicast, whereas IEEE 802.15.4 only supports broadcast). A multicast IPv6 packet is transmitted using IEEE 802.15.4 frames with the required destination PAN ID and the broadcast address 0xFFFF.

16.3 CONCLUSIONS

In this chapter, we reviewed in detail the 6LoWPAN adaptation layer that optimized the transport of IPv6 packets in IEEE 802.15.4 frames. 6LoWPAN allows the support of the necessary fragmentation and reassembly mechanisms considering the limited MTU of IEEE 802.15.4. Furthermore, the 6LoWPAN adaptation layer provides efficient header compression mechanisms avoiding information redundancy to dramatically reduce the IP overhead headers to a few bytes, which is particularly interesting on links that only support small frame sizes. 6LoWPAN is not a generic term referring to smart object networks but an adaptation layer to carry IPv6 packets over IEEE 802.15.4 frames.

RPL Routing in Smart Object Networks

17

17.1 INTRODUCTION

As already discussed in Chapter 14, the Internet Engineering Task Force (IETF) formed a new Working Group called ROLL (Routing Over Low-power and Lossy networks; http://www.ietf.org/dyn/wg/charter/roll-charter.html) in 2008 with the objective of specifying routing solutions for Low-power and Lossy Networks (LLNs). The first objectives of the Working Group were to produce a set of routing requirements (discussed in Section 17.2), determine whether or not existing IETF routing protocols would satisfy the requirements spelled out in the routing requirement documents, and establish a routing security framework and define new routing metrics for routing in LLNs. The Working Group quickly converged on the fact that none of the existing routing protocols would satisfy the fairly unique set of routing requirements for LLNs. Thus ROLL was re-chartered to design a new routing protocol called RPL (Routing Protocol for Low-power and Lossy Networks) explained in detail in this chapter. Note that the terminology used in ROLL specifications can be found in [248].

17.2 WHAT IS A LOW-POWER AND LOSSY NETWORK?

When not familiar with the environment of IP smart object networks interconnected by lossy links, one may wonder: How lossy is lossy? Ethernet and Optical links have remarkably low BERs. A lossy link is not just a link with higher BER uniformly distributed errors. Packet drops on lossy links are extremely frequent, and the links may become completely unusable for quite some time for a number of reasons such as interference. This observation has strong consequences on the protocol design. Indeed, knowing that link failures are frequent and usually transient also means that the routing protocol should not overreact to failures in an attempt to stabilize under unstable conditions. For example, if node A selected node B as its preferred next-hop, and as a result of temporary lack of connectivity between A and B, node A chooses an alternate next-hop C and immediately triggers a re-computation of the routing table. This would not only lead to routing instabilities but would generate a significant amount of control plane traffic impacting the entire network.

It is worth pointing out that by lossy link what immediately comes to mind are wireless links, but remember that Powerline communication (PLC) links are also lossy.

Interconnecting Smart Objects with IP. DOI: 10.1016/B978-0-12-375165-2.00017-X

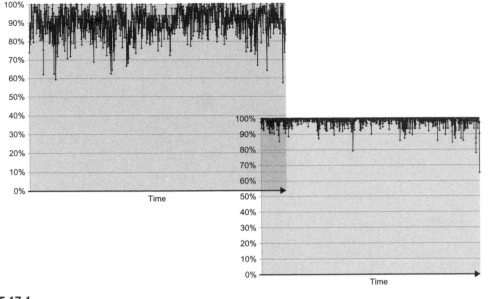

FIGURE 17.1

Packet Delivery Ratio for two IEEE 802.15.4 links.

Figure 17.1 shows the packet delivery ratio (PDR) for two low-power IEEE 802.15.4 links as a function of time (in seconds). The PDR significantly varies from 60 to 100%.

17.3 ROUTING REQUIREMENTS

When defining a new protocol, it is always tempting to start right away with the protocol specification, processing rules, packet encoding, etc. But without a clear understanding of the requirements, this unavoidably leads to further difficulties when trying to adapt the protocol as new requirements are added. To avoid such situations, IETF Working Groups usually produce requirement documents that follow the "informational" track (please refer to Chapter 14 for more details on standardization tracks). In the case of the ROLL Working Group one of the main challenges was to determine the scope of the work. In contrast with traditional IP networks (e.g., a core Service Provider network), LLNs can greatly vary from each other. A mobile Delay Tolerant Network (DTN) used to study wildlife does not have much in common with a dense "always on" network used for industrial automation. Thus the choice was made to limit the scope to four main applications: urban networks (including Smart Grid applications), building automation, industrial automation, and home automation. These applications are representative of other types of networks and there was an urgent need to design routing solutions for them. Thus it was believed that by addressing the routing requirements of these applications, a routing protocol for LLN would address the vast majority of routing requirements of smart object networks.

Requirement documents usually use normative language in IETF terms (see [23]): the MUST, SHOULD, and MAY in these documents indicate if a feature is mandated or simply desirable. MUST, SHOULD, and MAY are used in protocol specifications. For example, if a protocol document specifies that a feature MUST be supported then an implementation is not compliant with the RFC if it does not support the feature in question.

The ROLL Working Group has produced the following four routing requirements: [169], [24], [197], and [57]. These sections provide an overview of the major routing requirements spelled out in these documents (the MUST).

These routing requirements make no assumption on the link layer in use; they specify a list of routing requirements for networks made of LLNs.

- Unicast/anycast/multicast: Several requirement documents list the support of unicast, anycast, and multicast traffic as mandatory. The support of the multicast traffic is explicitly listed in the ROLL Working Group charter.
- Adaptive routing: Most requirements specify the need for adaptive routing where new paths are dynamically and automatically recomputed as conditions change in the network (e.g., link/node failure, mobility, etc.). Furthermore, the routing protocol must be able to compute routes optimized for different metrics (e.g., minimize latency, maximize reliability, etc.). [169] also specifies that the routing protocol must be able to find a path that satisfies specific constraints such as providing a path with a latency lower than a specified value.
- Constraint-based routing: All documents mention that the routing protocol has to support constraint-based routing to take into account various node characteristics used as constraints such as energy, CPU, and memory as well as link attributes ([197]) such as link latency.
- Traffic characteristics: There are a number of LLNs highly focused on data collection (e.g., telemetry) where most of the traffic is from leaf nodes such as sensors to a data collection sink. This type of traffic is also referred to as multipoint-to-point (MP2P) traffic. It is often necessary in these networks to also support point-to-multipoint (P2MP) traffic; for example, when the sink sends a request to all nodes in the network, acknowledgments in the context of reliable messaging are necessary or a central management tool performs a software update. Furthermore, as pointed out in [169] and [24], the routing protocol must support point-to-point (P2P) communication between devices in the network. The routing protocol must also support the computation of parallel paths (not necessarily disjoint) to absorb bursts of traffic more efficiently. In some cases ([197]) it was required to not just support Equal Cost Multiple Path (ECMP). Note that other routing protocols such as ISIS or OSPF only support ECMP (avoiding loops with non equal load balancing is somewhat challenging).
- Scalability: As discussed throughout the entire book, LLNs are composed of a very large number of nodes, thus scalability is very important. The routing protocol requirement documents indicate a number of nodes between 250 [24] to 1000 [169] and up to 10^4 in [57]. There are deployments that even require the support of millions of nodes (see Part III); in this particular case, the deployment of the routing protocol may follow specific rules (e.g., network partitioning).
- Configuration and management: As expected, there is a long list of requirements related to configuration. In most documents, it is clearly spelled out that the routing protocol must be able to auto-configure with minimal or even 0-configuration. In other words, the end user must be able to place the node in its environment without intervening in the configuration and the routing protocol must

be able to join the routing domain and start functioning from a routing perspective (see [197] for a detailed example). [24] also specifies that the routing protocol must be able to isolate a misbehaving node to limit/eliminate its impact on other nodes. [169] mentions that an application should not require any reconfiguration even after replacement of the devices (in other words, a new IP address must not be reassigned to the node).

• Node attribute: [169] mentions that when there are sleeping nodes in the network (a frequent situation with battery-operated nodes), the routing protocol must discover the capability of a node to act as a proxy. A packet could be delivered to a proxy that could relay the packet to the destination once awakened.

• Performance: Indicating performance numbers in requirement documents is always a risky proposition. Performance may not only greatly vary between implementations but is subject to potential changes as new applications emerge. A protocol should never be designed with hard numbers in mind to preserve its future use. Thus performance numbers in requirement documents should not be seen as "hard" numbers or bounds but simple indications providing some order of magnitude. For example, [197] mentions that the routing protocol must find routes and report success or failure within several minutes. In [24], the routing protocol must provide mobility with a convergence time below 0.5 s and it must converge within 0.5 s if no nodes have moved and within 2 s if the destination has moved. But again, these numbers should be seen as indicative as opposed to hard performance targets or bounds.

• Security: As discussed in Chapter 8 and shown in Part III, security is very important in most LLNs. There are some LLNs (e.g., Smart Cities telemetry networks) where minimal security is required, but in most cases (e.g., Smart Grid, building automation, industrial automation, etc.) security is absolutely critical. Authentication is listed as an absolute must in all documents. Encryption is also an absolute must. Note that [169] mentions that "the routing protocol must gracefully handle routing temporal security updates (e.g., dynamic keys) to sleeping devices on their 'awake' cycle to assure that sleeping devices can readily and efficiently access the network."

How should conflicting objectives be dealt with? It is always challenging to consider a set of requirements dictated by several applications that significantly differ from each other. The first naïve approach is to consider the union of all of the requirements. Unfortunately, such an approach is usually unrealistic or undesirable. The union of all requirements may not be possible considering the constrained nature of smart objects and the need to bound the complexity of the protocol. There are even cases where some of these requirements are contradictory. Even if all of these requirements were satisfied by a single routing protocol, the results may not be beneficial. Why would a routing protocol operating in a building have to support features needed for urban networks? It may be more advantageous to only support the required features to limit the resource (node and network) consumption in the network. The other approach adopted by RPL was to design a modular routing protocol where the core component of the application would be specified by the RPL specification with optional features activated only where and when needed. For example, RPL specifies how to build a destination oriented directed acyclic graph (DODAG), but the characteristics of the DODAG are specified by an objective function. For the time being, think of a DODAG as a logical routing topology over a physical network that is built by the routing protocol to meet specific criteria. How RPL builds DODAGs is further explored in detail in the rest of this chapter. It is even possible for a node to join multiple DODAGs (if the application requires different objectives that must be realized through the use of multiple DODAGs) and mark the traffic according to the DODAG characteristics in support of Quality of Service (QoS) awareness and constrained-based routing. Then applicability documents will be produced to provide guidance on how the core RPL protocol could be used, in conjunction with specific objective functions, and configured to meet specific requirements supporting the application and environment.

17.4 ROUTING METRICS IN SMART OBJECT NETWORKS

Routing metrics are a critical component of the routing strategy and have been studied for decades. Most of the IP routing protocols used in today's networks such as OSPF [179] or IS-IS [131] use static link metrics. The network administrator is responsible for configuring the link metrics, which may reflect the link bandwidth, delay, or combine several metrics. Some Service Providers are combining up to three metrics (e.g., delays, bandwidth, cost) in the link metric. Then the routing protocol computes the shortest path taking into account these static link metrics.

Several attempts were made to use dynamic link metrics. For example, extensive studies were made in ARPANET-2 to dynamically compute the link metric based on the averaged queue length to reflect the level of congestion. These strategies were abandoned due to the difficulty in designing stable systems. One of the main challenges with dynamic metrics is to carefully control the rate at which new metrics are advertised. Frequent link metric refreshers provide a high level of accuracy but may also lead to routing oscillation. For example, when the link metric reflects the link utilization, increasing the metric discourages traffic from traversing the link and triggers the rerouting of traffic in other parts of the network. As the link utilization decreases, the link metric also decreases thus attracting more traffic. If not controlled carefully, such strategies unavoidably lead to traffic oscillation and thus to jitter, potential packet reordering, and so on. Extreme care must be taken to limit the control traffic overhead in LLN where bandwidth and energy are usually scarce resources. In addition to the potential traffic oscillation, routing updates too frequently create congestion in the network that would drain energy, which may be a real issue for battery-operated nodes.

Another characteristic of the current routing protocol's metrics is that they are only related to links, which makes perfect sense in the current Internet because most core routers are not traffic bottlenecks.

In contrast, routing in LLN does require more sophisticated routing metrics strategies.

Let's clarify the distinction between routing *metric* and *constraint*. A metric is a scalar used to determine the best path according to some objective function. For example, if the link metric is representative of the link propagation delay, the path cost represents the total propagation delay to the destination and the objective function may specify finding the shortest path based on the propagation delay. Some metrics may not be additive; for example, the objective function may be to find the path where the minimum link quality is maximized. A constraint is used to include or eliminate links or nodes that do not meet specific criteria (this is usually referred to as *constraint-based routing*). For example, the objective function may not select any path that traverses a node that is battery-operated or a link that does not provide link layer encryption. The objective function may combine link/node metrics and constraints such as "find the path with the minimum delay that does not traverse any nonencrypted link." An example is provided in Section 17.5.

The set of link and nodes metrics/constrained for RPL are defined in [250] and discussed in the next section. [250] allows routing objects to be defined as constraints or metrics with a great deal of flexibility. Let's consider the link quality level (LQL). The LQL is an integer between 0 and 3 that characterizes the link quality (poor, fair, good). The objective function (OF) may stipulate to prune links with a "poor" quality level (LQL is used as a constraint) or to find the path that provides the minimum number of links with poor quality (LQL is used as a metric). This applies to all routing objects that can be used as a metric or constraint.

17.4.1 Aggregated Versus Recorded Routing Metrics

The path cost is defined as the sum of the cost of all links along the path. This implicitly makes use of aggregated metrics. For example, if the metric reflects the link's throughput where the metric is inversely proportional to it, the best path is the path with the lowest cost (the path cost is the sum of all link metrics along the path). On the other hand, in some cases it might be useful to record each individual link metric as opposed to an aggregated value. In the reliability metric, one approach adds the link's LQL along the path (aggregated metric), but this comes with a loss of information in which case it might be useful to record the LQL of all links along the path. [250] supports both aggregated and recorded metrics.

17.4.2 Local Versus Global Metrics

A metric is said to be local when it is not propagated along the DODODAG. In other words, a node would indicate its local cost (in contrast with a global metric), but the cost will not be propagated any further.

17.4.3 The Routing Metrics/Constraints Common Header

[250] specifies a common header for all metrics and constraints with several flags used to indicate whether the routing object refers to a routing metric or a constraint, if the routing object is local versus global, if the global metric is aggregated versus recorded, if a constraint is optional or mandatory, and if a metric is additive or reports a maximum/minimum.

17.4.4 The Node State and Attributes Object

The node state and attribute (NSA) object is used to report various node state information and node attributes.

Nodes may act as traffic aggregators. Knowing that a node can aggregate traffic may influence the routing decision in an attempt to reduce the amount of traffic in the network. It is likely that a single flag will not suffice and additional information will have to be specified.

Nodes may have limited available resources. Extensive discussions took place in the ROLL Working Group to define which node parameters should be provided. One scheme would have been to report the available CPU processing power, available memory, etc. But this would become extremely bandwidth intensive and irrelevant considering how quickly such metrics vary. It was thus decided to simply make use of a 1-bit flag set when a node sustainably experiences some level of congestion. It is the responsibility of the node to determine, according to local policy, when the flag should be set potentially triggering traffic rerouting to avoid that node.

17.4.5 **Node Energy Object**

Energy is a critical metric in LLNs, especially in the presence of battery-operated nodes. The approach taken by [250] provided several levels of granularity to characterize the node energy: (1) the node power mode, (2) estimated remaining lifetime and potentially, and (3) potentially some detailed set of power-related metrics and attributes.

1. The node power mode: Three flags are used to indicate whether the node is main-powered, battery-powered, or if the node is powered by energy scavenging (solar panels, mechanical, etc.).
2. The approach to estimated remaining lifetime provides some indication of the power level for both battery-operated and scavenging nodes. With the battery-operated node, the unit is the current expected lifetime divided by the desired minimum lifetime. [250] provides two examples of how to compute this value.

   If the node can measure its average power consumption, then H can be calculated as the ratio of desired max power (initial energy E_0 divided by desired lifetime T) to actual power $H = P\_max/P\_now$. Alternatively, if the energy in the battery E_bat can be estimated, and the total elapsed lifetime, t, is available, then H can be calculated as the total stored energy remaining versus the target energy remaining: $H = E\_bat/[E\_0 (T-t)/T]$.

   In the latter case (scavenger), the unit is a percentage (power provided by the scavenger divided by the power consumed by the application).
3. The detailed set of power-related metrics and attributes may potentially be used and is to be defined in the future.

17.4.6 **Hop-count Object**

The hop-count object simply reports the number of hops along the path.

17.4.7 **Throughput Object**

The throughput object is used to report the link throughput. When used as a metric, the throughput can be used as an additive metric or to report a maximum or a minimum.

17.4.8 **Latency Object**

The latency object is used to report the path latency. Similar to the throughput, latency can be used as a metric or a constraint. When used as a metric the latency object expresses the total latency (additive metric) and the maximum or minimum latency along the path. When used as a constraint, the latency can be used to exclude links that provide greater latency than predefined values.

17.4.9 **Link Reliability Object**

Routing protocols such as OSPF or IS-IS do not use reliability metrics simply because links used in the Internet such as SONET/SDH, Optical links, and Ethernet are extremely reliable with low error rates. They do fail and a plethora of fast recovery mechanisms have been defined, but the link quality usually expressed as BER for these types of links is not used for path selection. The situation is radically different in LLNs where links are lossy and not only can the BER be high, but the link states can vary quite significantly over time. Figure 17.1 illustrates the PDR for two links (indoor and outdoor) over time. This stresses the importance of considering the "lossyness" of a link when computing the best path to a destination. Very similar lossy characteristics can be shown in PLC links.

Many research papers have investigated a set of reliability metrics for lossy links such as low power links (e.g., [50], [85]). The most popular reliability metric thus far is the expected transmission (ETX) count metric, which characterizes the average number of packet transmissions required to successfully transmit a packet. The ETX is consequently tightly coupled to the throughput along a path. Several techniques have been proposed to compute ETX.

One method described in [50] sends regular probes in *each direction* to compute the delivery ratio for a specific link. ETX is defined as $1/(Df * Dr)$ where Df is the measured probability that a packet is received by the neighbor and Dr is the measured probability that the acknowledgment packet is successfully received. One way to compute Df and Dr is to send probes at regular time intervals, since both end points of the link know the frequency at which probes are sent. By reporting the number of received probes in the opposite direction, each node can easily compute both values. Other proposals have been made in [85] and [150].

It is important not to specify at the IETF the method for computing ETX values. The ETX is a link-specific quantity and the technique used to compute the ETX value should be independent of the link layer and not specified by the network layer that only carries it for routing protocol decisions. Some links may use link layer mechanisms, and in other cases probing techniques and the ETX value may be derived from one of these techniques or any combination.

The ETX for a path is computed as the sum of the ETX for each link along the path (e.g., RPL reports cumulative path ETX as discussed next).

17.4.10 Link Colors Attribute

There are circumstances where it may be useful to "color" a link to report a specific property. Such mechanisms have been defined in other protocols such as IS-IS, for example, to indicate that a link is protected with lower layer recovery mechanisms. A similar approach is adopted by RPL. The link color is encoded using a bit vector and the meaning of each color is left to the implementer. As described later in this section, RPL computes paths over a dynamically built DODAG. The DODAG root uses an OF required for each node along the path reporting path metrics to also report the set of colors of each link along the path. For example, suppose that the color blue is used to indicate the support of the link layer encryption. Upon receiving the path metric, if link colors are recorded, a node may decide to elect as a parent the parent reporting paths with encrypted links (blue links) or with the maximum number of blue links in the absence of a path exclusively made of blue links.

17.5 THE OBJECTIVE FUNCTION

The routing metric is insufficient for the routing protocol to compute the "best" path. The OF may be so simple that it could be implicit. For example, the OF of RIP [163] is to select the path with minimal hop count. OSPF or IS-IS would compute the paths that provide the minimum cost where the path cost is simply the sum of the static link cost along the path. In other cases such as MPLS TE the OF may be slightly more complex: "find the shortest path according to some metric such as the OSPF/IS-IS metric or the Traffic Engineering metric that satisfies some constraint such as the available reservable bandwidth or the type of recovery protection provided by the link." This is known as constraint-based routing. Still, the objective may be significantly more complicated. It is supported by the path computation element (PCE) architecture (http://www.ietf.org/dyn/wg/charter/pce-charter.html) to compute sophisticated MPLS Traffic Engineering Label Switch Paths (TE LSP). For example, the request might be to compute the shortest constraint path with multi-metric optimization (a Nondeterministic Polynomial (NP)-complete problem).

With LLNs there is strong interest in using several OFs because deployments greatly vary with different objectives and a single network may support traffic with very different requirements in terms of path quality. Consider the case of a mixed network with battery- and main-powered nodes, a variety of high and low bandwidth links, and two main applications (telemetry and critical alarms). This is a situation where it might be extremely useful for each node supporting both applications to be able to use two paths. These would include one "time sensitive" path for alarms where the objective is to have a short delay and a highly reliable path with no constraint on the type of nodes along the path to the destination, and another "not time sensitive path" for the telemetry traffic where it is beneficial to not traverse any battery-operated node to preserve energy and where the objective would be to minimize hops to avoid traffic congestion in the network. RPL addresses these requirements by building two DODAGs with each one having its own OF. The OF is used in conjunction with the routing metric to compute the path.

Consider Figure 17.2 which depicts an LLN. In this network, the link's LQLs are provided in addition to the latency and availability of link layer encryption. In addition, node 11 is battery-operated. The arrow shows the best computed path from the low-power and lossy network border router (LBR) to node 34 for two different OFs, OF1 and OF2, defined in the following:

> OF1: "Use the LQL as a global recorded metric and favor paths with the minimum number of low and fair quality links, use the link color as a link constraint to avoid non-encrypted links." Note that two paths are available with an equivalent aggregated LQL metric: 34-35-24-13-1 and 34-33-23-22-12-1. But because the OF specifies using a recorded metric, the path 34-33-23-22-12-1 is chosen since it only has two links of "fair" quality.
>
> OF2: "Find the best path in terms of latency (link latency is used as a global aggregated metric), while avoiding poor quality links and battery-operated nodes." Several paths have been pruned because they traverse battery-operated nodes (node 11) and traverse poor quality links (link 12-23). The best path (lowest latency) is 34-24-13-1.

17.6 RPL: THE NEW ROUTING PROTOCOL FOR SMART OBJECT NETWORKS

This section describes RPL (IPv6 Routing Protocol for Low-power and Lossy Networks), the newly specified IP routing protocol for smart object networks, in detail. RPL is still a work in progress and the IETF RFC should be used as the final reference. Various aspects may change or be added to the specification.

17.6.1 Protocol Overview

Similar to IETF specifications (see [214]), this section provides an overview of the RPL mode of operation.

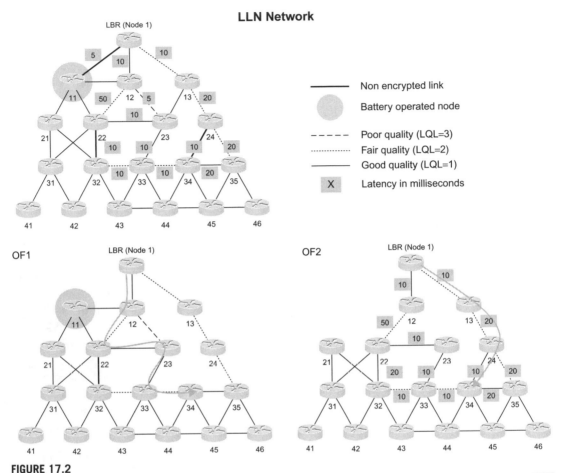

FIGURE 17.2

Examples with two different OFs.

Considering the wide set of routing requirements spelled out in the application-specific documents and discussed in Section 17.3, RPL was designed to be highly modular. The main specification [256] covers the intersection of these requirements. The prime objective is to design a highly modular protocol where the core of the routing protocol would address the intersection of the application-specific routing requirements, and additional modules would be added as needed to address specific requirements.

RPL was designed for LLNs where constrained devices are interconnected by (wireless and wired) lossy links. Many of the routing protocol design decisions were strictly driven by the unique characteristics of these networks. When observing the link failure profiles of the link layers in the Internet or private IP networks (Ethernet, Optical links, etc.), error rates are relatively low and the link error profiles show uniform distribution. Thus routing protocols designed for such link profiles quickly react to link failure with no risk of oscillation since link flaps are rare events. When failures do occur, various dampening techniques are used. This drove the design principles of various "fast reroute" mechanisms. As soon as the link failure is detected (thanks to link layer notification or fast keepalive mechanisms such as Bidirectional Forwarding Detection; BFD [144] or link layer triggers), the traffic is immediately rerouted onto a backup path to minimize the traffic disruption. The situation in LLN is rather different. Figure 17.1 shows the packet delivery ratio (PDR) for two wireless links and the situation is extremely similar to PLC links. Such link failure profiles are not uncommon and demonstrate that it is imperative to handle link failure in a very different manner in LLN. First, a node should try to determine whether or not the link should be considered as down (not an easy decision in LLNs) and, consequently, inadequate for traffic forwarding. The same reasoning applies to determining whether or not a link should be considered as usable in the first place (known as "local confidence"). This means that a node should carefully observe a link and start using it or determine whether to stop using it (thus triggering a global path recomputation in the network).

The lossy nature of these links is not the only LLN characteristic that drove the design decisions of RPL. Because resources are scarce, the control traffic must be as tightly bounded as possible. In these networks the data traffic is usually limited and the control traffic should be reduced whenever possible to save bandwidth *and* energy. Using a fast probing mechanism as with many other routing protocols is just not an option, and ideally the control traffic should decrease as the routing topology stabilizes. Nodes are constrained in nature, which implies that the routing protocol should not require heavy state maintenance.

Bearing in mind the lossy nature of links in LLN helps understand the RPL design choices made during the specification design.

RPL is a distance vector protocol that builds a DODAG where paths are constructed from each node in the network to the DODAG root (typically a sink or an LBR). There are a number of reasons why it was decided to use a distance vector routing protocol as opposed to a link state protocol. The main reason was the constrained nature of the nodes in LLNs. Link state routing protocols are more powerful (the detailed topology is known by all nodes) but require a significant amount of resources such as memory (Link State Database; LSDB) and control traffic to synchronize the LSDBs. An example of DODAG is shown in Figure 17.2. Various procedures described in Section 17.6.2 govern how the DODAG is constructed and how nodes attach to each other according to an OF. In contrast with tree topologies, DODAGs offer redundant paths, which is a MUST requirement for LLNs. Thus if the topology permits, RPL may provision more than one path between a node and the DODAG root and even other nodes in the network.

Before digging into the protocol specification, a high-level overview of the protocol is in order. First, one or more nodes are configured as DODAG roots by the network administrator. A node discovery mechanism based on newly defined ICMPv6 messages is used by RPL to build the DODAG. RPL defines two new ICMPv6 messages called DODAG information object (DIO) messages and destination advertisement object (DAO) messages. DIO messages (simply referred to as DIO) are sent by nodes to advertise information about the DODAG, such as the DODAGID, the OF, DODAG rank (detailed in the next section), the DODAGSequenceNumber, along with other DODAG parameters such as a set of path metrics and constraints discussed in the previous section. When a node discovers multiple DODAG neighbors (that could become parents or sibling), it makes use of various rules to decide whether (and where) to join the DODAG. This allows the construction of the DODAG as nodes join. Once a node has joined a DODAG, it has a route toward the DODAG root (which may be a default route) in support of the MP2P traffic from the leaves to the DODAG root (in the up direction).

RPL uses "up" and "down" directions terminology. The up direction is from a leaf toward the DODAG root, whereas down refers to the opposite direction. The usual terminology of parents/children is used. RPL also introduces the "sibling"; two nodes are siblings if they have the same rank in the DODAG (note that they may or may not have a common parent). The parent of a node in the DODAG is the immediate successor within the DODAG in the up direction, whereas a DODAG sibling refers to a node at the same rank. Back to the example in Figure 17.2, 13 is a parent of 24, 22, and 23 are siblings, and 43 and 44 are children of 33. A DODAG is said to be grounded if it is connected to what RPL calls a "goal," which can be a node connected to an external (non-LLN) private IP network or the public Internet. A non-grounded DODAG is called a floating DODAG.

RPL uses iterations controlled by the DODAG root to maintain the DODAG; the DODAGSequenceNumber is a counter incremented by the DODAG root to specify the iteration number of the DODAG.

A mechanism is now needed to provide routing information in the down direction (for the traffic from the route to the leaf) and for the P2P direction since the DODAG provides defaults routes to the DODAG root from each node in the network. For this mechanism, RPL has defined another ICMPv6 message called the DAO message. DAO messages (simply referred to as DAO) are used to advertise prefix reachability toward the leaves. DAOs carry prefix information along with a lifetime (to determine the freshness of the destination advertisement) and depth or path cost information to determine how far the destination is. Note that the path in this direction is dictated by the DODAG built by RPL in the other direction. In some cases DAOs may also record the set of visited nodes. This is particularly useful when the intermediate nodes cannot store any routing states, which is discussed later in Section 17.6.6. If a parent receives destination advertisements that can be aggregated from multiple children, local policy may be used to perform prefix aggregation in an attempt to reduce routing table and the size of DAO messages. Note that redundant DAO messages are aggregated along the DODAG. An OF may be specifically designed to maximize prefix aggregation.

What about P2P traffic? RPL supports P2P traffic. When node A sends a packet destined to node B, if B is not in direct reach, it forwards the packet to its DODAG parent. From there, if the destination is reachable from one of its children, the packet is forwarded in the down direction. In other words, the packet travels up to a common ancestor at which point it is forwarded in the down direction toward the destination. An interesting optimization periodically emits link-local multicast IPv6 DAOs. Thus if the destination is in direct range (one hop away), a node can send the packet directly to the destination without following the DODAG. The degree of optimality for P2P traffic is discussed in Section 17.6.10.

Sending DIO and DAO messages is governed by the use of trickle timers. The trickle timers use dynamic timers that govern the sending of RPL control messages in an attempt to reduce redundant messages as discussed in detail later in Section 17.6.10. When the DODAG is unstable (e.g., the DODAG is being rebuilt) RPL control messages are sent more frequently (the DODAG becomes inconsistent). On the other hand, as the DODAG stabilizes messages are sent less often to reduce the control plane overhead, which is very important in LLNs.

Once the DODAG is built and routing tables are populated, routing is fully operational. As links and nodes fail, paths are repaired using local and global repair mechanisms. Local repairs quickly find a backup path without an attempt to globally reoptimize the DODAG entirely, whereas global repairs rely on a reoptimization process driven by the DODAG root.

RPL also supports the concept of DODAG instances identified by an Instance ID called the RPLInstanceID. It might be useful to form different topologies according to various sets of constraints and OFs. An RPL node may join multiple DODAG instances; for example, one DODAG optimizes for high reliability and another DODAG optimizes for low latency. Data packets are then forwarded along the appropriate DODAG according to the application requirements.

17.6.2 Use of Multiple DODAG and the Concept of RPL Instance

As previously discussed, a DODAG is a set of vertices connected by directed edges with no directed cycles. As shown in Figure 17.2, RPL builds DODAGs forming a set of paths from each leaf to the DODAG root (typically an LBR). In contrast with tree topologies, DODAGs offer redundant paths, a MUST requirement for LLNs. Thus if the topology permits, there is always more than one path between a leaf and the DODAG root.

The notion of DODAG instance is quite straightforward and similar to the concept of multi-topology routing (MTR) supported by other routing protocols such as OSPF and IS-IS. The idea is to support the construction of multiple DODAGs over a given physical topology. Why more than one DODAG? This is done to steer traffic to different paths optimized according to the requirements. Consider the case of a physical network made of a series of links with different qualities (e.g., reliability, throughput, latency) and nodes with different attributes (e.g., battery-powered vs. main-powered). If the network carries traffic with different QoS requirements, it might be useful to build one DODAG optimized for low latency and another DODAG optimized to provide high reliability while avoiding battery-operated nodes. In this case, RPL can build two DODAGs according to two different OFs. *If a node carries both types of traffic it may then decide to join both DODAGs (DODAG instance).* When a delay-sensitive packet must be sent along the DODAG, it is flagged (in the packet header) with the appropriate DODAG instance and forwarded along the appropriate DODAG. This decision is made by the application.

Figure 17.3 shows how two DODAGs are built from a given physical topology. DODAG 1 (instance 1) is built to optimize the path reliability while avoiding battery-operated nodes, whereas DODAG 2 (instance 2) is optimizing the latency. Depending on the sequence event, RPL may not compute the exact same routing topology. Also note that only preferred parents are depicted on the picture along with siblings.

A destination-oriented DODAG (DODODAG) is a DODAG rooted at a single destination. Within an instance, the LLN routing topology can be partitioned among multiple DODAGs for a number of reasons such as providing a greater scalability. Figure 17.4 shows multiple DODAGs in a specific DODAG instance.

A node can only join a single DODODAG within a DODAG instance.

A DODAG is identified by its instance (RPLInstanceID). A DODAG is uniquely identified by the combination of the DODAG instances (RPLInstanceID) and the DODAGID (the identifier of the DODAG that must be unique within the scope of a DODAG instance in the LLN). A DODAG iteration is uniquely identified by the tuple {RPLInstanceID, DODAGID, DODAGSequenceNumber}.

17.6.3 RPL Messages

A good way to gain further insight into a protocol after a protocol overview is to look at the protocol packet formats. RPL specifies three messages (using the same ICMPv6 codepoint): the DODAG

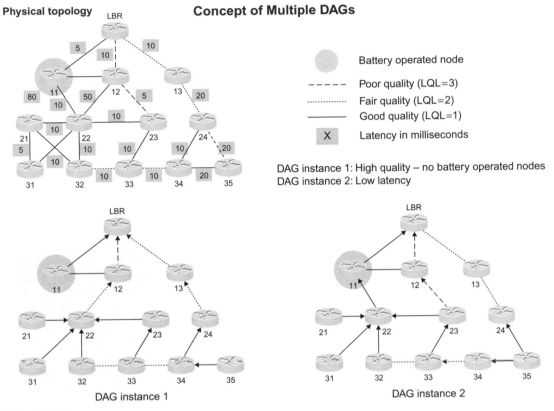

FIGURE 17.3

RPL DODODAG and instance.

Information Object (DIO), the DODAG Destination Advertisement Object (DAO), and the DODAG information solicitation message (DIS).

17.6.3.1 DIO Messages

DIO messages are sent by RPL nodes to advertise a DODAG and its characteristics, thus DIOs are used for DODAG discovery, formation, and maintenance. DIOs carry a set of mandatory information augmented with options.

The DIO base option is mandatory and may carry several suboptions. The following flags and fields are currently defined:

- Grounded (G): Indicates whether the DODAG is grounded, in other words, the DODAG root is a goal for the OF (e.g., the DODAG root is connected to a non-LLN IP network such as a private network or the public Internet).
- Destination Advertisement Trigger (T): The T bit is used to trigger a complete refresh of the routes in the down direction (downward routes).

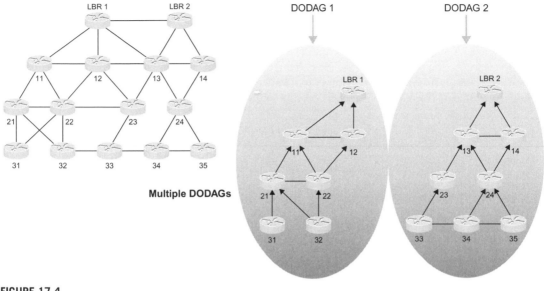

FIGURE 17.4

RPL multiple DODAGs within a DODAG instance.

- Destination Advertisement Stored (S): The S bit is used to indicate that a non-root ancestor is storing routing table entries learned from DAO messages.
- Destination advertisement supported (A flag): The A flag is set when the DODAG root supports the collection of prefix advertisements and enables the advertisement of prefixes in the DODAG.
- DODAGPreference (Prf): The Prf is a 3-bit field set by the DODAG root to report its preference. It can be used to engineer the network and make some DODAGs more attractive to join.

The DODAGSequenceNumber is the sequence number of the DODAG that characterizes the DODAG iteration and is exclusively controlled by the DODAG root.

The RPLInstanceID is used to identify the DODAG instance and is provisioned at the DODAG root.

The Destination Advertisement Trigger Sequence Number (DTSN) is an 8-bit integer set by the node sending the DIO. The DTSN is used by the procedure to maintain the downward routes as discussed in Section 17.6.6.

The DODAGID is a 128-bit integer set by the DODAG root and that uniquely identifies the DODAG.

The DODAG Rank is the rank of the node sending the DIO message.

The rank determines the relative position of a node in the DODAG and is used primarily for loop avoidance. The rank is computed according to the OF and is potentially subject to local node policy. The rank (although potentially derived from routing metrics) is not a metric. For example, a node that first joins a DODAG may not select the node with the lowest rank as a parent (closer to the DODAG root) should there be an alternate node with a deeper rank advertising a path with a lower cost. Once the rank has been computed, the node cannot join a new parent with deeper rank for loop avoidance except under specific circumstances discussed in Section 17.6.7.

When two nodes have the same rank, the nodes are said to be siblings (they are located at a similar level of optimality in the DODAG). It is highly desirable to make the rank a coarse value to favor the use of siblings. A sibling is a node that has the same rank and is used to increase connectivity. If the OF chooses to use the path ETX as the rank, more than likely the nodes will all have a different rank and thus the probability of finding a sibling will be very low. A rounded ETX (a coarse-grained value derived from the ETX) helps to increase the probability of finding siblings. A node may forward a packet to one of its siblings, if the link to its most preferred parent is not viable, at the risk of forming a loop (loop detection mechanisms can then be used to detect such a loop).

17.6.3.1.1 Use of the Rank for DODAG Parent Selection

If Rank (A) < Rank (B), then node A is located in a more optimal location than node B and it is safe for B to select A as a DODAG parent with no risk of forming loops.

On the other hand, if Rank(A) > Rank(B), it is not safe for B to select A as a parent (unless B joins the DODAG for the first time) since A may be in B's sub-DODAG. Selecting A as a parent would potentially form a routing loop. This may be allowed in a limited manner according to the max_depth rule explained in Section 17.6.7 to allow for local repair.

Note that the rank is a monotonic scalar. The rank of a node is always higher than the rank of any of its parents.

The rank is a 16-bit value used for the number of purposes described in detail in this chapter. At the time of writing, [256] suggests to consider the rank as a fixed point number, where the position of the decimal point is determined by value advertised by the DODAG root called the MinHopRankIncrease. The MinHopRankIncrease represents the minimum amount that a rank can increase on each hop and is used to detect siblings. The integer portion of the rank is called floor (Rank/MinHopRankIncrease).

A node A has a rank less than the rank of a node B if floor (Rank(A)/MinHopRankIncrease) is less than floor (Rank(B)/MinHopRankIncrease).

A node A has a rank greater than the rank of a node B if floor (Rank(A)/MinHopRankIncrease) is greater than floor (Rank(B)/MinHopRankIncrease).

Two nodes A and B are siblings if: floor (Rank(A)/MinHopRankIncrease) == floor (Rank(B)/MinHopRankIncrease). In other words, A and B are siblings if the integer portion of their rank is equal.

This can be better illustrated with an example. If MinHopRankIncrease is equal to, say, $2^5 = 32$ and the rank is equal to 953, then the integer portion of the rank is equal to int(953/32) = 29. All the nodes with a rank between 928 and 959 will have the same integer part for their rank, so they will be siblings.

Note that this may still change but this would not affect how the notion of rank is used in [256].

The DODAGID is a 128-bit integer that uniquely identifies the DODAG and is set by the DODAG root. If the DODAG root uses an IPv6 address, the same IPv6 address must not be used by any other uncoordinated DODAG root within the LLN for the same DODAG instance.

Several suboptions are defined for DIOs. One of the most important is the DODAG metric container suboption used to report the path metrics described in the previous section.

A second important suboption is the destination prefix suboption used for prefix advertisement in the down direction (thus to provision state to route a packet in the up direction) for prefixes other than the default route. This may be useful to advertise prefixes other than the default route. The prefix is accompanied by a preference field compliant with [59] and a prefix lifetime.

The third important suboption is the DODAG configuration suboption used to advertise several DODAG configuration parameters such as trickle timers. Sending of RPL messages is governed by trickle timers and a detailed description of the trickle algorithm can be found later in Section 17.6.10. To ensure consistency across the DODAG, the trickle timer's configuration is advertised by the DODAG root. Since these timers are unlikely to change in the DODAG, a node may decide not to include the DODAG timer suboption in every DIO, except if the DIO is sent in reply to a DIS. The three parameters advertised in the DODAG timer configuration suboption include DIOIntervalDoubling, DIOIntervalMin, and DIORedundancyConstant. These are discussed in detail in Section 17.6.9. Other DODAG parameters such as the DAGMaxRankIncrease used by the local repair mechanism (specified in Section 17.6.7) and the MinHopRankIncrease are also advertised. Other parameters are likely to be added in further revisions of RPL to support additional features.

17.6.3.2 DAO Messages

DAO messages are used to propagate destination information along the DODAG in the up direction to populate the routing tables of ancestor nodes in support of P2MP and P2P traffic. The DAO message includes the following information:

- DAO sequence: A counter incremented by the node owning the advertised prefix each time a new DAO message is sent.
- RPLInstanceID: The topology instance ID as learned from the DIO.
- DAO rank: Corresponds to the rank of the node that owns the prefix.
- DAO lifetime: It is expressed in seconds and corresponds to the prefix lifetime.
- Route tag: 8-bit integer that can be used to tag "critical" routes. The priority could be used to indicate whether the route should be stored by the nodes with a lower rank (closer to the DODAG root), which could be useful if nodes have limited memory capacities and must be selective about which destination information to cache. Note that the size of that field has been changed several times and is subject to further changes.
- Destination Prefix: The Prefix Length field contains the number of valid leading bits in the prefix.
- Reverse Route Stack: The RRS is discussed in detail in Section 17.6.6, and contains a number of RRCount (another field of the DAO message) IPv6 addresses used in LLNs with nodes that cannot store routing tables.

17.6.3.3 DIS Messages

DIS messages are similar to the IPv6 router solicitation (RS) message, and used to discover DODAGs in the neighborhood and solicit DIOs from RPL nodes in the neighborhood. A DIS has no additional message body.

17.6.4 RPL DODAG Building Process

In this section, the DODAG building mode of operation for RPL is discussed. The DODAG formation is governed by several rules: the RPL rules used for loop avoidance (based on the DODAG ranks), the advertised OF, the advertised path metrics, and the policies of the configured nodes. A node may be part of several DODAG instances, and within a DODAG instance there may be several DODAGs rooted by different nodes.

DIO messages are sent upon the expiration of the trickle timer (see Section 17.6.10 for more details). The basic idea is to send DIOs more frequently when a DODAG inconsistency is detected (e.g., when the node receives a modified DIO with new DODAG parameters such as a new OF, new DODAGSequenceNumber, or the parent advertises a new DODAG Rank, etc.), a loop is detected (e.g., the node receives a packet from a child that is intended to move down along the same child according to its routing table), or the node joins a DODAG with a new DODAGID or has moved within a DODAG. When a DODAG inconsistency is detected the node resets its trickle timer to cause the advertisement of DIO messages more often. As the DODAG stabilizes and no inconsistency is detected, DIO messages are sent less frequently to limit the control traffic.

When a node starts its initialization process it may decide to remain silent until it hears a DIO advertising an existing DODAG. Alternatively, the node may issue a DIS message to probe the neighborhood and receive DIO messages from its neighbors more quickly. Another option is to start its own floating DODAG and to begin multicasting DIO messages for its own floating DODAG (note that this may be desired if it is required to establish and maintain inner connectivity between a set of nodes in the absence of a goal/grounded DODAG). Unicast DIOs are sent in reply to unicast DIS messages and also include a complete set of DODAG configuration options.

The G-bit is only set if the DODAG root is a goal. If the advertising node is the DODAG root, the rank is equal to the RPL variable called the ROOT_RANK (equal to 1).

Upon receiving a DIO message, a node must first determine whether or not the DIO message should be processed. If the DIO message is malformed, it is silently discarded. If not, the node must then determine whether the DIO was sent by a candidate neighbor. The notion of a candidate neighbor is tightly coupled with the notion of local confidence, and that important notion is implementation specific and used to determine if a node is eligible for parent selection. For example, when a node first hears about a neighbor it may choose to wait for a period of time to make sure that the connecting link is sufficiently reliable.

Then the node determines whether the DIO is related to a DODAG it is already a member of.

If the rank of the node advertising the DIO is less than the node's rank plus some RPL configurable value called the DAGMaxRankIncrease, then the DIO is processed. This rule is called the max_depth rule and is explained in detail in Section 17.6.7.

If the DIO message is sent by a node with a lesser rank and the DIO message advertises a (different) DODAG that provides a better path according to the OF, then the DIO message must be processed.

The DIO must also be processed if it is originated by a DODAG parent for a different DODAG than the node belongs to since the DODAG parent may have jumped to another DODAG.

A collision may occur if two nodes simultaneously send DIOs to each other and decide to join each other. This is why DIO messages received during the risk window are simply not processed. Because of the random effect of the trickle timers, it is expected that the next DIO messages are not likely to collide again.

For the DODAG root operation on the DODAGSequenceNumber the DODAGSequenceNumber is only incremented by the DODAG root. It may be incremented upon the expiration of a configurable timer, upon a manual command on the DODAG root, or upon the reception of a signal from downstream (yet to be determined by the RPL specification). A node may safely attach to a parent regardless of the advertised rank if the parent in the next DODAG iteration (the DODAGSequenceNumber is higher than the node's current one) since that parent cannot possibly belong to the sub-DODAG of that node. This is further discussed in Section 17.6.8.

17.6.4.1 A Step-by-step Example

The DODAG building process is illustrated by Figure 17.5, which shows the physical network topology and how the DODAG is built. The link metric is the ETX and the OF finds the path minimizing the path ETX where the path ETX is defined as the sum of the ETX for all traversed links. The OF specifies an additional constraint of avoiding battery-operated nodes and the rank is based on the hop count. Note that the OF could have been different; for example, it could have been computed as a function of the ETX (e.g., Rank = int(ETX*10)/10).

> Step 1: The DODAG root starts sending link-local multicast DIO messages. This is one possible event sequence. One of the nodes could also decide to send a DIS message, in which case the DODAG root (LBR) would immediately send the DIO in reply to the DIS message.

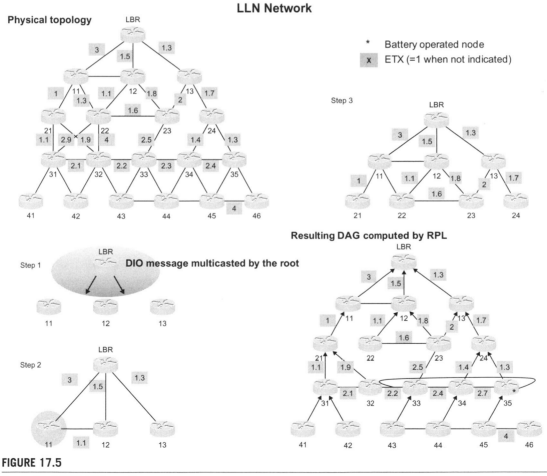

FIGURE 17.5

Example of DODAG formation.

Step 2: Nodes 11, 12, and 13 receive the LBR DIO. Upon processing the DIO (which comes from a lower ranked node thus a lower rank value), nodes 11, 12, and 13 select LBR as their DODAG parent (note that nodes 12 and 13 may have waited for some period of time to build enough local confidence). At this point, nodes 11, 12, and 13 compute their new rank based on the hop count and the path ETX value is computed. Node 11 also selects node 12 as a sibling and vice versa (same rank).

Step 3: Shows the resulting DODAG after another round of iteration. Note that link 22-11 has been pruned from the DODAG since node 12 is a better parent considering the OF (minimize the path ETX). Node 23 has selected two parents offering equal cost paths (ETX = 3.3).

Step 4: Shows the final DODAG. Node 46 has not selected node 35 as a best parent since the OF specifies the constraint of not traversing a battery-operated node. Local policy may be used to indicate whether constraints also apply to siblings (in this example, node 34 did select node 35 as a sibling). A potential sibling loop 33-34-35-33 has formed (discussed in Section 17.6.7).

The shape of the resulting DODAG depends on the event sequence ordering.

17.6.5 Movements of a Node Within and Between DODAGs

There are a few fundamental rules that govern movements within a DODAG:

1. A node is free to jump to any position in any other DODODAG that has not been previously visited at any time. For example, a node may decide to select a new node as a parent that belongs to a new DODAG regardless of the rank. The new DODAG may be the same DODAG (same DODAGID, same RPLInstanceID) but with a higher DAGSequenceNumber or it may be a different DODAG (different DODAGID and/or different RPLInstanceID). It is recommended to jump to another DODAG only when all queued packets have been transmitted along the previous DODAG. Jumping back to a previous DODAG is similar to moving inside a DODAG. This is why a node should remember its DODAG identified by the RPLInstanceID, DODAGID, and DODAGSequenceNumber along with its rank within that DODAG. Jumping (moving) back should then honor the rules of the previous position so as not to potentially create a loop (max_depth rule).

2. A node may advertise a lower rank at any time when it has jumped to another DODAG.

3. Within a DODODAG iteration a node must not advertise a rank deeper than L+DAGMaxRankIncrease where L is the lowest rank. The DAGMaxRankIncrease is an RPL variable advertised by the DODAG root, and a value of 0 has the effect of disabling this rule. There is one exception to this rule; the poison-and-wait rule where the node advertises an infinite rank that is described right after. The reasons for this rule are further discussed in Section 17.6.7.

When a node prepares to move to a new DODAG iteration it may decide to defer the movement to see if it could join another node with a better path (even if the rank is higher) cost according to the OF.

It is perfectly safe for a node to move up in the DODAG and select new parents with a lower rank than its current parents' rank. In this case, the node must abandon all prior parents and siblings that have now become deeper than the node in the DODAG and potentially select new ones.

If a node wants to move down in its DODODAG causing the rank to increase, it may use the poison-and-wait rule discussed in Section 17.6.7.

What if a node receives a DIO message specifying an OF that it does not support or recognize? The two options are either not to join the DODAG or to join as a leaf. Such a node may not join as a router since the node would then be incapable of propagating an appropriate metric, which may lead to a DODAG using an inconsistent metric. Thus when a node joins as a leaf node, it can receive and process DIO messages and send DAO messages. But it should not send DIO messages and thus cannot act as an RPL router.

17.6.6 Populating the Routing Tables Along the DODAG Using DAO Messages

As the DODAG is being built, the next task is populating the routing tables along the DODAG in support of the down traffic (toward the leaves). DAO messages are used to propagate prefix reachability along the DODAG.

DAO operation is still being discussed within the IETF ROLL Working Group. More than likely several changes will take place and the mechanisms described in this section reflect the DAO mode of operation at the time of writing: the reference should be the final RFC for RPL.

A sequence number is included to detect the freshness of the information and outdated or duplicate messages are simply discarded. The sequence number is incremented by the node that owns the prefix. A node sends unicast DAO to its preferred parent only (note that this is the option taken by RPL at the time of writing; further revisions of RPL may suggest sending the DAO messages to a set of parents, which would require extensions to the DAO message propagation rules). Allowing for sending DAO messages to more than one parent would enable load balancing in the down direction of the DODAG.

The DAO message contains the rank of the node owning the advertised prefix. That rank may be used by a node who received multiple DAO from different children for the same destination prefix as a selection criteria to select the next-hop that provides the more optimal route, although the rank may not reflect the actual path cost to the advertising node. RPL also supports the inclusion of the DAG Metric Container in DAO messages to provide the path cost.

Note that RPL supports the ability to prune a route by sending a prefix with a lifetime set to 0. This is also called a "no-DAO" message.

17.6.6.1 Use of the Reverse Route Stack in DAO Message

Some nodes in the network may have significant constraints regarding memory and may be incapable of storing routing entries for downward routes. Although not an issue in support of the MP2P traffic, such nodes cannot store routing states upon receiving DAO messages from their children and, consequently, the P2MP traffic or P2P traffic cannot be routed to the destination leaf. Thus RPL has specified extensions to accommodate this type of node (also called non-storing nodes) in LLNs. The mechanism records paths traversing memory-less nodes when forwarding the DAO. Let's consider Figure 17.6 where nodes 22 and 32 cannot store any routing updates. P1 and P2 are two IPv6 prefixes owned by nodes 42 and 43, respectively, and advertised to node 32 by means of DAO. Upon receiving the unicast DAO message, node 32 appends the IPv6 prefix of node 42 to the reverse route stack of the received DAO. Upon receiving the DAO from node 32, node 22 (which is also memory-less) performs a similar operation and appends the IPv6 address of node 32. Each time, the RRCount counter is incremented. Once the DAO message reaches a node capable of storing routing states (node 12), the node detects that the DAO has traversed a region with nodes incapable of storing routing states by observing the presence of the reverse route stack in the DAO. Then node 12 simply extracts the set of

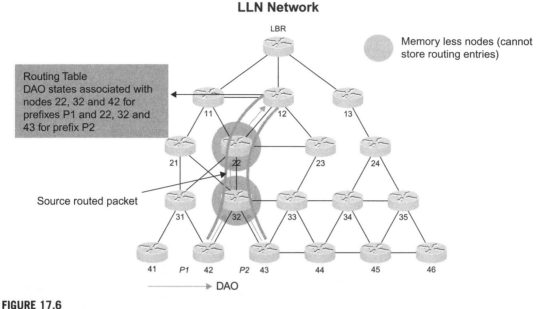

LLN Network

Memory less nodes (cannot store routing entries)

Routing Table
DAO states associated with nodes 22, 32 and 42 for prefixes P1 and 22, 32 and 43 for prefix P2

Source routed packet

→ DAO

FIGURE 17.6

Use of reverse route stack in DAO message.

hops associated with the advertised prefix, stores them locally in its routing table, and then clears the reverse stack header and the RRCount counter. Upon receiving a packet destined to, say, prefix P1, node 12 consults in the routing table and makes use of source routing to send the packet to node 42. This allows reaching the final destination with intermediate nodes incapable of storing states. This mechanism can be generalized to a network exclusively made of memory-less nodes thus leading to a situation where all node-to-node communication would transit via the DODAG root.

Thus DAO message can be used to propagate reachability information and also to record routes for regions comprising non-storing nodes. These two mechanisms could also be decoupled.

The source routing mechanisms used by RPL have not yet been defined. They could be based on IPv6 source routing, which would require a new extended header (potentially with compressed IPv6 addresses) or labels. Furthermore, the mechanism described here is subject to change and RPL may evolve to not allow for the mix of storing and non storing nodes in the same network in an attempt to simplify the specification.

17.6.6.2 Routing Table Maintenance

If a node loses routing adjacency with a child for which it has an associated prefix, it should clean up the corresponding routing entry and report the lost route to it parents by sending a no-DAO message for the corresponding entry.

Prefixes may be in three different states: (1) connected (prefix locally owned by the node), (2) reachable (prefix with a non-0 lifetime received from a child), and (3) unreachable (prefix that has timed out for which a no-DAO message will be sent to the parent the node had previously advertised that prefix to).

Two timers have been specified for the processing of DAO messages:

- DelayDAO timer: This timer is armed each time there is a trigger to send a new DAO message (e.g., reception of a DIO message that requests to receive new DAO messages). At the time of writing, the DelayDAO timer is set to a random value between [DEF_DAO-LATENCY/ Rank(Node)] and [DEF_DAO_LATENCY/Rank (parent's node)] for nodes deeper in the DODAG to advertise their prefixes first. By attempting to order the sequencing of DAO, the chances to aggregate prefixes along the DODAG in an attempt to reduce the number of DAO messages and routing table size increase.
- RemoveTimer: This timer is used to remove stale prefixes that are no longer advertised by nodes in the sub-DODAG. There is a mechanism that allows a node to request DAO to be sent to refresh the states. In the absence of replies after n requests, the timer is started and upon its expiration routes are removed in the absence of DAO advertising these routes. The node then also informs its own parent with a no-DAO.

One event that triggers the sending of a DAO message (or more precisely arming the DelayDAO timer) is the reception of a new DIO message from a parent.

All routes learned through DAO messages are removed if the corresponding interface or the routing adjacency for these prefixes is determined as down.

DAOs are sent as unicast messages to DODAG parents, but they can also be sent to the link-local scope all-nodes multicast address (FF02::1). In the case of multicast messages, the node only advertises its own local prefixes, and these prefixes can also be advertised by a node to its DODAG parent using a unicast DAO. A node is not allowed to advertise prefixes learned from one of its children using multicast DAO. The main purpose of multicast DAO is to help with the "one-hop" P2P traffic between two nodes that can communicate directly with each other even when the link does not belong to the DODAG.

As illustrated in Figure 17.7, a multicast DAO is received by the node from node 23 advertising prefix P1. Thus if a packet received or originated by node 32 is destined to prefix P1, it is sent directly to node 23 without having to follow the DODAG. In the absence of multicast DAO, such a packet would first be sent to the parent of node 32 (node 22), which would relay the packet to its parent (node 12). At this point, node 12 would have P1 in its routing table due to the DAO message received from its child, node 23. Thus the path would have been 32-22-12-23.

In its current form there is exactly one prefix per DAO message. But as prefixes travel along the DODAG, a node can factor out some of their common attributes. For example, prefixes advertised at the same rank could be packed in the same DAO message with a unique rank without needing to repeat the same rank for each prefix. The same reasoning applies to many other prefix attributes. Thus by packing prefixes into the same message and factoring out their common attributes, the control traffic overhead is reduced and wasting bandwidth is avoided. More than likely DAO packing will be added to the RPL specification.

17.6.7 Loop Avoidance and Loop Detection Mechanisms in RPL

Routing loops are always undesirable and one of the objectives of routing protocols is to avoid the formation of loops whenever possible.

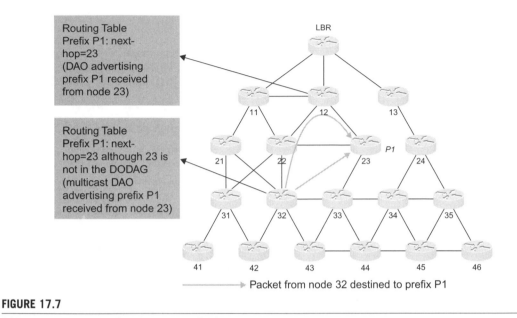

FIGURE 17.7

P2P routing in a DODAG with multicast DAO.

In high-speed networks, the packet TTL is decremented at each hop so a looping packet is quickly destroyed even if the loop has a short duration. Even with link state routing protocols such as OSPF and IS-IS, temporary loops (often called micro-loop due to their limited lifetime) may form during network topology changes due to the temporary lack of synchronization of the node's LSDB. At high data rates, even a short duration loop can lead to packet drops and link congestion. Various mechanisms have been proposed to avoid such loops.

In LLNs, the situation is somewhat different. First the traffic rate is generally very low, thus a temporary loop may have a very limited impact. Second, it is extremely important not to overreact in the presence of instability. In contrast with "traditional" IP networks where fast reaction (reconvergence) is very important, it is crucial not to react too quickly in LLNs. Thus loops may exist; they must be avoided whenever possible and detected when they occur. RPL does not fundamentally guarantee the absence of temporary loops, which would imply expensive mechanisms for the control plane and may not be appropriate to lossy and unstable environments. RPL instead tries to avoid loops by using a loop detection mechanism via data path validation.

17.6.7.1 Loop Avoidance
One of the RPL's rules, the max_depth rule, states that a node is not allowed to select as a parent a node with a rank higher than the node's rank+DAGMaxRankIncrease. Let's explain why this rule exists by considering the network depicted in Figure 17.5.

The first reason is simply to reduce the risk of a node attaching to another node that belongs to its own sub-DODAG, thus leading to a loop that may require counting to infinity. For example, in Figure 17.5 if node 24 loses all of its parents and decides to select node 46 as a parent, since the path to the root from node 46 is via node 24, a loop would form and node 24 has no way to learn that node 46 actually belongs to its own sub-DODAG. As explained in Section 17.6.8, the max_depth rule does not prevent loops from occurring, but it limits the loop sizes and allows the detection of such a loop without having to count to infinity.

Another RPL rule requires that the rank to increase the set of feasible parents should not be increased to avoid a "greediness" effect. Consider again Figure 17.5. Suppose that nodes 22 and 23 are both at rank 3, share a common parent (node 12), and there is a viable link between them (nodes 22 and 23 are siblings). Suppose that both nodes 22 and 23 try to increase their set of feasible successors to have alternate routes in case of link failure with their preferred DODAG parent (e.g., by detaching and moving down in a controlled manner). Suppose that node 22 first decides to select nodes 23 and 12 as DODAG parents (the new rank is now 4, the highest rank of both parents). Suppose now that node 23 does not follow the RPL rule and processes the DIO from node 22 (which now has a deeper rank than node 23). Node 23 may then decide to select both nodes 12 and 22 as DODAG parents, thus increasing its rank to 5. Then node 22 may reiterate the process until counting to infinity and restarting the process.

This explains two fundamental loop avoidance rules of RPL (except in specific conditions such as attempts to perform a local repair as explained next): (1) a first node is not allowed to select as a DODAG parent a neighboring node that is deeper in the DODAG than the first node's self rank+DAGMaxRankIncrease and (2) a node is not allowed to be greedy and attempt to move deeper in the DODAG to increase the selection of DODAG parents (possibly creating loops and instability). Indeed, suppose that node 23 is now allowed to, and for some reason (temporary better metric) decides to, select node 43 as a DODAG parent. This leads to a loop …

Still, even with the loop avoidance mechanisms stated earlier, loops may take place in a number of circumstances within a DODAG. DODAG loops can take place when a DIO message is lost (examples are given in Section 17.6.8), but these are not the only type of RPL loops. DAO loops may occur when a node fails to inform its parents that a destination is no longer reachable. If the DAO message is lost, the parent may keep the route to that destination in its routing table. If the child wants to send a packet to that destination, the parent would send it back to the child thus leading to a loop. One proposal is to use acknowledgments for DAO messages, which would dramatically reduce the risk of DAO loops. Another possible type of loop is a sibling loop. Consider again Figure 17.5. In case of multiple failures of links toward the root (e.g., links 35-24, 34-24, and 33-23), a packet sent by node 35 to the LBR may very well loop (35-34-33-35) since siblings are by definition at the same rank. If one link fails (e.g., 35-24) and node 35 reroutes a packet destined to the root to node 34, the packet will then be forwarded to the root by node 34 with no loop, but in a multi-failure scenario like the one described above a sibling loop may form. In most cases routing protocols may experience similar issues during multiple failures and do not even try to solve the problem.

How about loops between RPL DODAG instances? When a host sends a packet for a destination it also selects an RPL DODAG instance according to the path objectives. RPL states that once a packet is forwarded along an RPL instance (specified by the RPLInstanceID in its header), it should not be rerouted along another DODAG instance even if the corresponding DODAG is "broken," which is precisely to avoid such loops. RPL might be extended at some point to allow defaulting to a "wide" connectivity DODAG with minimal constraints to increase the chance of at least one valid path to the root, in which case, it will be necessary to specify a rule to avoid loops between DODAG instances.

17.6.7.2 RPL Loop Detection Mechanism

In the previous section we showed that routing loops are hardly avoidable, thus loop detection mechanisms must be available. The loop detection mechanism piggybacks routing control data in data packets by setting flags in the packet header (this is sometimes referred to as data path validation).

The exact location where these flags are carried is not yet defined (e.g., flow label, existing, or even new IPv6 extended header). The idea is to set a flag in the packet header that is used to verify that the packet is making forward progress in order to detect loops, or to detect a DODAG inconsistency.

For example, when a packet is rerouted to a sibling, a flag is set in the packet header to indicate that the packet has been forwarded to a sibling. When it reaches the next hop, if the packet has to be forwarded again to another sibling because there is no available link toward the root, then the packet is dropped. In its current revision, RPL allows for a one-hop sibling path (only 1 bit is used) since it is believed that in most cases a one-hop sibling will provide a viable path to the root but that a single bit could be extended to a counter. The idea is to limit the number of hops along a sibling path to avoid sibling loops. Similarly, DAO loops can be detected by using a "down" bit. When a packet is sent in the down direction, the bit is set. Upon receiving a packet with the "down" bit set, if the routing table of the node indicates to send it in the up direction, the DODAG is inconsistent (there may be a loop) and the packet may be discarded. Such inconsistency triggers the resetting of the DIO trickle timers. As further optimization, the child that has received the packet in error can send it back to the parent with an "error" bit set to trigger the cleanup of the route by the parent that will in turn send the packet again to another child or sibling. That process allows recursive routing table cleanup. The same mechanism could be used for other types of loop detection and routing table cleanup.

17.6.8 **Global and Local Repair**

Repair mechanisms are key components of routing protocols. As the network topology changes because of link and node failures or link/node metric changes, it is imperative to dynamically update the routing decision to adapt to topological changes. To that end, various mechanisms have been defined to rebuild the DODAG upon network topology changes. The first case to handle is *DODAG repair* when a network element (e.g., such as a link or a node) fails. RPL must then rebuild a new DODAG according to the new topology. Repairs must be handled with care in lossy environments to avoid rebuilding a DODAG upon a transient failure, since rebuilding a DODAG has a global impact on the network and nodes resources. Overreacting would potentially compromise routing stability.

RPL specifies two complementary repair mechanisms: a *global* and a *local* repair technique. There are many other routing protocols that use local repair strategies to quickly find an alternate path (which may momentarily not be optimal) deferring the global repair of the entire topology. This is the approach taken by RPL: when a link is considered nonviable and an alternate path must be found (as opposed to being a transient failure that does not require any action), the node triggers a local repair to quickly find an alternate path, even if the alternate path is not optimum (local optimum). Then in a second step, which may be deferred, the DODAG is rebuilt for all the nodes in the network (global optimum).

- Local repair: To quickly find an alternate path when the most preferred path or all other alternate paths are no longer available with a minimal attempt to find an optimal path.
- Max_depth rule: A node cannot advertise a rank less than or equal to any of its parents. It may advertise a rank lower than in a previous advertisement if the node has jumped in the DODAG to improve its position. The max_depth rule also states that within a DODAG iteration a node must not advertise a rank deeper than L+DAGMaxRankIncrease, where L is the lowest rank that the node has advertised within the DODAG iteration. Note that the DAGMaxRankIncrease is an RPL variable advertised by the DODAG root and a value of 0 has the effect of disabling this rule. There is one exception to this rule: the poison-and-wait rule where the node advertises an infinite rank.

Although this has already been discussed, let's re-explain why such as rule was introduced: one of the main risks when joining a parent is to be on the path of that node to the DODAG root (in other words, to attach to one of a children). Should that happen, a loop would be formed and the rank would then continuously increment until reaching the "infinite" value for the rank at which point the nodes would detach from each other. This is also referred to as the "count-to-infinity" problem that also exists in other distance vector routing protocols because with this type of routing protocol a node does not have global visibility of the network topology. Thus the idea is to introduce a mechanism that reduces the number of iterations of successive increments, in other words, avoid waiting to count until "infinity." A node triggering a local repair is allowed to choose as a parent a node whose rank is less than L+DAGMaxRankIncrease where L is the lowest rank value that has been advertised within the DODAG iteration. Once again, the DODAG root may decide to set the DAGMaxRankIncrease value to 0. If at some point the rank of the node exceeds L+DAGMaxRankIncrease, the rank is considered equal to infinity and the loop is broken. This mechanism is illustrated using Figure 17.8.

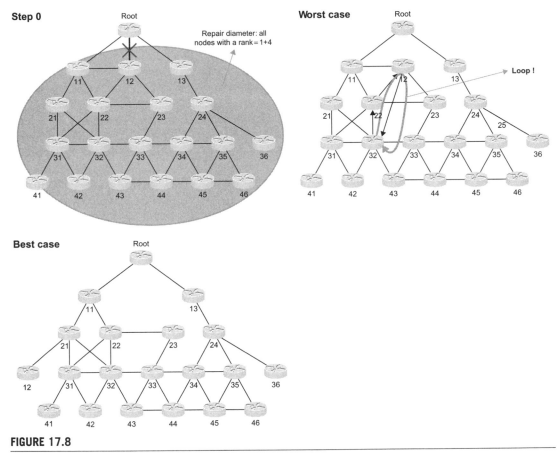

FIGURE 17.8

Illustration of the use of the DAGMaxRankIncrease value.

Suppose that the link between node 12 and the root fails and DAGMaxRankIncrease = 5. In this example suppose that node 12 has a rank of 2. That means node 12 can join any node with a maximum rank of (rank_of_node 12) + 5 = 7. This includes all nodes in the network (in this simple example). In the best case, node 12 selects a node that does not belong to its sub-DODAG and no loop is formed (e.g., if node 12 decides to join node 21). Let's now suppose that node 12 attaches to a node in its sub-DODAG, say node 32 (note that the line between node 12 and 32 is oriented in the 12->32 direction). What happens next is that node 12 sends an updated DIO reflecting its new rank 5. Node 22 in turn updates its rank to 6, node 32 updates its rank to 7, and node 12 updates its rank to 8, which exceeds the maximum allowed value. At this point the loop will be broken and the node will detach. This illustrates how the use of the DAGMaxRankIncrease avoids counting to infinity (0xFFFF).

In addition, RPL has defined another mechanism known as "poisoning," which is useful when performing local repair while trying to avoid loops.

The poison-and-wait mechanism considers the situation of a node running out of parents after a network element failure. According to the local policy the node may simply decide to root a new "floating" DODAG (in this case the G-bit of the DIO must be cleared) after having set its rank to 1 (it is the DODAG root) and the DODAGPreference (the node may decide to lower its preference). Alternatively, the node may decide to try to rejoin the DODAG by selecting a new parent. According to the RPL rules it cannot join a node if that makes its rank higher than L+DAGMaxRankIncrease in the DODAG iteration that it has left. Note that if the DAGMaxRankIncrease value is set to 0 by the DODAG root, the node cannot join any node that would increase its rank. The "poisoning" mechanism sends a poisoning DIO message to all children to be removed as a parent and trigger a new parent selection so the node is not an ancestor of any of the nodes in its sub-DODAG. This mechanism is illustrated in Figure 17.9.

Suppose link 24-13 fails. Node 24 does not have any alternate parent or sibling. In this case, it resets its trickle timer to trigger the sending of a new DIO, and upon expiration of the trickle timer it sends a DIO with Rank = Infinite (value = 0xFFFF). As the new DIO travels in the sub-DODAG, nodes act to potentially select another parent. For example, node 36 becomes isolated, node 35 starts using node 23 as a new parent, so does node 34, etc. The end result is that the former children of node 24 no longer use node 24 as an ancestor. Note that an implementation may choose to send multiple DIO poisoning messages should one of them get lost. After the expiration of a local timer (to give a better chance for all nodes in the sub-DODAG to change their next-hop decision), it becomes safe for node 24 to call the OF and select a new parent *regardless of its rank* as long as the max_depth rule is respected. The poisoning message may be lost resulting in attaching to a child, which may lead to a loop (but the max_depth rule would avoid counting to infinity). Step 2 in Figure 17.9 shows node 24 then joining the DODAG via node 34 before advertising its new rank.

⚠ Although the poisoning node advertises an infinite rank, it retains its original rank to be compliant with the max_depth rule exposed earlier.

The poisoning approach is not "guaranteed"; the poisoning DIO may be lost resulting in loop formation that could be broken faster because of the max-depth rule without having to count to infinity.

Global repair is achieved by RPL when the DODAG root generates a new DODAGSequenceNumber. As the DIO messages are propagated down the DODAG, each node detects the new DODAG SequenceNumber, the OF function is reevaluated, and nodes potentially select new parents.

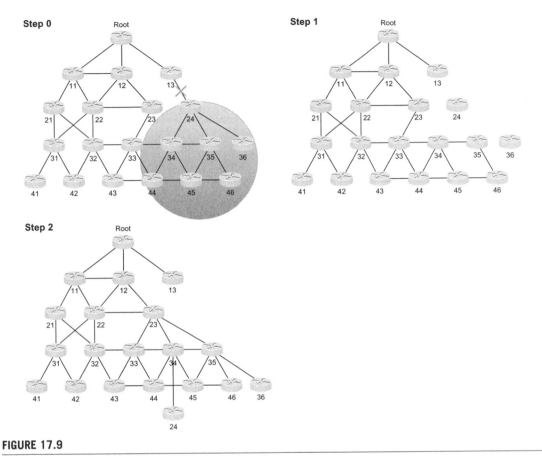

FIGURE 17.9

Illustration of the Poison-And-Wait Approach.

Note: This allows bypassing the RPL rule that states a first node must not process the DIO and select as a parent a second node that would result in the first node increasing its rank above L+DAGMaxRankIncrease. If a node using the old DODAGSequenceNumber receives a DIO with a new DODAGSequenceNumber from a second node with a rank too high according to the max_depth rule, there is no risk that the second node lies in the sub-DODAG of the first node, because the second node is in the new DODAG iteration and, consequently, there is no risk of loop. Thus the DODAG is recomputed entirely according to the OF creating an entirely new DODAG iteration. Such a global repair is not only used to effectively "repair" a DODAG but also to reoptimize it. Indeed, once a node has selected a parent, it continues to ignore DIO from other nodes in its current iteration resulting in an increase in its rank above L+DAGMaxRankIncrease. But what if one of these nodes effectively advertises a more optimal route according to the OF? That better path would then be ignored until a new DODAGSequenceNumber was originated by the DODAG root. Thus the global repair mechanism is not only used to repair a DODAG but also to reoptimize it.

Global repair rebuilds the DODAG. As such it is not only used as a repair mechanism but also a reoptimization technique for the DODAG. It requires extra cost regarding control traffic and is driven by the root. Mechanisms could be added to request the DODAG root to trigger the global repair. Still, local repair is useful since the effect is localized and may occur more rapidly. As with any distance vector protocol, the risk of reattaching anywhere in the DODAG is forming loops. Thus the max_ depth rule has been defined to limit the impact of forming loops, and to avoid counting to infinity should a loop be formed. Additionally, RPL supports the poisoning mechanism triggered by a node with no parent to avoid any node in its sub-DODAG to use it as an ancestor. At this point it would be safe for the node to locally repair by joining any node regardless of its rank as long as the max_depth rule is honored for that DODAG iteration. Finally, the ability of forming a floating DODAG upon losing connectivity with parents, in an attempt to preserve inner connectivity between a set of nodes in the network, is supported by RPL.

17.6.9 Routing Adjacency with RPL

Routing adjacency in RPL definitely deserves its own section. With routing protocols such as OSPF or IS-IS a routing adjacency between two neighbors is established once the neighbors have exchanged and agreed on various routing protocol parameters (e.g., protocol version, frequency of hellos, dead-timers) and once the LSDBs have been synchronized. From that point, routing adjacencies are maintained thanks to the exchange of "hello" packets sent every X seconds (X being configurable). If no hello is received after n * X seconds (n configurable) then the routing adjacency is considered as down, which triggers a routing protocol convergence. The situation in LLNs is radically different since the exchange of "hellos" between nodes would drain energy from the nodes as well as potentially cause congestion on limited bandwidth links in LLNs, which is highly undesirable when energy and bandwidth are scarce resources.

The approach taken by RPL recommends using a probing technique based on IPv6 Neighbor Discovery (ND); namely sending IPv6 solicitations messages (see Chapter 15). The use of ND implies neighbor reachability verification when data traffic is to be sent. The routing adjacency is then considered valid upon receiving a neighbor advertisement message with the "solicited" flag set. Other probing techniques could also be used. Alternatively and/or additionally other types of active probing are used according to the network characteristics and design.

If the most preferred parent is temporarily unavailable, then the node forwards the packet to an alternate parent (if available). In the absence of an alternate parent the node selects a sibling (if there is a sibling available).

Some implementations may choose to use algorithms to keep track of the number of recorded failed probes within a specific time window. It is important not only to consider the percentage of failed probes but also the time period during which the percentage of failed probes has been calculated in the presence of lossy links. It is not rare for a failure to be transient, which should not disqualify the parent. Thus an implementation should obverse the percentage of failed probes against the time frame. The reception of any message such as a DIO from a neighbor may be used as probes (failed or successful) if the link can be trusted to be symmetrical.

17.6.10 RPL Timer Management

Timer management is an important component of any protocol and RPL is no exception. The DIO timers used by RPL rely on the trickle algorithm proposed by [160], and other RPL timers may use the same algorithm in the future. Most routing protocols send keepalives to maintain routing adjacency and any other control packets necessary to update their routing tables without explicitly trying to limit the control protocol overhead. This is done because the required bandwidth is negligible compared to the data traffic in "classic" IP networks. But such an approach would be problematic in LLNs where links are unstable and network resources are scarce. The issue is that limiting the control traffic also impacts the ability to maintain synchronization, the ability to quickly react to network changes, and so forth.

The trickle algorithm uses an adaptive mechanism to control the sending rates of control plane traffic such that nodes hear just enough packets to stay consistent under various circumstances. In the presence of change nodes send protocol control packets more often and control traffic rates are reduced when the network stabilizes. The trickle algorithm does not require complex code and states in the network. This is an important property considering the constrained resources on the nodes (some implementations only require 4–7 bytes of RAM for state maintenance).

RPL treats the DODAG construction as a consistency problem and makes use of trickle timers to decide when to multicast DIO messages. When an inconsistency is detected RPL messages are sent more often, and then as the network stabilizes RPL messages are sent less often.

Trickle behavior is controlled by several parameters:

- I: Current length of the communication interval.
- T: Timer value; T is in the range [I, I/2].
- C: Redundancy counter.
- K: Redundancy constant (learned from the DODAG root).
- I_{min}: Smallest value of I learned via the DIO message. $I_{min} = 2^{DIOIntervalMin}$ ms where DIOIntervalMin is advertised by the DODAG root in DIO messages.
- $I_{doubling}$: The number of times I may be doubled before maintaining a constant multicast rate. $I_{doubling}$ is advertised as DIOIntervalDoubling by the DODAG root in DIO messages.
- I_{max}: Largest value of $I_{max} = I_{min} * 2^{Idoubling}$.

In RPL trickle a node sets the trickle variable I_{min} and $I_{doubling}$ to the original values learned from the DIO messages, C = 0, I = I_{min}, and a random value is chosen for T in the range [I/2,I]. Each time a node receives a consistent DIO message from a DODAG parent, the C counter is incremented. When the timer expires, C is compared to the RPL constant (K = DEFAULT_DIO_REDUNDANCY_CONSTANT) to decide whether or not to multicast a DIO message. When the communication interval I expires, I is doubled, the C counter is reset, and a new value of T is chosen until I reaches the maximum value of I_{max}. The RPL specification explicitly states that the variable C may not be incremented. Indeed in some cases it may be beneficial not to increment C to avoid the suppression of some RPL control messages (this aspect is still under consideration).

When is the RPL trickle timer reset? The trickle timer has to be reset each time a DODAG inconsistency is detected to increase the frequency at which DIO messages are sent to quickly update the DODAG: when a new node joins the DODAG, when it receives a multicast DIS message from another node, when the node moves within a DODAG, when a node receives a modified DIO message from a DODAG parent reflecting some changes in the DODAG, when a potential loop is detected (e.g., a DODAG parent receives a packet that it would have forwarded inward), when the rank of a DODAG parent has changed, and so forth.

By tuning the values of I_{min} and I_{max} it becomes possible to achieve some trade-off between the need for consistent DODAG, speed to propagate changes, and the protocol overhead. Some simulations indicate that by setting I_{min} and I_{max} to a few dozen milliseconds and 1 hour, respectively, the control traffic could be reduced to up to 75% compared to a fix beacon value of 30 s. Knowing this, applicability statement documents combined with the specifics of the network where RPL is deployed should provide further guidance. For example, in some cases it may not be advantageous to set the I_{min} value too small (e.g., with low power MAC layers) to avoid simultaneous sending of DIO messages. The expected effect of using the trickle algorithm on control traffic is shown via simulation in the next section.

17.6.11 Simulation Results

Although only real-life deployments provide actual data on the efficiency of a protocol, there are a number of tools that a protocol designer can use during the design process, and simulation is undoubtedly one of the most useful. Although simulators are not "formal" mathematical proofs, they do provide useful data and help improve the level of confidence on the design choices. Furthermore, in most cases, there is no mathematical model that can be used to simulate the level of complexity of the protocol and real-life conditions.

During the design process of RPL, a number of simulations were performed. [239] is undoubtedly one of the major contributions in this area. A discrete event simulator has been developed based on OMNET++ [254] and the Castalia module for Wireless Sensor Networks within OMNET++.

One of the major challenges when developing a smart object network simulator is model link behavior. With lossy links such as low-power wireless links or PLC links, none of the mathematical models such as Markov Chains are applicable. Thus the approach taken in [239] uses real-life link traces as input to get high-fidelity results representative of real networks. Hundreds of link traces were gathered to build a link failure model database for both indoor and outdoor low-power lossy links. Each trace provided the PDR at different times. For some links, the received signal strength indication (RSSI) was available and due to the correlation between the RSSI and the PDR [254], it was possible to derive the PDR from the RSSI.

The simulator reads a topology database and randomly selects real-life traces when simulating RPL, thus providing very useful results that can be trusted. When a packet is to be transmitted by a node, the PDR of the link is read from the database and the packet is dropped with a probability equal to 1-PDR (different random number generators are used for all links to avoid link correlation).

Several networks have been simulated with consistent results and the results for one of them are provided in this section (the simulated network is depicted in Figure 17.10).

Data traffic is "constant bit rate" with a configurable rate. In the simulation run, the constant data traffic rate was set to 5 packets per second (a fairly high traffic rate for LLNs, but the idea was to stress the network to exacerbate some protocol characteristics).

Link failures are directly read from the link behavior database to which random failures were added according to an M/M/1 Markov Chain model (the interarrival times were set to a mean of 1 per hour).

In these simulations, 25% of packets were destined to the root and 75% to other nodes. In most networks a good proportion of the traffic is sent to the root or sink behind the root. In these simulations we chose to have a fairly high proportion of P2P traffic to study the efficiency of P2P routing with RPL.

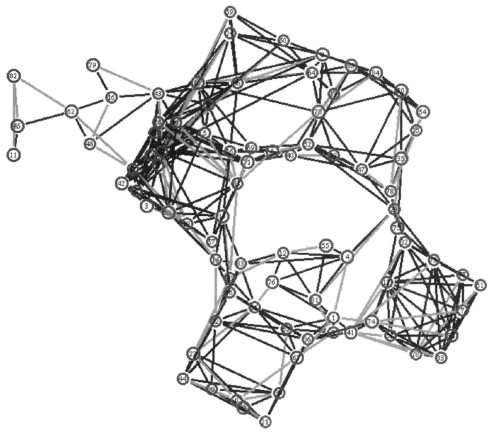

FIGURE 17.10

Topology of the simulated network.

The objective was to observe RPL behavior in a number of conditions (steady state, high stress) regarding several metrics for a single DODAG instance computed using the network topology shown in Figure 17.11. The RPL metric is the ETX (as described earlier) and the OF consists of minimizing the ETX path cost.

Several RPL characteristics were studied: control traffic, routing table size, path efficiency, and failure handling.

17.6.11.1 Control Traffic

In "classic" IP networks, the control traffic overhead (the routing protocol in this case) is generally not problematic considering the bandwidth available on high-speed links and is negligible compared to the data traffic. This is in contrast with LLNs where it is imperative to minimize the control traffic overhead and try to bound the control traffic to the data traffic. It is also imperative to reduce the traffic control load as the network stabilizes, which is the main motivation for using dynamic trickle

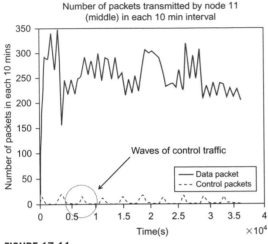

FIGURE 17.11

RPL control versus data traffic.

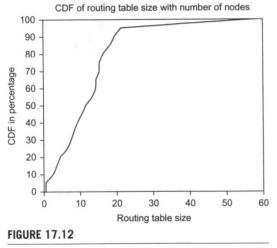

FIGURE 17.12

RPL routing table sizes.

timers. The values of the trickle timers for I_{min} and $I_{doubling}$ in these simulations were 1 and 16 seconds, respectively. Figure 17.11 shows how the data and control traffic varies over time.

The first observation is that the control traffic is clearly negligible compared to the data traffic (for that data traffic assumption, which is more true as we get closer to the DODAG root), but more importantly as the DODAG stabilizes the control traffic decreases significantly. This illustrates the desired effect of the trickle timers. We can observe waves of the control traffic. Each time an inconsistency is detected in the DODAG such as a path cost change, new parent after a failure, or a global repair mechanism triggered by the DODAG root (the DODAG root increments the DODAGSequenceNumber), the DIO changes and the trickle timers are reset. These factors explain the waves of control traffic. As expected and desired, when the DODAG stabilizes the traffic control is reduced accordingly as expected because of the trickle timers.

17.6.11.2 Routing Table Size

Nodes in LLNs have constrained memory. In extreme cases, some nodes cannot even store a routing table. RPL supports the insertion of such nodes in the network as discussed in the previous sections. In other cases routing tables may potentially contain dozens of entries, but nodes have limited memory for the storage of the routing table compared to IP core routers that can easily store hundreds of thousands of BGP routes. Thus, it is interesting to observe the memory requirements of RPL regarding routing table sizes. Figure 17.12 shows the Cumulative Distribution Function (CDF) for the number of required routing table entries (the number of routing entries increases as we get closer to the sink). Note: these results are in the absence of route aggregation in the network. There is tremendous interest in coupling RPL with route aggregation to limit the routing table sizes, and this work is currently in progress.

17.6.11.3 Path Efficiency

The DODAG computed by RPL is a sub-topology of the physical connectivity graph just like any other routing protocol. In other words, there are paths that the traffic has to follow along the DODAG

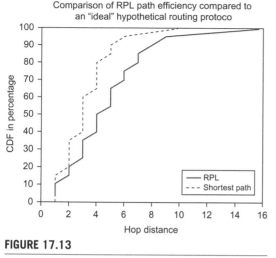

FIGURE 17.13

Path efficiency.

although a more optimal path may actually exist (outside of the DODAG) in the physical connectivity. This is particularly true for P2P traffic where the traffic from node A to node B must meet a common ancestor before being redirected down to the DODAG toward the destination (node B), with the exception of the P2P traffic between two nodes that are in direct range because of the use of multicast DAO. Thus the idea is to see how "suboptimal" the path computed by the DODAG for P2P traffic is compared to an "ideal" routing protocol that would systematically compute the best available path between A and B based on the actual connectivity.

⚠ Note: it is critical to remember that although RPL builds a DODAG this is not a P2MP or MP2P routing protocol: RPL fully supports P2P routing. RPL has even been enhanced with mechanisms such as multicast DAO to provide shortcuts for nodes in direct range and optimized P2P routing.

RPL provides a good quality path for the majority of cases. Still additional mechanisms may be added in the future with regards to P2P routing. As a reminder, these are simulations results and as such cannot be generalized. The results are shown in Figure 17.13. Other simulations on that particular subject are in progress.

17.6.11.4 Failure Handling

The ability of a routing protocol to compute an alternate path in the presence of network element failures has always been a critical characteristic of a routing protocol. Unfortunately, there is always tension between the control traffic cost, the environment, and the ability to quickly reroute the traffic. In a highly stable high-speed network, routing protocols use fast failure detection mechanisms to quickly detect a failure and reroute the traffic along a backup path. In contrast, in lossy environments in the presence of frequent failures the routing protocol should not constantly recompute paths (thus leading to high control traffic, oscillations, etc.), which is what RPL achieves as explained in detail earlier in this chapter. RPL makes use of two different repair mechanisms that have been discussed in Section 17.6.8: global repair triggered by the DODAG root and local repair where nodes locally handle the failure. We provide several simulation results showing both mechanisms. The metric used to illustrate the effect of RPL repair mechanisms is the amount of time during which no path was available when having to send a packet during the course of the simulation. For example, Figure 17.14 shows that in 80% of the cases the period of time without path was around 20 s **for the specific RPL parameters used in these simulations, of course**. In Figure 17.14 we also show the CDF for the failure period when first using global repair only.

Figure 17.14 shows the failure time for two different frequencies of global repair: in the first case, global repair (generation of new DODAGSequenceNumber) is set to 1 hour and in the second case it is reduced to 1 mn. As expected, this allows reduction in the failure time at the cost of increasing the control traffic cost (we can observe an increase of the control traffic, looking at node 11 in the

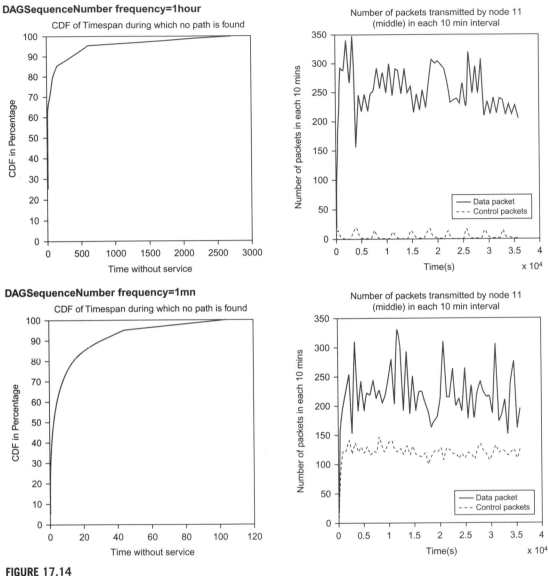

FIGURE 17.14

Time without service with global repair only.

middle of the network). As discussed earlier, it was decided to add a local repair mechanism to reduce the failure time. This way, the local repair mechanism quickly provides an alternate path followed by global repair to further reoptimize the DODAG. This is shown in Figure 17.15 where the global repair mechanism is set to 1 hour and local repair is activated. We observe that the failure time is reduced *dramatically*. The traffic control is *slightly* increased with local repair but localized (not even visible on the simulation run).

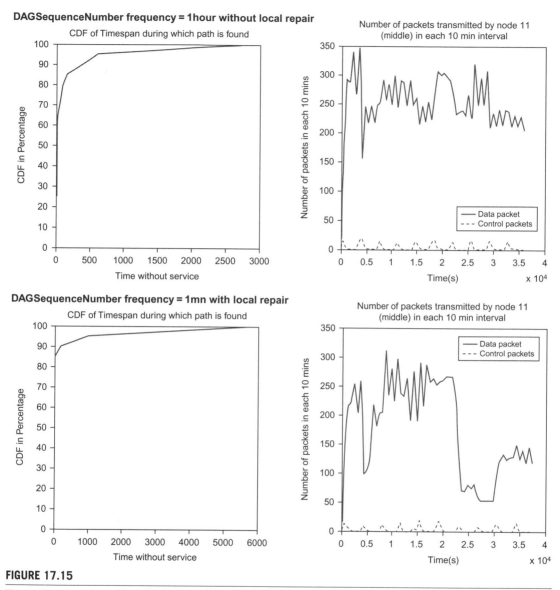

FIGURE 17.15

Time without service with global and local repair.

17.7 CONCLUSIONS

This chapter was entirely devoted to RPL, the new routing protocol for IP smart object networks developed by the IETF ROLL Working Group. A series of novel mechanisms have been designed to make RPL an efficient distance vector routing protocol for smart object networks in support of

P2P, MP2P, and P2MP traffic designed for LLNs. RPL has been designed as highly modular, with a very small footprint, and able to support a wide range of metrics and constraints according to the environments of interest while operating in constrained environments thus reducing the control traffic whenever possible. RPL can even be deployed to support multiple routing topologies according to the objective function (e.g., optimize reliability, minimize latency, etc.). Furthermore, several mechanisms referred to as global and local repair have been designed to provide alternate paths in the presence of failures and to reoptimize the routing topology on a configurable periodic basis while ensuring a high degree of robustness and flexibility. Early implementations show that RPL will only require a few kilobytes of Flash and a very few KB of RAM in its current specification.

The IP for Smart Object Alliance

18

18.1 MISSION AND OBJECTIVES OF THE IPSO ALLIANCE

As discussed in Chapter 14, the Internet Engineering Task Force (IETF — http://www.ietf.org/) is the standardization body in charge of producing the technical specification for the IP protocol suite.

Companies such as Cisco, ArchRock, Proto6, SICS, Atmel, and others that from the beginning believed in the benefits of an end-to-end IPv6 solution to make the "Internet of Things" a reality were faced with the following realities:

- The only available technical documents were related to protocol designs or detailed technical requirements produced by the IETF. They were difficult for engineers not involved in the IETF on a daily basis to read. There was clearly an absence of white papers and tutorials showing how the IP protocol suite specified by the IETF and, in particular for smart objects networks, could be used and deployed in a variety of environments such as building automation, Smart Cities, and Smart Grids, just to mention a few.
- There was no interoperability event showing how a network of smart objects could be built using a variety of devices from different vendors thus demonstrating the benefit of using an open standard such as IP. Other existing alliances (sometime specifying semi-closed protocols) were organizing events to certify products. Furthermore, the IETF considered the existence of interoperable and independent implementations in the Internet as a necessary condition to promote an RFC to a high level of standard, as discussed in Chapter 14.
- Building an IP ecosystem for smart objects considering the number of companies involved in building solutions for smart object networks such as chipset suppliers, integrators, automation systems (home, building, etc.), telecommunication companies, software vendors, and also end users (utilities, large companies, telecommunication service providers) and research institutions was paramount to collectively contribute to such a new alliance, gather input from all members to fill the potential gaps, and quickly increase the number of members speaking with a common voice.

Thus it quickly became necessary to form a new open, worldwide industry alliance to promote the use of IP as the open and interoperable standard for smart objects. This led to the formation of the IP for Smart Objects alliance (IPSO — www.ipso-alliance.org).

The IPSO alliance was formed in September 2008 by the founding members shown in Figure 18.1 and has been growing at an impressive rate since its formation with about 50 members as of October 2009.

Interconnecting Smart Objects with IP. DOI: 10.1016/B978-0-12-375165-2.00018-1

Founding members   iPSO
                                                          Alliance

- Arch Rock   - Kinney Consulting
- Atmel   - Nivis
- Cimetrics   - PicosNet
- Cisco   - Proto6
- Duke Energy   - ROAM
- Dust Networks   - SAP
- Électricité de France R&D   - Sensinode
- Eka Systems   - SICS
- Emerson Climate Technologies   - Silver Spring Networks
- Ericsson   - Sun Microsystems
- Freescale   - Tampere University
- Gainspan   - Watteco
- IP Infusion   - Zensys
- Jennic

FIGURE 18.1

Initial founding members of the IPSO alliance.

The mission of IPSO is not to specify protocols (this is done at the IETF) but to promote the use of IP for smart objects:

- Create awareness of existing and new IP-based technologies designed for smart objects. How many times have we heard "Yes, IP is a great technology that could be used in smart objects such as sensor and actuators in the future…"? No, it is *there* and the key mission of the IPSO alliance is to show that sophisticated interoperable systems composed of IP-enabled smart objects can be built today, using the same protocol as in existing IP networks with no compromise on performance and efficiency compared to existing proprietary approaches.
- White papers and tutorial are needed. Indeed, IETF RFCs and Working Group documents are not always easy to read so the IPSO alliance produces white papers and webinars focusing on technologies (tutorial) and use cases. To date, the alliance has produced the following white papers:
  - IP for Smart Objects: This white paper provides a high-level overview on why IP is the protocol of choice for smart object networks.
  - Lightweight IPv6 Stacks for Smart Objects: The Experience of Three Independent and Interoperable Implementations: This white paper covers key implementation aspects based on the experience of three implementations of IPv6 stacks.
  - 6LoWPAN: Incorporating IEEE 802.15.4 into the IP Architecture: This white paper introduces the key concepts of the 6LoWPAN adaptation layer (support of IPv6 on IEEE 802.15.4 links) and provides a good overview of several of its functionalities such as header compression and fragmentation as well as the 6LoWPAN adaption layer overall architecture.
  - Neighbor Discovery in IPv6: This document discusses several optimization mechanisms to the IPv6 Neighbor Discovery Protocol for efficient usage of IPv6 in the low-power networks that may or may not support multicast at the link layer.
  - Security in Low-power and Lossy Networks (LLNs): A survey of the security issues encountered in LLNs along with the existing IP-based security mechanisms that can be used in LLNs.

- Low-Power Technologies in Smart Object Networks: Provides the general characteristics of three low-power technologies for smart objects: IEEE 802.15.4, low-power WiFi, and a low-power Powerline communication (PLC) technology (Homeplug, WPC). Further revisions of this white paper will cover additional low-power technologies that will be defined for smart objects in the future.
  - Several new white papers are in progress such as "embedded web services," "smart cities," etc.
- Link companies that provide IP-based smart objects for control and actuation (hardware and software).
- Support and organize interoperability events, which is a key activity of the IPSO alliance.

The IPSO alliance is also actively working on an IP for smart object certification and more details will be available in the near future.

18.2 IPSO ORGANIZATION

The IPSO alliance is very lightweight and straightforward (see Figure 18.2), with an objective to be similar to IETF by being open and having low subscription fees.

To date, the IPSO Board of Directors is composed of nine members (one member per company) and each company has to be an IPSO promoter member. In contrast to the IETF, IPSO members represent companies, not individuals. Half of the Board of Directors is renewed every year. The Board of Directors is responsible for defining the strategy of the alliance and also defines the goals and objectives as well as controlling the operation of the alliance (budget, meeting, press release, etc.). The Board of Directors is helped in its mission by several committees and the Technology Advisory Board (TAB).

IPSO committees are formed when a specific task has to be performed under the governance of the Board of Directors and with the help of the TAB. Each committee has a charter along with milestones to help track deliverables. The target, set of deliverables, and duration greatly vary between committees. For example, the Marcom committee is a long-lived committee that drives the communication strategy of the alliance. Other committees can be formed to perform a specific task before disbanding. A security committee and a building automation were formed to exclusively focus on the security aspects to show that many well-proven IP security mechanisms are already available that can be implemented on smart objects.

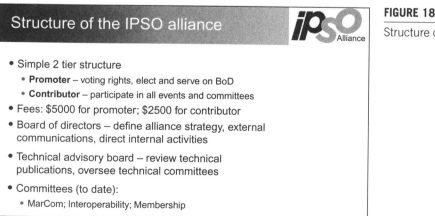

FIGURE 18.2

Structure of the IPSO alliance.

The TAB, whose objective it is to be the "technology arm" of the IPSO alliance, is nominated by the Board of Directors. It can produce white papers and tutorials in the form of webinars on request or decide to produce its own white papers. In addition, the TAB oversees some of the technical white papers produced by the different committees. TAB members also represent IPSO in various technology conferences and support alliance liaisons with other technology standardization bodies.

18.3 A KEY ACTIVITY OF THE IPSO ALLIANCE: INTEROPERABILITY TESTING

Fostering interoperability between native IP smart objects around the IP protocol specifications produced by IETF is one of the most critical missions of the IPSO alliance. Showing large test beds with a variety of smart objects communicating with each other *using IP without any protocol translation gateway* is a key activity of IPSO.

A first series of tests including several media (such as IEEE 802.15.4 or IEEE 802.11) was completed in March 2009 in Palo Alto, California. The objective of that first interoperability event was to show a global system composed of a number of IP-native devices communicating with each other. The interoperability committee will organize further events with more complex scenarios involving all the layers on the IP protocol stack beyond IP connectivity, but that first interoperability event was a key milestone.

As shown in Figure 18.3, the test bed included the following components:

- IPv6 web server
- A set of IPv4 and IPv6 network clouds connected to the Internet composed of several types of smart objects

Note that "border routers" are not performing any form of protocol translation. *The traffic is IP end-to-end.* The IPv6 network did communicate with the web server natively whereas IPv6 clouds were interconnected using 6to4 tunnels (see Chapter 15 for a description of 6to4 tunnel mechanisms).

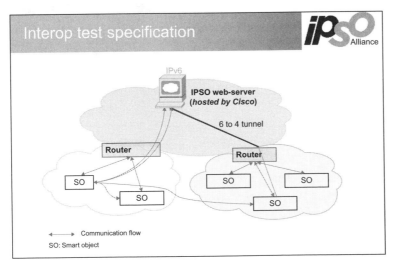

FIGURE 18.3

Interop test specification.

A series of tests was made up of the following steps, strictly complying with the IPv6 specification:

Step 1: Autoconfiguration of an IPv6 link local address.

Step 2: Discovery of the default router by the IP smart object and autoconfiguration of the global IPv6 address (due to the RA messages sent by the router).

Step 3: Direct communication between smart objects using ICMP Echo Request/Reply messages to demonstrate inter smart object connectivity. Such ICMP packets were exchanged within subnetworks, between smart objects lying in different subnetworks across the Internet, and finally with the IPv6 web server connected to the Internet (all communication flows are depicted by the arrows in Figure 18.3).

Step 4: Data communication. Each smart object sent data to the web server. In this case it was temperature reading, but the type of data could be vibration, humidity, gas detection, light, temperature, etc. Note that the protocol transport used in this experiment was UDP and a simple application running over UDP was designed for that purpose.

Step 5: Consisted of sending command/response between smart objects effectively enabling native inter-device IP communication.

Figure 18.4 illustrates the displays of data received on the IPv6 web server. Note that not all smart objects were using the same link layer. This is the beauty of IP: media agnosticism. In this particular case, two link layers were used: IEEE 802.11 and IEEE 802.15.4 (900 MHz and 2.4 GHz). It is expected that other link layers (such as the PLC link) will be used in further interoperability events.

In May 2009, IPSO announced the world's first interoperability test event between IP smart objects with 11 participants at NETWORLD+INTEROP 2009. The test bed included four different wireless physical layers and media access communication protocols: Primex wireless, Gainspan Low power WiFi, Nivis 6LoWPAN (IPv6 over IEEE 802.15.4), and Sigma Design's wireless home control technology based on the Zwave chipset radio. Note that all stacks were native IP stacks over various PHY/MAC with no layer 3 protocol translation.

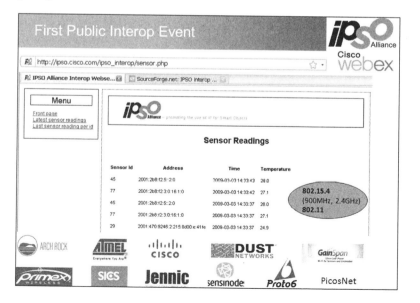

FIGURE 18.4

First public Interop event of IPSO, March 2009.

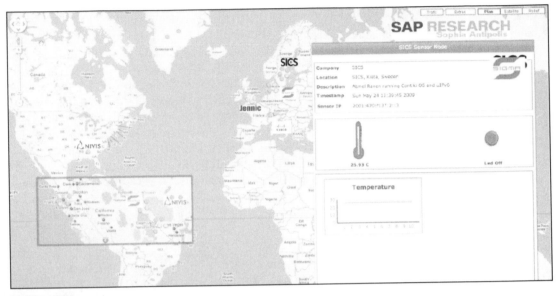

FIGURE 18.5

IPSO demonstrator at NETWORLD+INTEROP 2009.

FIGURE 18.6

IPSO — Best Invention of 2008 by *TIME* magazine.

One company, SAP, had developed software for data gathering displaying all the data gathered from the various smart objects connected around the world through the Internet, as shown in Figure 18.5 (in this figure the smart object was a temperature sensor but other types of sensors and actuators were connected to the network). In March 2008, the IPSO alliance announced the first interop demonstration of the RPL routing protocol discussed in Chapter 17.

IPSO was even listed as one of the best inventions of 2008 by *TIME* magazine (Figure 18.6).

18.4 CONCLUSIONS

Without a doubt, the IPSO alliance will continue to grow at an impressive rate and its success clearly demonstrates the unanimous momentum for the use of IP for smart object networks. By providing white papers, tutorials, and webinars and organizing interoperability events, the IPSO alliance shows that the use of IP for smart objects is not a futuristic or idealistic vision of what is sometimes referred to as the "Internet of Things," but a technology that can be used *today* using open standards without the need for costly proprietary solutions.

Non-IP Smart Object Technologies

19

Before the consensus to adopt IP for smart objects became a reality, several non-IP solutions were developed and deployed, and are still being deployed. Until recently, the IP architecture was often considered too heavyweight to use for low-power short-range networks. Therefore, a number of custom protocol stacks and architectures were developed. In this chapter, we provide a high-level overview of two such protocol specifications: ZigBee and Z-Wave. Both have been developed for specific low-power, short-range, and low-bit-rate radios, and smart objects are their main application areas.

In general, custom protocol stacks are incompatible with the IP architecture. As discussed in Chapter 3, there are a number of disadvantages with these architectures when they are to be connected to IP networks. For this reason, many of the custom low-power radio specifications are currently moving toward an IP-based model. In the summer of 2009, ZigBee announced that the specification would be amended with IP for the smart energy profile.

In addition to ZigBee and Z-Wave, there are a number of protocol specifications for the smart object domain that we do not cover here. The WirelessHART stack is designed for low-power and high-reliability industrial monitoring networks. WirelessHART is defined on top of the IEEE 802.15.4 radio standard and uses a time-synchronized protocol to provide very low power consumption as well as a channel hopping mechanism to maintain low radio interference [196]. WirelessHART networks are controlled by a central network manager that computes the channel hopping, timing schedules, and routing for the entire network. The ISA100a standard is also designed for low-power industrial wireless monitoring. ISA100a is similar to WirelessHART in many aspects, but is built on the network layer of IPv6.

19.1 ZIGBEE

ZigBee is a proprietary specification for wireless communication between smart objects based on the specific IEEE 802.15.4 radio link layer. The ZigBee specification is owned by the ZigBee Alliance. For noncommercial projects, the ZigBee Alliance provides the specification for download from their web site [263]. For commercial projects, a membership in the ZigBee Alliance is required.

The ZigBee Alliance was formed in 2002 as a nonprofit organization. ZigBee Alliance membership is open to any company. The alliance has three membership levels: promoter, participant, and adopter. The membership fee is higher for promoter members and participants, but lower for adopter members.

Implementations of the ZigBee protocols stack have been developed as stand-alone libraries that are intended to be used without an operating system, and for smart object operating systems such as Contiki and TinyOS [50,231]. Independent open source implementations also exist [5].

There are four versions of the ZigBee specification: ZigBee 2004, ZigBee 2006, ZigBee 2007, and ZigBee Pro. Both ZigBee 2004 and ZigBee 2006 are considered deprecated and are not used in new products. ZigBee 2007 is currently the most used version of the specification, and is often simply called "ZigBee." ZigBee 2007 adds a number of features that were not present in the 2006 version such as support for packet fragmentation and the ability to dynamically switch physical radio channels. ZigBee Pro increases the amount of devices in each network from 31,101 to 65,540 and adds a number of network mechanisms such as multicasting and source routing. Finally, an extension to the ZigBee 2006 specification, called ZigBee residential, is also available but is not widely used.

ZigBee is based on the IEEE 802.15.4 standard and does not provide any alternatives as underlying radios. The ZigBee protocols are defined around the concepts and addressing modes provided by the underlying IEEE 802.15.4 radio, making it difficult to adapt the ZigBee protocols to other radios.

19.1.1 ZigBee Device Types

ZigBee specifies three different device types: the ZigBee Coordinator (ZC), the ZigBee Router (ZR), and the ZigBee End Device (ZED). These three devices play different roles in a ZigBee network as shown in Figure 19.1.

A ZigBee network has exactly one ZC device. The ZC coordinates the actions of the network as a whole and is responsible for bootstrapping the network. The ZRs build a network between themselves through which packets are exchanged. The ZEDs are logically attached to a ZR. ZEDs communicate only with their ZR, but cannot communicate between each other.

Each of the ZigBee device types has been designed for a specific deployment. ZCs and ZRs have a higher power requirement than ZEDs and cannot be battery-powered. The ZED has a lower power requirement and achieves a long lifetime on batteries. Regarding IEEE 802.15.4, ZC and ZR are fully functional devices (FFDs), whereas the ZEDs are reduced function devices (RFDs).

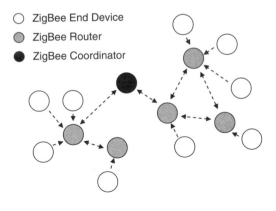

FIGURE 19.1

A ZigBee network consists of three device types: the ZigBee Coordinator, of which there is exactly one in each network, ZigBee Routers, and ZigBee End Devices.

The ZC is responsible for bootstrapping the network. During the bootstrapping process, the ZC chooses the personal area network (PAN) identifier that will be used by the network, as well as the physical radio channel on which the network will operate. After bootstrapping, the ZC acts as a normal ZR device.

ZEDs are off most of the time, thus they are not able to receive any traffic sent to them. Instead, they periodically wake up and check for messages at the ZR with which they are associated. The ZR buffers data sent to their ZED nodes and sends these data whenever they get a poll request from a ZED. The ZED transmits data to the ZR at any time, since the ZR is always awake. The wake-up schedule for ZED is defined by the application developer, not by the ZigBee specification. The number of ZEDs associated with a ZR is limited. In the ZigBee 2007 specification, a ZR can handle a maximum of 14 ZEDs.

19.1.2 Layers in the ZigBee Stack

The ZigBee specification is divided into five layers, as shown in Figure 19.2: the physical (PHY) layer, the medium access control (MAC) layer, the network (NWK) layer, the application support (APS) layer, and the application framework (AF) layer. In addition to the five layers, a cross-layer entity called the ZigBee Device Object (ZDO) is also present in the architecture. Of these layers, PHY and MAC are not part of the ZigBee specification; they are taken from the IEEE 802.15.4 radio standard. The NWK, APS, and AF layers are part of the ZigBee specification, as is the ZDO.

The layering of the ZigBee stack is reminiscent of the layers in the IP stack. Just like in the IP architecture, each layer in the ZigBee stack has a specific purpose. There is, however, one major difference between the layering in the IP architecture and the layering in the ZigBee stack: in the ZigBee stack, the layers cannot be changed. The IP architecture is built to allow multiple types of MAC and PHY layers. The same protocols can be used even if the specific radio standard changes. In contrast, the ZigBee specification is designed specifically for the IEEE 802.15.4 MAC and PHY layers. Also, the upper layer protocols make explicit use of mechanisms provided by the radio layer. For example, instead of providing its own NWK layer addressing scheme, ZigBee uses IEEE 802.15.4 MAC layer addresses even at the NWK layer.

We will now discuss the ZigBee layers in more detail.

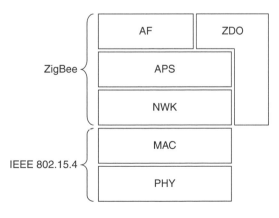

FIGURE 19.2

The ZigBee protocol stack builds upon the MAC and PHY layers from the IEEE 802.15.4 radio standard. The NWK, APS, AF, and ZDO are part of the ZigBee specification.

19.1.3 **PHY and MAC Layers**

The PHY layer transports bits across the physical radio medium. The MAC layer mediates access to the medium so that multiple transmitters do not transmit at the same time.

Because ZigBee uses IEEE 802.15.4 for its MAC layer, ZigBee also uses the same addressing format at 802.15.4. ZigBee supports the short addressing mode in which addresses are 16 bits wide. This allows each ZigBee network to support at most 65,536 nodes. In practice, the number of possible nodes is reduced because a number of addresses are reserved. In ZigBee 2004 and 2006, a network includes a maximum of 31,101 nodes, whereas in ZigBee 2007 and ZigBee Pro, the maximum number of nodes in a network is 65,540.

The ZigBee stack uses IEEE 802.15.4 for the MAC and PHY layers, but does not use every aspect of the standard; most notably, ZigBee does not make use of its beacon mode. The beacon mode builds a time-synchronized schedule of all nodes. Avoiding the beacon mode helps reduce the complexity of ZigBee implementations.

ZigBee uses a carrier sense multiple access with collision avoidance (CSMA/CA) scheme for its MAC layer. Before a packet is sent, the MAC queries the PHY for other current radio transmissions. If another node is currently sending a packet, the node refrains from sending its own packet. Instead, it sets a timer and tries to resend the packet at a later time.

The MAC layer does hop-by-hop acknowledgments for all ZigBee packets except broadcast packets. The acknowledgment uses the standard IEEE 802.15.4 acknowledgment mechanism. If an acknowledgment is not received, the packet is retransmitted up to three times. ZigBee also performs end-to-end acknowledgments at the application support sublayer, as described next.

ZigBee does not use any duty cycling mechanisms at the MAC layer. Instead, nodes have either their radio turned on all the time or turned off all the time, except when sending data. ZRs and ZCs have their radios constantly on, whereas ZDEs may keep their radio off all the time. Nodes that have their radio turned on all the time have a significantly higher energy consumption and therefore cannot be battery-operated. Only nodes that keep their radios turned off have a low enough power consumption to be battery-operated.

The IEEE 802.15.4 standard is described in more detail in Chapter 12.

19.1.4 **NWK**

The NWK layer performs addressing and routing and is the equivalent of the IP layer in the IP architecture. The ZigBee network layer provides two forms of data delivery: broadcast and unicast. Multicast is also supported, but multicast data are delivered using broadcast with software filtering of the incoming packets at the receiver. Broadcast delivery is a form of network flooding, which sends a packet to all nodes on the network. The packet can be tagged with a maximum hop count that determines how far the packet can travel in the network. Because the broadcast packet reaches every node in the network, a broadcast is an expensive operation. Unicasts, on the other hand, are sent only to the node to which they are addressed. Both broadcasts and unicasts can travel up to 30 hops.

The ZigBee stack has two schemes for routing unicast packets: network routing and source routing. In network routing, the network takes care of finding the best route for the packet to take through the network. In source routing, the sender must explicitly state through which nodes the message should pass to reach its destination. Source routing is useful for large networks where each node in the network may not be able to maintain large routing tables for all nodes. Instead, the ZC node, which is assumed to have significantly more memory than the other nodes, can maintain all routing information for all nodes. This reduces the memory load for the network at the expense of a slight overhead in each packet. But as node addresses are short in ZigBee, this overhead is small. To keep the overhead to a bounded value, source routing is limited to five hops. Source routing is available only in the ZigBee Pro version.

There are two types of network routing: mesh and tree routing. Mesh routing builds a connected mesh between the ZR devices and transports data in a point-to-point fashion. The tree routing scheme builds a tree where the ZC is the root of the tree and ZEDs are the leaf nodes. Tree routing is not available in ZigBee Pro.

The ZigBee mesh routing algorithm is an adaptation of the Internet Engineering Task Force (IETF) standard protocol Ad hoc On-demand Distance Vector (AODV) Protocol [194]. AODV is a reactive on-demand protocol, which means that routes are not established until they are needed; that is, nodes do not know about each other until the first packet is sent. When a packet is sent, the originating node broadcasts a routing request packet. This routing request reaches all nodes in the network.

Nodes set up a reverse path to the originating node as part of the route request procedure. When a node receives a routing request packet, it adds an entry for the originating node in its routing table. The routing table entry is filled with the address of the originating node as well as the address of the node from which the route request came. This packet should be sent to this node to reach the originator. Thus a reverse path is built in the network.

When the route request reaches the requested node, this node sends a unicast route reply back to the originator of the request. Since the nodes in the network have built a reverse path, the network knows how to reach the originator node. As the nodes on the path forward the unicast route reply, they add the destination node to their routing tables along with the node from which they received the route reply. When the route reply reaches the originator, the route is set up and the originator and the destination begin exchanging packets.

The network routing mechanism works well for small networks, but as the network grows, the amount of state each node has to maintain increases. In large networks with hundreds or thousands of nodes, the routing tables in the memory-constrained nodes begin to overflow. Additionally, the network flooding of the route request packets becomes problematic. In such situations, the source routing mechanism can be used instead.

19.1.5 APS Sublayer

The APS sublayer is equivalent to the transport layer in the IP architecture. It is a thin layer that acts as an intermediary between the NWK layer and the application layer. The purpose of the APS is to do end-to-end acknowledgments and to filter out duplicate packets.

The APS layer has a connection between two nodes called a binding. A binding is unidirectional — a node is bound to another node, but the other node is not necessarily bound back to the first node.

19.1.6 AF

The ZigBee application layer is called application framework (AF) and runs on top of the APS layer. The AF supports multiple applications and demultiplexes incoming data between the registered applications. Some of the applications are defined by the ZigBee specification, whereas others are implemented independently by vendors. In ZigBee, an application is called a profile.

ZigBee profiles are identified with an integer between 0 and 240, called an end point. This is the equivalent of the port number in the IP architecture. When the AF layer processes a packet, it demultiplexes the packet based on the end point identifier. Applications register with an end point identifier at the AF layer. If a packet arrives for an end point identifier that is not registered, the packet is silently dropped. If the application has been registered, the packet is passed to the application layer.

ZigBee profiles are used in cases for which the ZigBee technology is intended. For example, the ZigBee Alliance has defined a profile for home automation, smart energy management, building automation, and toys.

There are two types of application profiles: public and vendor-specific. Each application profile is identified by an integer between 1 and 240. This integer is called a profile end point. The profile with end point zero is the ZDO and it is used for network configuration and setup. Profile identifiers are allocated and managed by the ZigBee Alliance. Public profiles are intended to be interoperable across different vendors, whereas vendor-specific profiles are intended to be used only by products from one specific vendor.

The ZDO profile is responsible for network maintenance. It provides mechanisms for interacting with the NWK and APS layers, which is done during network configuration. The ZDO is therefore drawn as a prolonged horizontal box as seen in Figure 19.2.

19.1.7 Network Setup

The ZigBee network setup process involves all layers of the ZigBee stack. This process establishes a physical communication link between the nodes in the network, distributes address information between the nodes in the network, and discovers and binds the services on the nodes.

The network setup process begins at the PHY layer. The ZC starts by scanning the 16 available physical radio channels of the IEEE 802.15.4 radio to find the channel that has the least current radio energy. This channel is assumed to be the one with the least interference from other equipment. Since IEEE 802.15.4 runs on the unlicensed 2.4 GHz band, there are several sources of interference such as WiFi networks and microwave ovens. The channel scan samples each channel for 0.5 s. Thus the process takes eight seconds and gives only a snapshot of the channel activity. When the scan is complete, the ZC chooses the channel with the least activity for the network. This channel is retained through the lifetime of the network.

After the PHY layer channel selection is complete, the MAC layer creates a new PAN ID for the network. The PAN ID is a 16-bit integer selected at random by the ZC. Once the ZC has selected a PAN ID, it begins to announce its presence on the selected channel and with the selected PAN ID through repeated beacon messages. When the physical channel and PAN ID have been selected, the network formation is said to be complete.

Once the ZC has formed the network, ZRs and ZEDs begin to join it. Nodes join a network by sending out their own beacon messages. If a ZR or ZC hears a beacon from a node that is not part of a network, it responds by sending a beacon message back. The node collects all answers it receives and decides which network and ZR it should try to associate with. The process by which the node chooses its network and parent is application-specific. If network security is enabled, after a node has selected a network and a parent, it authenticates itself with the parent. Now the node is fully part of the network.

19.1.8 **ZigBee Is Migrating to IP**

The layers of the ZigBee stack loosely correspond to the layers of the IP stack. The ZigBee stack is, however, incompatible with the IP architecture. This causes severe problems when ZigBee networks are deployed together with existing IP-based services and applications. There is no way for the ZigBee network and the IP-based services to communicate except through custom gateways. A gateway needs to run both the full ZigBee stack and an IP stack, which effectively doubles the memory requirement for the gateway device. Additionally, these gateways require installation, custom hardware, and custom software, inducing significant costs. These problems are not specific to ZigBee, however; we discuss these generic problems at length in Chapter 3.

To reduce the costs and trouble of integrating ZigBee networks with IP-based networks and services, the ZigBee Alliance announced in mid-2009 that ZigBee will move toward an IP-based infrastructure for the latest application profile for smart energy metering. By incorporating IP into the ZigBee architecture, the hope is that existing ZigBee applications will be able to run over IP instead of over the custom NWK layer in the current ZigBee specification. This reduces the cost of integrating with existing IP networks. In addition, there is ongoing work outside of the ZigBee Alliance to adopt the existing ZigBee application profiles to run over a UDP/IP [237], allowing the ZigBee application profiles to become applications running on top of the IP architecture. How the ZigBee Alliance will progress with the migration toward IP was not decided at the writing of this book.

19.2 **Z-WAVE**

Z-Wave is an alliance that developed its own patented low-power RF technology for home automation and small residential environment. The Z-wave technology is not IP-based and has its own physical, MAC, networking, transport, and application layers. The application layer makes use of command classes that describe devices and the language used to communicate with these devices. The information discussed next is based on the public information available on the Z-Wave/Zensys web site.

The main application of Z-Wave products is home automation such as garage doors, alarm systems, door locks, sensors for HVAC and energy management, lighting and windows, home healthcare, sprinklers, and other home applications. Z-Wave provides a developer kit that allows developers and original equipment manufacturers (OEMs) to develop products using the Z-Wave technology due to the use of an API and handles its own certification program.

Z-Wave technology has been designed to be plug and play, requiring minimal manual intervention to connect new devices that expand the meshed network. The Z-Wave technology has been designed to be low power so it is used on both main-powered and battery-operated nodes such as smoke detectors or other types of sensors.

The RF Z-Wave technology uses binary frequency shift keying (B-FSK) modulation and operates in the sub-1 GHz band. Since 2008 it also supports the 2.5 GHz band for a throughput between 9.6 and 40 Kilobits/s (performances indicated by Zensys). The MAC layer uses link layer acknowledgment and retransmission with collision avoidance and checksum for error detection.

The ZM3102 Z-Wave® Module is an integrated RF communication module using the unlicensed short-range frequency band 902—928 MHz in the United States and 868.0–868.6 MHz in Europe. The

Z-W0301 Single Chip is a chipset made of the following components: an RF transceiver, the 8-bit 8051 microcontroller unit (MCU) core from Texas Instruments equipped with 32 K of flash memory, 2 K of RAM for the Z-Wave protocol, and OEM application software. The Zensys 300 series power consumption is 2.5 µA in sleep mode, 21 mA in receive mode, 5 mA (MCU "on" and radio "off"), transmission of 23 mA (at −5 dBm), and 37 mA (at 0 dBm).

Z-Wave products support the basic device class protocol libraries and command classes that reference the command exchanges between the devices. Home automation can be performed via an Internet connection through an IP/Z-Wave protocol translation gateway since Z-Wave does not natively support the IP protocol. The role of the gateway is then to connect the Z-Wave world to the Internet.

The technology is supported and promulgated by the Z-Wave Alliance (www.z-wave.com).

19.3 CONCLUSIONS

Several non-IP protocol specifications for smart objects have been developed. The ZigBee specification, developed by the ZigBee Alliance, is based on the IEEE 802.15.4 radio standard and provides a set of mechanisms for creating networks of nodes as well as the establishment of applications on top of the network. The ZigBee specification is owned by the ZigBee Alliance and vendors need to join the alliance to commercialize ZigBee technology.

Z-Wave is another specification for low-power communication in wireless smart object systems. It is patented and owned by the Z-Wave Alliance. Z-Wave specifies an entire network stack from the physical layer to the application layer. The application layers are tailored to specific market segments such as home automation or energy management.

Neither ZigBee nor Z-Wave are compatible with IP, which is a significant problem for emerging systems that need to integrate with IP-based networks and services. To alleviate these problems, the ZigBee Alliance announced in mid-2009 that it would work towards allowing ZigBee to use IP, enabling seamless integration between ZigBee networks and IP networks.

Smart Grid

20.1 INTRODUCTION

The power grid is the electrical network delivering electricity to houses, offices, and industrial users. As shown in Figure 20.1, electricity is produced by plants (nuclear, coal, solar, geothermal, wind) and transported through a hierarchical power grid network where electricity flows from power generation sources to homes after a succession of voltage transformations performed by substations. Electricity is generated and transported over long distances at high voltage (between 110 and 400 kV) to reduce line loss. The line voltage is then stepped down by transformers located in a primary substation (typically to 40–60 kV) until it reaches pole top transformers (United States) or a secondary substation (Europe)

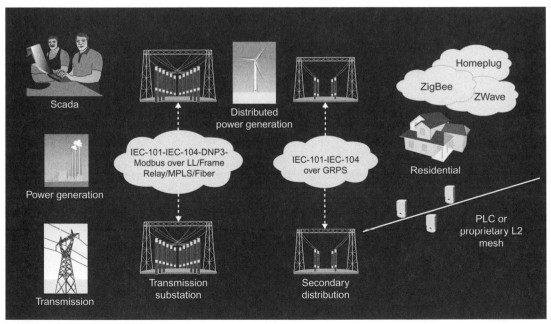

FIGURE 20.1

Current grid infrastructure.

Interconnecting Smart Objects with IP. DOI: 10.1016/B978-0-12-375165-2.00020-X

where the voltage is further stepped down to 110/220 V (see Figure 20.2). Power lines may either be overhead or underground depending on the voltage and country.

The approximate number of primary substations in Europe is several thousands and the number of secondary substations is as large as several hundreds of thousands in the largest countries.

Since there is one smart meter per house and several per building, there are hundreds of millions of meters in the world.

Thus far, the power grid has been mostly managed and designed according to power consumption forecasts using monodirectional information flows. In the past few decades power demand was highly stable and predictable. With increasing environmental concerns to reduce CO_2 emission and the cost of energy, the end user has changed its power consumption behavior, thus making the power demand less predictable. Additionally more users have access to electricity leading to an increase in energy consumption. Even more important is the change of power production in the grid with the generation of power from distributed renewable energy sources referred to as "distributed generation" both within the grid or downstream of the smart meter (at medium and low voltage). Distributed generation refers to solar panels, wind turbines, or micro combined heat and power (CHP) equipment that can convert waste heat with gas micro-turbines or fuel cells (significantly more efficient than combustion-based generation).

It is predicted that 20% of produced power will be from renewable sources in Europe by 2020. In some countries that proportion has already exceeded 40%. Power generation from unpredictable

United States transmission grid

kV
115
138
161
230
345
500

FIGURE 20.2

US power grid.

(Source: FEMA.)

distributed generation sources and user power consumption behavior changes increased the level of unpredictability. This requires fine-grained monitoring and management of the grid to maintain a high level of reliability and reduce the number of network outages. This type of management is not always deployed in today's grid networks. Furthermore, power is injected in parts of the grid that are not always monitored, such as the medium voltage (MV) and low voltage (LV) areas, which adds to the requirement for widespread advanced monitoring and control systems in the grid.

Power grid operators (also called utilities) are facing difficult challenges when managing the grid for the previously mentioned reasons as well as governmentally imposed restrictions on greenhouse gas emission. There is a strong requirement to design the next generation of the "greener" grid with a reduced carbon footprint in an increasingly more complex environment with increasing demand, power consumption changing patterns, and in the presence of a distributed sources generation that considerably reduces the level of predictability.

The introduction of a potentially large number of electric cars (plug-in hybrid electric vehicles; PHEV) is undoubtedly a unique opportunity, but it brings its own challenges to the grid network. Smart mechanisms will be required to smooth out the energy consumption and draw power from the grid when it is appropriate according to power production. Note that it may also be interesting to use the millions of car batteries as a future electricity storage buffer for peak shaving.

Figure 20.3 shows the number of minutes of outage in the distribution grid.

Each minute of network outage has economical consequences. The current grid "consists of more than 9,200 electric generating units with more than 1,000,000 MW of generating capacity connected to more than 300,000 miles of transmission lines.... Today's electricity system is 99.97% reliable, yet still allows for power outages and interruptions that cost Americans at least $150 billion each year — about $500 for every man, woman and child."[1]

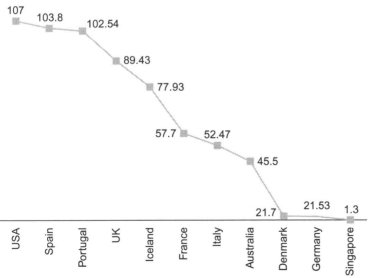

FIGURE 20.3

Yearly outages in the transmission/distribution grid.

[1]See *The Smart Grid: An Introduction*, US Department of Energy, at http://www.oe.energy.gov/1165.htm.

The consequence of these outages is the need for an advanced networking infrastructure in the Smart Grid from generation to distribution and finally homes and buildings. Such an infrastructure is made of billions of smart objects performing sensing and actuating in the grid to provide "real-time" information about the grid health and consumer demand to optimize the grid operation. Based on this set of data, the network will be able to adjust in "real time" to perform load shedding and accurate grid management with the objective of increasing grid reliability by reducing grid outages while reducing carbon footprint and cost.

Smart objects such as sensors and actuators will collect data across the network to feed analytical tools to better manage the network and also to trigger various actions within the network (e.g., power consumption regulation based on dynamic interaction between the end user and the grid, fault isolation, etc.). Several scenarios are further analyzed in Section 20.3 of this chapter. Some of these actions will be triggered from within the network (using distributed in-network intelligence) while others will be managed using centralized systems (e.g., SCADA applications).

Thus grid reliability is one of the most critical priorities for utilities. The grid should be managed by an extremely reliable communication network that provides the necessary infrastructure of real-time monitoring and distributed grid management to reduce network outages: without a doubt IP networks have demonstrated their ability to meet these requirements.

The forecast of investments from utilities in Smart Grid networks exceeds $42 billion, and some forecasts are significantly higher.

Power grid networks are designed for future use, thus providing a great deal of flexibility with extremely high reliability and security.

Security is undoubtedly another priority for Smart Grid designers since advanced networks supporting critical infrastructure may be prone to various forms of attacks. The good news is that a plethora of existing IP security technologies are used to safeguard the overall networking infrastructure.

20.1.1 How Can We Define the Smart Grid?

There is no single definition of the Smart Grid. Instead, there is a set of expectations that must be met to face the wide range of new requirements exposed in the previous section. The Smart Grid must enhance the current grid network with advanced sensing actuators and a highly secure networking infrastructure to improve grid efficiency, performance, and reliability as well as to support a wide range of new services (e.g., better knowledge of power consumption profiles, use of PHEV, distributed sources such as solar panel and residential power generation, and smart home appliances).

The Smart Grid is one of the major applications for smart object networks, and the IP protocol will be central to them. As described through several use cases explored in this chapter, most of the expectations and requirements for the Smart Grid involve smart object networks: sensors (e.g., measuring the current, voltage, phase, or reactive power) and actuators (e.g., circuit breakers, etc.) to efficiently monitor and control the power grid, sensing in smart meters to measure power consumption, and a number of smart devices used in homes, buildings, and factories that communicate via specialized energy management devices with the grid for efficient energy management.

A typical power grid architecture from power generation to the home/building is depicted in Figure 20.4: power is generated by plants and then distributed to the end user through a distribution network. The particularity of the grid network lies in its hierarchical structure. High voltage (HV) lines are connected to (primary) substations where the voltage is reduced to MV before being even further reduced to LV using pole tops (United States) or secondary substations (Europe). Finally, electricity is delivered to the end user where a smart meter is used to monitor energy usage (and to perform many other functions).

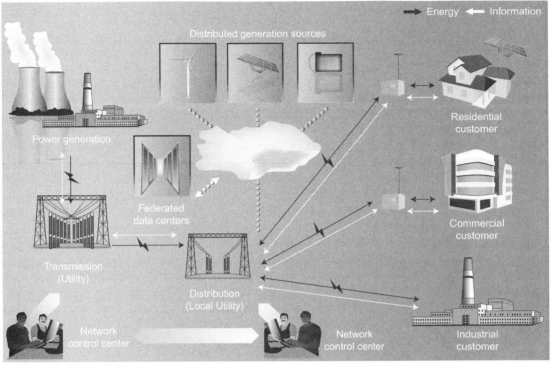

FIGURE 20.4

Overview of the Smart Grid network.

In each part of the network, smart objects are used to provide a myriad of services that are described in Section 20.3.

In this chapter we outline several use cases for smart object networks in Smart Grid networks:

- Substation monitoring and control
- Smart metering
- Home energy management

20.2 TERMINOLOGY

There are several common terms used when referring to Smart Grid architectures:

- Substation automation/integration (SA/I): The core grid network from power generation to power distribution. It includes the primary and secondary substations.
- Neighbor area network (NAN): Refers to the network between the substations and the homes. It includes the concentrators and smart meters.
- Home area network (HAN): The home network including smart appliances, home energy controller (HEC), etc.

20.3 CORE GRID NETWORK MONITORING AND CONTROL

This first use case shows the role of sensors and actuators in the core grid for monitoring and control.

Monitoring and control undoubtedly deserves its own book considering the number of applications involving smart objects that utilities need to use to effectively monitor and control the power grid. The objective of this section is to provide an overview of three applications:

- Substation monitoring and control
- Substation condition-based maintenance (CBM)
- Line dynamic rating

20.3.1 Use Case 1: Secondary Substation Monitoring and Control

As discussed previously, secondary substations are used to step down the power voltage from medium (40–60 kV) to low voltage (110/220 V). As shown in Figure 20.4, a substation hosts transformers as well as a number of devices called intelligent end devices (IEDs) such as circuit breakers, voltage sensors, reclosers, and surge protectors. IEDs are currently mostly managed by a centralized system located at the network control center (NCC) called the Supervisory Control and Data Acquisition (SCADA) application.

As shown in Figure 20.5, in Europe secondary substations are equipped with transformers and remote terminal units (RTUs) that receive data from sensors and trigger local actions (referred to as substation monitoring and control). In addition, the substation may also host a smart meter

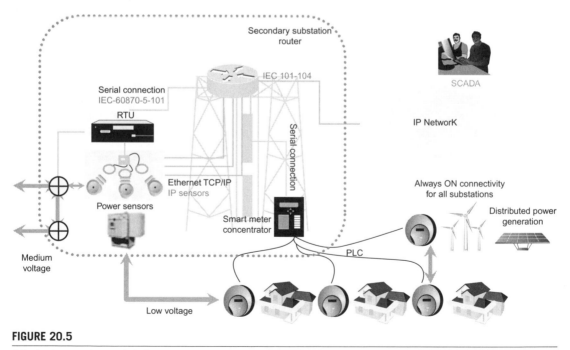

FIGURE 20.5

A typical secondary substation.

concentrator that collects data from the meters and performs local processing to report information back to the SCADA system as discussed later in Section 20.4. Substations are connected to a data network using various types of networking technologies.

Sensed data can trigger local actions performed within the substation or they can alternatively be reported to the SCADA application where the appropriate action is taken. Smart Grid networks tend to introduce distributed intelligence in the grid in contrast with a purely centralized system.

Smart objects such as sensors are primarily used to monitor the MV and LV power lines and report a number of quality metrics such as the voltage and current levels for each phase. Other metrics of interest for utilities can then be derived such as the active and reactive power (known as the P and Q values). Such metrics can either be computed by the sensor, the RTU, a smart router located in the substation, or the SCADA application. Sensors also report ground faults, fuse status, cable temperature, and voltage or current values exceeding some pre-configured thresholds that are sent to the SCADA application. They are also potentially stored in equipment within the substation (e.g., smart routers).

Smart objects in a substation are not limited to sensors: circuit breakers (actuators) are also used for substation control and can either be controlled by the RTU or by the operator in charge of the SCADA application.

In some grid networks, distributed algorithms can be used between substations (primary and secondary) to perform automatic failure recovery. Upon detecting a fault, the distributed algorithm automatically locates the fault and isolates the faulty line thus providing a fully automatic error recovery mechanism.

The RTU has historically been using protocols defined by IEC[2] such as IEC 60870-5-101 and IEC 60870-5-105 (mostly in Europe), or DNP3 (Distributed Network Protocol) and Modbus in primary substations in the United States, but there is clearly a trend toward a truly end-to-end IP architecture from smart objects such as sensors and actuators to the SCADA application. Such smart objects already exist and could then directly be connected to a smart router that performs various tasks (such as hosting distributed algorithms to trigger local actions by sending orders to actuators such as circuit breakers) in addition to routing the IPv6 traffic to the SCADA application and between substations. This is represented by the "direct" lines between the sensor and the router, thus replacing the traditional (usually analog) connection between sensors and RTUs and thus opening the door to a myriad of new services.

In addition to providing critical information to utilities regarding grid health, these smart objects greatly contribute to the reduction of the number of grid network outages. As shown by the secondary substation in Figure 20.5, smart objects are an integral part of the central nervous system of the power grid.

20.3.2 Use Case 2: Substation CBM

The use of sensors to proactively determine the need for equipment maintenance based on the health condition of the device is one of the most prevalent uses of smart objects in industrial networks; substation automation and control is not an exception. By monitoring the device, utilities can perform maintenance before a failure occurs, thus saving the cost of the device but also indirect costs due to network outages. The alternative approach based on preventive maintenance with regular preplanned maintenance is not only usually less effective but more costly.

[2] IEC: International Electrotechnical Commission — http://www.iec.ch/.

CBM includes the periodic sending of health reports (from a few minutes to hours) by a smart object, such as a sensor, to a central system in addition to sending alarms triggered by specific events. The number of such smart objects used for CBM in a substation is impressive. Here is a small subset of the wide set of sensors used in today's environments:

- Partial discharge detectors
- Infrared thermographic imaging monitors
- Vibration sensor on rotating equipment
- Acoustic emission defect sensors
- Moisture in oil sensors
- Load current measurement sensors
- Backscatter sensors
- Wind speed sensors
- Temperature sensors
- Humidity sensors
- Dissolved gas analysis sensors
- Self-reporting distribution transformer (health metric life odometer)
- Liquid leaks
- Low oil levels
- Overhead cable ice load, swing, and tilt sensors

The analysis of a set of reported values by sensors (due to well-known equations) is used to detect anomalies. For example, knowing the load and other parameters, utilities can determine the expected temperature of the system. When exceeding a threshold, an indication that maintenance is required is triggered, thus potentially avoiding expensive failures in equipment such as transformers. Another typical example is the use of dissolved gas analysis sensors to monitor transformers. The analysis of various dissolved gases in transformers such as oxygen hydrogen, methane, ethane, ethylene, carbon monoxide, and dioxide can help identify a transformer failure. Smart objects (sensors) allow for very regular (once a day or even every hour) analysis in contrast to the usual yearly on-site samplings that were sent to a laboratory for further analysis.

The benefits of CBM are clear. Not only will CBM prolong the life of expensive devices and in some cases even increase their effectiveness, it will also avoid catastrophic failures that lead to costly grid network outages. The use of smart objects for CBM also reduces the cost of preventive maintenance and increases workforce effectiveness in many ways. Whereas CBM solutions have been in use for years for local purposes usually using proprietary solutions, the need to generalize their use across the network involving extended communication between a myriad of devices shows the need for using a unified communication infrastructure to support the required level of services. IP is undoubtedly the ideal candidate for that purpose supporting a wide range of devices: from large computers to smart objects.

20.3.3 Use Case 3: Line Dynamic Rating

Line dynamic rating is yet another use case where IP smart objects can significantly improve the effectiveness of the power grid. With the emergence of distributed generation, it is common to face situations where power generation exceeds the grid transmission capacity. For example, in a region of New York 1200 MW of generation is already operational with 8000 MW of generation planned for the future.

Transmission line capacity is limited. Resistive heating melts conductors at too high a current and voltage cannot be increased infinitely. If the power line load is increased, the conductor temperature also increases leading to sagging through thermal expansion. This may cause line damage in addition to affecting the transformer efficiency. The grid transmission capacity is usually expressed in static ratings using worst-case weather scenarios (high air temperature and minimal wind: typically full sun with a high temperature of 40°C (104°F) and wind speed perpendicular to the conductor of 1.4 mph). Utilities may decide to increase the static ratings by 10 to 20% during extreme situations for a short period of time on the basis of weather reports. But static ratings do not take into account real-time conditions, thus imposing static bounds to the power flows even when weather conditions allow for an increase in the grid capacity.

Unlike static rating, dynamic rating makes use of real-time measurements of parameters such as temperature. It has been found that during high wind conditions, conductor thermal capacity could be increased for a period of time thus leading to more efficient use of wind generation.

Dynamic rating makes use of various techniques. First, it can be based on weather because of equations using air temperature, solar heating, and wind speed. This technique does not require sensors mounted on the power line, thus it does not consider the effective line load. The weather monitoring equipment must be appropriately placed to reflect the weather parameters of the line. Other dynamic rating techniques involve the use of several sensors on the line. For example, real-time conductor temperatures can be converted to an equivalent wind speed used with a series of other parameters to compute the dynamic line rating. To be effective this technique requires the use of several sensors along the power line that communicate with each other, which is another piece of smart object networks. Another dynamic rating technique is based on sag/tension monitoring that provides real-time data converted to equivalent wind speed.

The Electric Power Research Institute (EPRI) has developed monitor sagometers and backscatter conductor temperature sensors in addition to a new rating calculation equation (dynamic thermal circuit rating; DTCR) to optimize the power transmission capacity of existing lines at moderate cost. The New York Power Authority (NYPA) has been working with EPRI to use real-time or historical weather and electrical load data to compute dynamic ratings. Required real-time data involve a variety of smart objects: temperature/backscatter sensors, video sagometers, and tension sensors installed on HV lines exposed to high wind capacity connected to the line.

Depending on the study, it was shown that the gain in power transmission capacity can vary between 10 and 20% and even up to 30% in some cases. The Electric Reliability Council of Texas (ERCOT), who started to use dynamic rating in 2005, reported significant power transmission gains: during a typical winter day, improvement ranged from 10% (South Houston) to 30% (North West) and even reached 128% in a South North region.

Most of the smart objects (sensors) used for dynamic rating are equipped with radio communication and when not main-powered, solar panels can be used as a local source of energy power. Power supply typically is provided by solar panels, but emerging alternatives include contactless power scavenging from the electromagnetic (EM) field around high voltage, high current cables.

20.3.4 Technical Characteristics and Challenges

Most core grid monitoring and control applications have common characteristics and present similar technical challenges.

20.3.4.1 The Networking Environment

Most of these smart object networks operate in fairly harsh environments due to high temperature or strong electromagnetic interferences (EMI), especially in HV and MV substations, due to inductive load switching, lightning strikes, electrostatic discharges, and radio frequency interferences. Furthermore, the power grid covers vast areas of operation including many outdoor networks that have their own source of disturbance. This means that the plethora of smart object networks used in the core grid for monitoring and control are operating in harsh conditions but must still provide a very high level of reliability, thus imposing difficult challenges to software and hardware engineers.

20.3.4.2 Traffic Flows and Network Topologies

20.3.4.2.1 Substation Monitoring and Control

Historically most of the traffic flows have been between sensors and the RTU that communicates with the centralized SCADA application. Local traffic flows are typically between IEDs and RTUs in both directions (sensors reporting various metrics and RTUs or smart routers sending orders to actuators such as circuit breakers).

With the emergence of new standards such as IEC 61850 and distributed intelligence in the Smart Grid, we can clearly anticipate a strong increase of the traffic between smart objects residing within substations (smart object to smart object communication).

Consequently, traffic flows tend to move from a hub and spoke model (between substations and the SCADA application) to a more distributed model (between smart objects and local processing devices and between smart objects residing in different substations).

20.3.4.2.2. CBM Applications

CBM reports can be sent as often as every minute for highly critical equipment monitoring and up to hours or even weeks for less critical or less stressed devices. In some circumstances critical alarms may be sent upon detecting an anomaly requiring immediate action. For example, a dissolved gas analysis sensor is expected to send data to the data concentrator in the substation once a day, but this transmission rate could be increased to once every hour if the transformer exceeds its static rating.

Data are usually collected by a central system that stores all reports and alarms for immediate processing to identify the set of immediate required actions and also for further processing for failure profile analysis, assets management, and so forth.

Although most of the flows are multipoint to point (from the smart objects to the central system), some of them may be locally processed within a substation for immediate local processing. An alarm may require an immediate local action on an actuator (another smart object).

Finally, some scenarios may involve point-to-point traffic between smart objects to collectively determine the required set of actions.

20.3.4.2.3 Dynamic Ratings

Two main applications hosted in the Network Operating Center are involved in dynamic rating operations: the Dynamic Line Rating System (DLRS) and the Dynamic Transformer Rating System (DTRS).

- DLRS: Receives data from the sensors in the field and computes the dynamic rating of the power line. It then compares the calculated line dynamic rating to the current loading information gathered from sensors in the substation.

- DTRS: Receives data from the sensors in the field to compute the dynamic transformer rating. It then compares the calculated transformer dynamic rating to the current load information to determine if the transformer has exceeded its capacity.

Dynamic line rating sensors send reports to the data concentrator every minute that it transmits data to the DLRS. Note that other substation sensors (switch, circuit breakers) also send data to the DLRS to compute the dynamic rating since they could bottleneck if their rating is below the line's rating.

Dissolved gas analysis sensors typically send data to the DLRS once a day, but this frequency may be increased to once per hour if the transformer exceeds its static rating.

20.3.4.3 Smart Object and Link Characteristics

As in most industrial networks, smart objects designed for power grid automation are usually ruggedized and must be highly reliable to the critical nature of the applications. Sensors and actuators vary from fairly simple to highly sophisticated devices that have fairly constrained resources (CPU, memory, etc.).

Links interconnecting the smart objects are both wired (in substation) and wireless (for some outdoor applications), usually with low speed and with a relatively high error rate (also qualified as lossy links).

20.3.4.4 Quality of Service and Network Reliability

As with most industrial applications, Quality of Service (QoS) is a critical component of the overall architecture. Although some data are not critical, others such as critical alarms have real-time requirements and the networking infrastructure must guarantee reliable delivery, minimized delays, and bounded jitters, which makes IP highly suitable to these environments. IP supports high QoS due to a number of techniques discussed in Chapter 15 (traffic classification, shaping, scheduling, congestion avoidance, traffic engineering, etc.).

With CBM, the level of required QoS significantly varies with the nature of the report. Some data are clearly non-critical and a packet loss may not be a problem, whereas a critical alarm requires low networking delay and high network reliability. Most of the alarms in substation monitoring and control applications are critical. Similarly, dynamic rating is yet another example where QoS is vitally important. In many cases, the data sent every minute to the DLRS and DTRS must be reliably transmitted with moderate tolerance to delays.

IP networks also provide a wide range of QoS that make it attractive for these types of networks.

20.3.4.5 Scalability

The number of smart objects in Smart Grid networks is extremely high. As pointed out in the Introduction of this chapter, a single power network can be made up of hundreds of thousands of secondary substations/pole tops. With at the very least a few dozen smart objects per substation/pole top, in addition to thousands of sensors located on power lines, the number of smart objects could be several millions. Thus scalability is a prime concern, which again supports the use of protocols such as IP (and in particular IPv6) that largely proved their scalability. As discussed in detail in Chapter 17, IP protocols such as routing (RPL) for these types of smart object networks have been designed to be highly scalable.

20.3.4.6 Reliability Requirement

Reliability of the control network for the Smart Grid is highly critical and tightly coupled with the support of QoS. Not only must these smart object networks be operational at all times, they must also be able to recover various types of failures within usually bounded times.

20.3.4.7 Mobility

Mobility in Smart Grid networks is generally low to moderate. With the exception of the human workforce having to perform on-site maintenance, most of the smart objects are fixed powered devices.

20.3.4.8 Security

Security is undoubtedly one of the most critical concerns in Smart Grid networks considering the high criticality of power grid networks. As discussed in Part I, Chapter 8, IP has been enhanced with a number of security mechanisms and its degree of exposure through the public Internet helped reach a very high degree of security because of authentication, encryption, and non-repudiation techniques.

20.3.4.9 Network Management

Considering the number of smart objects and other devices *and* their critical concerns, network management is key and the grid has a long history of sophisticated network management with SCADA applications. Substation automation requires network management considering the number of devices, autoconfiguration, and device/service discovery is highly desirable.

20.4 SMART METERING (NAN)

20.4.1 Applications and Use Cases

Electrical meters have been greatly enhanced with added features whereas not so long ago (and this is still the case in many countries) metering management was limited to manual reading of electrical meters requiring periodic trips to each physical location.

The first set of enhancements, automatic meter reading (AMR), consisted of adding communication functionality to the meters to perform an automatic collection of power consumptions, load curves, alarms, and status from the NCC for automatic billing as well as device monitoring of the meters. Moreover, real-time power consumption helped provide accurate billing instead of using historical data coupled with predictions (the requirement is usually to provide meter reading every 15 minutes, although the data may only be downloaded once a day).

The next step consisted of equipping meters with more advanced functionalities such as sensing for power-quality monitoring and power fault reports, thus leading to the concept of Advanced Metering Infrastructure (AMI).

Communication between a central system and smart meters became truly two-way in support of a myriad of new and advanced applications such as dynamic pricing, demand-response (DR), and grid monitoring due to advanced sensing capabilities.

Dynamic pricing and demand-response allow the utility to perform load shedding, thus optimizing their infrastructure. Although dynamic pricing is likely to be provided by the smart meters to the end user (most likely to an HEC residing in the home), dynamic signals supporting DR may also be sent by other means such as the Internet.

Two-way communication is fundamental for the support of advanced services in AMI networks. The following list provides a subset of the information exchanged between smart meters and the central SCADA application:

- Dynamic pricing (new hour tariff)
- Load curves
- Actuation of a circuit breaker

- Closing delay on metrological fault
- Alarm reset
- Communication time out before circuit breaker opens

Data retrieved by the SCADA application from smart meters:

- Power consumption per hour tariff (kilowatt consumed for each tariff)
- Active alarms
- Logs of historical alarms
- Power supply remaining battery life
- Nominal battery life
- Circuit breaker state
- Smart meter parameters such as serial number, manufacturer identification, meter type, etc.

Furthermore, smart meters can also be used for several additional services that are of great interest for utilities:

- Geographic information system that keeps track of the meter location, phase the meter is connected to, automatic detection of any change in the LV network, and automatic data upload for newly connected meters.
- Grid monitoring where the smart meter is part of the grid and as such can be used for grid monitoring. For example, it could report alarms and help localize faults along MV feeders or could detect an absence of voltage on a phase that is not detected by the feeder breaker.
- Report power outage in near real time with the ability to perform fault location (grid vs. private installation side).
- Since the smart meter is also a sensing device, it can be used to provide load curves on any single phase to perform grid network engineering and reduce losses and voltage drops.

Several large-scale deployments of smart meters already took place and many are planned in the future. For example, in one of the largest deployments the entire customer base (over 27 million) was equipped with smart meters supporting a wide range of services such as real-time power consumption, the ability to change the maximum amount of power available at any given time, the ability to turn power on and off, automatic detection of power outage, and so forth.

In Japan, smart meters are equipped with various sensing capabilities.

In the United States Duke Energy, PGE, and several other utilities are deploying millions of smart meters with advanced AMI functionalities such as near real-time power consumption, dynamic pricing, etc. Several other countries also started similar deployments on very large scales (e.g., France, UK, Ireland, Nordic countries, Germany, Australia, New Zealand, Turkey, etc.).

Smart metering is not limited to electrical meters, it also applies to water and gas meters (since this chapter is devoted to Smart Grid networks, we focus mainly on electrical meters).

20.4.2 Technical Challenges and Network Characteristics

20.4.2.1 The Networking Environment

Although the networking environment is not as harsh as substations with HV or MV lines, smart meter networks are mostly outdoors and, as discussed in the next section, connectivity between smart meters may be greatly affected by the nature of the links used in these environments.

20.4.2.2 Traffic Flows and Network Topologies

Smart meter networks may have different topologies: star topologies up to a concentrator, meshed topologies made of routers, and smart meters acting as routers or a mix of both. These networks are usually hierarchical and concentrators are interconnected via a backbone network. The current trend is to migrate these networks to IP end to end.

20.4.2.3 Smart Object and Link Characteristics

In contrast with gas meters, electrical smart meters are main powered devices (equipped with a battery for redundancy purposes). Still, this does not mean that power consumption is not an issue. Furthermore, smart meters usually have moderate constraints in CPU processing and are required to have enough storage capacity not only to store information related to power consumption that could be less frequently downloaded by utilities, but also to store a detailed log of power outages. Regulation varies between countries, but it is common to require the storage of several months of historical faults, alarms, and power consumption.

Smart meters are thus smart objects forming a complex multi-hop network and act as end devices and routers. Meters are interconnected by wireless links (mostly in the United States) or Powerline communication (PLC) technology (in Europe although some meters are also using wireless technologies in Europe too). These networks are a perfect example of smart object networks and, more precisely, Low-power and Lossy Networks (LLNs). Indeed, smart meters are constrained in CPU power and memory as well as power consumption since utilities require drastically reduced energy consumption. Moreover, smart meters are interconnected by lossy links. When using wireless links, link reliability is usually quite low with a large amount of link flaps. This also applies to PLC links where the reliability can greatly vary for a number of reasons such as impedance variation, floor noise, and so forth, as discussed in Chapter 12. Link bandwidth is also fairly limited, from a few Kbits/s in the worst case to a few hundreds of Kbits/s in the very best case. The myriad of link layers in use also explains the suitability of IP as the convergence layer in smart meter networks, which allows for the use of PLC, high and low bandwidth wireless technologies, or a combination of both.

20.4.2.4 Quality of Service and Network Reliability

QoS and network reliability requirements are relatively low in smart metering networks. Meter reading is usually not a critical application and network outage of a few hours is usually not a major issue. With the emergence of new applications such as dynamic pricing and DR QoS and reliability, requirements tend to increase but are not likely to be very high.

20.4.2.5 Scalability

Smart meters are made of millions of devices, thus scalability must be extremely high. Once again, this is another compelling reason to use IP. New IP protocols such as RPL (discussed in Chapter 17) have been designed to support a large number of IP smart objects in a single network.

20.4.2.6 Mobility

There is no mobility requirement in smart metering networks.

20.4.2.7 Security

Smart metering networks is another area of the Smart Grid where security is a paramount concern, since the hacking of a smart meter could lead to cutting power to potentially thousands of homes.

Smart meter vendors actively work on the use of sophisticated authentication and encryption technologies.

20.4.2.8 Longevity

Smart meters are required to last for at least two decades, preferably with no human intervention. This requires the support of dynamic software upgrades but, more important, flexible hardware and software functionalities capable of supporting features that will be required in the next two decades.

20.5 HAN

20.5.1 Applications and Use Cases

As previously noted, solutions for energy management are currently extremely rudimentary. The only sensing device available for energy monitoring is the electrical meter reporting the total energy consumption in the home with no granularity.

Figure 20.6 shows a typical HAN configuration. The HEC is connected to the HAN on one side and to the grid on the other side either via the Internet or the smart meter. The HAN is composed of a variety of smart objects connected via both wireless (e.g., IEEE 802.11, IEEE 802.15.4) and PLC links forming a low-speed control command network. Note that some HANs will be wireless only, others will exclusively use PLC, and others will be made of a mix of wireless and PLC links.

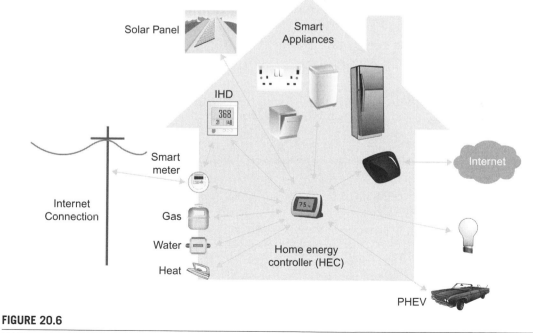

FIGURE 20.6

HAN.

20.5.1.1 The Role of Smart Objects

Smart objects are at the heart of the HAN and provide efficient energy management solutions:

- Smart appliance: An appliance equipped with a smart object(s) capable of sensing, actuating, and communicating with the HEC. The smart appliance typically reports energy consumption to the HEC (sensing) and could also be controlled by the HEC according to the DR signals (discussed later in Section 20.5.1.1.2) and to user-defined rules on the HEC. In some cases, a dialog could even take place between the smart appliance and the HEC to make appropriate decisions according to the situation. For example, it might not be wise to interrupt a washing machine cycle if the cycle is about to end. Restarting a new cycle after pausing for several hours may end up consuming more energy.
- Smart plugs: It may take some time before all appliances are equipped with smart objects. Thus an intermediate solution is to use an electrical wall-plug adaptor equipped with a sensor to measure the energy consumption in near real time and allow for appliance control (on/off action). Such smart plugs (or alternative form factor like a DIN rail mounting design) could be used for a variety of devices such as a pool pump, heater, HAVC, and so forth and can communicate with the HEC using PLC or wireless communication.
- Smart thermostats: Could control the temperature setting of the room based on the received DR signal from the HEC and could lower the temperature by several degrees for a period of time and report energy savings.

As discussed in the Introduction, the Smart Grid enables a myriad of new services from power generation to home and buildings. Although this section is mainly devoted to home energy management, it is fairly straightforward to figure out how similar services can be supported for building energy management (further discussed in Chapter 24 devoted to the Building Automation Use case).

There are two main applications of interest to the end user discussed in this section:

- Home energy management
- Demand-response

20.5.1.1.1 Home Energy Management

Many studies have shown that user energy saving ranges between 5 and 15% if the users were given the appropriate tools to accurately monitor their energy consumption at home. There is very limited data provided to the user who does not have access to accurate billing and does not know which devices in the home are the main sources of energy consumption. Thus it is imperative to provide user-friendly tools that allow access to the power usage in the home via a simple display as well as other forms of data access (PDA, Web Interface).

In addition to (real-time and historical) power usage, other useful information could be provided such as tips from utilities to help save energy and main sources of energy consumption in the home (HVAC, swimming pools, etc.). For example, the following set of data could be provided to the user: energy usage in kWh (total and per device), energy cost (total and per device), and CO_2 consumption. These data could be provided in real time and also with historical statistics over the past few hours, days, or even months.

Another service could be to detect a malfunctioning device by observing the power consumption and compare it to energy consumption profiles of similar devices. In some cases, it might even be useful to correlate the energy consumption and other external data such as weather. Observing the heat energy consumption and correlating the data with weather information could detect that the heater does not perform at its maximum level of efficiency or provide some indication of the level of thermal isolation of the home.

Furthermore, users should have the ability to act upon devices according to their consumption based on a series of rules such as time of the consumption, real-time energy pricing, and so forth.

Finally, it is envisioned that other services will emerge such as micro-generation management (information related to the energy produced by renewable energy sources such as solar panels and wind locally generated by the home) and PHEV (indication of energy consumption by a car, charging level, etc.).

20.5.1.1.2 Demand-Response

One of the main challenges utilities are facing is adapting the grid capacity to user demand and in particular handling peak loads. Peak load shaving can only be performed in two ways:

- Over-provisioning the grid capacity (clearly not a viable option)
- Spot purchase energy on the market, which turns out to be a costly option since energy bought "on the fly" is usually significantly more expensive than the normal price

The concept of DR is based on the ability of the grid to dynamically interact with the home (or a building) to regulate the power demand according to the grid capacity with some pricing incentive for the end user. Upon peak load on the grid, the utility sends a signal to the end user via the HEC requesting power consumption reduction to perform load shedding at peak times. Simplified DR programs have been in place in several countries for years; a signal is sent to the smart meter at specific times of the day (known by the end user) to indicate the energy price. By knowing that electricity costs X cents between 7:00 a.m. and 11:00 p.m. and Y cents during 11:00 p.m. and 7:00 a.m., there is a strong incentive for the end user to use high-impact appliances during low price periods whenever possible. Such static pricing shifts occurring at the same time are a bit more controversial since there is a tendency for all demanding energy appliances to simultaneously start thus leading to peak load on the grid. Some utilities then improved the system by shifting low price periods on a per region basis.

The concept of DR goes one step beyond with several additional features:

- Dynamic pricing: In accordance with the grid load, the energy price is dynamically adjusted and communicated to the HEC.
- Critical alarms: Such signals can be sent at any time to cope with unexpected events in the grid that require lower energy consumption (e.g., network outage). Such signals could also be sent in specific conditions for an entire day when price is at a maximum. Such signals have a higher priority than dynamic pricing signals.

DR is two-way communication: signals are sent to the HEC and energy consumption reduction reports (potentially validated due to meter readings) are provided back to the power grid. Such reports are then used for energy bill discounts. It is even envisioned for the HEC to be able to provide proactive information to the grid about energy consumption that could be off-loaded from the grid, should the grid run into peak load. Such information enables the grid to take appropriate actions upon peak loads.

Does that mean that utilities will control end-user appliances? No. Fortunately full control is given to the end user who may even decide to ignore near real-time pricing indications. This is where the HEC comes into play. As shown in Figure 20.5, the HEC controls the HAN and all of the connected devices and smart objects in general in the home. Functionally the HEC is connected to both the HAN where smart objects are connected (sensors, actuators) and the grid via either the smart meter or the Internet. DR signals are received from the grid to report dynamic energy pricing that is then processed by the HEC according to user-configured rules. For example, an end user may decide to reduce by X degree the temperature of a room if the energy price exceeds Y cents per kWh. It might also be possible to interact with the device to postpone a specific action (e.g., start a washing machine cycle) by several hours to avoid peak times. A friendly user interface can then be used by end users to control their devices and appliances in the home according to real-time energy pricing.

Needless to say, such an architecture opens the door to non-energy-related applications: appliance monitoring for health management, simulation using lighting management scenarios, and so forth. These applications fall into the category of home automation and are further discussed in Chapter 23.

20.5.2 Technical Challenges and Network Characteristics

20.5.2.1 The Networking Environment

The HAN environment is significantly less challenging than an HV substation environment. That being said, low-power wireless links such as IEEE 802.15.4 may also be subject to all sorts of interference due to other wireless radios (e.g., IEEE 802.11) and appliances. Similarly, the electrical wiring system may be of variable quality with noises creating various perturbations of the low-speed PLC, not to mention the issue of coexistence with other high-speed PLC technologies used for other purposes than control/command.

20.5.2.2 Traffic Flows and Network Topologies

The HAN topology is fairly straightforward. PLC should be able to reach out to almost all devices in the home (there are systems that provide connectivity across multiple phases while offering several Kbits/s of bandwidth). Smart objects could also be connected in a mesh wireless IP network. Home automation has been one of the targeted applications for the routing protocol in LLNs, which are discussed in great detail in Chapter 17.

Most of the traffic flow for energy management in the HAN is between smart devices and the HEC. There may be a few point-to-point flows between smart devices and the meter or the HEC and the meter. In the future, distributed energy management applications may require communication between smart objects to better optimize energy management in the home.

20.5.2.3 Smart Object and Link Characteristics

Smart objects in the HAN such as smart plugs, thermostats, or microcontrollers embedded in smart appliances are all fairly inexpensive (a few dollars for the communication engine and in the near future a few dozen cents), which also means limited CPU and memory. There is a mix of main- and battery-powered devices usually equipped with low bandwidth communication capabilities (a few dozen Kbits/s). The degree of constraints varies with cost, but simple devices such as light bulbs equipped with sensor/actuator capability are envisioned. In such a case where costs must be as low as possible, resources are likely to be extremely scarce. Note that resource constraints also have an impact on software design; for example, the routing protocol designed by the Internet Engineering Task Force (IETF; RPL) supports devices with extremely limited memory and new mechanisms have been designed to allow routing in a home network where nodes may not have any routing table storage capability.

20.5.2.4 Quality of Service and Network Reliability

The HAN for energy management is unlikely to be a multi-QoS network where packet prioritization is required in case of network congestion. Indeed, in contrast with applications such as substation or industrial automation, all messages have similar QoS requirements. Requirements for reliability are not high. A temporary HAN failure has limited consequences. The smart appliance or smart plug may be out of control for a period of time with no dramatic consequences.

20.5.2.5 Scalability

Scalability is not a primary concern, since in the foreseeable future HANs are expected to be limited to a few dozen smart objects, although that number may be higher (a few hundred) for multidwelling units.

20.5.2.6 Mobility

Mobility in the HAN is required but moderate. Most devices are fixed.

20.5.2.7 Security

Security requirements are high. Such networks must be secure. Authentication and encryption technologies are an absolute must.

20.5.2.8 Network Management

The HAN is a typical example of a network that must be self-managed and requires minimal configuration from the end user. Smart devices must be self-configured with autodiscovery, and several IP protocols are already available to perform this discovery (e.g., Bonjour protocol developed by Apple). Once installed the smart object starts to discover the network, be part of the routing protocol, and announce itself to the HEC that discovers the device's capabilities. Several powerful HAN management solutions with a very friendly user interface are already available.

20.5.3 Summary of the Technical Challenges

For each use case, we provided an overview of the technical challenges. Figure 20.7 provides a summary of the technical challenges and characteristics for the Smart Grid use cases discussed in this chapter. Note that the ranking may slightly vary between applications.

20.6 CONCLUSIONS

The worldwide Smart Grid initiative involves a complete transformation of the networking infrastructure used to manage the power grid with billions of connected devices to achieve better energy management, reduced carbon footprint, support of new sources of renewable energy with an extremely high level of reliability, and reduction of cost. The number of applications where smart objects will play a key role in our future is only bounded by our imagination. Smart Grid networks are an area where smart objects will definitely play a major role.

Sensors and actuators have been used in the current grid for years. Their number will dramatically increase over the next few years in all areas of the Smart Grid from distribution to homes and buildings. Their communication models will be based on IP, end to end, which undoubtedly meets all of the stringent requirements of Smart Grid networks.

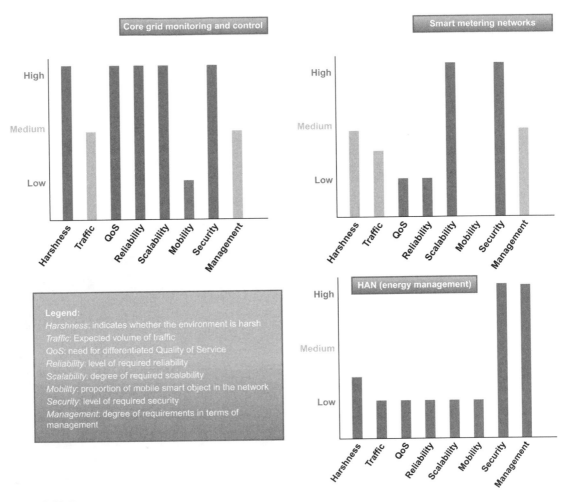

FIGURE 20.7

Summary of the technical challenges and characteristics for the use cases presented in this chapter.

Although a power grid managed by isolated/standalone communication control grid networks was a viable option a few years ago, the emergence of innovative applications for grid monitoring and control, DR, and many other applications makes the need for an end-to-end standardized-based communication protocol a must.

The adoption of IP end to end has a direct consequence on cost and manageability. The use of multiprotocol gateways interconnecting proprietary protocols is a non-starter considering the complexity of such a network, the scalability requirements, and cost pressure. IP-enabled smart objects connected to multi-service IP networks is a core component of Smart Grid networks, and these new generations of grid networks will dramatically change the way power is consumed for the better of our planet.

Industrial Automation

Industrial automation is the automation of industrial processes by means of modern computer-assisted technology. It is a broad industry comprised of many segments and application domains. A common way to divide the industrial automation market is according to the type and characteristics of the process:

- Process manufacturing (continuous processes) is the branch of manufacturing that deals with formulas and raw material. The output cannot be distilled back to its basic components, for example, food, paper, steel, ore.
- Discrete manufacturing (manufacturing of discrete units) is the branch that deals with orders and parts. The output is easily identifiable things, for example, cars, toys, computers.

The opportunities for wireless communication within the industrial automation market are growing at a rapid rate for several reasons. One reason is the available access to difficult locations and hazardous areas in the plant. For these applications, maintenance and diagnostic tasks can be accomplished more quickly, effectively, and safely using a wireless connection. Process manufacturing has an estimated growth rate of 32% per year, and is expected to become a $1.1 billion business by 2012 (see Figure 21.1). For discrete manufacturing the growth rate is estimated to be almost as high and is expected to grow from $400 million to over $800 million by 2012.[1]

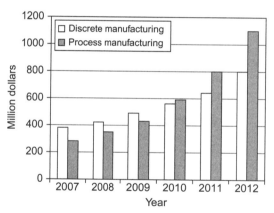

FIGURE 21.1

Worldwide market for wireless in discrete and process manufacturing.

21.1 OPPORTUNITIES

Industrial automation has always lagged behind telecommunications and consumer applications when it comes to adopting wireless communication technologies. This originates from the more stringent

---

[1]ARC Advisory Group, http://www.arcweb.com.

Interconnecting Smart Objects with IP. DOI: 10.1016/B978-0-12-375165-2.00021-1

performance and reliability requirements in industrial automation, and also from the conservative mind-sets in these industries. Wireless communication is, however, becoming more widespread in industry, especially since the recent ratifications of standards designed with industrial automation requirements in mind.[2]

During recent years, industrial automation vendors have moved forward and are now talking about *wireless infrastructure* as an important goal. The trend is to connect more than just sensors; the intention now is to provide a wireless backbone for everything in the plant from sensor information to portable human machine interfaces (HMIs) to mobile phones. However, it is important to note that most vendors currently see wireless technology as complementary to wired, and not as a replacement.

Discrete manufacturers are mainly focused on planning and deploying wireless infrastructures within their factories and assembly lines for measurement and service applications. In contrast, process manufacturers are focused more on cable replacement and mesh sensor networking technologies. Almost all standardization organizations have also made a clear distinction between these two industry segments and have created separate working groups to propose solutions that match their different requirements.

The use of wireless technologies in industrial automation provides new possibilities and advantages compared to the existing wired solutions. These technologies will enable easier access to more information related to the process and the equipment used in the process. Today, many plant automation installations only provide the basic process values, for example, temperature, flow, and pressure. There is a lot of valuable information such as the status and condition of the equipment and the addition of more process measurement points that offer a significant opportunity to increase the productivity of industrial installations. It is possible to access this information with wired sensors; however, the cost is prohibitive due to the required redesign, installation, and wiring. For some applications wiring is extremely expensive due to limited availability of space and hazardous areas, which puts requirements on the cables and connectors. This is where wireless technology provides a very attractive solution due to its nonintrusive nature. It is easier to retrofit wireless equipment on existing installations; they require no (or very little) wiring, which makes planning, design, and installation easier and more cost-effective.

Wireless technology also provides flexibility regarding scalability; it is easier to extend a network with more sensors than using wired technologies. Mobility is another attractive feature, which makes it easier to reconfigure a network by moving sensors to different positions if the application process is altered thus requiring sensors mounted in different locations.

Besides providing easy access to information, easier installation, and scaling, wireless technology opens up a range of new applications. It is now possible to mount sensors on rotating equipment such as rolling mills for paper and steel, robot swivels, and moving equipment. It is even more reliable to use wireless technologies since there will never be any cable or connector problems due to wear and tear, which often causes problems for swiveling equipment using wired solutions. Wireless also offers a cost-effective way to use temporary installations to fine-tune a process during a few months or collect statistical data and then remove the installation.

Recently the trend of industrial automation is to provide remote access possibilities to plants, or at least parts of plants (e.g., to remote control vehicles), and collect condition monitoring information. Wireless technology provides an easy way to connect to these industrial automation sites, especially sites located in remote parts of the world such as mines and onshore and offshore oil and gas fields.

---

[2]WirelessHART was ratified in September 2007 and ISA100.11a-2009 was ratified in September 2009.

With wireless access, the control room no longer has to be located on site; instead it can be located in or near population centers where people prefer to work and live. Actual personnel only need to travel to the site location for maintenance or if problems arise.

Wireless technology also enables a new field called the mobile workforce. In different vertical industries there are many areas where mobility can be leveraged to benefit a mobile workforce; for example, field maintenance, site survey, and localization. A wireless localization application makes it possible to find and track inventory and valuable assets and workers that are moving inside and outside of the plant. The ability to locate each worker quickly or to allow remote access to a site and the information it contains offers safety and productivity benefits.

All in all, wireless technology will open up many new possibilities within the industrial automation area.

21.2 CHALLENGES

For wireless communication technology to become successful in the industrial automation market there are many challenges that must be overcome. These challenges range from issues arising from the wireless communication technology, related technologies such as batteries and security, and plant automation control systems to the general mindset of people in the business.

One of the biggest hurdles wireless communication technology faces is the misconception of how easy the wireless communication is to compromise. This is because it is possible to sit outside the fence surrounding the plant site and eavesdrop on the plant traffic, inject fake traffic, or even jam the wireless signals. Therefore, all wireless communication technologies used in a plant must employ security mechanisms (e.g., encryption, authentication, integrity checking) to ensure unmolested communications.

The environment in which the wireless technology solution will operate is considered very harsh. A plant typically consists of metal constructions (pipes, walls, floors, machines, etc.) and moving equipment (forklifts), which create fading problems for wireless signals. In addition, there is electrical machinery (drives, welding), which affects the radio by causing electromagnetic interference (EMI) in the frequency spectrum.

Another important aspect is that the physical location of the wireless equipment is determined by the process that it monitors or controls, and not by where the radio communication environment is best.

In the face of these challenges it is important that wireless technology can deliver data reliably. Furthermore, many wireless industrial automation applications have very tough requirements for reliability such as wireless control and localization in safety critical areas. In wireless communication several different approaches for reliable communication exist. One solution is to employ mesh network topology; another approach is to add error control techniques.

As discussed in Section 21.1, industrial automation is a wide area that contains many applications and use cases, which in turn puts a wide range of requirements on the wireless communication. It is quite obvious that a single radio communication technology cannot satisfy all of the requirements on the physical layer; however, using a unified technology on a higher layer (IP) could be an advantage for many parts of the automation network, since there is a trend for wired communication (i.e., field buses) to use IP-based protocols.

Table 21.1 Generic Requirements for Industrial Automation Processes

Process attribute	Process manufacturing	Discrete manufacturing
Sensor types (data type)	Predominantly analog	Predominantly discrete
Production cycle length	100 days	Few hours to 1 day
Typical control loop times	1 to 1000 s	1 to 500 ms
Device density	Low	High
Devices per plant	10,000	10,000

Table 21.1 summarizes some of the important attributes of industrial automation processes. These attributes differ widely between the process and discrete manufacturing areas.

In the following list are some generic requirements that are important in industrial automation settings:

- Global availability: Industrial automation solutions have a requirement to be globally available, thus requiring the use of globally available frequency bands. Solutions are therefore operating in the unlicensed 2.4 GHz ISM band.[3] Unfortunately, this frequency band is used by many different communication technologies which in turn could cause potential interference problems.
- Coexistence: Industrial plants often contain many different wireless communication technologies that operate in the same frequency band, for example, IEEE 802.11- and IEEE 802.15-based technologies both operate in the 2.4 GHz ISM band. Thus, it is very important that a solution can coexist in a radio environment with a large amount of interference as well as limit its own disturbance.
- Lifetime: Most industrial automation systems have lifetimes measured in tens of years. During this lifetime equipment is expected to provide good availability and require a minimum of maintenance. Battery-powered wireless equipment is not expected to require a battery change more often than a few years, however, longer intervals are preferred.
- Security: As for all general wireless networking the security, authenticity (making sure data come from the correct sensor node), and integrity (making sure no one has tampered with the data) are very important.
- Interoperability: Using standardized equipment and communication is very important for most process plant owners. They want to be able to use equipment from different vendors, and they want it to work together seamlessly.

Preferably the new wireless technology should integrate into the existing plant automation system similar to wired technology. The challenge is that wireless technology will be used in new applications that take advantage of its features such as mobility and temporary installations. This is something that current plant automation systems cannot handle, so to capitalize on the wireless advantages these systems must be upgraded.

Different industrial applications will have very different requirements and will set different solutions, values, or bounds for each of these requirements. The solution developer must focus intently on

---

[3]ISM — Industrial, Scientific, and Medical, defined by the International Telecommunication Unit (ITU).

what the application requires. Then the challenge is to choose a set of network properties that will satisfy all application requirements (see Figure 21.2). The real objectives for any wireless industrial product are determined by the application in which it must perform, not by the technology deployed.

In industrial automation plants wireless technologies are deployed on a large scale, and the complexity of the wireless infrastructure is increasing. A major challenge is how to plan, deploy, and manage this in a cost-effective way. Multiple wireless technologies must be able to coexist in the same frequency band. One technology should preferably support multiple applications — for example, VoIP, video, and process data — on the same wireless network. To support this it must be possible to engineer and manage the infrastructure as well as guarantee minimum requirements on

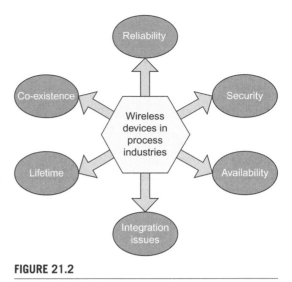

FIGURE 21.2

Key challenges in industrial automation.

Quality of Service, coexistence, positioning services, roaming, and security. The automation process in most cases is too costly to stop if a retrofit wireless installation is planned; therefore it should be possible to integrate it into the automation system without disturbing the running process.

21.3 USE CASES

With the use of wireless communication in industrial automation it is possible to access more information about the process and the devices connected to it. Furthermore, new use cases and applications arise that will improve the life cycle of the plant. This section describes three use cases in industrial automation with different requirements for latency, reliability, and data rate (see Figure 21.3).

21.3.1 Condition Monitoring

Condition monitoring is the first use case in which wireless technologies will be used for industrial automation. Condition monitoring is a very wide use case that contains many different applications. In general, it can be described as the collection

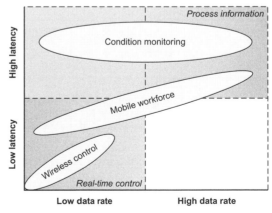

FIGURE 21.3

Three wireless use cases and their varying requirements.

of data related to the condition and status of machinery, which is used to predict failures, generate alarms, and schedule maintenance. Condition monitoring tasks are sometimes performed as manual labor; personnel have to travel to the site and manually collect data from the equipment or even visually inspect the condition.

A major driver for wireless condition monitoring is the ability to easily install a condition monitoring solution in an existing plant and hook it up to a condition analysis system. The condition monitoring system can be installed without interfering with the plant control system as a kind of add-on solution. Wireless technologies also make remote condition monitoring easier, as the condition information can be accessed from anywhere in the world.

There are many different parameters to monitor on the wide array of equipment and machinery used in industrial automation. It is very common to monitor the condition of rotating or swiveling equipment such as motors, pumps, fans, and robots that contain bearings. These are usually monitored using vibration analysis, but acoustic analysis is also used. Vibration is very common in industrial settings. Almost everything in a plant vibrates (machines, pipes, structures), which makes it a very good case for condition monitoring. Temperature is also a good indicator of the condition of the equipment, where a high temperature usually indicates a problem. Oil can be monitored to detect wear debris or even to detect release of certain gases detectable in the oil through gas chromatography, which is used to indicate equipment condition.

The following requirements are important for condition monitoring applications:

- Latency: The time delay from when data are produced (measured) to when they are available to the automation system, for example, distributed control or asset monitoring systems. The importance of latency varies, but it is not considered to be the most important requirement for condition monitoring. When it comes to actual latency requirements it is usually in the range of seconds or minutes.
- Duty cycle: The rate (period) with which new data are required to be produced and made available to the plant automation system. The duty cycle requirement varies from a few milliseconds to seconds to weeks (or even months) depending on the application. In some cases there is no strict cycle; instead the condition monitoring system or personnel determines (randomly) when measurements should be performed.
- Throughput: The bandwidth required to transport the data according to the duty cycle and latency requirements. The amount of data sent varies from application to application, ranging from sending a single temperature value once every few minutes to sending a full vibration time series collected over a few seconds every few seconds.
- Range: The range requirement for condition monitoring within a plant is usually a few hundred meters with line-of-sight to less than 100 m with no line-of-sight. For remote condition monitoring the range can be much longer. A range of several miles is required to connect to an offshore platform.

21.3.2 **Wireless Control**

Industrial automation control applications can be divided into two categories: real-time and event-based. For real-time control applications, process signals must be received within a specified amount of time to correctly operate the process. To support real-time control applications, networks often must be able to guarantee end-to-end communication deadlines. On the other hand, event-based control applications are more relaxed and wait until the signal is received (no deadline) before making any decisions.

For more than 30 years wired communication networks have been used for distributed control, but recent advances in wireless technologies have enabled wireless control to be used in industrial automation. The main benefits of introducing wireless networking in industrial control applications are cost, flexibility, and reliability. In many sites (chemical plants, refineries, oil platforms) distributed control systems are installed and a large number of controllers and instruments are distributed over the site and either connected by wired or wireless communication.

In process automation (i.e., chemicals, metals, and minerals) there are relatively slow-moving processes and the time constants range from seconds to minutes. One example is the flotation process. Flotation is a separation technique used in minerals, the paper industry, de-inking, and water treatment. The control program of the controller, for this kind of process, has a loop time of approximately 0.5 to 1 s, but the scan rate of analog or digital input/output devices (I/Os) is faster (in the range of 20 ms). The control is based on several measurements and control actions. The measured entities include conductivity, airflow, water flow, pH measurements, and tank levels. The control actions include air valves and water pumps and control loops such as level control, pump control (before and after the flotation series), and air- and slurry-flow control. A more challenging scenario is the metallurgy process of hot rolling, which must have control requirements in milliseconds. The rolling speed varies between passes: slow in the beginning and faster as the strip gets thinner. The speed may be as fast as 10 m/s and to reach the desired performance in the thickness control a sampling rate of 10 to 20 ms is usually needed.

Wireless control in discrete manufacturing differs quite substantially when compared to process automation, since the requirements at machine level are mission-critical and considerably more stringent than typical requirements for other areas. In an automotive assembly plant, up to 100,000 I/O points may be present in a dense area and small roundtable production machines can have up to ten devices per m^3 machine volume (300 per machine). Furthermore, fast response times are generally less than 15 ms, and it is important that coexistence is permitted in multiple cells; up to 300 devices in a single machine have to be supported. Most of the existing wireless systems/standards do not satisfy the needed balance of requirements such as latency versus data rate, reliability, power consumption, and node density. Some technologies are designed for high throughput applications between small numbers of terminals and have less stringent latency and power requirements.

Wireless communication systems for industrial automation and control must fulfill the following requirements:

- Device mounting: The orientation of the sensor and actuator nodes is very important and has a clear impact on reliability and latency. A misplaced device can cause decreased throughput or increased delay.
- Latency: Ranges from milliseconds to minutes depending on the specific application.
- Duty cycle: The rate (period) with which new data are required to be produced and made available to the control system. As mentioned, typical duty cycle requirements for control applications range from a few milliseconds to seconds.

21.3.3 Mobile Workforce

Information and Communication Technology (ICT) has a dramatic impact on the productivity of industrial installations. With the advent of wireless technologies, engineering tasks carried out through portable or detachable HMI units are now very common in all industries. Wireless technologies can improve productivity by effectively supporting more flexible work processes that are not hindered or limited by the location of plant personnel relative to the process and control equipment they need to install, configure, operate, and maintain. The main objective of the mobile workforce area is to optimize the workflow of a plant throughout its life cycle.

Asset tracking and local access to devices enable a faster installation and commissioning procedure. In addition, direct access to the maintenance and control systems while in the field can streamline the process even further, such as effectively supporting check-in/check-out processes where physical presence in the plant is required. Error-prone off-line work can be moved to online updates with support for automated validation and verification.

As a way to lower operation costs and improve product quality, the level of plant automation is increasing. This means that fewer operators (personnel) are required to run the plants, and that the role and scope of the operator are expanding to cover a larger part of the plant's operation. To support this, mobile access to plant information is essential as one person will need to handle device specifics while controlling the total system. If specific information or control actions are restricted to the control room, this type of operation is impossible. Also, as the number of dedicated people for specific process sections decreases, asset tracking and localization will play an important role to help guide operators and service personnel to the right place within the plant. Collaborative support functions will also become more important, as the experts will not necessarily be available on site when a problem occurs. Support for streaming (video, voice, and data) to a remote expert can help solve critical issues in a timely manner and avoid expensive emergency service calls (especially important for plants located in remote locations where travel is prohibitive).

The main benefits of asset monitoring and service come from two aspects:

- The mobility aspect is access to any information, at any time, from anywhere. It enables online integrated access to computerized maintenance systems (CMMS). This eliminates error-prone off-line double work as the data can be updated and validated during a service or maintenance task.
- The ability to automatically identify and locate devices supports asset tracking and audit tasks. Location-dependent services help speed up routine maintenance as well as troubleshooting tasks. Information and actions can be dynamically adapted based on the service person's location in the plant, and the location-dependent service can highlight that a device in close proximity needs a maintenance check.

The ability to precisely locate a person within a plant can also be used to improve the safety of the workforce. Proximity to a potentially dangerous situation on the plant floor can be signaled to the worker. Virtual safety functions can be implemented so that the mobile worker is able to safely stop the operation of the plant within a defined proximity. This improves productivity as the shutdown can be limited (in a dynamic manner) and improves safety as the worker always has an emergency stop on hand.

Sensors carried by workers can be used to monitor their health and signal if an emergency situation occurs (notify other plant personnel, or even initiate a shutdown in the area where the worker is located).

The following requirements are important to mobile workforce applications:

- Latency: This is important to certain aspects of the mobile workforce such as localization to warn personnel when entering dangerous areas or performing emergency shutdowns. On the other hand, accessing system documents when inspecting faulty equipment does not require minimum latency.

- Throughput: For the mobile workforce it is important to have access to all data in the system such as voice, video, and sensor data. High-quality video streaming could have a fairly high requirement on the throughput (as well as latency).
- Range: The range for a localization service within a plant usually requires coverage of the plant size (tens of thousands of square meters), while remote maintenance range requirements are several miles, or possibly even global access.
- Multiprotocol: When plant operators move around in the plant it is important that they have access to the plant information wherever they are using whatever wireless technology is operating in the vicinity. It is not feasible to have to change equipment (PDA, phone, laptop) just to be able to communicate; the portable communication equipment must be able to seamlessly switch between different technologies.

21.4 CONCLUSIONS

Industrial automation has traditionally been performed with wired systems. Wireless communication is rapidly emerging in industrial communication due to the increased ease of installation with wireless systems as well as the ability to install systems in locations where wired systems are cumbersome or impossible. Examples of such places are rotating machinery or highly mobile systems.

Industrial automation systems are used for condition monitoring, control applications, and the mobile workforce. Common to all industrial automation applications are the requirements for global availability of components, coexistence between wired and wireless technologies, lifetime, security, and interoperability. Wireless technology is rapidly emerging to meet these needs.

Smart Cities and Urban Networks

22

22.1 INTRODUCTION

In 1900, only 13% of the world's population lived in cities. By 2050, that number will have risen to 70%. Vibrant and creative cities drive economic, social, and cultural development. This urbanization is both an emblem of our economic and societal progress and a challenging strain on the urban infrastructure.

The integration of Information and Communication Technology (ICT) with development projects can change the urban landscape by developing Smart Cities. Smart Cities can dramatically improve their citizens' quality of life, encourage business to invest, and create a sustainable urban environment. As illustrated throughout this chapter by means of several use cases, smart object networks will play a critical role in making Smart Cities a reality.

A number of cities have started to enable smart object networks in support of a number of new services. Transport officials in Singapore, Brisbane, and Stockholm are using smart systems to reduce congestion and pollution. Public safety officials in major cities like New York are not only able to solve crimes and respond to emergencies, but also to help prevent them. City managers in Albuquerque, New Mexico, have achieved a 2000% improvement in efficiency in sharing information across agencies, keeping citizens informed, and providing critical municipal services from residential and commercial development to water to public safety. A large hospital organization in Paris is implementing an integrated patient-care-management solution to facilitate seamless communication across its business applications enabling them to track every stage of a patient's stay in the hospital. Many cities in the world have deployed smart object networks to efficiently manage outdoor lighting management systems, thus performing proactive maintenance and significantly reducing energy consumption. Personal Travel Assistant, a company launched in Seoul, South Korea, helps residents reduce personal carbon footprint, transit costs, and travel time via their new, web-based service. Furthermore, this company is developing a metropolitan area sensor network in Beijing for high-resolution monitoring of urban environments. These are just a few examples of new services improving the quality of life of citizens in cities, reducing the carbon footprint, and contributing to green initiatives because of innovative smart object networks.

Smart Cities require a large ubiquitous IP network interconnecting a myriad of devices via various links (fixed and wireless) in support of a number of new services[1] such as

- Transport: Traffic flow management, speed control, congestion charging, information systems, vehicle tracking, onboard safety, parking management

---

[1] See *Smart City*, PA Consulting Group at http://www.paconsulting.com/.

Interconnecting Smart Objects with IP. DOI: 10.1016/B978-0-12-375165-2.00022-3

- Public safety and security: Access control systems, alarm monitoring, emergency warning, and situation management
- Public services: Remote patient monitoring, patient records management, education/learning networks
- Identity: Biometric/smart card systems
- Utilities: Facilities management (e.g., energy, water), climate control, energy generation and storage management, water/gas leak detection, and network management
- Environment: Data collection and monitoring (noise, pollution, etc.)
- Social networking

This chapter specifically focuses on smart object networks; needless to say that high-speed networks are also needed to support other services such as video, telephony, etc.

Smart object networks will consist of smart objects of a different nature such as magnetic, thermal, visual, seismic, infrared, acoustic, and radar, which are able to monitor a wide variety of ambient conditions that include temperature, humidity, sunlight, soil makeup, air makeup, noise levels, pollution, energy, presence or absence of certain kinds of objects, mechanical stress levels, and so on.

In the rest of this chapter, three use cases for smart object networks in Smart Cities are considered: urban environmental monitoring, social networking, and intelligent transport systems.

22.2 URBAN ENVIRONMENTAL MONITORING

Pervasive computing (in particular, sensing and actuation) can be used to monitor and control various natural and infrastructure systems that affect the urban environment. The following use cases provide an overview of several pervasive sensing applications and their use in the context of urban environmental monitoring.

22.2.1 Urban Ecosystem Monitoring

We are living in an increasingly urbanized world. Further increases in size and rates of population growth will no doubt increase the stress on the environment. While urbanization is an important driver of environmental changes, it is not the only urban-related influence. The conversion of land to urban uses, the extraction and depletion of natural resources, and the disposal of urban wastes as well as urbanization in general are having a global impact.[2] To provide a "healthy" environment both for citizens and for the natural ecosystem, the city should be viewed as an organic body with metabolic processes.[3] Inputs and outputs should be measured by pervasive sensing, and this information can help determine the source of pollution and the appropriate action to preserve the environment.

This requires the deployment of a dense smart object network across the city to implement pervasive and multifunctional monitoring. Such networks are comprised of various sensors (temperature, humidity, radiation, light intensity, etc.) deployed in cities to enable real-time monitoring of the urban ecosystem. These smart objects, mounted on buildings, streetlights, and cars, gather data autonomously transmitted to data centers via a private IP network or the Internet for further analysis. As discussed in Chapter 10, data may also be interpreted by the network (referred to as "local processing"). Note that in some cases, mobile sensors and actuators may require location-positioning systems.

---

[2] World Resources Institute, 1997.
[3] Abe Wolman, 1965.

There are many implemented systems and ongoing research projects of environmental smart object networks. The US Department of Natural Resources and Parks has built water-quality monitoring systems in King County, Washington.[4] The UK government supports an urban pollution monitoring project comprised of a number of mobile sensing systems that give a broader and denser picture of how pollution affects urban spaces and the people within them.[5] In Singapore, the Singapore-MIT Alliance for Research and Technology (SMART) has been working on the use of a wireless sensor network for the continuous monitoring of water distribution systems. This research includes a low-cost wireless sensor network for high data rate collection and online monitoring of hydraulic parameters within large urban water distributed systems. Water-quality parameters (i.e., pH, chlorine residual, turbidity, conductivity, and dissolved oxygen) are also monitored. The system can use high-frequency pressure measurements of hydraulic transient events to detect leaks and predict pipe bursts remotely.[6]

The amount of environmental data of interest is very large and fast growing: air-quality monitoring, water-quality monitoring, temperature and humidity monitoring, microenvironmental sunlight monitoring, weather condition monitoring, environmental pollution monitoring, exhaust emission monitoring, waste discharge monitoring, and soil pollution monitoring.

Information can be accessible to citizens or may exclusively be used by the city. This highlights the need for various information management models that have different security requirements.

22.2.1.1 Resource Management

Energy and water management (see examples illustrated in Figure 22.1 and 22.2) are critical resources that must be managed with great care in large cities.

Home and building energy management is absolutely critical and Smart Grids will play a key role in energy saving and carbon footprint reduction. Efficient energy management systems developed for

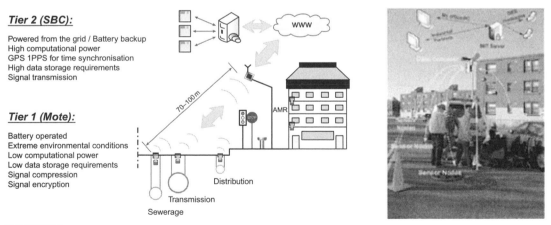

Tier 2 (SBC):

Powered from the grid / Battery backup
High computational power
GPS 1PPS for time synchronisation
High data storage requirements
Signal transmission

Tier 1 (Mote):

Battery operated
Extreme environmental conditions
Low computational power
Low data storage requirements
Signal compression
Signal encryption

70–100 m

AMR

Distribution

Transmission

Sewerage

FIGURE 22.1

Prototype monitoring system for water distribution network.

[4] http://www.kingcounty.gov/environment/data-and-trends/monitoring-data.aspx.
[5] http://www.equator.ac.uk/index.php/articles/563.
[6] http://censam.mit.edu/research/res2/index.html#s1.

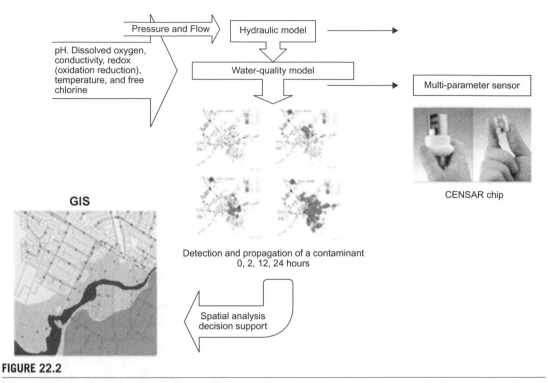

FIGURE 22.2

Integrated hydraulic and water-quality monitoring system.

homes in the context of the Smart Grid also apply to buildings in cities (see Chapters 20 and 22). Additionally, public infrastructures such as road lighting can be more efficiently managed due to the deployment of IP smart object networks. Networks where each light is equipped with a sensor have been deployed to perform proactive maintenance and even dynamic lighting management according to several external factors such as the local environment, the presence of cars or citizens in the areas, etc., with the objective of reducing cost but also providing a better lighting service to citizens. Systems such as ROAM [122] provide a complete lighting management system as shown in Figure 22.3.

Water management in large cities is also a key component and an important expense. Similar to the energy management systems, smart object networks can be used to optimize water consumption in the city and detect water leaks in the ground, which is a fairly frequent source of water wastage.

Such networks are usually static, with mostly multipoint-to-point traffic patterns with moderate Quality of Service (QoS) requirements. One of their prime characteristics is to be large scale. Such road lighting management networks have been deployed with millions of nodes.

22.2.2 Natural Hazards Monitoring and Early Detection

Natural hazards monitoring and forecasting is another important application for smart object networks. In contrast with urban ecosystem monitoring, natural hazards monitoring needs to meet more stringent and complicated design requirements. The monitoring network must cover large

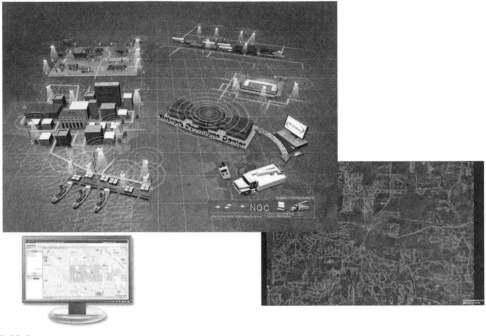

FIGURE 22.3

ROAM lighting management networks.

geographical regions in which natural hazards may occur while avoiding "blind zones." The system must operate throughout long disaster-free periods, measure a variety of variables contributing to the hazard, and communicate over potentially large geographical regions. When the event damages the environment, such as with floods or hurricanes, this further complicates the requirements. This system must withstand the event, which usually poses a hazard to network survival and survival of the smart objects directly measuring the event. Typical smart objects used in hazard monitoring include volcano monitoring sensors, seismic sensors, tsunami early warning systems, slope deformation monitoring sensors, and so forth.

Early warning flood detection is one type of natural hazard monitoring. In many developing countries, current systems for flood detection still rely on human observations. People read the river level off of markings and the rain level from water collecting gauges several times a day and manually send their reports. Comparison with previous records provides some indication of potential hazards that may occur. Overall, this detection system is not very reliable, because there is a lack of enough measurements, quick aggregation, and accurate prediction. More sophisticated smart object networks performing continuous measurements are required to improve the level of prediction.

Forest fire modeling and early detection are important to control and prevent this natural hazard. Traditionally, forest fires are detected using fire lookout towers located at high points. Charged coupled device (CCD) cameras and infrared (IR) detectors are installed on top of towers. In case of fire or detection of smoke, the system alerts local fire departments, residents, and industries. But the accuracy of these systems is largely affected by weather conditions, and it is difficult to avoid blind zones with a small number of towers. Smart object networks are critical for building near real-time forest fire detection systems. Large-scale wireless sensor networks can be easily deployed with good coverage using airplanes. Sensors can then monitor a variety of variables including temperature, relative humidity, and smoke that help to precisely detect fire. The communication range of the sensor node is usually limited to save power and increase lifetime. Similar to the other examples, such distributed smart object networks can be self-formed using IPv6 as the networking protocol and RPL (see Chapter 17) as the routing protocol.

Figure 22.4 shows a typical forest fire detection system. Nodes are self-organized into "clusters" where cluster heads aggregate collected data and report to a data processing center. Some sensor nodes are kept in idle or sleep mode to save energy. The shaded area represents a forest zone with higher fire potential that needs to be monitored by more active sensors. Smart object networks can make use of the Internet or any other private IP networks to send their report to data centers. This can be seen as an example of overlay network as discussed in Chapter 10.

22.2.3 Technical Characteristics and Challenges

Smart object networks used for urban ecosystem monitoring and natural hazards monitoring present a series of technical challenges.

22.2.3.1 The Networking Environment

Urban environmental networks are mostly outdoor networks and the connectivity between smart objects may be greatly affected by the nature of the links used in these environments. Multipath effect and channel fading vary significantly with the environment. For example, a wireless channel on a

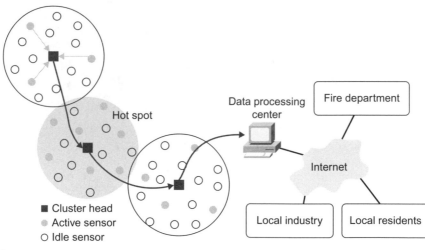

FIGURE 22.4

Architecture of a typical forest fire detection system.

(Source: MOHAMED HEFEEDA. Forest Fire Modeling and Early Detection Using Wireless Sensor Networks. Simon Fraser University, Canada.)

rainy day is much worse than on sunny days. Moreover, the shielding of buildings and other spatial factors will cause significant asymmetry in a wireless channel. This is one of the reasons why Powerline communication (PLC) is used in some cases.

22.2.3.2 Traffic Flows and Network Topologies
In general, traffic flows are between nodes and information collectors (that may be distributed in the network for local data processing) and data centers. The up-streaming traffic flows are significantly higher than the down-streaming ones. There are also scenarios where data are exchanged directly between sensors and actuators for immediate actions. Networks have different topologies, but mesh network topologies are very frequent.

22.2.3.3 Smart Object and Link Characteristics
As discussed in length in Chapters 11 and 12, sensor technology has dramatically progressed over the past decade regarding size, power consumption, and reliability. However, miniaturization, cost reduction, and low-power consumption are still necessary for environmental sensors, which will undoubtedly be developed soon. The additional requirement for natural hazard monitoring applications is the high level of sensitivity, stability, and accuracy of sensors even in extremely harsh environments.

Environmental smart object networks are complex wireless multi-hop networks. Sensor nodes are usually deployed in harsh environments, and these networks are usually unattended in remote geographic areas; thus links may be unstable and vulnerable to interferences.

22.2.3.4 QoS and Network Reliability
QoS and network reliability requirements greatly vary with applications. Urban environment monitoring is usually delay-tolerant and a network outage of a few hours is usually not a major issue. In contrast, natural hazard monitoring requires low latency and a high level of reliability.

22.2.3.5 Scalability
The number of sensor nodes deployed in monitoring environments may be of the order of hundreds or thousands or even millions of nodes. Moreover, the network used in urban sensing must be scalable from medium scale (district area) to large scale (metropolitan area).

22.2.3.6 Mobility
Recent advances in mobile communications trigger research in mobile wireless sensor networks, and hybrid structures provide more effective and flexible networks with a mix of fixed and mobile nodes. Fixed nodes with higher computational and power resources can be deployed as urban infrastructure in some hot spots, whereas mobile nodes (usually more constrained) are used to augment the sensing coverage.

22.2.3.7 Security
Security requirements are very high. Such networks must be highly secured to prevent tampering, both at the hardware level as well as data and management levels. Authentication and encryption technologies are mandatory.

22.2.3.8 Network Management
Because of the large networking scale and its vital function to the population, network management is a key concern. Most systems today have been produced as research platforms and require

considerable technical expertise to be deployed and managed. There are ongoing efforts in self-management and self-configuration to evolve toward remote and unattended usability.

22.3 SOCIAL NETWORKS

In the first decade of the twenty-first century, Social Network Services (SNSs) have captured the attention of millions of people and millions of dollars from investors all over the world. They have encouraged new ways to communicate and share information. Until now, most SNSs were web based and offered similar basic functions such as a network of friends, blogging, e-mail, instant messaging, discussion forums or communities, commenting, and media uploading. Facebook, MySpace, Twitter, LinkedIn, Tagged, as well as content-sharing web sites like YouTube and Flickr, are all fast growing social networks that provide a variety of ways for users to interact for various social and professional purposes, transforming the Web into a social platform.

Smart objects performing a variety of tasks (e.g., activity recognition, location, condition sensing) are now available by the millions embedded in mobile devices (e.g., cellphones, PDAs, laptops, devices on personal vehicles). Considering the increasing popularity of SNSs, along with the increasing usage of instant messages as a replacement to e-mails in the business world and otherwise, there is undoubtedly a strong incentive for sharing information learned from sensed data as well. Recently, applications that integrated social networks and smart object networks such as Wireless Sensor Networks (WSNs) that enabled novel developments in communications have been a high topic of interest. A few key applications of successful integration of SNSs and smart object networks are the extension of web-based SNSs for monitoring the elderly and kids. There are many other examples such as a mobile sensing system for outdoor game communities.

22.3.1 Extension of Web-based SNSs

Online SNSs have been extensively used by millions of people and the extension of web-based SNSs that take advantage of smart objects (e.g. sensors) is definitely appealing. In this section, we introduce two applications to show how WSNs bring the SNSs from the Internet into daily lives. CenceMe and the identification of social acquaintances in localized areas are examples of WSNs.

CenceMe is a component of the MetroSense Project [174], a collaborative project sponsored by Dartmouth College, NSF, Intel, Nokia, and Motorola, that is developing new applications, classification techniques, privacy approaches, and sensing paradigms for mobile phones to establish a global mobile sensor network capable of societal-scale sensing. CenceMe is a personal sensing system that enables members of social networks to share their sensing presence with their friends in a secure manner. A sensing presence captures a user's status regarding activity (e.g., sitting, walking, meeting friends), disposition (e.g., happy, sad, doing okay), habits (e.g., at the gym, coffee shop today, at work), and surroundings (e.g., noisy, hot, bright, high ozone). CenceMe injects a sensing presence into popular social networking applications such as Facebook, MySpace, and IM (Skype, Pidgin) allowing new levels of "connection" and implicit communication (albeit nonverbal) between friends in social networks. The CenceMe system is implemented, in part, as a thin-client on a number of standard and sensor-enabled cell phones and offers a number of services that can be activated on a per "buddy" basis to expose different degrees of a user's sensing presence including: life patterns, presence, friend feeds, social interaction, significant places, buddy search, and buddy beacon.

Currently, a number of mobile devices have been integrated into the CenceMe system: the Nokia N800 Internet Tablet, Nokia N95, Nokia 5500 Sport, Moteiv Tmote Mini (above the N95), and the prototype BlueCel accessory (above the 5500). Each sensing client is configured to periodically push its sensed data to the CenceMe core. All of a user's processed sensor data can be viewed via a web browser by logging into the user's account on the CenceMe portal. Additionally, a subset of the user's status information is made available to the user's buddies (subject to his configured sharing policies) through their CenceMe portal pages, and through plug-ins to popular social networking applications. Figure 22.5 shows a snapshot of a user's data page on the CenceMe portal. Figure 22.6 shows the architecture of the CenceMe system.

Identifying social acquaintances in localized areas was an idea put forward by the W3C workshop on the future of social networking [123]. Today at conferences a social network site or forum is often supplied by the organizers to let attendees define and maintain their social network and discuss particular topics. When an attendee finds someone sharing similar interests, there is no other way to have a face-to-face conversation apart from sending e-mails and organizing a meeting at a certain place at a certain time. Equipped with smart devices integrating WSNs and SNSs, the attendees can make the experience much more efficient and convenient. Benefiting from the system, which can indentify

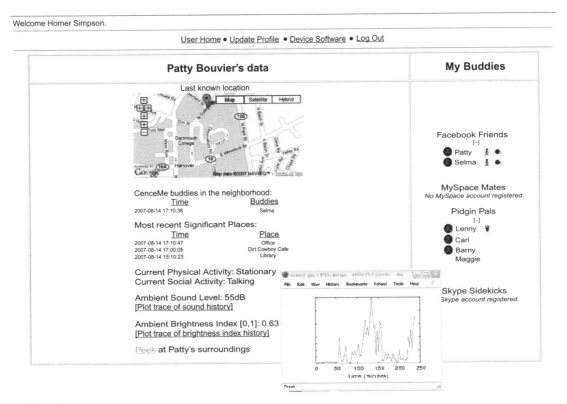

FIGURE 22.5

Snapshot of the CenceMe portal.

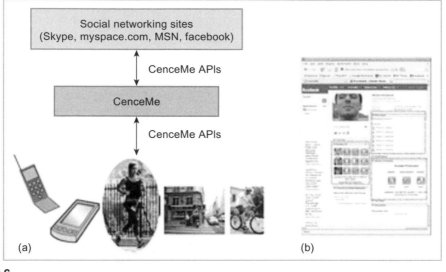

FIGURE 22.6

Architecture of CenceMe.

users' precise locations and define information from the social network sites, people can be reminded when they come across someone special. For instance, one might receive an alert on his mobile phone as soon as someone he wants to meet or exchange messages with on a forum appears in a shared place.

22.3.2 Monitoring the Elderly and Kids

Applications in this section show another usage of smart objects for monitoring the elderly and kids, which helps with family healthcare and communications. Without a doubt such applications will grow very quickly.

Social networks and WSNs can also be combined to support independent living and healthcare for the elderly [130]. By deriving a semantic presence based on context from sensor-enabled social networking devices, useful tasks can be carried out for the elderly. For example, for daily living purposes the network can check the status of friends and find shopping or walking buddies to promote mobility. By using semantic representations of information from smart objects, one can build on the idea of connecting people through shared activities and interests. More important, the system can send alerts based on abnormal activity patterns or a change in life dynamics. Through sensor readings of body position or health measurements, requests can be issued for attention not just to clinicians but to nearby friends in the elderly person's social network. Social science and medical research have consistently pointed to social engagement as an important indicator and predictor of health status.

Monitoring kids is another important application. The new *num8* watch by *Lok8u* has a GPS tracking device and satellite positioning system concealed inside so that parents can locate the wearer to within 10 feet on Google maps. The watch can be tightly fastened to a kid's wrist and it can send an alert if forcibly removed. Parents can see the location of their child on Google maps by clicking "where r you" on a secure web site or texting "wru" to a special number. Safe zones can also be programmed with parents alerted if their kids stray outside this zone. The makers of the *num8* watch claim it gives peace of mind to parents and makes children more independent.

22.3.3 Technical Characteristics and Challenges

Most of the smart object networks integrated with social networks share common characteristics and present similar technical challenges.

22.3.3.1 The Networking Environment

Most smart object networks operate in fairly harsh environments due to the channel uncertainty and complex, strong interferences in the ISM band. In indoor networks, the prediction for transmission fading is rather difficult while the power decay is considerable. Considering common urban use cases, a variety of disturbances (i.e., other radios used for other purposes) exist in personal areas and the multipath effects are obvious due to the reflection and shelter of obstacles (e.g., buildings, vehicles). In outdoor networks, link quality is highly dependent on the environment.

22.3.3.2 Traffic Flows and Network Topologies

For social network communications, most traffic flows are burst traffic embedded with audio, video, or SMS services. Traffic flows greatly vary from point-to-multipoint (P2MP), multipoint-to-point to point-to-point (P2P), and P2P traffic is certainly very common.

22.3.3.3 Smart Objects and Link Characteristics

Smart objects used in these networks share the same characteristics: cheap, flexible, spatially distributed, and autonomous. The smart objects used in social networks are mostly embedded in users' portable devices such as mobile phones and laptops, thus they can be recharged periodically. However, this does not mean that power consumption is not an issue. Sensors used for social communication are highly information-rich and should monitor various types of quantities including temperature, sound, slope, healthy parameters, images, and so on.

22.3.3.4 QoS

The social wireless network is a multi-QoS system. The required QoS varies with the application. Real-time data (e.g., sounds, images, texts) are usually quite demanding regarding throughput, delay, jitter, and so on. At the other end of the spectrum, short messages and location reports do not require high QoS.

22.3.3.5 Scalability

Scalability is not a pivotal characteristic in social applications. The scalability of these smart object networks is usually limited to a few dozen or a few hundred smart objects.

22.3.3.6 Reliability Requirement

As for requirement on reliability, it is not as high as that of public applications. But the requirement of security, especially privacy, is quite essential for human-involved systems.

22.3.3.7 Mobility

In social sensing, the support of tracking and sensing of mobile targets with mobile sensing devices is essential. Mobility is one of the keys to success for the integration of smart object networks and

SNSs. With the exception of a few fixed sensors such as smart objects equipped at the checkpoints in orienteering resorts, most of the sensors keep moving together with the users. Thus it is a real challenge to build and maintain mobile sensing systems in both complex urban environments and outdoor terrains.

To improve the ability of spatial network organization and management, it is essential to model the mobility of an ad hoc network. Seeing the tight link between the mobility of an ad hoc network and human movement, research focusing on modeling users' movement patterns has been performed (see [182]). This research reported that movement of humans is strongly impacted by the need to socialize in one form or another. Humans are known to associate in particular ways that can be mathematically modeled. Research also proposed a new mobility model founded on social network theory. [139] studies the internal relation between the relative movement of mobile users and users' social attributes. By quantizing users' social attributes, the studies created the Attractor Matrix, which described the relationship of human relative movements as a guide for modeling the user mobility for ad hoc networks.

22.3.3.8 Security
Needless to say, security is another priority of social applications. As social networks become increasingly smarter, great concerns about the privacy of the information shared among peers on social network services arise. Indeed, people want to keep a clear view and total control on what is shared and with whom. With the ability to set sensing presence information on user profiles dynamically on these services from mobile applications directly, users are more concerned about what the system really knows about them and shares with others. Note that location tracking is already possible with existing cell phones, but the amount of shared data is further increased in this case. These concerns tend to inhibit innovation in social network services because most new usages allowed by location techniques or context-aware information retrieval give users the impression of a loss of control [86].

22.3.3.9 Network Management
WSNs in social applications are a typical example of networks that must be self-managed and require minimal configuration from the end user. Smart devices must be self-configured with autodiscovery and automatic computing.

22.4 INTELLIGENT TRANSPORT SYSTEMS
As the demand of transportation increases, traffic congestion becomes a major concern in most large cities. Thus Intelligent Transportation System (ITS) is one of the key challenges for the future. ITS varies in technologies applied from basic management systems such as car navigation to dynamic traffic signal control systems, variable message signs, automatic car plate recognition, and speed cameras to monitoring applications such as security CCTV systems to even more advanced applications that integrate live data and feedback from a number of other sources such as parking guidance and information systems, weather information, and bridge deicing systems. Smart object networks play an important role in most of those systems. Most ITSs rely on smart object networks for communication; for example, the dynamic traffic light sequence system relies on the sensor nodes distributed both on roadside and vehicles to define the traffic flow condition. The car navigation system relies on

the wireless sensor network established among vehicles and control center to monitor and control the traffic condition, and most automatic road enforcement and charging systems identify the vehicles with RFID.

The following use cases provide an overview of the applications of smart object networks in traffic monitoring and automatic charging systems.

22.4.1 Traffic Monitoring and Controlling

22.4.1.1 Dynamic Traffic Light Sequence

Traffic congestion and tidal flow management were recognized as major problems in modern urban areas and have caused much frustration and loss of man hours. Several technologies have been developed to ease the frustration. The image processing system gives the quantitative description of traffic flow by processing the image of vehicles captured by roadside cameras. The major problem with this system is the high false acceptance rate (FAR) and high false rejection rate (FRR) under the situation of jam-packed traffic due to the aliasing between the images of different vehicles. The second technique is called the beam interruption technique, which determines the number of vehicles by counting the times the beam is interrupted and sends it from one side of the road and receives it on the other side. The problem with this technique is that parallel vehicles would be counted only once; furthermore, in a multi-driveway road, the interruption caused by the vehicle closer to the beam sender could be possibly continued by vehicles on the driveway relatively far from the sender without interval. This makes a long-lasting interruption so the system struggles to determine exactly how many vehicles passed by. The WSN solution suffers none of these problems.

New technologies based on smart objects have been developed. In one of these systems, each vehicle is identified by a WiFi Access Point (WAP) from an RFID tag, thus forming a wireless sensor network. The WAP then collects and relays the information through the wireless network to the data center, which analyzes and processes it for optimized traffic light sequence. Dynamic traffic light sequence has circumvented or avoided the problems that came with previous systems that used image processing and beam interruption techniques. RFID technology with appropriate algorithms and databases were applied to multi-vehicle, multi-lane, and multi-road junction areas to provide an efficient time management scheme. A dynamic time schedule was worked out for each car lane.

RFID together with WSN technologies are anticipated to create a revolution in traffic management and control systems. The database contains online statistical information, which can be used by operators and planners to develop better models in the future.

This system relies on algorithms based on the traffic flow model. Simulations show that a proper strategy makes a remarkable improvement. However, it is difficult to find a general model that performs well in all traffic conditions, especially when traffic conditions change throughout the day. Ideally the system should be self-adaptive, which means that historical data should be memorized and taken into account.

22.4.1.2 Traffic Condition Monitoring and Control

One of the main objectives of ITS is to monitor and control traffic conditions. One of the well-known approaches is a system called COOPERS in which WSNs play an important role (see [121] for further reference). COOPERS is an acronym for CO-OPerative systEms for intelligent Road Safety and is a European research and development and innovation activity within the Call 4 (Co-operative

Systems and in vehicle integrated safety systems) of the 6th Framework Program by the European Commission–Information Society and Media. The COOPERS approach extends the concepts of in-vehicle autonomous systems and vehicle-to-vehicle communication (V2V) with tactical and strategic traffic information provided in real time by the infrastructure operator. Infrastructure to vehicle communication (I2V) in this respect will significantly improve traffic control and safety via effective and reliable transmission of data fully adapted to the local situation of the vehicle (ensemble of vehicles). I2V will extend the responsibility of the infrastructure operator compared to today regarding accuracy and reliability of information to drivers. The highest effect of I2V communication will be achieved in areas of dense traffic areas where risk of accidents and traffic jams is extremely high. Conversely, the real-time communication link between infrastructure and vehicle can also be used for V2I (vehicle to infrastructure) communication utilizing vehicles as floating sensors to verify infrastructure sensor data as a primary source for traffic control measures.

Given that traffic condition monitoring and control requires high accuracy and real-time information, the networking infrastructure is essential. A pure noncentralized network can hardly meet the demand because of stability, delays, and accuracy. However, the V2V communication as a supplement to the system shows the characteristics of self-organizing networks, which makes it a typical smart object network.

22.4.1.3 Vehicle Coordination Calculating and Sharing

The ideal solution to traffic condition informing is a coordination system in which vehicles are able to calculate and share their own coordination and velocity by communicating with other vehicles or a fixed facility through a wireless network. As soon as the coordination system is established, drivers become aware of the traffic condition of a certain area by the density of vehicles with the coordination within the area.

There are three types of nodes installed in this system: the vehicle unit on the individual vehicle; the roadside unit along both sides of a road, and the intersection unit on the intersection. The vehicle unit (installed in every vehicle) measures the vehicle parameters and transfers the data to the roadside units. The roadside unit gathers the information of the vehicles in the neighborhood and transfers it to the intersection unit. (Roadside units are installed on the lampposts along both sides of the road approximately every 50 to 200 m according to the wireless cover range.) The intersection unit receives and analyzes the information from other units and passes them to the strategy subsystem. Such a system is depicted in Figure 22.7 where the intersection unit, roadside units, and vehicle units are denoted as A, B, and C. Roadside units broadcast messages every second. The message includes its identifier (ID) and its relative location to the intersection. The vehicle unit is put in the listening mode. When a vehicle receives the broadcast message, the vehicle unit switches to active mode. If a vehicle unit receives messages from more than three nodes, it can calculate the location (x, y) and velocity v. Then, the vehicle unit sends the information (x, y, v) to the roadside unit nearby. The roadside units collect and compute the information from the vehicle nodes around, and pass on the information to the intersection unit one by one remotely. Since a massive amount of data is received from the vehicles, the roadside units aggregate the data before transferring them. The intersection unit is connected to the strategy subsystem directly. Then the strategy subsystem calculates an optimized scheme to control and/or guide the execution subsystem. This subsystem provides information such as signal light, variable message sign, GPS navigation system, and so on. The roadside unit distributes on both sides of a road. A roadside unit only collects vehicle information in one direction.

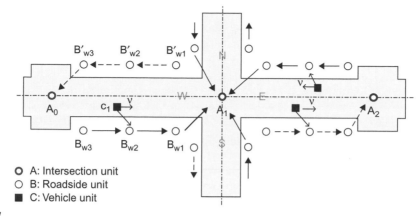

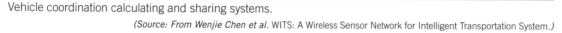

FIGURE 22.7

Vehicle coordination calculating and sharing systems.

(Source: From Wenjie Chen et al. WITS: A Wireless Sensor Network for Intelligent Transportation System.)

22.4.1.4 Parking Lot Monitoring

Many existing systems that monitor parking lot occupancy require installation during the construction of the structure. Systems implemented in existing lots typically require complex installation. Furthermore, the information captured by these systems is typically confined to the structure in which it is captured. A smart object network such as a WSN typically provides a cheap infrastructure that can be easily installed after construction. For example, UCLA implemented a low-cost, easy-to-install parking lot occupancy monitoring system that integrates with an online database to provide parking space information locally and remotely. This system provides incoming cars with information about parking availability with online access using computers and cell phones. It provides an overall occupancy count for the parking structure as well as more detailed zone-level information. Sensors are placed at each entrance, exit, and transition points between the zones. Sensors at the entrance and exit points wirelessly transmit data on entering and exiting vehicles to a central base station at the exit kiosk. Sensors monitoring the transition points between zones detect traffic and direction to determine if vehicles are moving between zones. The sensors send these data to the central base station, which analyzes all incoming data to give a real-time count of total available parking spots and counts for each zone. After the initial installation, the designers enhanced the system so that the base stations can upload information as well as download data from other "linked" parking lots to help drivers choose a parking lot if the one they are in is fully occupied. The primary target for expanded deployment would be the same parking level of the medical building as well as the adjacent parking structure. LED display signs in the parking structures are another improvement of the system. The displays automatically provide availability information to the incoming cars.

22.4.2 Automatic Charging and Fining

22.4.2.1 Automatic Road Enforcement

The prime objective of the Automatic Electronic Enforcement Project is to reduce the number of road accident victims by deploying automatic electronic enforcement mechanisms to detect traffic law violations.

This project includes a comprehensive survey of the published literature, a research study evaluating driver behavior, a mapping of junctions and roads where cameras and other equipment might potentially be sited, and an analysis to establish the cameras' optimum distribution among many other criteria.

Statistics showed that from 2002–2003 18% of all fatal accidents were caused by excessive speed; speed that was either illegally high or excessive given the circumstances or conditions on the road. A number of research studies have demonstrated that speed cameras or traffic light cameras can significantly reduce the number of accidents. Digital speed-limit enforcement cameras that detect and identify speeding motorists have already been found efficient and effective in the United States, England, Scotland, Australia, New Zealand, and Spain. Such systems have been deployed in a number of countries on roads and traffic light junctions subject to frequent accidents. Data collected by the devices are then sent to the database of the administrator wirelessly in a direct or indirect way (i.e., relayed by other nodes). The objective is to reduce the number of people killed and injured on the roads by altering driving norms by inducing drivers to be more observant of the traffic laws, chiefly speed limits, and of traffic lights.

22.4.2.2 Automatic Congestion Pricing for Cordon Zones

Congestion pricing is considered an effective way to improve transportation system performance. Many transportation experts believe that congestion pricing offers promising opportunities to cost-effectively reduce traffic congestion, improve the reliability of highway system performance, and improve the quality of life for residents. However, the low-efficiency of manual-toll facilities would be intolerable during rush hour, which may overwhelm the benefit delivered by the strategy. Thus automatic charging technology is crucial to the effectiveness of the strategy. Automatic License Plate Recognition (ALPR) is one of the solutions. ALPR technology is used on most electronic tolling facilities around the world both in free-flow and toll-lane-based situations (some lanes are not free of use and subject to charge, thus less congested). ALPR is based on captured images of vehicle license plates, which are then processed through optical character recognition software to identify the vehicle by its license plate. Some systems use front- and rear-located cameras to capture the images to improve identification rates. Once identified, the facility sends the data to a data center and the required charge or permit-checking processes are undertaken.

22.4.3 Technical Characteristics and Challenges

22.4.3.1 The Networking Environment

Most of these smart object networks operate in open roadside environments, which means the shelter effect of buildings is low, but the interference is reasonably high.

For on-vehicle nodes, the mobility causes other problems. One problem is the Doppler effect, which is caused by rapid movement of transmitters and/or receivers. The other problem is transient connectivity, which requires very efficient interactions among mobile nodes.

22.4.3.2 QoS and Network Reliability

Generally, the requirement of QoS in ITS is relatively high due to the need for real-time traffic information. For example, real-time data such as images, video streams, and short messages are quite demanding regarding throughput, delay, and jitter. In contrast, some data like statistical reports do not have stringent QoS requirements.

22.4.3.3 Scalability

The scale of the network depends primarily on the scale of the urban area, which makes networks in large cities like Beijing and New York harder to establish.

22.4.3.4 Reliability Requirement

Reliability requirement in ITS is moderate. Many experiments of WSN for ITS have been done by universities and companies all around the world, however, the reliability of most of these networks is far from the level needed for business application. The value of the intelligent transport system depends on its reliability though.

22.4.3.5 Mobility

As mentioned before, the WSN for ITS is a mixture of both mobile and fixed nodes where fixed nodes are used to collect and relay the information generated by the on-vehicle sensors.

22.4.3.6 Security

Because of urban critical infrastructure, the security level required by ITS is relatively high, although security issues have not been a primary concern thus far. However, it is predictable that methods to protect a person's privacy and defend the attack of malicious nodes will quickly become a prime concern.

22.4.3.7 Network Management

Management of such large-scale networks, whether in a centralized or a distributed manner, is essential for a successful ITS. The deployment and maintenance of such systems may be costly but it is a necessity. There are a number of projects currently working on the management of such large-scale networks.

22.5 CONCLUSIONS

Smart Cities will significantly improve the quality of life in large cities due to a wide range of innovative services. This chapter showed several examples of such applications. Environmental monitoring, increased public safety and security, efficient resources management such as energy and water, ITS, and the development of new social networks are just a few examples.

All of these new applications rely on the deployment of IP smart object networks offering a high degree of scalability, reliability, and security in (most of the time) harsh and unattended environments. This is why the use of IP technologies is central to the successful deployment of such networks. There is a strong need for the support of a variety of media and a true end-to-end IP architecture avoiding complex and hard to manage multiprotocol gateways. This wide spectrum of applications requires the deployment of IP multiservice networks with differentiated services regarding QoS, reliability, and security while ensuring a great deal of flexibility considering the number of future applications. In some cases, Virtual Private Network (VPN) technologies can be deployed to logically separate the flows if needed.

The hardware and software technologies are available and the deployment of IP smart object networks in Smart Cities will undoubtedly take place on a large scale in the near future.

Home Automation

23.1 INTRODUCTION

Home automation is not a novel subject. Instead, home automation products (such as X10 products) have been on the market for more than 25 years. Nonetheless, home automation has not yet reached the mass consumer market. A large and growing market for home control solutions has emerged for high-end solutions, especially in the United States. Such solutions cost $20,000–30,000, with typical projects easily costing between $50,000 and 100,000. With the Custom Electronic Design and Installation Association (CEDIA; a largely American trade organization leads this segment) certifying over 2000 professionals and conducting a large trade show on an annual basis, the significance of this market segment is undisputed. However, homes in this high-end market segment typically cost more than $1–2 million. Attempts to shift from this segment toward the mass market thus far have yielded only a limited market segment expansion.

On the other end of the spectrum, there is a market segment largely driven by enthusiasts. Most of them are buying the corresponding products through the Internet or "historically" through mail order. With products in this segment significantly cheaper than in the high-end market and with installations typically performed by skilled customers, total solution cost is an order of magnitude lower. However, it is obvious that the size of this market segment is strongly limited by the number of skilled customers who are willing to perform their own integration work.

The overall market opportunity has been estimated by various industry analysts (OnWorld, Parks Associates, and InStat) to be huge. Typical calculations set the potential number of devices in the long term as high as 50–100 per home then multiply this number with a number of target households in the range of 200–300 million worldwide. Slightly more conservative approaches estimate the need for one device for every 80–100 square feet (or approximately one device for every 8–10 square meters) in the home and still reach the market potential of several billion devices.

Standardization plays a pivotal role in approaching the mass market, and the lack of standardization thus far is one of the main reasons why systems were so costly. Several initiatives have attempted to set the standard for home control and unlock access to the mass consumer market. X10, one of the earliest to try and set an industry standard based on Powerline communication (PLC), has arguably been closest to succeeding with products in mass retail outlets such as Radio Shack. Today, from the perspectives of feature set, manufacturer support, and robustness, X10 must be seen as outdated. Members of the Electronics Industry Association have built CEBus, a standard for home automation with a spread spectrum modulation-based power line technology providing more features than X10. However, finally released in 1992, CEBus failed to play a visible role in the market.

Interconnecting Smart Objects with IP. DOI: 10.1016/B978-0-12-375165-2.00023-5

KNX, which goes back to the Instabus or EIB, Batibus, and the European Home Systems Protocol (EHS), is well accepted for building control and leads the wireline home automation market in the high-end segment in Europe. However, its wireless variant KNX RF has failed to gain any significant market momentum.

23.2 MAIN APPLICATIONS AND USE CASES

Home automation is an area of multiple and diverse applications that include lighting control, security and access control, comfort and convenience, energy management, remote home management, and aging independently and assisted living (see Figure 23.1). Note that the term "home automation" appears to be used more frequently than "home control." However, most customers are not drawn toward a fully automated home in the "Jetson's" style. Instead most consumers clearly indicate that they want solutions that help them easily and conveniently control their home.

23.2.1 Lighting Control

Lighting automation was probably the first application area in the home automation space. In terms of sales it is still the largest segment. With future growth, it may be expected that lighting control

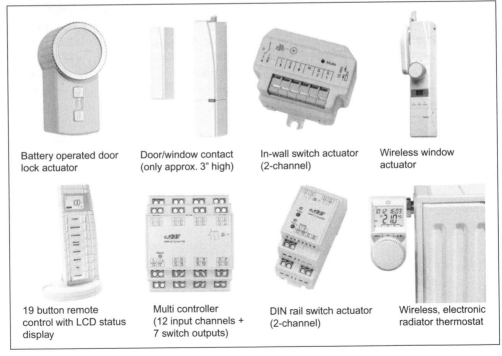

FIGURE 23.1

An overview of some home control devices.

(Source: ELV/eQ3 group.)

devices will be the device types with the largest number of units deployed. The types of lighting control devices in the market are as diverse as the application scenarios. Key differentiations in lighting control device types include:

Type of device:

- Controllers: Handheld controls, key fobs, in-wall controllers, room occupancy sensors, movement sensors, etc.
- Actuators: Switches, dimmers (leading edge, trailing edge, universal dimmers), LED lighting actuators

  Key differentiations:

- Mounting location: Switch panel (e.g., in DIN rail form); gang box, wall-mount box
- Number of channels: Single channel, dual channel, multichannel actuators and controllers
- Power source: Main-powered, battery-operated, energy "scavenger"

23.2.2 Safety and Security

Alarm systems may immediately come to one's mind when considering this solution area. In fact, the integration of alarm systems with home automation is one potential path the industry may take. However, "safety and security" in home automation is often seen from a slightly different angle. Instead of focusing on burglar alarms and adding protection against other risks, the actual *and* perceived safety are moved to the center of attention. Key use cases include situations like wirelessly turning on the lights before opening the garage and/or leaving the car, creating a safe path of light into the home, providing a panic button to turn on all lights, or creating a lived-in look for a home when traveling.

Devices for safety and security include movement sensors and door and window contacts as well as RF-based smoke detectors, gas sensors, and water leakage sensors.

Access control is sometimes seen as an application space in home automation on its own, yet is sometimes seen as an extension of safety and security. Key devices include garage door openers as control solutions for garage door drives and electronic door locks. With electronic door locks one key challenge in the consumer market is how devices can be retrofit, especially when no wires can be installed and when the door is not going to be changed.

23.2.3 Comfort and Convenience

"Comfort and convenience" is often used as a term in home automation for a solution area. This is also an area where home automation can bring significant value. It usually encompasses devices from multiple areas starting with lighting control, adding energy conservation, access control, and safety and security. Actuators to control motorized blinds, shutters, and curtains are often counted in this area, although the devices are also used in various use cases; for example, window actuators can be seen as devices that increase comfort and convenience for home owners. However, such devices also have a strong use case for conserving energy and protecting buildings from mold and mildew. In energy-efficient houses, the buildup of humidity and subsequent problems with mold are on the rise. This is not only a concern because it is very expensive to repair, but even more so as a large health risk for the occupants.

23.2.4 **Energy Management**

With energy prices increasing and the attention for CO_2 reduction growing both on a public and private level, efficient energy management has become the main focus for home automation. See Chapter 20 for more details.

As a brief reminder, solutions typically focus on controlling heating, ventilation, and air conditioning (HVAC) in homes. The primary use case here is to integrate the control of the HVAC thermostat into overall home automation. Examples include switching the thermostat into setback mode when the house is not occupied and to turn it back into comfort mode just before family members return. Another driver is the convenience of programming the (typically weekly) temperature profile with a graphical user interface in a PC or web browser. As pointed out in Chapter 20, such control could be driven by the home energy controller (HEC) according to the dynamic pricing information provided by the power utility.

Usually lighting control is added from an energy conservation perspective. Controlling the entry of sunlight into buildings with shades and blinds and controlling heat dissipation with roller shutters are additional examples of home automation used to conserve energy.

In Europe, one type of heating control plays a pivotal role: more than one billion mechanical radiator thermostats are installed in both residential and commercial environments. Water-based heating with radiators is regulated with valves that are controlled by these radiator thermostats. The thermostat head can be exchanged without changing the valve, allowing for installation by end users without requiring a professional installer. Electronic thermostats with timed programs can save as much as 30% of the heating energy. Wireless communication enables remote control of thermostats and allows integrating window contacts, providing further opportunities for energy savings. While mechanical thermostats act based on the temperature next to the radiator, a wall-mounted wireless room thermostat can improve the regulation by measuring the temperature in a more relevant location to actual room usage. Furthermore, wireless electronic thermostats enable the added convenience of using remote controls to set all thermostats in a room or in the home without having to walk up to every individual unit.

This application area is highly challenging with its demand for battery-to-battery communication (see Figure 23.2). Unlike thermostats in HVAC applications in the United States, the room thermostat, plus the valve actuator, window sensors, and remote controls need to be battery-operated. This is creating a strong need for battery-to-battery communication on a regular basis that is typically not found in home automation applications in the United States.

23.2.5 **Remote Home Management**

Remote home management puts another angle on the other types of use cases in home automation and is seen by several Service Providers as an interesting opportunity to enrich their services portfolio. It typically describes the ability to control home automation devices from outside the home. With access to the Internet so ubiquitous, remote home management can be provided at very low cost, creating a simple, yet powerful business case. Applications include checking on the home from abroad, receiving alarms from smoke sensors, door contacts, movement detectors or water leakage sensors, controlling heating and HVAC before returning back home, and use cases in aging independently and assisted living.

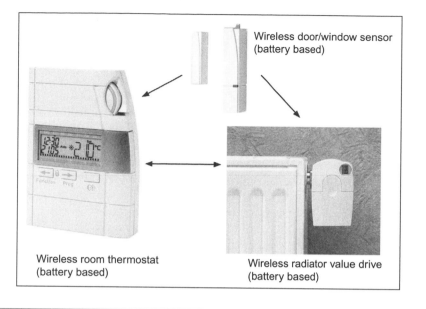

FIGURE 23.2

Battery-to-battery communication.

(Source: ELV/eQ3 group.)

23.2.6 Aging Independently and Assisted Living

With the demographics rapidly changing in North America, Europe, and even more so in countries such as Japan and China, supporting older people through home automation quickly becomes an important application for emergency assistance or monitoring changes in life dynamics. The objective is for people to stay longer in their private residences with the help of home automation applications, thus reducing the burden on public funding of retirement homes and increasing the quality of life for the people involved.

Home automation sensors can also be used for assistance applications that monitor activity and health of people, providing for added safety for elderly people in homes. More complex systems can also be used to aggregate a set of data to detect any change in the life dynamics.

23.3 TECHNICAL CHALLENGES AND NETWORK CHARACTERISTICS

At first the technical requirements and network characteristics appear straightforward for home automation. Compared to other applications fields such as building control or industrial sensor applications, home automation appears significantly less demanding. The key success factor will be the emergence of a universally accepted standard for home automation such as IP.

23.3.1 Type of Topology and Traffic Matrix

From a home automation user's perspective, the paramount requirement is that devices can be installed anywhere in the home. With the advent of mesh networking solutions in the early 2000s, home automation was seen as an easy field for its application. Unfortunately several non-IP solutions designed for home devices underestimated several technical challenges. On the other hand, solutions such as HomeMatic have proven that a full scale mesh networking solution may not be required to provide RF coverage for an entire home. The same is true for early implementations of the 868 MHz modes of the 2006 version of the IEEE 802.15.4 standard, most notably the so-called Parallel Sequence Spread Spectrum (PSSS) communication modes. Also true is that direct communication only appears not to be sufficient in all circumstances. It is also expected to see the use of mixed media such as wireless and PLC. Communication topologies in home automation are mixed. On one hand, many use cases require communication between a central controller and/or gateways device from and to sensor and actuator devices. On the other hand, sensor and actuator devices are required to communicate directly with each other. Both need to be easily and reliably accommodated.

Communication occurs infrequently on a per-device basis. Practically no home automation application requires more than a single message per minute per device when wireless communication is used. Remote controls may be used to rapidly conduct multiple settings and also to control dimming of the device by holding buttons for longer periods of time. However, remote controls in home automation are not expected to be used for "zapping" like TV remotes. Even with the low number of per-device messages, traffic may concentrate at gateway and central controller devices.

23.3.2 Number of Devices

The majority of deployments is expected to be in the range of 50 to 100 nodes. Larger homes and more advanced solutions scenarios may see an increase of up to 150 to 200 nodes. Although not yet common, there are already deployments with over 200 nodes in a single home. It is obvious that IP provides all of the necessary ingredients and is proven for just these types of networks.

23.3.3 Degree of Mobility

The vast majority of devices are stationary in home automation. Devices such as remote controls can be considered as portable devices. In contrast with truly mobile devices, remote controls do not need to support communication while being moved (it may be assumed that devices that have sent a command will typically stay in the same location until they have received responses).

23.3.4 Robustness and Reliability

Hard real-time requirements basically do not exist in home automation and individual packets may be lost and retransmitted in most circumstances. However, robustness and reliability of the overall communication are paramount to consumer acceptance and market success. Furthermore, note that typical installations will not be performed by skilled and trained installers, which means that home automation networks must be easy to install and extremely reliable.

For reasons of reliability, robustness, and ease of configuration, confirmed two-way communication is strongly preferred over unidirectional links.

23.3.5 Requirements for Quality of Service

Requirements for fine-grained control of Quality of Service (QoS) are relatively rare in home automation. One could distinguish immediate control commands where response time is observed by a user from background control algorithms, status reporting, and setup functions that could operate with longer round-trip delay and more jitter in response times. However, based on the concurrent requirement for low cost and low complexity, functions for QoS may be traded in favor of meeting other requirements.

23.3.6 Battery Operation

Long-term battery operation is a key requirement in home automation. This includes initiating and accepting communication to, from, and also between battery-based devices. Battery-to-battery communication was added later in some proprietary solutions. However, the solution was optimized for infrequent, ad hoc use by remote controls to switch battery-operated devices. This key application was designed mainly for door locks. However, adding such battery-to-battery communication late has resulted in most remote controls on the market implemented on earlier versions of the technology without these modes.

Battery-less operation in devices on a long-term basis would be desirable for home automation devices. The vision is that energy could be collected at a device and used for device operation communication. Examples include devices from EnOcean that use piezo elements in wall switches to generate electricity or thermostats and other sensor devices with photovoltaic cells. Note that PLC is also an interesting option for this type of device. However, for residential home automation, several challenges remain to be solved for battery-less devices to become more attractive such as cost, limited amount of energy available via scavengers, and product lifetime (still limited for currently available battery-less devices).

23.3.7 Operating Environment

The operating environment for home control is in several aspects much less demanding than, for example, the environments in which industrial controls are deployed. This is, for example, true for operating temperature ranges, dust and dirt, chemicals in the environment, electromagnetic interferers, or vibration. However, there may be one exception where the environment for home automation is very challenging. In densely populated areas the use of licensed RF bands is rapidly growing. This is especially the case for the 2.4 GHz band where WLAN has reached a level of deployment that already saturates the spectrum in certain regions. For devices that need to operate on batteries on a multiyear basis, this is a very serious concern since it is practically impossible to predict the development of the use of the 2.4 GHz band even for the lifetime of the first set of batteries in a device. Depending on the crowdedness of the 2.4 GHz band, frequent retransmissions in a battery lifetime may be affected. It may be noted that practically all significant wireless home control technologies in Europe are using the 868 MHz band, where the risk of interference is much lower because it is less crowded.

23.3.8 Security

Originally, the level of security required in home control applications was seen as low. As a matter of fact, none of the home control solutions or industry standards in the market provides security in all devices. Even most wireless alarm systems do not use security technologies in their protocol stacks. Security is provided today in home automation typically in devices for access control only. This is the case in dedicated garage door opener solutions with both rolling code systems and bidirectional authentication solutions. In some technology platforms security has been added just recently. There are a few products that currently provide the implementation of AES-128-based authentication. Even a plug-in switch device can be configured to require authentication.

It remains to be seen how market and customer requirements regarding security will develop in the home automation space. While the operational needs remain much lower than for industrial applications, building control, or smart meter and Smart Grid applications, it can be expected that products without security will be unsuccessful.

23.3.9 Ease of Installation and Setup

Especially in the consumer market, easy setup and configuration are critical for success, and the solution must truly be plug and play. This is very different from the main market segments for home automation.

23.4 CONCLUSIONS

The lack of a universally accepted standard that can meet all relevant market and customer requirements is among the key obstacles for adoption of home automation with its associated application fields in the consumer market. Compared to analyst predictions just 4–6 years ago, the development of this market is disappointing.

The IP protocol suite and especially IPv6 provide many of the ingredients that could prove essential for success in home automation. The IP protocol work conducted by the 6LoWPAN, ROLL IETF Working Groups (as discussed in detail in Chapter 17), and other working groups fully applies to home automation smart object networks.

Building Automation

24

With ever-increasing energy costs, energy savings have become critical in buildings. Building automation is a way to save energy in buildings and provide critical functions such as fire emergency evacuation. Smart objects are rapidly entering this market because of the reduced installation costs that wireless systems provide.

Building automation is the instrumentation, mechanization, and data aggregation of a variety of discrete building systems to make monitoring and controlling of building equipment more efficient. Building Automation Systems (BAS) automatically adjust heating ventilation and air conditioning (HVAC) and lighting systems to meet the targeted environmental conditions for the building, while minimizing energy cost. Building automation also increases the security and safety of the building environment by monitoring and controlling the installed physical security and fire systems. BAS is often interchangeably called Facility Management Systems (FMS), Building Management Systems (BMS), Energy Management Systems (EMS), or Intelligent Building Systems (IBS).

Traditionally, BAS and enterprise network systems were separately installed and maintained by the facility and IT organizations, respectively. The cost of supporting two complex pervasive networks within a building has led to the integration of the facility equipment onto the IT network. This convergence has brought about economic advantages but also highlighted differences in the performance, latency, and other operational characteristics of mission-critical systems with that of office networks.

BAS is deployed in a variety of commercial vertical markets including universities, hospitals, government, lower education (K–12), hospitality, and manufacturing. The building types serving these markets include single tenant and multi-tenant owner occupied and leased buildings; multi-building single site environments such as university campuses, and widely dispersed multi-building multi-site environments such as franchise operations. Full-blown BAS typically target buildings ranging in size from 100 K square feet structures (five-story office buildings), to multimillion square feet skyscrapers. Buildings sized from 50 to 100 K square feet fall into the "mid-market" sector. These buildings are typically instrumented with preconfigured HVAC, lighting, and security solutions using either residential or commercial grade sensors and controllers.

Smart objects have a clear place in the building automation ecosystem by providing both the sensors that the BAS needs, as well as the actuators that affect the physical environment. Smart object networks installed as part of BAS can be either wireless using radio communication, or wired using Powerline communication (PLC) or Ethernet.

To accomplish this spectrum of building topologies and sizes, the BAS must be able to meet the nuances of each specific facility. This chapter provides an overview of the BAS architecture for larger

Interconnecting Smart Objects with IP. DOI: 10.1016/B978-0-12-375165-2.00024-7

buildings describing the various components, systems, and their interrelationship giving context to the needed technical, networking, and performance requirements.

24.1 BAS REFERENCE MODEL

Before discussing the applications of building automation, we present a common reference model that we use throughout this chapter. This reference model describes the BAS from the lowest layer to the highest layers in the hierarchy. Each section describes the basic functionality of the layer, its networking model, power requirements, and a brief description of the communication requirements. The entire section references the block diagram seen in Figure 24.1.

Figure 24.1 shows the five major logical subsystems that make up a BAS. These subsystems have layered solutions starting at the sensor layer moving upward in complexity toward the enterprise. While these five subsystems are common to most facilities, they are by no means the exhaustive list — a chemical facility may require a complete fume hood management system, a manufacturing facility may require interfacing to the programmable logic controllers subsystems, or a multi-tenant facility might require a comprehensive power management subsystem. The objective in the overall design is to integrate all common functions into the system yet allow maximum flexibility to modify these systems and add other systems as dictated by the job requirements.

To understand the network systems requirements of a BAS in a commercial building, there is a framework for the basic functions and composition of the system. A BAS is a horizontally layered system of sensors and controllers. Additionally, a BAS may also be divided vertically across alike but different building subsystems as noted next.

Other than the sensors and actuators layers, much of a BAS is optional and all upper layers have stand-alone functionality. These devices can be tethered together to form a more synergistically

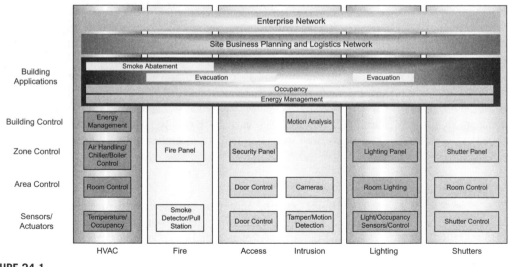

FIGURE 24.1

BAS functional domains.

robust system. The customer decides how much of this vertical "silo" should be integrated to perform the needed application within the facility. This approach also provides excellent fault tolerance since each node is designed to operate in an independent mode if the higher layers are unavailable.

As shown in Figure 24.1, HVAC, fire, security, lighting, and shutter control are components that can be woven together into applications tailored to the customer's requirements. Shutter control is an emerging application domain prevalent in the European market. These major subsystems are connected logically through application software called building applications. This horizontal stack follows the vertical stack design in that each silo is optional. The customer can integrate all the subsystems at once or add them as the facility or budget dictates.

24.2 EMERGING BUILDING AUTOMATION APPLICATIONS

In addition to HVAC applications, there are numerous emerging applications of building automations technology. Such applications are encoded by the building application layer, which is a software layer that binds the various system silos into a cohesive systemic application. This discussion is meant to show a snapshot of emerging use cases and describe how these diverse systems can be coordinated with holistic building automation applications.

24.2.1 Occupancy and Shutdown

A major energy saving technique in commercial buildings is to automatically commence HVAC and lighting operations prior to building occupancy. Conversely, building shutdown allows the systematic reduction in HVAC and lighting operations as the building goes unoccupied.

The HVAC system is usually charged with defining occupied and unoccupied times. The fire and security operations are always operable and lighting is most often subservient to the HVAC. These times are typically programmed into the system by facility operations; however, it could be learned adaptively by the security's access control system. The target occupancy time drives the HVAC subsystem to turn on all ventilation equipment at an optimal time so that each space is ready for occupancy at the prescribed time. These algorithms will be adaptive over time but also include systemic instrumentation such as outdoor air and relative humidity to turn on the equipment at the last possible moment yet still meet the target environmental needs just before occupancy. The lighting systems will also be turned on just prior to occupancy.

Conversely, the HVAC systems will also determine the earliest possible time it can shut down heating/cooling yet still control the set points to meet the requisite parameters. Lighting again is easier since the lights can be extinguished as soon as they are no longer needed. Building owners may use the lighting systems to pace the janitorial service providers by defining a strict timetable that the lights will be on in a given area; the janitorial service providers will need to keep in step to complete their work prior to the lights being turned off.

The system may also include a telephone or computer interface that allows any late workers to override the normal HVAC and lighting schedules simply by dialing into the system and specifying their locale. The lights and fan system will continue to operate for a few extra hours in the immediate vicinity. The same applies to occupancy sensors in meeting rooms. Either by automatic sensing or a simple push of the occupied switch, the HVAC and lighting schedules will extend the normal schedule for the meeting room.

24.2.2 Energy Management

The occupancy/shutdown applications noted above optimize the runtime of large equipment. This is a major energy saving component. However, even during occupancy large equipment can be modulated or shut off temporarily without affecting environmental comfort. This suite of applications runs in the HVAC domain; however, the HVAC silo will interact with the lighting system to reduce the lighting load to help in the overall reduction of energy.

The load-rolling and demand-limiting applications permit the sequencing of equipment to reduce the overall energy profile or to shave off peak energy demands in the facility. The BAS will constantly monitor real-time energy usage and automatically turn off unneeded equipment (or reduce the control set point) to stave off peaking the facility's electrical profile. Demand peaks set by commercial facilities are frowned upon heavily by utilities and are often accompanied by huge energy charge increases for one year.

24.2.3 Demand Response

Recently real-time pricing has furthered the incentives to save energy. This allows a facility to proactively use or curtail energy based on its current price. Again, the HVAC subsystem takes the lead in this application by polling the current and future pricing structures from the electrical utility company via the Internet. The array of data is automatically analyzed and energy strategies are executed to defer or reduce energy use until the price rate drops.

24.2.4 Fire and Smoke Abatement

In the United States, most local building codes now require commercial buildings to incorporate comprehensive fire and life/safety systems into a building. It is well documented that loss of life in a building is mainly caused by smoke inhalation and not the actual fire. The product safety standardization organization, Underwriters Laboratories (UL), has a fire certification program (UL-864) that governs fire and smoke operations in commercial buildings. This program requires rigorous interactive testing with UL to obtain certification. In addition to the obvious need to minimize life/safety situations in a building, facility operators are highly encouraged to implement these systems to receive insurance cost reductions.

The UL fire and smoke systems operate in either a manual or automatic mode. The manual mode provides critical fire and smoke information on a display to be controlled by a Fire Marshal. The automatic mode is a preprogrammed set of events that automatically control the fire. In practice, the fire system will be set to automatic mode and operate accordingly until the Fire Marshal arrives. At that point the system is normally overridden to manual mode so that the Fire Marshal can control operations from the command center as deemed necessary.

The fire certification program UL-864 is comprised of fire system operations (UOJZ) and smoke control (UUKL). UOJZ certification allows all fire and smoke operations, events, and alarms to be controlled from a Fire Workstation. Local fire panels can only be accessed and commanded from this workstation. Operator authentication and command authorization are required for all operations. Alarms can only be acknowledged from this device. One and only one Fire Workstation can ever govern a given area at a time to assure that destructive control operations cannot inadvertently occur by two operators simultaneously controlling a space.

The smoke abatement certification, UUKL, is an adjunct function of the fire system that automatically or manually purges the fire and directs smoke safely out of the building. This is done by exhausting smoke from exit passageways and refuge areas by judicially adjusting pressures and dampers in the affected areas. Furthermore, it will actually assist in putting out the fire by starving the fire of oxygen in the affected area while simultaneously routing smoke out the building in the adjacent areas.

While the smoke abatement operation could be the province of the fire system alone, economics dictates that the fire system off-load the smoke abatement operation to the HVAC system. In practice, the fire system will receive the initial fire indication by one or more of its smoke detectors. It will then inform the HVAC system of the physical locale of the fire. The HVAC system will then take charge of the smoke abatement operation by automatically adjusting the air handlers and dampers. The HVAC system must incorporate a comprehensive prioritization scheme throughout its system. This prioritization scheme must allow all smoke operations to take control precedence over all other control operations including manual operator control. All affected devices must support a supervision policy that assures that all operations requested were executed properly. The system will automatically return to normal operation once the smoke situation has abated.

Many buildings also trigger the evacuation application (see the next section) coincidentally with a smoke control situation. The evacuation application assists building inhabitants in safely leaving a building. Elevator control policies may restrict inhabitants from calling for the elevators while simultaneously posting the elevators to the ground floor for use by fire personnel.

24.2.5 Evacuation

Evacuation is a systemic operation that may be activated as part of the fire/smoke control application, or may be activated for other reasons such as terrorist threats. Evacuation requirements most often activate subsystems of the fire, security, and lighting silos. The fire system normally supports the intercom subsystem in the facility. The intercom system will then trigger the recorded voice evacuation instructions. This may be in concert with the fire system audio indications if a fire situation is active or stand-alone. The lighting subsystem will be activated to turn on the lights and evacuation paths to aid in the evacuation. The security system coincidentally opens all doors to allow a smooth safe egress from the building. If the building also supports elevator control, the elevators operate as directed by a preprogrammed evacuation policy.

24.3 EXISTING BUILDING AUTOMATION SYSTEMS

Existing BAS is typically installed using wired connections. Although wired connections provide good efficiency when the system is deployed, wired systems are difficult and expensive to install and update if the building changes. For this reason, wireless mechanisms are emerging. Before discussing wireless technology, we review existing BAS.

EIA-485 and Ethernet are the dominant media used in BAS. Sensors, actuators, area controllers, zone controllers, and building controllers are connected via EIA-485 three-wire twisted pair serial media operating nominally at 38,400 to 76,800 baud. This will run to 5000 ft without a repeater. With the maximum of two repeaters, a single communication trunk could serpentine 15,000 feet dropping as many as 255 control devices along its path. Wired sensing devices that typically had been hard-wired to the controller are increasingly placed on an EIA-485 sensor bus.

The HVAC, fire, access, intrusion, lighting, and shuttering subsystems are often integrated using LAN-based Ethernet technology. These enterprise devices connect to standard CAT-5 through work-group switches.

In the past five years, wireless technologies such as 802.15.4, WiFi, and Powerline communication (PLC) have been deployed for sensor and controller networks. Figure 24.2 depicts a wired network and an equivalent wireless network. WiFi is deployed to extend the enterprise layer for portable user interface communications. WiFi communications replace the Ethernet connection if the application

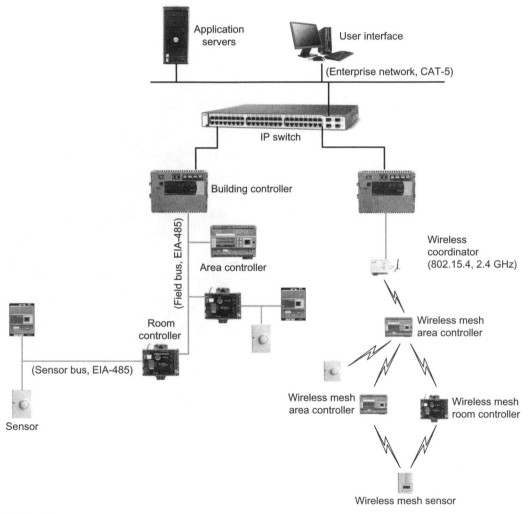

FIGURE 24.2

BAS wired and wireless topological hierarchy including controller types and networks.

operates within the WiFi performance characteristics. Multi-building sites also connect onto the facility intranet or over the Internet if the available performance matches the application requirements.

24.3.1 **Existing Control Protocols**

Sensors, actuators, area controllers, zone controllers, and building controllers all typically coexist on an EIA-485 multi-drop network. EIA-485 provides the proper communication speed and flexibility at a reasonable cost. Through the early 1990s the protocols running on these networks were proprietary. However, in mid-1990 the Building Automation Control Network (BACnet) and Local Operating Network (LON) protocols were developed by the HVAC industry consortia that defined electrical interfaces as well as a standard set of objects, properties, and services for sensing and controlling devices. The emergence of these protocols allowed vendor interoperability of these devices. Since their inception these protocols have been augmented to include energy management, lighting, security, and fire support. Other protocols such as Digital Addressable Lighting Interface (DALI) have also been developed to increase interoperability for targeted markets.

24.3.1.1 *BACnet*

BACnet is an ISO standard protocol designed to maximize interoperability across many products, systems, and vendors in commercial buildings. BACnet was conceived in 1987 and first released in 1995 as an HVAC protocol. Standard objects, properties, and services were defined supporting device and object discovery, object creation, the reading and writing properties of objects, event notification, network security, and routing. Since its first release fire, security, and lighting functionalities have been added. BACnet currently supports six media types including Ethernet (802.3 and UDP/IP), EIA-485, Arcnet, LON, RS-232, and ZigBee. The BACnet object set is very generic supporting object types such as analog input and binary input. The definition maximizes flexibility but obfuscates semantic meaning. Hence, the system integrator must have a priori knowledge of the object's use. Without it, the integrator could easily reference the boiler temperature point instead of the outdoor air temperature point.

24.3.1.2 *LON*

LON competes with BACnet most often at the sensor and field bus layers. LON is an ISO/IEC standard that was originally developed by the Echelon Corporation and that typically is used with ISO/IEC 14908.2. Whereas BACnet is purely a software protocol that runs on standard communication hardware, many LON implementations use specialized chips that implement the protocol. Unlike BACnet, which has very loose binding, LON has defined standard device profiles with rich semantic meaning. This assures interoperability albeit at a slight decrease in flexibility.

24.3.1.3 *DALI*

DALI is a lighting protocol standard defined within IEC 62386. This protocol was created to allow interoperable control of digital lighting for small areas and applications. It provides for multiple types of lights including fluorescent, emergency, HID, low voltage halogen, incandescent, and LEDs. Commands include ON/OFF and UP/DOWN. Predefined scenes can be configured and saved for later recall. Communication occurs over a two-conductor cable (no shield is required). The effective transmission rate is 1200 bps for longer distance and reliability.

24.4 BUILDING AUTOMATION SENSORS AND ACTUATOR CHARACTERISTICS

Sensor and actuator performance is dictated by the class of device. Table 24.1 illustrates examples of the real-time performance required of the sensor and controller network. As noted, the sensor to actuation time can be as short as 100 ms for some applications. Many applications such as smoke detection and smoke purge actuation must occur within a few seconds. Less critical applications such as room temperature control can take minutes. Application performance requirements span many orders of magnitude. The mission-critical nature of these applications is the reason that the control networks and IP networks have yet to completely merge onto the enterprise network.

Fire sensing and response is considered the highest priority function in BAS. Security systems rank second followed by HVAC and lighting applications. Historically, fire and safety subsystems have been hardwired or implemented on completely dedicated infrastructures to ensure that the fire and security systems are not affected by the HVAC and lighting subsystems. Market and customer pressure, however, is changing this approach since customers want application interaction across these systems with the HVAC and lighting subsystems.

24.4.1 Area Control

An area describes a small physical locale (300–500 ft^2) within a building, typically a room. Room and area control are terms often used interchangeably, although the former is confined to the application set defined within a room; the latter encompasses areas outside a room such as auditoriums, atria, and stairways. Common sensors feeding area controllers include temperature, occupancy, ambient lighting load, and smoke detectors. Sensors found in specialized areas (such as chemistry labs) might also include air flow, pressure, CO_2, and CO particle sensors. Actuation includes temperature set point, airflow adjustment, lights, and blinds/curtains.

The controllers deployed within an area are most often stand-alone devices that provide the necessary functionality without further assistance by the higher layers of the architecture. However, when these devices are connected to the higher layers, these layers provide additional functionality including manual override and time series and event data for further analysis. Likewise, the enterprise level can then override the local control from a centralized location. When connected to the higher layers, the controllers deploy a fail-soft algorithm that reverts to local control if the higher order communication is lost.

Room temperature controllers are soft real-time devices implementing nominally 60 s control loops. Environmental data are provided to the controller by its sensors each minute in either a polled

Table 24.1 Sensor Expected Performance Characteristics	
Sensor type	**Expected response time**
Space temperature	10 min
Duct temperature	1 min
Fire detection	3 s
Occupancy	1 s
Door access	1 s
Static pressure	100 ms

or event-driven fashion. The controller then analyzes the data and modulates the actuators accordingly to meet the application requirements.

Ambient lighting sensors and solar sensors periodically sample the room's light load. This information is forwarded to the lighting panel. The lighting panel then automatically adjusts the light level to the desired set point by modulating the external solar light load with the interior lighting, typically minimizing electrical demand. When available a room occupancy sensor will override the algorithm whenever the room is unoccupied. The solar sensor may also forward radiant heat infiltration to the HVAC control. The HVAC controller then includes these data in the heating or cooling load requirement.

Room lighting control also requires real-time performance. Room lights need to have near instantaneous response to a light switch activation. The lighting operator expects to see some change in the scene within 300 ms after a complex lighting command has been executed.

Door control requires much higher performance. Persons entering a facility will expect a latency of no more than 300 ms between swiping the access card and entry approval. Camera pan-tilt-zoom commands need to execute with less than 250 ms latency.

24.4.1.1 Area Controller Communications

Area and room controllers need to communicate to higher order (zone) controllers as well as subordinate sensors and actuators. The controllers operate on a field bus. Although the field bus is often implemented with the same EIA-485 physical network as the sensor bus, the communication rates, packet size, buffering, and fragmentation are increased to handle the larger packet transmissions. The protocol on the field bus is most often a peer-to-peer protocol to ease sharing controller data across the controllers.

24.4.2 Zone Control

Zone control supports a similar set of characteristics as the area control, albeit to an extended space. A zone is normally a logical grouping or functional division of a commercial building that also coincidentally maps to a physical locale such as a floor. Table 24.2 illustrates zones for the various functional domains within a commercial building.

Zone control may have direct sensor inputs (smoke detectors for fire), controller inputs (room controllers for air handlers in HVAC), or both (door controllers and tamper sensors for security). Like

Table 24.2	Examples of Commercial Zones
Functional domain	**Zone**
HVAC	Air handler is the area served by a single fan system; typically a floor or adjacent floors in a building.
Lighting	A bank of lights that all operate consistently.
Fire	An area of a facility that operates consistently when fed by the same fan system or covered by the same set of smoke detectors or follows the same pressurization and alarm annunciation rules. The zone may also be a functional grouping when a certain area is governed by a set of fire dampers.
Security	A subset of the building operating in a similar fashion such as a logical collection of lockable doors.

area/room controllers, zone controllers are stand-alone devices that operate independently or may be attached to the larger network for more synergistic control.

Zone controllers may have some onboard sensor inputs and also provide direct actuation; however, they also direct the actions of their underlings via commands as well as respond to environmental changes reported by those same underlings. For example, an air handler controller might directly sample the duct pressure, the supply air temperature, and return air temperature. However, it may also send commands to other networked devices querying the outdoor air temperature and relative humidity. Similarly, a fire panel may have all the smoke detectors directly wired, yet send commands to other adjacent fire panels to request their status if a fire condition arises. A list of zone controller characteristics is defined in Figure 24.2.

24.4.3 Building Control

Building controllers (BCs) provide the overall orchestration of the system. While the sensor and area controllers provide real-time focused applications; the BCs provide broad systemic functionality. The BCs also provide the view ports into the embedded real-time systems for the operator, integrators, and enterprise applications. The BCs cache and archive important real-time data from the area controllers and act as an agent to Enterprise Application Servers for long-term data archival and retrieval.

BCs are completely field programmable devices that are designed to integrate into all system control operations. HVAC BCs often must map a wide variety of legacy protocols into a single object model for a single representation of the building's data to the user. HVAC BCs also provide sophisticated applications such as energy management, alarm annunciation, trending time series data, and scheduling all activities during the week.

The fire subsystem application is stand-alone and in many cases dictated by the fire codes. However, the BCs may monitor the fire subsystem as a secondary reporting device. Here the smoke detectors, pull boxes, strobes, and evacuation subsystems that are under the control of the fire controller are also integrated into the HVAC BC for viewing and monitoring by building operations. By regulation, the HVAC system cannot affect changes to the fire system.

The fire subsystem may be further integrated into the HVAC BC in cases where the HVAC system operates in concert with the fire subsystem to provide a smoke abatement application.

From a control point of view, the security subsystems are stand-alone. As noted earlier, local door controllers support building entry algorithms. Cameras may be controlled from a centralized location. An optional centralized video server is deployed to allow remote wireless viewing of cameras. This server also supports motion alerts on unexpected changes in the camera's view. The security system can also be tied into the HVAC system to facilitate the experience of someone entering a facility. This application is discussed in Section 24.2.

Lighting applications are most often localized to a room or area. Lighting manufacturers do not deploy server-level devices to control the entire facility; they provide application "hooks" into the lighting panels that allow the BAS to monitor and override the local lighting algorithms.

Emerging shuttering systems are often extensions of the lighting system, which works in concert with the shuttering system to control the required light levels while reducing overall energy. Since energy management is the province of the HVAC silo, the HVAC BC monitors and overrides both of these systems as needed to meet the needed energy savings targets.

24.5 EMERGING SMART-OBJECT-BASED BAS

Wireless communication and smart object technology have the potential to significantly reduce installation costs for BAS. This is increasingly important for modern buildings in which rooms and walls are reconfigurable by customers. With a wireless BAS, the reconfiguration of walls is easily managed without requiring reinstallation of a wired BAS.

Wireless networks have recently become economically feasible for building control applications. Wireless communication reduces installation cost by easing sensor installation and eliminating wiring material and labor costs. Since the sensors monitor the environment and inject status data onto the network, these devices can be deployed using battery power. This is not true for their actuator counterparts. Actuators change the environment by modulating dampers and opening and closing doors as well as other similar activities. The very nature of these devices most often deems battery power insufficient to perform the task.

A recent addition to sensor technology is battery-less sensors. These devices use power scavenging from the environment such as mechanical activation, ambient light, or vibration to create enough energy to transmit its packets. As this technology matures it will surely become a required addition to BAS.

24.5.1 Emerging Sensors, Actuators, and Protocols

Sensors and actuators are often the leaves of the network tree structure. The actuators are the sensors' counterparts modifying the characteristics of the system based on the input sensor data and the application control deployed. Traditionally, sensors were hardwired devices deployed on proprietary networks. Lately, economics have allowed sensors to be connected using a wireless smart object network. Installing addressable sensors on its own network eliminates the need for homerun wiring from the sensor to the controller, reducing installation cost. Addressable sensors also allow applications to readily accept many sensor inputs rather than a few providing better environmental control and comfort.

24.5.1.1 EnOcean

EnOcean is an emerging wireless communication device and communication protocol that allows point-to-point communication without the use of conventional power sources. EnOcean devices scavenge the power necessary to communicate by means of mechanical activation, temperature differentials, vibration, or solar load.

24.5.2 IP-based Enterprise Protocols

Multiple protocols are supported at the enterprise level of the BAS since this layer supports not only the embedded control operation but also the user interface and end user enterprise applications.

24.5.2.1 Peer-to-peer Controller Communication

BCs, often called supervisory controllers, orchestrate the overall BAS operation. Control and data access functions implemented on the enterprise level typically use BACnet or LON. DALI and EnOcean protocols are room-level protocols that do not surface at the enterprise layer. BACnet supports IP intrinsically, hence, controller and enterprise communication is seamless via BACnet routing. LON utilizes IP gateways to move LON controller data onto the enterprise network.

24.5.2.2 *Enterprise Communication*

The control protocols used on the control and sensor networks typically are not viable for user access at the enterprise layer. Web services and SNMP have been added to the enterprise layer in many implementations to assist in integration with end user applications and Network Management Systems, respectively.

Some vendors have developed public web services to allow third-party application access to the building data. BACnet has recently defined a set of web services that cleanly map the BACnet object model data to standard web services. Other groups, such as Open Building Information Exchange oBIX), have developed other sets of web services and are working with standards bodies such as the Organization for the Advancement of Structured Information Standards (OASIS) toward standardization.

24.6 CONCLUSIONS

BAS use sensors and actuators dispersed in buildings to control their heating, ventilation, and air conditioning. With more efficient integration techniques, new applications have emerged such as advanced energy management and intelligent fire and evacuation control.

Existing BAS is typically deployed using wired communication technology. With the advent of efficient wireless communication and smart object technology, this is changing. Due to the reduced installation costs of wireless technology, BAS is moving in the direction of wireless smart object network systems. Wireless sensors can be deployed with battery-less, power-scavenging technology.

Structural Health Monitoring

25

25.1 INTRODUCTION

The world is full of stationary structures — some small, some huge, others new, most of them very old — such as buildings, damns, or bridges. Buildings include office complexes, apartment buildings, or power plants. The commonality between these large structures is that they are critical in everyone's day-to-day life: bridges are used by pedestrians, cars, trucks, and trains and millions of people live in buildings. Any damage in these structures may result in life-threatening situations and serious financial loss. Thus, monitoring the health of these structures with smart object networks is imperative to detect any irregularities or anomalies that could be a sign of damage and lead to problems in the future.

Structural health monitoring (SHM) defines an abstract condition for a physical structure such as a bridge, crane, tower, or other physical object or even heavy machinery. Measurement data are used to monitor physical quantities and computer models are used to analyze the data and classify the current state of the structure and trigger alerts if necessary. SHM typically becomes a part of the structure for its entire lifetime, and the structure's condition will be inferred from its physical measurements. Due to the lifetime requirements and physical size of the objects, wiring of the sensors recording physical quantities is not a preferred solution or even possible, especially for existing structures not equipped with wiring. Enabling SHM on such structures would be a major investment and effort. In most cases, smart objects are interconnected via low-power wireless links, a solution that avoids costly and error-prone wiring within the structure.

The bridge shown in Figure 25.1 is used for research purposes. The acceleration sensors transmit the acceleration measurements using a wired network.

One of the main challenges with SHM is that the structure health is not determined by a single measured quantity. There is no single sensor that tells directly if, for example, a bridge is going to collapse. The only viable methodology consists of periodically measuring a series of physical quantities and then using various data analysis and data mining techniques to analyze the data and find irregularities or changes that could be a sign of an emerging problem.

The structure's condition must be described by the physical quantities measured from the structure. Typical physical quantities include accelerations, strains, pressure, temperature, wind speed, flow, position, orientation, chemical quantities, and wave propagation quantities. Timely availability of the measurements has a large effect on the delay of detection, therefore near real-time measurements are used. This also sets requirements on the transmission bandwidths of the network. While

Interconnecting Smart Objects with IP. DOI: 10.1016/B978-0-12-375165-2.00025-9

FIGURE 25.1

Experimental bridge used for SHM studies.

monitoring the structure, only the output measurements are available, without knowing the state (or condition) of the structure or the input that caused the damage. In the subsequent analysis phase, it is assumed that these measurements are representative of the normal condition of the structure.

In civil engineering studies, a typical sampling frequency is often less than or equal to 100 Hz. Nyquist theorem states that to detect signal frequencies up to a frequency f, the sampling frequency has to be double that frequency ($2*f$). A typical SHM application includes vibration measurements (accelerometer) sampled at 100 Hz for 10 minutes at a time. With existing hardware, it is possible to sample at up to 8 kHz, which could lead to nearly 5 million samples per sensor for one measurement event; this repeats once or a few times per day. If each sample uses 16-bit encoding that means 9.6 MB. Yet, new sensors are already moving to kHz sampling frequencies, which produce 10 times more data. In this case the data are stored in flash memory.

Even for a stand-alone sensor with memory to store measurements, this many samples is a real issue. With 1 kHz sampling frequency, existing hardware stores measurements for a 30 s period; for example, with 16-bit samples the overall main memory needed is 60 KB, but storing measurements for a 10 minute period is not yet possible within the main memory. Thus, the data often need to be stored in an external flash memory, which increases processing and energy consumption overhead. Typically a wireless sensor node cannot sample, process, transmit, and receive simultaneously; it executes one of these functions at a time.

For many applications of the measured data (e.g., data analysis) time synchronization is required. The accuracy of timing after synchronization is in the scale of microseconds, but due to clock drifts, the synchronization needs to be done regularly (maybe every half a minute). Due to local processing of the data, the sampling is done in an asynchronous way (no continuous sampling), but at least the neighbor nodes should perform synchronized measurements. This can be achieved by running a time synchronization algorithm in the network requiring communication from sensors/cluster heads to sensors.

There are two distinct methods for analyzing the sensor data: online and off-line applications, where the data are either processed at the scene or off-line. The choice of mode greatly affects the networking solutions. There is also an obvious trade-off in local data processing versus data transmission. The rule of thumb is that energy-wise transmitting one byte is as expensive as running 8000 CPU cycles. This means that computation should be done as close to the measurement point as possible, such as locally on the nodes. Only the fused information should be transmitted to those nodes that need the information (e.g., certain covariance information might be needed in another node to be able to perform Kalman-filtering, etc.). The computing capabilities of the nodes are very constrained. The microprocessor in many sensor products is a TI MSP430 with 10 kB of RAM and 256 kB flash memory running at 8 MHz. The node also has a 4 Mbit serial data flash memory. The nodes are typically equipped with a 6LoWPAN (IPv6 over IEEE 802.15.4 links, as discussed in Chapter 16) protocol stack.

A study performed for one sensor type showed that the power required to transmit 1 bit roughly corresponded to 74 CPU cycles of computing. Such a number cannot be generalized but provides a good sense of the cost ratio between data transmission and CPU cycle cost for existing sensors.

Often the positions of sensors needs to be known. Sometimes they need to be very accurately fixed in advance, and sometimes the sensors need to be installed exactly in the same locations as was done previously. Location is not only important for data analysis, but also for networking. Hence localization support might be needed, which means that the nodes would have to be equipped with GPS or ultrasound sensors, because the radio signal strength-based localization results in low accuracy if the device does not have direct and constant line-of-sight to satellites.

Sensors used to measure physical quantities of the structure are located in different physical locations in the structure. To have a holistic view on the entire structure, the detector (software and model used to analyze the data) must have access to all of the data. Two alternative architectures are possible: centralized and decentralized. With centralized architecture the data are mediated through the wireless sensor network to a central node. The centralized node is then responsible for assessing the structure's condition based on the measurements. In a decentralized architecture, there is more analysis local to the sensors.

Two modes of measurement can be differentiated: periodic and continuous. In a periodic type of a measurement, a fixed period of time (e.g., 10 minutes) is dedicated to the measurements after which the data are mediated to a central location and analyzed. In a continuous measurement mode, the condition of the structure is continually measured parallel to the data mediation and its analysis. This sets stringent requirements on the throughput of the network as well as the response time for the detector. For example, consider a sensor network with 50 sensors measuring vibrations with 1 kHz frequency and 16-bit samples. Each of the 50 sensors produces 2 bytes of data 1000 times per second. Overall, this results in 100 kB/s data traffic. Taking a media access control (MAC) layer payload of 100 bytes, each sensor would need to send 20 packets per second or 1000 packets per second in the whole network. Again, if we have only a couple of data sinks, each sink would need to handle hundreds of packets per second.

Two modes of analysis can be used. The data-based mode uses measurement data to estimate a model of the normal behavior and use it to assess the condition of the structure. Statistical time-series models are well suited for this task. The model-based approach relies on a computer-based model of the physical structure and finite element method to derive results on the behavior of the structure. Such complex calculations can only be performed on high-performance servers.

25.2 MAIN APPLICATIONS AND USE CASE

In this section, a use case is presented to illustrate the use of network-based monitoring techniques in civil structures. This use case monitors a bridge using a smart object network.

The smart object network is made of sensors measuring the desired physical phenomena, based on which the damage detection of the bridge structure is accomplished. One of the approaches uses acceleration sensors to record acceleration, or vibration, of the structure. Temperature could also be recorded, since there are known connections between vibration profiles and the temperature, although these may be structure-dependent. As mentioned in the Introduction, other quantities that could be recorded include strains, pressure, temperature, wind speed, flow, position, orientation, chemical quantities, and wave propagation quantities. Pinning down a specific set of features requires interaction with domain specialists who know the theory of structures, or an extensive set of redundant measurements and an empirical work in data analysis to select what measurements are useful in practice [236]. While the latter approach may be interesting to researchers, it is too costly to be used in practical use case scenarios.

Data acquisition and data analysis are discussed in Section 25.4. Let's now assume that we have a model that supplied the data to estimate or approximate the probability of the damage present in the bridge. For estimating the global probability of the damage, all the data must arrive where the model probability computation takes place. Alternatively, the computation may be performed in a distributed fashion, since the probability computation is decomposable due to the conditonal independence assertion done in the model. This is a basic building block in constructing Bayesian networks.

Once the probability computation is realized, a cut-off point for a decision must be set. All the probabilities exceeding the threshold cause an alarm. What to do with the alarms is essentially a question of business logic and at best should be separated from making the best possible decision in the model.

25.3 TECHNICAL CHALLENGES

Based on the previous description of the functionalities required for SHM, this section highlights the functional requirements and technical challenges required of smart object networks. A Wireless Sensor Network (WSN) is required in this case, but some structures may be monitored with wired smart object networks.

There are two fundamental properties of the SHM that put pressure on how the smart object network must work. First, the WSN for SHM produces *large amounts of data* at various intervals. Typical applications do not produce a small amount of continuous data or frequent small bursts, rather every 8 hours a relatively large amount of data must be transferred from the sources to one or more sinks. This does not happen all over the network at one time, but a certain section of the network needs to transfer the data at a given time. Secondly, SHM is used in many areas where lives could be lost. Thus, once a section of the sensor network starts to transfer data, the data must get to their destination with a *high reliability*.

An SHM WSN is not only about periodic one-way transmission of measurement data. If the data mining reveals a possible problem in the structure, advanced applications would control the sensors to continue measuring the structure at a redefined frequency and data delivery interval. Additional functionality of an SHM smart object (sensor) network includes service discovery; sensors need to find sinks, or nodes performing data fusion, and the sinks must be able to find the sensors.

As discussed in the previous section, there are two types of modes for data mining, off-line and online. In this section we mainly focus on the off-line mode, where data are not analyzed within the sensor network but instead are transmitted to sinks/gateways and from there onto servers. Online mode makes similar requirements on the network: large amounts of data must be periodically sent to an entity, either a sink or gateway to external networks, or a place for data fusion and online data mining.

Designing the network structures and data routing is ultimately about choices, one performance aspect rules out another one, all functional design decisions affect performance in some way. SHM is about static deployments and use cases. Thus, support for highly dynamic networks is not needed. We can expect the network to bootstrap itself in a matter of hours or even days, rather than seconds. Also, once the network routing has started, changes include nodes just dying out and nodes replaced at a very modest frequency.

We can also consider, sometime in the distant future, that structures could be built with the wireless sensors already embedded into the building materials. Such a network would need to bootstrap itself, configure each node's role (e.g., by elections), and be able to run for a very long time.

SHM applications do not require extremely large sensor networks. One network might consist of up to a few hundred nodes. If larger structures need to be monitored, multiple independent sensor networks could be used.

25.3.1 Autoconfiguration

The network should be able to automatically configure itself and the routing paths. There are usually no strict requirements on timeliness. To make accurate measurements from multiple sensors at the exact same instance, time synchronization with accuracy in the order of milliseconds is usually required, possibly over multiple hops.

25.3.2 Multicast Support

To create the bootstrapping function, and also save energy, routing should support multicast (as in the case of RPL, the routing protocol developed by the IETF ROLL Working Group discussed in Chapter 17). This is especially needed for the service/node discovery.

25.3.3 Routing

Since SHM produces large amounts of data at one time, the routing protocol should be able to support more than one routing path between a data producer and the sinks. This requirement is not mandatory, since the use of multiple paths can be simulated on a higher layer by a sensor sending its data to multiple sinks. This helps to use different paths if the sinks are carefully placed, for example, each sensor would send every second packet to a different data sink or sensors are configured to use different sinks. *Reliability* is key in SHM networks: when a group of sensors provides their data for further processing (data mining), these data must be routed/transported in a reliable way. If one part of the data is lost, the entire sampled data may be useless. This requirement is more important than real-time operation. Also, bandwidth problems can be partly solved by using multiple data sinks. In such a case, the routing metric used by RPL is likely to be the reliability metric (see Chapter 17). The routing protocol should be aware of the energy levels of the sensor nodes and seek to balance the energy consumption of the whole network. Note that RPL also supports energy awareness in its routing decision. It is required for the routing protocol to find alternate routes in case of link and node failures as well as to compute new routes as new links and nodes are added in the network. It is desirable for the change to be localized and not visible all around the sensor network. RPL addresses this requirement by relying on local repair combined with global repair (reoptimization). There are no tight constraints on the time for repairing the network unlike in the bootstrapping phase.

25.3.3.1 Coupling with Radio Resource Management (RRM)

Since the sensor nodes need to save power, they will sleep most of their lifetime. Because the hardware typically only supports one function at a time (measuring or data transmission/reception), nodes are not always able to receive data. Thus, the routing protocol should consider the node availability regarding the radio interface and each node's ability to further forward or route packets. It is of little use to send data on a certain path if that path will be truncated as hops down the path will be sleeping.

25.3.4 Network Topology

Typically a sensor network deployed for an SHM application would follow a DAG (directed acyclic graph)-like topology with multiple routes. For example, there could be a set of sensors around one pole of a bridge connected over multiple paths and hops to sinks.

25.3.5 Network Scalability

An SHM application typically requires tens or at most a few hundred nodes. Most of these would be running the measurement applications, while the rest are used for routing only purposes.

25.3.6 Degree of Mobility

Bridges and buildings typically do not move, neither do the sensors. Thus, support for mobility is not required.

25.3.7 Link and Device Characteristics

SHM requires reliable data delivery. If the links are lossy, per-hop acknowledgments and retransmissions, forward-error correction, or other reliability mechanisms such as bi-casting are required at the link layer. Wireless sensor networks are usually required because of the absence of wiring infrastructure. This also means that there are no power cables either. Conversely, in the presence of wiring infrastructure to supply power to the sensors, it is possible to also install wired communications. A common setup requires that the sensors are battery-operated, but the sinks, or gateways to external networks, are main-powered. Sinks pass so much data, they would need huge batteries to last any sensible time period. As the sensors are wireless, the power source must be local as well. To avoid frequent servicing of the nodes, energy levels should be sustained at an operating level of the sensor and the associated radio as long as possible. To alleviate the problem, energy harvesting could be used. Energy can be harvested from solar radiation using solar cells, vibration scavengers, or even from radio waves, as is done in some environmental monitoring applications.

25.3.8 Traffic Profile

As discussed earlier, SHM produces a large amount of traffic bursts. Thus, once sensors have collected enough data, they need to transfer those data to the sinks. This event may take a very long time.

25.3.9 Quality of Service

SHM does not have any particular need for Quality of Service (QoS). The issue is mainly about reliable data delivery when monitoring information needs to be transmitted to a sink.

25.3.10 Security

Monitoring the health of structures saves lives and allows timely response to emerging problems. The data provided by sensors are thus very important. Not only must the network provide reliable data delivery, but it also must support the ability to verify the data source. When measurement data of a structure are collected, one must be able to trust the data. Thus, data origin authentication is a security feature that must be available. Encryption of the transmitted data and eavesdropping is not a primary concern. The sensor data are mostly public information.

25.3.11 Deployment Environment

The environment where SHM applications are deployed may significantly vary from harsh outdoor environments to less demanding indoor locations. Both cases still demand unattended operation for as long as possible. Device failure is the only reason for a serviceman to appear. Unrelated to the sensor network, if the data mining of the sensor data reveals potential damage to the structure a full-blown investigation will be carried out.

25.4 DATA ACQUISITION AND ANALYSIS

As mentioned in the Introduction, two modes can be characterized according to the analysis model used. In the off-line mode, data are gathered from sensors without any guarantee of the timeliness of the sensor data samples. Usually, this type of solution is used when developing the actual algorithms to detect novelty or to characterize the sensor signals as normal or faulty. The sole purpose in the off-line mode is to gather representative data from the structure under observation. These data are then analyzed to learn how to detect damages from observed data or how to classify states of normal or faulty conditions. This research phase may take months to two years.

If the experimental conditions can be manipulated, such as in research structures in a laboratory environment, then these conditions need to be stored with the time information. The time information is particularly necessary when the conditions are aligned with the measurement time series. This is a prerequisite for simulating an online detection system, where the detection decisions take place as soon as data are available (real-time or near-real-time detection). The online mode would be the preferred mode in a real environment, although practical considerations may hinder making real-time or near-real-time decisions.

There is an interesting trade-off between the computation accomplished in nodes and the communication needs between the sensor nodes. If data analysis can be performed, even at a low level, the amount of communicated data sent from a node may be reduced. For example, some form of compression may be used to summarize data before sending the data over to the central node. The form of compression may vary depending on the models used in detection. Recent results with compressive sampling [31] suggest that lower sampling frequencies may be used without losing essential information.

Assuming that a database of sensor network measurements is available, the estimation of the model may proceed. Once the data analyst has decided what model class to use, he can learn or estimate the parameters of the model from the database. The detection model must be assessed according to two criteria: the probability of false alarms and the probability of true detection. Estimating these measures requires the truth of the state of the bridge at the same time as decisions are made. As mentioned earlier, damages can be simulated in laboratory conditions to create labeled data (data where the operating condition, damage or no damage, is known). To assess the overall diagnostic accuracy, Receiver Operating Characteristic (ROC) analysis can be used [233]. In ROC analysis, the true positive rate is compared with the false-positive rate for varying decision cut-off points. To optimize the decisions for unseen data, so-called generalization must be achieved. It is then possible to estimate generalization accuracy by simulation using cross-validation techniques. In cross-validation, data that have not been a part of the training set will be used to measure the detector's ability to alert alarming situations outside the training data, and therefore the model building effort as a whole. The best model is the one that has the best generalization ability among all models.

25.5 FUTURE APPLICATIONS AND OUTLOOK

One can expect a growing body of applications around networked monitoring of structures, both small and large. Interesting applications can be seen in ski lifts, ferris wheels, roller coasters, etc. The key factor in these applied use cases is the health and safety of humans in man-made structures.

25.6 CONCLUSIONS

SHM is yet another key area where smart object networks will play a central role. Structures such as buildings, bridges, dams, or heavy machinery are expensive and used by millions of people in their everyday life, thus monitoring their health is critical. Various models to sense and process the data have been presented (off-line vs. distributed) to carry large amounts of bursty traffic with a high level of reliability; a must have in these networks.

Although sensors may be retrofitted in existing infrastructures using wireless sensor networks, sensors will more than likely become part of the structure and be powered by energy harvesting.

Container Tracking

In the information age, it is easy to forget that global trade is as much about physical items being moved across the world as it is about information being transferred across the Internet. Every day there are over 6 billion tons of goods transported in over 12 million containers across the world. In the United States alone over 17,000 containers are loaded and unloaded every day.

Approximately 90% of the world's traded goods are shipped inside so-called intermodal containers used for loading goods onto ships, trains, and freighter airplanes. Intermodal containers come in several formats, some of which are specified by ISO standards. For intermodal container shipping, there is a large installed base infrastructure of loading cranes, shipping docks, and freighter ships.

Smart object technology is increasingly being used to track the movement of containers as they are transported on ships, at ports, and through exchange points at places around the world. Smart objects can be installed in the containers, in container locks, or in devices that are attached to the inside or outside of the containers. The ability to retrofit existing containers with smart objects is a key requirement, as the predicted lifetime of a container is many years.

The ability to track the goods as they are shipped across the world is tremendously beneficial for both the shipping company as well as its customers. The shipping companies are able to verify that the location of the goods is what the company expects it to be, as well as to gauge the time delay, should there be problems with the shipment. Likewise, customers are able to track their goods as they are transported by the shipping company providing an added value to the customer.

Container tracking is not only about tracking the location of the containers, however. With the ability to track goods and containers, additional services can be added. Container security is perhaps the most apparent one. With container security tracking, the shipping company is informed instantly when the integrity of its container is breached. Thus the shipment can be immediately stopped and inspected at the next port or exchange point.

Security tracking is not the only application of smart object container tracking. The goods inside the containers can be monitored using sensor-equipped smart objects placed inside the containers. These sensors can monitor temperature, humidity, and vibration conditions for the goods in the containers. This information helps the customers assess the status of their goods after shipment is complete. This is of particular interest for the shipment of foodstuffs and other goods that are sensitive to the transportation environment. The sensor information can be stored by the smart object and transmitted as the goods are unloaded, or transmitted in real time to the shipping company.

Container tracking has previously been implemented using bar codes and bar code readers allowing a coarse-grained tracking of the goods. Bar codes require a substantial amount of human labor, however, increasing the cost of the solution. Subsequently, RFID tags have been used for similar purposes. RFID readers are available at ports and unloading points and can automatically scan large numbers of RFID tags, reducing the handling costs.

Bar codes and RFID tags can only be used to track the location of containers at each unloading location. They cannot be used for real-time tracking or for additional services such as lock security or sensor monitoring. For these services, smart objects are needed.

Two commercially deployed smart object-based container tracking systems, the GE CommerceGuard system and the IBM Secure Trade Lane system, are discussed next.

26.1 GE COMMERCEGUARD

The GE CommerceGuard system provides global tracking of containers as well as immediate notification if the security of the container is breached. The system is semi-IP-based where the end devices are not IP end points, but communicate with fixed readers that are IP end points. The CommerceGuard system was developed in 2002 by the company AllSet Marine Security AB and sold to General Electric in 2005. Its container security device and attachment to an intermodal container are shown in Figure 26.1.

The CommerceGuard system consists of two components: container security devices and readers. The container security devices are placed on the containers and communicate with the readers. Readers are placed both at ports and reloading locations as well as on the ships. There are also mobile readers that are attached to mobile phones or laptops.

The readers communicate with the container security device using a low-power radio and a proprietary protocol. The readers are connected to the Internet and communicate using TCP/IP over an Inmarsat satellite connection. The readers have contact with a database that maintains the location of all container security devices in the system. Customers and users can interact with the system through the database. The CommerceGuard architecture is shown in Figure 26.2.

The container security device consists of a microprocessor, a radio transceiver, a power source in the form of a battery, and a set of sensors. Different container security devices have different configurations of the sensors, but all container security devices have a sensor that detects the opening and closing of the door. The door sensor can also detect if someone is trying to open the door, but fails.

FIGURE 26.1

The CommerceGuard container security device (left) and the lock installed in an intermodal container (right).

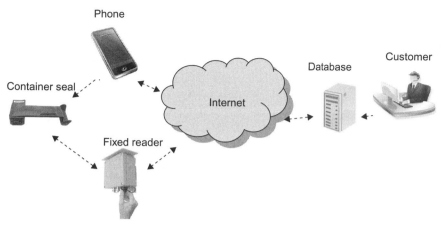

FIGURE 26.2

CommerceGuard architecture: container security devices communicate either with dedicated, fixed readers, or with a phone, and the reader or phone sends the packets over the Internet to a database from which customers download tracking data.

FIGURE 26.3

Fixed reader.

Container security devices can be equipped with additional sensors such as temperature, humidity, vibration, radioactivity, and motion. A particular set of sensors is configured depending on the goods transported in the container. The sensors collect data for storage and act on the data according to a set of application-specific rules.

The radio transceiver on the container security device is duty cycled to provide a long lifetime when running on batteries. The reader and security device communicate using an out-of-band protocol to establish a duty cycle that fits the activities of the location at which the reader is deployed. Readers on a ship, where containers are likely to be present for a longer time and where there is no container mobility, announce a duty cycle that allows the security devices to keep the radio off most of the time. In contrast, readers placed at a busy sea port with high container mobility announce a high duty cycle. Thus security devices keep their radio on for longer amounts of time, allowing for more frequent communication with readers. This allows the readers to communicate with security devices as they are moved between ships and freighter trucks while maintaining low-power consumption for the security devices.

Readers are either stand-alone fixed readers as shown in Figure 26.3 or implemented as an add-on to a phone. The purpose of the reader is to communicate with the container security device using the short-range radio. The readers run the uIP IP stack [64]. The IP stack enables IP-based communication with the device. This reduces the need for custom communication software, leading to lower deployment costs.

Users and customers interact with the CommerceGuard system using a web browser, as shown in Figure 26.4. The user interacts with the database that contains information about the security device's location and physical conditions inside the containers to which they are attached.

26.2 IBM SECURE TRADE LANE

The IBM Secure Trade Lane (STL) system was recently developed for container tracking and secure management for IBM by ETH in Zürich in 2006 [58]. The STL system consists of a container security device called the tamper-resistant embedded controller (TREC), which communicates with a database that tracks the movement of the container to which the TREC is attached.

FIGURE 26.4

The user interface of the CommerceGuard system running on a laptop.

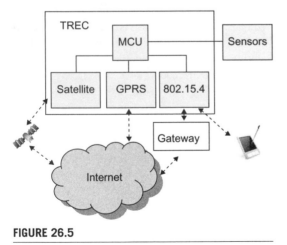

FIGURE 26.5

A block diagram of the TREC and its connections.

Similar to the CommerceGuard system, the TREC device contains a microprocessor, sensors, and several communication options. Unlike the CommerceGuard system, which required a reader device to communicate with the security devices, the TREC is able to directly communicate with the Internet using its on-board General Packet Radio System (GPRS) communication device. A block diagram of the TREC is shown in Figure 26.5.

The TREC contains three different communication devices: a GPRS interface that provides Internet connectivity when the device is within range of a mobile telephony system; a satellite communication system that allows Internet connectivity when the device is at sea, where there is little or no GPRS coverage; and an 802.15.4 low-power radio transceiver, which is used for short-range communication such as with a mobile reader terminal. Additionally, the 802.15.4 device can be used for communicating with a gateway device, which in turn connects to the Internet.

All communication devices are used to send information about the system to a database server over the Internet. The ability to use the Internet to transport information significantly reduces management overhead due to the ubiquitous presence of Internet connectivity.

The CommerceGuard system and the IBM STL system show the transition from semi-IP-based systems to fully IP-based systems. The CommerceGuard system used IP at the readers but did not fully run IP to the end points. The more recent IBM STL system runs IP all the way into the containers, making management of the system easier.

26.3 CONCLUSIONS

Global trade relies on the efficient shipment of goods since 90% of all goods are shipped in containers. The ability to track the location of such containers and to continuously and remotely inspect their status helps both shipping companies and their customers. Because of its success, smart object technology is increasingly being used for global container tracking.

We provide an overview of two container tracking systems: the GE CommerceGuard, developed in 2002, and the IBM Secure Trade Lane, developed in 2006. The GE CommerceGuard is semi-IP-based where IP end points are located at ships and ports, but the containers are not IP end points. The IBM STL system places the IP end points at every container, relying on the now-established infrastructure of Internet connectivity through satellite and GPRS connections. These are both examples of IP-based smart object systems that show the trend of pushing IP further into the actual devices.

References

1. Abeillé J, Durvy M, Hui J, Dawson-Haggerty S. Lightweight IPv6 Stacks for Smart Objects: the Experience of Three Independent and Interoperable Implementations; January 2009. IPSO Alliance White Paper 2. Available from: <www.ipso-alliance.org/>.

2. Abley J, Savola P, Neville-Neil G. "Deprecation of Type 0 Routing Headers in IPv6"; December 2007. Available from: <www.ietf.org/>.

3. Aboba B, Thaler D, Esibov L. Link-Local Multicast Name Resolution (LLMNR). Internet informational RFC4795; January 2007.

4. Adya A, Howell J, Theimer M, Bolosky WJ, Douceur JR. Cooperative task management without manual stack management. In: *Proceedings of the USENIX Annual Technical Conference*; 2002:289–302.

5. Akiba. Freaklabs — Open Source ZigBee. Web page. <http://www.freaklabs.org/>.

6. Alkabani Y, Koushanfar F. Active hardware metering for intellectual property protection and security. In: *Proceedings of 16th USENIX Security Symposium on USENIX Security Symposium, SS'07*. Berkeley, CA: USENIX Association; 2007:1–16.

7. Allman M, Paxson V. On estimating end-to-end network path properties. In: *Proceedings of the SIGCOMM '99 Conference*. Cambridge, MA; September 1999.

8. Allman M, Paxson V, Stevens W. TCP congestion control. RFC2581, Internet Engineering Task Force; April 1999.

9. Alvestrand H. RFC3710, "An IESG charter". Available from: <www.ietf.org/>.

10. Alvestrand H. RFC3935, "A Mission Statement for the IETF". Available from: <www.ietf.org/>.

11. Anderson R. Why cryptosystems fail. In: *CCS '93: Proceedings of the 1st ACM conference on Computer and Communications Security*. Fairfax, VA; 1993:215–227.

12. Anderson R, Kuhn M. Tamper resistance: a cautionary note. In: *Proceedings of the 2nd Conference on Proceedings of the Second USENIX Workshop on Electronic Commerce, WOEC'96*. Berkeley, CA: USENIX Association; 1996:1.

13. Asynchronous Transfer Mode Signaling Private Network-to-Network Interface.

14. Awduche D, Berger L, Gan D, Li T, Srinivasan V, Swallow G. RFC3209, "RSVP-TE: Extensions to RSVP for LSP Tunnels"; December 2001. Available from: <www.ietf.org/>.

15. Balakrishnan H, Seshan S, Amir E, Katz R. Improving TCP/IP performance over wireless networks. In: *Proceedings of the First ACM Conference on Mobile Communications and Networking*. Berkeley, CA; November 1995.

16. Blake S, Black D, Carlson M, Davies E, Wang Z, Weiss W. RFC2475, "An Architecture for Differentiated Services"; December 1998. Available from: <www.ietf.org/>.

17. Migrating to IPv6: A Practical Guide to Implementing IPv6 in Mobile and Fixed Networks by Marc Blanchet: Wiley.

18. Bormann C, Burmeister C, Degermark M, et al. RFC3095, "RObust Header Compression (ROHC): Framework and four profiles: RTP, UDP, ESP, and uncompressed"; July 2001. Available from: <www.ietf.org/>.

19. Braden R. Requirements for internet hosts — communication layers. RFC1122, Internet Engineering Task Force; October 1989.

20. Braden R, Clark D, Shenker S. RFC1633, "Integrated Services in the Internet Architecture: an Overview"; June 1994. Available from: <www.ietf.org/>.

21. Braden R, Zhang L, Berson S, Herzog S, Jamin S. RFC2205, "Resource ReSerVation Protocol (RSVP) — Version 1 Functional Specification"; September 1997. Available from: <www.ietf.org/>.

22. Bradner S. RFC2026, "The Internet Standards Process — Revision 3"; October 1996. Available from: <www.ietf.org/>.

23. Bradner S. RFC2119, "Key words for use in RFCs to Indicate Requirement Levels"; March 1997. Available from: <www.ietf.org/>.
24. Brandt A, Buron J, Porcu G. draft-ietf-roll-home-routing-reqs, "Home Automation Routing Requirements in Low Power and Lossy Networks", Work in progress. Available from: <www.ietf.org/>.
25. Buettner M, Yee GV, Anderson E, Han R. X-MAC: a short preamble MAC protocol for duty-cycled wireless sensor networks. In: *SenSys '06: Proceedings of the 4th International Conference on Embedded Networked Sensor Systems*. Boulder, CO; 2006:307–320.
26. Buettner M, Prasad R, Sample A, et al. RFID sensor networks with the Intel wisp. In: *Proceedings of the 6th ACM Conference on Embedded Network Sensor Systems*; 2008:393–394.
27. Burri N, von Rickenbach P, Wattenhofer R. Dozer: ultra-low power data gathering in sensor networks. In: *IPSN '07*; 2007.
28. Bush R, Meyer D. RFC3439, "Some Internet Architectural Guidelines and Philosophy", December 2002. Available from: <www.ietf.org/>.
29. Cain B, Deering S, Kouvelas I, et al. RFC3376, "Internet Group Management Protocol, Version 3"; October 2002. Available from: <www.ietf.org/>.
30. Callon R. "Use of OSI IS-IS for routing in TCP/IP and dual environments", RFC1195; December 1990.
31. Candès EJ, Wakin MB. An Introduction to Compressive Sampling. *Signal Process Mag*. March 2008.
32. Carpenter B. RFC2775, "Internet Transparency"; February 2000. Available from: <www.ietf.org/>.
33. Carpenter B. RFC2850, "Charter of the Internet Architecture Board (IAB)". Available from: <www.ietf.org/>.
34. Carpenter B, Moore K. RFC3056, "Connection of IPv6 Domains via IPv4 Clouds"; February 2001. Available from: <www.ietf.org/>.
35. Cheng TE, Fonseca R, Kim S, et al. A modular network layer for sensornets. In: *Proceedings of OSDI*; August 2006.
36. Cheshire S, Aboba B, Guttman E. Dynamic configuration of ipv4 link-local addresses. Internet standard RFC3927; May 2005.
37. Christian A, Healey J. Gathering motion data using featherweight sensors and TCP/IP over 802.15.4. In: *Proceedings of the IEEE International Symposium on Wearable Computers, On-Body Sensing Workshop*. Osaka, Japan; October 2005.
38. Claise B. RFC3954, "Cisco Systems NetFlow Services Export Version 9"; October 2004.
39. Clark D. "THE DESIGN PHILOSOPHY OF THE DARPA INTERNET PROTOCOLS", ACM; 1988.
40. Clark DD. Window and acknowledgement strategy in TCP. RFC813, Internet Engineering Task Force; July 1982.
41. Clausen T, Jacquet P. RFC3626, "Optimized Link State Routing Protocol (OLSR)"; October 2003. Available from: <www.ietf.org/>.
42. Conta A, Deering S, Gupta M. RFC4443, "Internet Control Message Protocol (ICMPv6) for the Internet Protocol Version 6 (IPv6) Specification", March 2006. Available from: <www.ietf.org/>.
43. Cooprider N, Archer W, Eide E, Gay D, Regehr J. Efficient memory safety for TinyOS. In: *Proceedings of the 5th International Conference on Embedded Networked Sensor Systems*. New York, NY: ACM; 2007:205–218.
44. Crawford M. RFC2464, "Transmission of IPv6 Packets over Ethernet Networks"; December 1998. Available from: <www.ietf.org/>.
45. Crockford D. The application/JSON media type for JavaScript object notation (JSON). Internet RFC4627; July 2006.
46. Culler D, Dutta P, Cheng TE, et al. Towards a sensor network architecture: Lowering the waistline. In: *Proceedings of the International Workshop on Hot Topics in Operating Systems (HotOS)*; 2005.
47. Cunha A, Koubaa A, Severino R, Alves M. Open-ZB: an open-source implementation of the IEEE 802.15. 4/ZigBee protocol stack on TinyOS. In: *IEEE International Conference on Mobile Ad hoc and Sensor Systems, 2007. MASS 2007*; 2007:1–12.

48. DARPA INTERNET PROGRAM, RFC791, "Internet Protocol"; September 1981. Available from: <www.ietf.org/>.

49. Understanding IPv6, Second Edition by Jospeph Davies: Microsoft Press.

50. De Couto D, Aguayo D, Bicket J, Morris R. A high-throughput path metric for multi-hop wireless routing. In: *Proceedings of the 9th Annual International Conference on Mobile Computing and Networking.* New York, NY: ACM; 2003:134–146.

51. De Rosa M, Goldstein S, Lee P, Campbell J, Pillai P. Programming modular robots with locally distributed predicates. In: *Proceedings of the IEEE International Conference on Robotics and Automation ICRA '08*; 2008.

52. Steve Deering, "Watching the Waist of the protocol Hourglass", IETF-51 London IETF-51.

53. Deering S, Hinden R. RFC2460, "Internet Protocol, Version 6 (IPv6) Specification"; December 1998. Available from: <www.ietf.org/>.

54. Deering S, Hinden R. RFC3513, "Internet Protocol Version 6 (IPv6) Addressing Architecture"; July 1998. Available from: <www.ietf.org/>.

55. Dierks T, Allen C. RFC2246, "The TLS Protocol – Verion 1"; January 1999. Available from: <www.ietf.org/>.

56. Dierks T, Rescorla E. The Transport Layer Security (TLS) Protocol Version 1.2. Internet standard RFC 5246; August 2008.

57. Dohler M, Watteyne T, Winter T, Barthel D. RFC5548, "Routing Requirements for Urban Low-Power and Lossy Networks". Available from: <www.ietf.org/>.

58. Dolivo F. The IBM Secure Trade Lane Solution. ERCIM News no. 68; January 2007.

59. Draves R, Thaler D. RFC4191, "Default Router Preferences and More-Specific Routes"; November 2005. Available from: <www.ietf.org/>.

60. Droms R. Dynamic host configuration protocol. Internet standard RFC2131; March 1997.

61. Droms R. RFC3736, "Stateless Dynamic Host Configuration Protocol (DHCP) Service for IPv6"; April 2004. Available from: <www.ietf.org/>.

62. Droms R, Bound J, Volz B, Lemon T, Perkins C, Carney M. RFC3315, "Dynamic Host Configuration Protocol for IPv6 (DHCPv6)"; June 2003. Available from: <www.ietf.org/>.

63. Droms R, Bound J, Volz B, Lemon T, Perkins C, Carney M. RFC3315, "Dynamic Host Configuration Protocol for IPv6 (DHCPv6)"; July 2003. Available from: <www.ietf.org/>.

64. Dunkels A. Full TCP/IP for 8-bit architectures. In: *Proceedings of The First International Conference on Mobile Systems, Applications, and Services (MOBISYS '03)*; May 2003.

65. Dunkels A. Protothreads web site. Web page; 2004. Visited 20.12.09.

66. Dunkels A, Vasseur JP. IP for Smart Objects; September 2008. IPSO Alliance White Paper 1. Available from: <www.ipso-alliance.org/>.

67. Dunkels A, Voigt T, Alonso J. Making TCP/IP Viable for Wireless Sensor Networks. In: *Proc. EWSN'04 work-in-progress session*; January 2004.

68. Dunkels A, Voigt T, Bergman N, Jönsson M. The Design and Implementation of an IP-based Sensor Network for Intrusion Monitoring. In: *Swedish National Computer Networking Workshop.* Karlstad, Sweden; November 2004.

69. Dunkels A, Finne N, Eriksson J, Voigt T. Run-time dynamic linking for reprogramming wireless sensor networks. In: *ACM Conference on Networked Embedded Sensor Systems (SenSys 2006).* Boulder, CO; November 2006.

70. Dunkels A, Schmidt O, Voigt T, Ali M. Protothreads: Simplifying event-driven programming of memory-constrained embedded systems. In: *Proceedings of the Fourth ACM Conference on Embedded Networked Sensor Systems (SenSys 2006).* Boulder, CO; November 2006.

71. Dunkels A, Österlind F, He Z. An adaptive communication architecture for wireless sensor networks. In: *Proceedings of the Fifth ACM Conference on Networked Embedded Sensor Systems (SenSys 2007).* Sydney, Australia; November 2007.

72. Durand A, Huitema C. RFC3194, " The Host-Density Ratio for Address Assignment Efficiency: An update on the H ratio"; November 2001. Available from: <www.ietf.org/>.

73. Durvy M, Abeillé J, Wetterwald P. et al. Making Sensor Networks IPv6 Ready. In: *Proceedings of the Sixth ACM Conference on Networked Embedded Sensor Systems (ACM SenSys 2008)*. Raleigh, NC; November 2008:421–422.

74. Eastlake 3rd D, Jones P. "US Secure Hash Algorithm 1 (SHA1)", RFC3174; September 2001. Available from: <www.ietf.org/>.

75. Eastlake 3rd D, Schiller J, Crocker S. "Randomness Requirements for Security", BCP 106, RFC4086; June 2005. Available from: <www.ietf.org/>.

76. El-Hoiydi A, Decotignie JD, Enz CC, Le Roux E. WiseMAC, an ultra low power MAC protocol for the WiseNet wireless sensor network. In: *SenSys*; 2003:302–303.

77. Eriksson J, Dunkels A, Finne N, Österlind F, Voigt T. Mspsim — an extensible simulator for msp430-equipped sensor boards. In: *Proceedings of the European Conference on Wireless Sensor Networks (EWSN), Poster/Demo Session*. Delft, The Netherlands; January 2007.

78. Estrin D, Farinacci D, Helmy A, et al. "Protocol Independent Multicast-Sparse Mode (PIM-SM): Protocol Specification"; June 1998. Available from: <www.ietf.org/>.

79. "Federal Information Processing Standards Publication", (FIPS PUB) 180-1, Secure Hash Standard; 17 April 1995.

80. Feeney L, Nilsson M. Investigating the energy consumption of a wireless network interface in an ad hoc networking environment. In: *IEEE Conference on Computer Communications (Infocom'01)*; April 2001.

81. Fenner W. RFC2236, "Internet Group Management Protocol, Version 2"; November 1997. Available from: <www.ietf.org/>.

82. Ferrari G, Stuber J, Gombos A, Laverde D, eds. *Programming Lego Mindstorms with Java with CD-ROM*: Syngress Publishing; 2002.

83. Fielding R, Gettys J, Mogul J, et al. Hypertext transfer protocol — http/1.1. Internet RFC2616; June 1999.

84. Floyd S, Jacobson V. Random Early Detection gateways for Congestion Avoidance, IEEE/ACM Transactions on Networking, V.1 N.4; August 1993:397–413.

85. Fonseca R, Gnawali O, Jamieson K, Levis P. Four-bit wireless link estimation. In: *Sixth Workshop on Hot Topics in Networks (ACM HotNets-VI)*. Atlanta, GA; November 2007.

86. Antoine Fressancourt, Colombe Hérault and Eric Ptak: Tangibility in social networks.

87. Fu K. Inside risks, reducing the risks of implantable medical devices: A prescription to improve security and privacy of pervasive health care. *Commun ACM*. 2009;52(6):25–27.

88. Fuller V, Li T. RFC4632, "Classless Inter-domain Routing (CIDR): The Internet Address Assignment and Aggregation Plan"; August 2006. Available from: <www.ietf.org/>.

89. Ganti R, Jayachandran P, Abdelzaher T, Stankovic J. Satire: a software architecture for smart attire. In: *MobiSys '06: Proceedings of the 4th International Conference on Mobile systems, Applications and Services*. New York, NY: ACM; 2006:110–123.

90. Gay D, Levis P, von Behren R, Welsh M, Brewer E, Culler D. The nesC language: A holistic approach to networked embedded systems. In: *Proceedings of the ACM SIGPLAN 2003 Conference on Programming Language Design and Implementation*; 2003:1–11.

91. Gilligan R, Nordmark E. RFC2893, "Transition Mechanisms for IPv6 Hosts and Routers"; August 2000. Available from: <www.ietf.org/>.

92. Glenn R, Kent S. RFC2710, "The NULL Encryption Algorithm and Its Use With IPsec"; November 1998. Available from: <www.ietf.org/>.

93. Gnawali O, Jang K, Paek J, et al. The tenet architecture for tiered sensor networks. In: *SenSys '06: Proceedings of the 4th International Conference on Embedded Networked Sensor Systems*; 2006.

94. Gnawali O, Fonseca R, Jamieson K, Moss D, Levis P. Collection tree protocol. In: *Proceedings of the 7th ACM Conference on Embedded Networked Sensor Systems (SenSys)*; 2009.

95. Goldstein S, Mowry T. Claytronics: An instance of programmable matter. In: *Wild and Crazy Ideas Session of ASPLOS*. Boston, MA; October 2004.

96. Goodspeed T. Extracting keys from second generation ZigBee chips. In: *Proceedings of Black Hat USA 2009*. Las Vegas, NV; July 2009.

97. Grossman D. RFC3260, "New Terminology and Clarifications for Diffserv"; April 2002. Available from: <www.ietf.org/>.

98. Gummadi R, Gnawali O, Govindan R. Macro-programming wireless sensor networks using Kairos. In: *Proc. of Distributed Computing in Sensor Systems (DCOSS)'05*. Marina del Rey, CA; June 2005.

99. Gupta V, Wurm M, Zhu Y, et al. Sizzle: A standards-based end-to-end security architecture for the embedded internet. *Pervasive Mobile Comput J*. December 2005:425–445.

100. Gutierrez JA, Naeve M, Callaway E, Bourgeois M, Mitter V, Heile B. IEEE 802.15.4: A developing standard for low-power low-cost wireless personal area networks. *IEEE Netw*. September/October 2001;15(5):12–19.

101. Guttman E, Perkins C, Veizades J, Day M. Service Location Protocol, Version 2. Internet RFC2608; June 1999.

102. Haberman B. RFC3307, "Allocation Guidelines for IPv6 Multicast Addresses"; August 2002. Available from: <www.ietf.org/>.

103. Haberman B, Thaler D. RFC3306, "Unicast-Prefix-based IPv6 Multicast Addresses". Available from: <www.ietf.org/>.

104. IPv6 Essentials by Silvia Hage, O'Reilly.

105. Hain T. RFC2993, "Architectural Implications of NAT"; November 2000. Available from: <www.ietf.org/>.

106. Handley M, Kouvelas I, Speakman T, Vicisano L. RFC5015, "Bidirectional Protocol Independent Multicast (BIDIR-PIM)"; October 2007. Available from: <www.ietf.org/>.

107. Harrington D, Presuhn R, Wijnen B. RFC2571, "An Architecture for Describing SNMP Management Frameworks"; April 1999. Available from: <www.ietf.org/>.

108. Harrington D, Presuhn R, Wijnen B. RFC3411, "An Architecture for Describing Simple Network Management Protocol (SNMP) Management Frameworks"; December 2002. Available from: <www.ietf.org/>.

109. Hartel P, Abelmann L, Khatib M. Towards tamper-evident storage on patterned media. In: *Proceedings of the 6th USENIX Conference on File and Storage Technologies, FAST'08*. Berkeley, CA: USENIX Association; 2008:1–14.

110. Heidemann J, Estrin D, Govindan R, Kumar S. Next century challenges: scalable coordination in sensor networks. In: *Proceedings of the Fifth Annual ACM/IEEE International Conference on Mobile Computing and Networking*. Seattle, WA; 1999:263–270.

111. Heidemann JS, Silva F, Intanagonwiwat C, Govindan R, Estrin D, Ganesan D. Building efficient wireless sensor networks with low-level naming. In: *Symposium on Operating Systems Principles*. 2001:146–159.

112. Heinanen J, Baker F, Weiss W, Wroclawski J. RFC2597, "Assured Forwarding PHB Group"; June 1999. Available from: <www.ietf.org/>.

113. Hill J, Szewczyk R, Woo A, Hollar S, Culler D, Pister K. System architecture directions for networked sensors. In: *Proceedings of the 9th International Conference on Architectural Support for Programming Languages and Operating Systems*; November 2000.

114. Hinden R, Deering S. RFC1884-IP Version 6 Addressing Architecture. Available from: <www.ietf.org/>.

115. Hinden R, Deering S. RFC2375 "IPv6 Multicast Address Assignments"; July 1998. Available from: <www.ietf.org/>.

116. Hinden R, Deering S. RFC4291, "IP Version 6 Addressing Architecture"; February 2006. Available from: <www.ietf.org/>.

117. Hinden R, Haberman B. RFC4193, "Unique Local IPv6 Unicast Addresses"; October 2005. Available from: <www.ietf.org/>.

118. Housley R. Using Advanced Encryption Standard (AES) CCM Mode with IPsec Encapsulating Security Payload (ESP). Internet standard RFC4309; December 2005.

119. Holbrook H, Cain B. RFC4606, "Source-Specific Multicast for IP". October 2006. Available at HYPERLINK <http://www.ietf.org/>.

120. Howard M, Sontag C. Bringing the internet to all electronic devices. In: *Proceedings of the Workshop on Embedded Systems on Workshop on Embedded Systems, WOES'99*. Berkeley, CA: USENIX Association; 1999:5.

121. http://www.coopers-ip.eu/.

122. http://www.roamservices.net/index.html.

123. http://www.w3.org/2008/09/msnws/papers/sensors.html.

124. Hui J, ed. draft-ietf-6lowpan-hc, "Compression Format for IPv6 Datagrams in 6LoWPAN Networks". Available from: <www.ietf.org/>.

125. Hui J, Culler D. IP is Dead, Long Live IP for Wireless Sensor Networks. In: *Proceedings of the 6th international Conference on Embedded Networked Sensor Systems*. Raleigh, NC; November 2008.

126. Huitema C. RFC1715, "The H Ratio for Address Assignment Efficiency"; November 1994. Available from: <www.ietf.org/>.

127. Huitema C, Carpenter B. RFC3879, "Deprecating Site Local Addresses"; September 2004. Available from: <www.ietf.org/>.

128. IANA. RFC3330, "Special-Use IPv4 Addresses"; September 2002. Available from: <www.ietf.org/>.

129. IEEE Computer Society, "IEEE Std. 802.15.4-2003"; October 2003.

130. Integrating Social Networks and Sensor Networks, W3C Workshop on the Future of Social Networking, 15–16 January 2009, Barcelona.

131. "Intermediate System to Intermediate System Intra-Domain Routing Exchange Protocol for use in Conjunction with the Protocol for Providing the Connectionless-mode Network Service (ISO 8473)", ISO 10589.

132. International Telecommunication Union. Code-independent error-control system; 1988. ITU-T Recommendation V.41.

133. Ishii H, Wisneski C, Brave S, et al. ambientROOM: integrating ambient media with architectural space. In: *The CHI 98 conference summary on Human factors in computing systems*. New York, NY: ACM; 1998:173–174.

134. Jacobson V. Congestion avoidance and control. In: *Proceedings of the SIGCOMM '88 Conference*. Stanford, CA; August 1988.

135. Jacobson V. Compressing TCP/IP headers for low-speed serial links. RFC1144, Internet Engineering Task Force; February 1990.

136. Jacobson V, Braden R, Borman D. TCP extensions for high performance. RFC1323, Internet Engineering Task Force; May 1992.

137. Jacobson V, Nichols K, Poduri K. RFC2598, "An Expedited Forwarding PHB"; June 1999. Available from: <www.ietf.org/>.

138. Jeong J, Park S, Beloeil L, Madanapalli S. RFC5006, "IPv6 Router Advertisement Option for DNS Configuration"; September 2007. Available from: <www.ietf.org/>.

139. Jing-xin W, Jian Y, Zhen-ming F, Can-feng C. A Users Social Attributes Based Mobility Model for Ad Hoc Network Research, CWSN; 2009, to be published.

140. Johnson D, Perkins C, Arkko J. "Mobility Support in IPv6"; June 2004. Available from: <www.ietf.org/>.

141. Johnson D, Hu Y, Maltz D. RFC4728, "The Dynamic Source Routing Protocol (DSR) for Mobile Ad Hoc Networks for IPv4"; February 2007. Available from: <www.ietf.org/>.

142. Kahn JM, Katz R, Pister K. Next century challenges: mobile networking for "smart dust". In: *MobiCom '99: Proceedings of the 5th annual ACM/IEEE International Conference on Mobile Computing and Networking*. New York, NY: ACM; 1999:271–278.

143. Karn P, Partridge C. Improving round-trip time estimates in reliable transport protocols. In: *Proceedings of the SIGCOMM '87 Conference*. Stowe, VT; August 1987.

144. Katz D, Ward D. draft-ietf-bfd-base, "Bidirectional Forwarding Detection", work in progress. Available from: <www.ietf.org/>.

145. Kent S. IP Encapsulating Security Payload (ESP). Internet standard RFC4303; December 2005.

146. Kent S, Atkinson R. RFC4302, "IP Authentication Header"; December 2005.

147. Kent C, Mogul J. Fragmentation considered harmful. *SIGCOMM Comput Commun Rev*. 1995;25(1): 75–87.

148. Kent S, Seo K. Security Architecture for the Internet Protocol. Internet standard RFC4301; December 2005.

149. Khare R, Lawrence S. RFC2817, "Upgrading to TLS Within HTTP/1.1", May 2000. Available from: <www.ietf.org/>.

150. Kim KH, Shin KG. "On Accurate Measurement of Link Quality in Multi-hop Wireless Mesh Networks". Mobicom; 2006.

151. Kleinrock L. *Communication Nets: Stochastic Message Flow and Design*: McGraw-Hill; 1964.

152. Kohler E, Handley M, Floyd S. Datagram Congestion Control Protocol (DCCP). RFC4340; March 2006.

153. Kompella K, Rekhter Y. RFC4202, "Routing Extensions in Support of Generalized Multi-Protocol Label Switching (GMPLS)"; October 2005. Available from: <www.ietf.org/>.

154. Kompella K, Rekhter Y. RFC4203, "OSPF Extensions in Support of Generalized Multi-Protocol Label Switching (GMPLS)"; October 2005. Available from: <www.ietf.org/>.

155. Kompella K, Rekhter Y. RFC4305, "Intermediate System to Intermediate System (IS-IS) Extensions in Support of Generalized Multi-Protocol Label Switching (GMPLS)"; October 2005. Available from: <www.ietf.org/>.

156. Kushalnagar N, Montenegro G, Schumacher C. RFC4919, "IPv6 over Low-Power Wireless Personal Area Networks (6LoWPANs): Overview, Assumptions, Problem Statement, and Goals"; August 2007. Available from: <www.ietf.org/>.

157. Lauer HC, Needham RM. On the duality of operating systems structures. In: *Proc. Second International Symposium on Operating Systems*; October 1978.

158. Levis P, Gay D. *TinyOS Programming*: Cambridge University Press; 2009.

159. Levis P, Patel N, Culler D, Shenker S. Trickle: A self-regulating algorithm for code propagation and maintenance in wireless sensor networks. In: *Proc. NSDI'04*; March 2004.

160. Levis P, Brewer E, Culler D, et al. "The Emergence of a Networking Primitive in Wireless Sensor Networks." In: *Communications of the ACM*. Vol. 51, Issue 7; July 2008.

161. Levis P, Tavakoli A, Dawson-Haggerty S. Overview of existing routing protocols for low power and lossy networks; 2009. Internet-draft, work in progress.

162. Madden S, Franklin M, Hellerstein J, Hong W. Tag: a tiny aggregation service for ad-hoc sensor networks. In: *OSDI '02: Proceedings of the 5th Symposium on Operating Systems Design and Implementation*. New York, NY: ACM; 2002:131–146.

163. Malkin G. RFC2453, "RIP Version 2"; November 1998. Available from: <www.ietf.org/>.

164. IPv6 Network Administration by David Malone (Author), Niall Richard Murphy, O'Reilly.

165. Mann S. Wearable computing: A first step toward personal imaging. *Computer*. 1997;30(2):25–32.

166. Manner J. Coupling of Service and Neighbor Discovery in 6LowPAN; October 2009. draft-manner-6low-app-sdnd, Internet-draft, work in progress.

167. Maróti M, Kusy B, Simon G, Lédeczi A. The flooding time synchronization protocol. In: *Proceedings of the 2nd International Conference on Embedded Networked Sensor Systems*. New York, NY: ACM; 2004:39–49.

168. Marrón P, Minder D, Lachenmann A, Rothermel K. TinyCubus: An adaptive cross-layer framework for sensor networks. *IT — Inf Technol*. 2005;47(2):87–97.

169. Martocci J, De Mil P, Vermeylen W, Riou N. draft-ietf-roll-building-routing-reqs, "Building Automation Routing Requirements in Low Power and Lossy Networks", Work in progress. Available from: <www.ietf.org/>.

170. Mathis M, Mahdavi J, Floyd S, Romanow A. TCP selective acknowledgment options. RFC2018, Internet Engineering Task Force; October 1996.

171. McCann J, Deering S, Mogul J. RFC1981, "Path MTU Discovery for IP version 6"; August 1996. Available from: <www.ietf.org/>.

172. McKusick MK, Bostic K, Karels MJ, Quarterman JS. *The Design and Implementation of the 4.4 BSD Operating System*. Reading, MA: Addison-Wesley; 1996.

173. Melkonian M. Get by Without an RTOS. *Embedded Syst Program*. September 2000;13(10).

174. MetroSense Project Web Page. <http://metrosense.cs.dartmouth.edu/>.

175. Mills D. "Network Time Protocol (Version 3) Specification, Implementation and Analysis", RFC1305; March 1992. Available from: <www.ietf.org/>.

176. Montenegro G, Kushalnagar N, Hui J, Culler D. Transmission of IPv6 Packets over IEEE 802.15.4 Networks. Internet proposed standard RFC4944; September 2007.

177. Moore N. RFC4429, "Optimistic Duplicate Address Detection (DAD) for IPv6"; April 2006. Available from: <www.ietf.org/>.

178. Moreira L, Souza S, Spiess P, et al. SOCRADES: A Web Service based Shop Floor Integration Infrastructure. In: *Proceedings of Internet of Things 2008 Conference*. Zurich, Switzerland; March 2008.

179. Moy J. RFC2328, "OSPF Version 2"; April 1998. Available from: <www.ietf.org/>.

180. Mulligan G. The 6lowpan architecture. In: *Proceedings of the 4th Workshop on Embedded Networked Sensors*. New York, NY: ACM; 2007:78–82.

181. Musaloiu-E R, Liang CJM, Terzis A. Koala: Ultra-Low Power Data Retrieval in Wireless Sensor Networks. In: *IPSN '08*; 2008.

182. Musolesi M, Hailes S, Mascolo C. An Ad Hoc mobility model founded on social network theory[C]. In: *Proceedings of MSWiM'04*: ACM Press; October 2004:20–24.

183. Naone E. Meters for the smart grid. *MIT Technol Rev*. 2009.

184. Narten T, Draves R, Krishnan S. RFC4941, "Privacy Extensions for Stateless Address Autoconfiguration in IPv6"; September 2007. Available from: <www.ietf.org/>.

185. Narten T, Nordmark E, Simpson W, Soliman H. RFC4861, "Neighbor Discovery for IP version 6 (IPv6)"; September 2007. Available from: <www.ietf.org/>.

186. Newton R, Arvind, Welsh M. Building up to macroprogramming: An intermediate language for sensor networks. In: *Proc. IPSN'05*. Los Angeles, CA; April 2005.

187. Ogier R, Templin F, Lewis M. RFC3684, "Topology Dissemination Based on Reverse-Path Forwarding (TBRPF)"; February 2004. Available from: <www.ietf.org/>.

188. Oliveira L, Kansal A, Priyantha B, Goraczko M, Zhao F. Secure-TWS: Authenticating node to multi-user communication in shared sensor networks. In: *Proceedings of the 2009 International Conference on Information Processing in Sensor Networks, IPSN 2009*; 2009:289–300.

189. Österlind F, Dunkels A, Eriksson J, Finne N, Voigt T. Cross-level sensor network simulation with COOJA. In: *Proceedings of the First IEEE International Workshop on Practical Issues in Building Sensor Network Applications (SenseApp 2006)*. Tampa, FL; November 2006.

190. Ostmark A, Lindgren P, van Halteren AT, Meppelink L. Service and device discovery of nodes in a wireless sensor network. In: *Proceedings of the 3rd IEEE Consumer Communications and Networking Conference, CCNC 2006*. Las Vegas, NV; January 2006.

191. Paisley J, Sventek J. Real-time detection of grid bulk transfer traffic. In: *Proceedings of the 10th IEEE/IFIP Network Operations Management Symposium*. Vancouver, Canada; April 2006.

192. Pajic M, Mangharam R. Anti-jamming for embedded wireless networks. In: *IPSN '09: Proceedings of the 2009 International Conference on Information Processing in Sensor Networks*. San Francisco, CA; April 2009:301–312.

193. Paxson V. End-to-end internet packet dynamics. In: *Proceedings of the SIGCOMM '97 Conference*. Cannes, France; September 1997.

194. Perkins C, Belding-Royer E, Das S. Ad hoc on-demand distance vector (AODV) routing. RFC3561, Internet Engineering Task Force; 2003.

195. Pfleeger C, Pfleeger S. *Security in Computing*. 4th ed. Upper Saddle River, NJ: Prentice Hall PTR; 2006.

196. Pister K, Doherty L. TSMP: Time Synchronized Mesh Protocol. In: *Proceedings of the IASTED International Symposium on Distributed Sensor Networks (DSN08)*. Orlando, FL; November 2008.

197. Pister K, Thubert P, Dwars S, Phinney T. RFC5873, "Industrial Routing Requirements in Low-Power and Lossy Networks". Available from: <www.ietf.org/>.

198. Polastre J. Java technology meets the real world: Intelligence everywhere; 2008. Presented at JavaOne. Number TS-5428.

199. Polastre J, Hill J, Culler D. Versatile low power media access for wireless sensor networks. In: *SenSys '04: Proceedings of the 2nd international Conference on Embedded Networked Sensor Systems*. New York, NY: ACM Press; 2004:95–107.

200. Polastre J, Szewczyk R, Culler D. Telos: Enabling ultra-low power wireless research. In: *Proc. IPSN/SPOTS'05*. Los Angeles, CA; April 2005.

201. Deploying IPv6 Networks by Ciprian Popoviciu, Eric Levy-Abegnoli, Patrick Grossette, Cisco Press.

202. Postel J. User datagram protocol. RFC768, Internet Engineering Task Force; August 1980.

203. Postel J. RFC792, "Internet Control Message Protocol", September 1981. Available from: <www.ietf.org/>.

204. Postel J. Transmission control protocol. RFC793, Internet Engineering Task Force; September 1981.

205. Postel J, Reynolds J. RFC959, "File Transfer Protocol"; October 1985. Available from: <www.ietf.org/>.

206. Presuhn R. RFC3418, "Management Information Base (MIB) for the Simple Network Management Protocol (SNMP)"; December 2002. <www.ietf.org/>.

207. Priyantha B, Kansal A, Goraczko M, Zhao F. Tiny web services: design and implementation of interoperable and evolvable sensor networks. In: *Proceedings of the 6th ACM Conference on Embedded Network Sensor Systems (SenSys '08)*. Raleigh, NC; 2008:253–266.

208. Ramakrishnan K, Floyd S. RFC2481, "A Proposal to add Explicit Congestion Notification (ECN) to IP"; January 1999. Available from: <www.ietf.org/>.

209. Ramakrishnan K, Floyd S, Black, D. RFC3168, "The Addition of Explicit Congestion Notification (ECN) to IP". September 2001. Available at HYPERLINK <http://www.ietf.org/>.

210. Reed DP. UDP length field. E-mail to the end-to-end discussion mailing list; April 2001. <http://www.postel.org/pipermail/end2end-interest/2001-April/000425.html/>.

211. Reese R, Bruce J, Jones B. *Microcontrollers: From Assembly Language to C Using the PIC24 Family*. Rockland, MA: Charles River Media, Inc.; 2008.

212. Rekhter Y, Li T, Hares S. RFC4271, "A Border Gateway Protocol 4 (BGP-4)"; January 2006. Available from: <www.ietf.org/>.

213. Rekhter Y, Moskowitz B, Karrenberg D, de Groot GJ, Lear E. RFC1918-Address Allocation for Private Internets. Available from: <www.ietf.org/>.

214. Rescorla E. RFC4101, "Writing Protocol Models"; June 2005. Available from: <www.ietf.org/>.

215. Rivest R. RFC1321, "The MD5 Message-Digest Algorithm"; April 1992. Available from: <www.ietf.org/>.

216. Römer K, Blum P, Meier L. Time synchronization and calibration in wireless sensor networks. In: Stojmenovic I, ed. *Handbook of Sensor Networks: Algorithms and Architectures*: John Wiley and Sons; September 2005:199–237.

217. Rosen E, Rekhter Y. RFC4364, "BGP/MPLS IP Virtual Private Networks (VPNs)"; February 2006. Available from: <www.ietf.org/>.

218. Saltzer JH, Reed DP, Clark DD. End-to-end arguments in system design. *ACM Trans Comp Syst*. November 1984;2(4):277–288.

219. Savola P, Haberman B. RFC3956 "Embedding the Rendezvous Point (RP) Address in an IPv6 Multicast Address"; November 2004. Available from: <www.ietf.org/>.

220. Schulzrinne H, Casner S, Frederick R, Jacobson V. RFC3550, "RTP: A Transport Protocol for Real-Time Applications"; July 2003. Available from: <www.ietf.org/>.
221. Shelby Z, Bormann C. *6LoWPAN: The Wireless Embedded Internet*: Wiley; 2009.
222. Shelby Z, Mähönen P, Riihijärvi J, Raivio O, Huuskonen P. NanoIP: The Zen of Embedded Networking. In: *Proceedings of ICC 2003*; May 2003.
223. Simon D, Cifuentes C, Cleal D, Daniels J, White D. Java™ on the bare metal of wireless sensor devices: the squawk Java virtual machine. In: *Proceedings of the 2nd International Conference on Virtual Execution Environments*. New York, NY: ACM; 2006:78–88.
224. Sollins K. RFC1350, "THE TFTP PROTOCOL (REVISION 2)"; July 1992. Available from: <www.ietf.org/>.
225. Stajano F. *Security for Ubiquitous Computing*: John Wiley and Sons; February 2002.
226. Stajano F, Anderson R. The resurrecting duckling: Security issues for ad-hoc wireless networks. In: *Security Protocols Workshop*; 1999:172–194.
227. Standard and Extended X10 Code Protocol. <http://software.x10.com/pub/manuals/xtdcode.pdf/>.
228. Stevens W. *TCP/IP Illustrated Volume 1*. Reading, MA: Addison-Wesley; 1995.
229. Stewart R. RFC4960, "Stream Control Transmission Protocol"; September 2007. Available from: <www.ietf.org/>.
230. Sturek D. Service Discovery for 6LowApp; October 2009. draft-sturek-6lowapp-servicediscovery, Internet-draft, work in progress.
231. Suarez P, Renmarker C, Dunkels A, Voigt T. Increasing ZigBee Network Lifetime with X-MAC. In: *Proceedings of REALWSN 2008*; April 2008.
232. Sun Y, Gurewitz O, Johnson D. RI-MAC: A Receiver-Initiated Asynchronous Duty Cycle MAC Protocol for Dynamic Traffic Loads in Wireless Sensor Networks. In: *Proceedings of the 6th ACM Conference on Embedded Network Sensor Systems (SenSys '08)*. Raleigh, NC; 2008.
233. John A. Swets, Measuring the Accuracy of Diagnostic Systems. *Science*. 1988;240:1285–1293.
234. The HomePlug Powerline Alliance. HomePlug AV White Paper; 2005.
235. Thomson S, Narten T, Jinmei T. RFC4862, "IPv6 Stateless Address Autoconfiguration"; September 2007. Available from: <www.ietf.org/>.
236. Toivola J, Hollmén J. Feature extraction and selection from vibration measurements for structural health monitoring. In: Adams NM, Robardet C, Siebes A, Boulicaut JF, eds. Lyon, France: Springer-Verlag; August/September 2009:213–224. *Proceedings of the 8th International Symposium on Intelligent Data Analysis of Lecture Notes in Computer Science*; Vol. 5772.
237. Tolle G. A UDP/IP Adaptation of the ZigBee Application Protocol. Internet Draft draft-tolle-cap-00.txt; October 2008, work in progress.
238. Topolcic C. "Experimental Internet Stream Protocol, Version 2 (ST-II)"; October 1990. Available from: <www.ietf.org/>.
239. Tripathi J, De Oliveira J, Vasseur JP. draft-tripathi-roll-rpl-evaluation, "Performance Evaluation of Routing Protocol for Low Power and Lossy Networks (RPL)", work in progress. Available at HYPERLINK <http://www.ietf.org/>.
240. Troan O, Droms R. RFC3633, "IPv6 Prefix Options for Dynamic Host Configuration Protocol (DHCP) version 6"; December 2003. Available from: <www.ietf.org/>.
241. Tsiftes N, Dunkels A, He Z, Voigt T. Enabling Large-Scale Storage in Sensor Networks with the Coffee File System. In: *Proceedings of the 8th ACM/IEEE International Conference on Information Processing in Sensor Networks (IPSN 2009)*. San Francisco, CA; April 2009.
242. Turley J. The Two Percent Solution. *Embedded Systems Design*; December 2002.
243. Running IPv6 (Hardcover) by Iljitsch van Beijnum, APress.
244. van Dam T, Langendoen K. An adaptive energy-efficient MAC protocol for wireless sensor networks. In: *Proceedings of the First International Conference on Embedded Networked Sensor Systems*. Los Angeles, CA; November 2003.

245. Varga A. "The OMNeT++ Discrete Event Simulation System. In: *Proceedings of the European Simulation Multiconference (ESM'2001)"*; June 2001.
246. Network Recovery: Protection and Restoration of Optical, SONET-SDH, IP, and MPLS (The Morgan Kaufmann Series in Networking) by JP Vasseur, Mario Pickavet and Piet Demeester; July 2004.
247. Definitive MPLS Network Designs by JP Vasseur, Francois Le Faucheur and Jim Guichard; March 2005, Cisco Press.
248. Vasseur JP. draft-ietf-roll-terminology, "Terminology in Low power And Lossy Networks", Work in progress. Available from: <www.ietf.org/>.
249. Vasseur JP. Stefano Previdi, RFC5029, "Definition of an IS-IS Link Attribute Sub-TLV". Available from: <www.ietf.org/>.
250. Vasseur JP, Kim M, Pister K, Chong H. draft-ietf-roll-routing-metrics, "Routing Metrics used for Path Calculation in Low Power and Lossy Networks", work in progress. Available from: <www.ietf.org/>.
251. Vida R, Costa L. RFC3810, "Multicast Listener Discovery Version 2 (MLDv2) for IPv6"; June 2004. Available from: <www.ietf.org/>.
252. Wang AY, Sodini CG. On the energy efficiency of wireless transceivers. In: *IEEE International Conference on Communications*. Istanbul, Turkey; June 2006.
253. Want R, Hopper A, Falcao V, Gibbons J. The active badge location system. *ACM Trans Inf Syst.* 1992;10(1):91–102.
254. Watteyne T. Thesis on "Energy-Efficient Self-Organization for Wireless Sensor Networks"; 2008.
255. Weinrib A. RFC2014, "IRTF Research Group Guidelines and Procedures". Available from: <www.ietf.org/>.
256. Winter T, Thubert P, Vasseur JP, et al. draft-ietf-roll-rpl, "RPL: IPv6 Routing Protocol for Low power and Lossy Networks", work in progress. Available from: <www.ietf.org/>.
257. Woo A. A new embedded web services approach to wireless sensor networks. In: *Proceedings of the 4th International Conference on Embedded Networked Sensor Systems (SenSys '06)*. Boulder, CO; 2006:347–347.
258. Woo A, Tong T, Culler D. Taming the underlying challenges of reliable multi-hop routing in sensor networks. In: *SenSys '03: Proceedings of the 1st International Conference on Embedded Networked Sensor Systems*. New York, NY: ACM Press; 2003:14–27.
259. Wood A, Stankovic J, Zhou G. DEEJAM: Defeating Energy Efficient Jamming in IEEE 802.15.4-based Wireless Networks. In: *Proceedings of IEEE SECON 2007*; June 2007.
260. Yazar D, Dunkels A. Efficient Application Integration in IP-Based Sensor Networks. In: *Proceedings of the ACM BuildSys 2009 Workshop,* in conjunction with *ACM SenSys 2009*; November 2009.
261. Ye W, Heidemann J, Estrin D. An Energy-Efficient MAC Protocol for Wireless Sensor Networks. In: *Proceedings of the 21st International Annual Joint Conference of the IEEE Computer and Communications Societies (INFOCOM 2002)*. New York, NY; June 2002.
262. Ye W, Silva F, Heidemann J. Ultra-low duty cycle MAC with scheduled channel polling. In: *SenSys '06: Proceedings of the 4th International Conference on Embedded Networked Sensor Systems*. New York, NY: ACM Press; 2006:321–334.
263. ZigBee Alliance. Zigbee. Web page. <http://www.zigbee.org/>.

Index